THE RULE OF LAW

STUDIES IN LEGAL HISTORY

Published by The University of North Carolina Press
in association with the American Society for Legal History

Editor: Morris S. Arnold

Editorial Advisory Board

THE RULE OF LAW:
ALBERT VENN DICEY,
VICTORIAN JURIST

BY RICHARD A. COSGROVE

The University of North Carolina Press
Chapel Hill

© 1980 The University of North Carolina Press

All rights reserved

Manufactured in the United States of America

ISBN 0-8078-1410-5

Library of Congress Catalog Card Number 79-18027

Library of Congress Cataloging in Publication Data

Cosgrove, Richard A   1941–

  The rule of law.

  (Studies in legal history)

  Bibliography: p.

  Includes index.

  1. Dicey, Albert Venn, 1835–1922.   2. Lawyers—Great Britain—
Biography.   I. Title.   II. Series.

KD631.D5C67   340'.092'4 [B]   79-18027

ISBN 0-8078-1410-5

FOR MY FAMILY:

WIFE, CHILDREN, PARENTS, IN-LAWS

CONTENTS

ILLUSTRATIONS

ACKNOWLEDGMENTS

For permission to consult and quote from collections of private papers, I am indebted to L. D. O'Nions, Browning Papers; Lord Cromer, Cromer Papers; the Trustees of the Chatsworth Settlement, Devonshire Papers; the Warden and Fellows of New College, Milner Papers; the Beaverbrook Foundation, Strachey and Bonar Law Papers; Professor Grant Gilmore and the Harvard Law School Library, O. W. Holmes, Jr., Papers; Department of Western MSS, Bodleian Library, Bryce Papers; His Grace the Archbishop of Canterbury and the trustees of Lambeth Palace Library, Selborne Papers; the trustees of the National Library of Scotland, Elliot Papers; Mrs. Dorinda Maxse, Maxse Papers; the Harvard Corporation, A. L. Lowell and C. W. Eliot Papers; the Houghton Library, Harvard University, E. L. Godkin, C. E. Norton, and William James Papers; the Marquess of Salisbury, Salisbury Papers; and Miss Sibella Bonham-Carter, the letters of Albert Venn Dicey.

I am also grateful to the following individuals for their aid in many different circumstances: Pauline Adams, Somerville College, Oxford; J. Baldwin, Glasgow University Library; Alan Bell, National Library of Scotland; B. S. Benedikz, University of Birmingham; E. G. W. Bill, Lambeth Palace Library; Victor Bonham-Carter of London for the illustrations that adorn these pages; Erika S. Chadbourn, Harvard Law School Library; Elizabeth Darbury, Historical Manuscripts Commission; Peter Day, Devonshire Collection; Rodney Dennis, Houghton Library; Clark Elliot, Harvard University Archives; Sandra Feneley, New College, Oxford; Patricia Gaffney, Cornell University Library; Patricia Gill, West Sussex County Record Office; Mary Hudson, the Macmillan Company; J. W. Igoe, Beaverbrook Library; T. L. Ingram, Baring Bros. Ltd.; Pauline Maclean, Scottish Record Office; J. F. A. Mason, Christ Church College, Oxford; David Muspratt, Working Men's College, London; D. S. Porter, Bodleian Library; Olive Prentice, London; E. V. Quinn, Balliol College, Oxford; W. E. Salmon, Somerset House; J. S. G. Simmons, All Souls College, Oxford; James J. Storrow, the *Nation*; Martha Vogeler, California State University, Fullerton.

I owe a special debt to the staffs of the Bodleian Library, the

Acknowledgments

Oxford Law Library, and the Working Men's College, London, for all their cheerful assistance.

For his careful work at my behest I thank my research assistant at the University of Arizona, Brian Templet; and for their careful preparation of several stages of the manuscript I am indebted to Marilyn Bradian and Wiladene Stickel.

The American Philosophical Society provided a grant which made much of this research possible, and for this I thank the Society.

For their suggestions in the preparation of the manuscript I would like to thank my colleague at the University of Arizona, Jack D. Marietta, and Richard W. Davis of Washington University, St. Louis.

Finally, for their friendship to me and my family during our stay in England, I would like to thank Enid and Gordon Shepherd and Ann Dykes of Forest Hill, Oxfordshire.

INTRODUCTION

Historians write frequently of the neglected figure upon whom posterity bestows a posthumous importance; such was not the case of Albert Venn Dicey, whose intellectual reputation stood highest in his own lifetime but has now declined sharply. In four separate areas Dicey wrote books of instant popularity that helped sustain his position as a leading figure in Victorian life. *Conflict of Laws* (1896) pioneered that legal specialty, shaping the development of the subject in England. Lawyers and political scientists have long recognized *Law of the Constitution* (1885) as a classic textbook on constitutional law. Historians have relied upon *Law and Opinion in the Nineteenth Century* (1905) as the departure point for the study of the relationship between ideas and governmental development during that century. Dicey's best book on politics, *England's Case against Home Rule* (1886), testified to the heat of a controversy abandoned eventually during World War I. In each of these works Dicey applied the tools of legal positivism for the purpose of deriving general principles about the subject in question. His steadfast adherence to this methodology worked well when applied to some aspects of the law and the constitution, but led to unsatisfactory results in other areas. His major works, therefore, have not stood the test of time well.

Readers may be surprised at the length with which Dicey's involvement in the Home Rule controversy is treated in this book, as it may seem at the expense of his more famous legal contributions. This emphasis on Dicey and Ireland reflects the passionate attachment Dicey had to the Union and the way Dicey himself apportioned his time: defense of the Union counted for more than his scholarly work. He followed the course of politics feverishly but only as an observer, never an actor. Dicey's political enthusiasms led him into a field where he possessed no experience, with the result that he gave lower priority to the law, where his expertise was greatest.

Despite the fact that his life contained one political disappointment after another, Dicey concerned himself with problems that have endured beyond his lifetime. Long the sole English supporter of the referendum, its debut in 1975 vindicated at far remove his enthusiasm for its use. The election of Mrs. Thatcher as leader of the Conservative party, and then as prime minister in 1979, marked the increasing participation of women in British politics, a process Dicey had vigorously denounced in his later years. Government planning for subordinate assemblies in Scotland and Wales has raised anew the question of the integrity of the United Kingdom, a concept for which Dicey fought his entire life. The ambiguous future of devolution in 1979 testifies to the strength of the idea of unity that claimed so much of Dicey's life. The prospect of parliaments in Cardiff and Edinburgh would have roused his wrath as surely as the proposed parliament in Dublin did in his own lifetime. Enduring troubles in Northern Ireland emphasize the historical continuity of Irish problems, as bitter in Dicey's day as at present. Finally, modern politicians have often invoked the magical phrase "rule of law," as in the case of the Heath government against the miners or its frequent repetition in the process that ended in the resignation of President Nixon. So commonplace has the phrase become that few recognize that its shorthand use for "equality before the law" derives from its popularization by the forgotten Dicey. The definition of the rule of law has altered drastically in the modern world, but its continued permutations accent its fertility as a basic concept of global politics.

In an essay on Dicey, former Vinerian Professor H. G. Hanbury pointed out the lack of a Dicey biography, writing correctly that the memoir by Robert S. Rait (1925) was just that, a remembrance without an attempt to appraise Dicey's career. The Rait book is valuable for the printing of a portion of Dicey's correspondence, the more so because Dicey rarely retained letters sent to him or copies of letters he wrote. On three occasions (to Mrs. E. L. Godkin, 15 May 1903; to the executors of Goldwin Smith, 26 October 1910; and to James Bryce, 23 March 1921), Dicey admitted that early in life he had adopted the habit of destroying his correspondence. Fortunately, many of his letters were preserved in other collections, so, though there is no single Dicey archive, many of the letters are extant. Emerging from this abundant correspondence is a picture of a man whose basic values were fixed in youth, when he imbibed the conventional beliefs of the mid-Victorian generation unquestioningly. He displayed an enduring fidelity to that code throughout his life.

Although he lived until 1922, this fact is so central to the interpretation of Dicey's career that we can call him a mid-Victorian. No other description conveys the essential elements of his life so well.

THE RULE OF LAW

Albert Venn Dicey, 1835–1922
(Courtesy of Victor Bonham-Carter)

CHAPTER ONE

THE BALLIOL YEARS,

1835–1861

A LBERT VENN DICEY came from a family whose first known forebear was Thomas Dicey, born in Leicestershire about 1660 and a journeyman of no great accomplishment. Toward the end of the seventeenth century Thomas entered into a profitable partnership with a Londoner named Sutton to produce certain patent medicines, especially "Daffy's Elixer," which peddlers sold on their circuits through the countryside. Thomas Dicey apprenticed his two sons, William and Cluer, to the printing trade, and the older, William, decided that these itinerant venders might well carry newspapers on their rounds. After one unsuccessful publishing venture in 1718 at St. Ives, William Dicey helped found the *Northampton Mercury*, first published on 2 May 1720, which formed the basis of Dicey family fortunes until well into the nineteenth century.

At the start of the eighteenth century the family also inaugurated the publication of chapbooks, the cheap printed literature that exercised a potent influence in the education and, it was hoped, the moral elevation of the poorer classes. Chapbooks were the special province of Cluer Dicey, who supervised their production and made the format attractive to a growing readership.[1] For half a century the Diceys dominated this field and inspired a host of imitators. The family prospered because of these successful printing ventures, which raised them from the obscurity of the previous century.

Throughout the eighteenth century the Diceys passed the newspaper from generation to generation until Albert's grandfather, Thomas Dicey, took over management in 1776. By 1792 Thomas Dicey enjoyed a fortune large enough to enable him to purchase Claybrook Hall, near Lutterworth in Northamptonshire. In 1807, on the death of his father, Thomas Edward Dicey assumed authority

1. John Ashton, *Chap-Books of the Eighteenth Century*, p. ix.

3

over the *Mercury*, though his personal direction began only after his graduation from Cambridge in 1811. He retained the editorship of the paper until his death in 1858. In 1814 Dicey married Anne Mary Stephen, daughter of James Stephen, a step that brought the Dicey family within the orbit of the Clapham sect. This marriage united two dynamic movements that reached their zenith in nineteenth-century England, the political liberalism of the husband and the Evangelical zeal of the wife. The combination made the Diceys a paramount example of the Victorian intellectual aristocracy.[2] Through this marriage the Diceys entered the world of such famous Evangelical families as the Venns and Stephens; Albert Dicey's middle name was taken from Evangelical leader John Venn.

Albert Venn Dicey was born at Claybrook Hall on 4 February 1835, the third of four brothers. Family tradition holds that the muscular weakness that plagued Dicey all his life stemmed from an obstetrical error at the time of his premature birth. Though his appearance always had a touch of the ridiculous because of his inability entirely to control his physical movements, Albert enjoyed good health for most of his long life and learned early in childhood never to strain his limited powers. He matured into a tall, angular young man, and surviving photographs invest him with a somber, almost forbidding air. On account of his youthful precarious health he enjoyed a more subdued childhood than most, as his cousin John Venn testified: "As a boy I had not your sense of proportion or of historic dignity."[3] In adulthood Dicey matured into a gifted conversationalist whose watchword was that it was better to be flippant than dull, a piece of advice he had appropriated while an undergraduate.[4] From early childhood, his parents' belief in the value of education and health considerations pointed him exclusively toward the intellectual life.

In later life Dicey recalled that his earliest memories possessed none of the melancholy associated in popular imagination with an

2. Lord Annan, "The Intellectual Aristocracy," in J. H. Plumb, ed., *Studies in Social History*, pp. 243–87.

3. John Venn to Albert Venn Dicey, 13 August 1919, General Manuscripts 508(28), Glasgow University Library.

4. Albert Venn Dicey, "Suggestions on Academical Organisation," p. 418.

Evangelical upbringing.[5] The portrait he left described a household of boys who received a strict education tempered by affection and merriment. Until he was seventeen years old his education took place at home, primarily under the aegis of his mother. Frequent trips to the Continent constituted the only outside influence in this personal and tightly structured system of education. Both parents, according to Dicey, had inherited "grave suspicions" of the public schools from their Evangelical background.[6] By the 1840s the public school system, in their estimation, still possessed defects that far outweighed its virtues, and thus his parents educated all their children at home.[7] Dicey never resented this sheltered education, for he often attested to the value of his close relationship with his parents. Friends of the family also contributed to his educational experience, particularly his cousins, Sarah Stephen and Caroline Emilia Stephen.[8] Friends and relations afforded the young man a unique opportunity to share the intellectual life of his parents, and they focused his attention on political affairs from an early age.

From this domestic education emanated two of the most fundamental influences on Dicey's personal growth. From his father he derived a commitment to classical liberalism that later events shook but never destroyed. Dicey never wrote of his father without the greatest reverence for the political and moral attitudes he had expressed during his long editorship. His father's keen sense of justice, exhibited in his unswerving detestation of every kind of unfairness, oppression, and cruelty, made him a paragon of wisdom to the son.[9] The elder Dicey combined the approval of reform without revolution, devotion to free trade, and belief in the value of the free exchange of ideas to which Dicey adhered for the remainder of his life. At the time of his departure from the parental household Albert possessed a liberalism characterized not only by specific

5. Albert Venn Dicey, "Autobiographical Fragment," in Robert S. Rait, ed., *Memorials of Albert Venn Dicey*, p. 13.

6. Dicey to James Bryce, 17 July 1920, James Bryce Papers, Bodleian Library, Oxford.

7. Dicey, "Autobiographical Fragment," in Rait, *Memorials*, pp. 14–15.

8. Mrs. R. B. Litchfield, "Recollections," in Rait, *Memorials*, p. 293.

9. Albert Venn Dicey, "Thomas Edward Dicey," in W. W. Hadley, ed., *The Bi-Centenary Record of the Northampton Mercury 1720–1920*, p. 49.

doctrines but also by an approach to life that held human reason capable of resolving the manifold problems facing society.

His mother exercised no less an influence upon the young Dicey. She had guided his education and stressed instruction in Greek, Latin, French, and German. She possessed a talent for teaching and adjusted her lessons to the capabilities of each child. Dicey often remembered with gratitude "the immense patience and care his mother expended in trying to teach his incapable fingers to do their work."[10] In the case of Albert, she carefully framed assignments in the form of conversation so as not to overtax his limited strength.[11] Her common sense approach to education doubtless benefited Albert more than the rigors of a public school.

Important as this aspect of her maternal care was, the most influential legacy Dicey obtained from his mother was a secularized version of Evangelical enthusiasm. He was never a practicing Christian in the ordinary sense, for he retained its spirit but "cared less than nothing for dogma."[12] Dicey never lost interest in religion as part of the human experience, but conventional religious beliefs vanished under a withering rationalism. He later termed his religious views "so vague & so dubious that 'synthesis' or belief of any kind is the last thing to be expected from me."[13] Formed in a crucible of rationalism, he could not tolerate faith without intellectual justification. From his earliest days he distrusted enthusiasm, and this made him throughout his life a warrior against the evils of fanaticism associated with emotional religiosity. He played no favorites, as Catholic and Protestant bigotry alike aroused his wrath, whether too great power in Catholic Ireland or denial of free speech to Catholics in other parts of the United Kingdom.

The primary indication of his mature religious tendencies may be seen in his membership in the Synthetic Society, a group of prominent late Victorians who met sporadically from 1898 to 1908 in order to find common doctrine among Christians divided by controversy.[14] Dicey found the meetings too diffuse for his taste, but the discussions of the society stimulated his curiosity about the histor-

10. Litchfield, "Recollections," in Rait, *Memorials,* p. 293.
11. Dicey, "Autobiographical Fragment," in Rait, *Memorials,* pp. 14–15.
12. Lord Annan, *Leslie Stephen,* p. 122.
13. Dicey to Bryce, 9 March 1896, Bryce Papers.
14. Kenneth Young, *Arthur James Balfour,* pp. 161–62.

ical evidence for Christian dogma.[15] His speculations about the early history of Christianity reflected intellectual concern only, for he concluded that none of the usual beliefs about the first Christian century had any historical basis.[16] On these grounds he emphasized the role of myth in the eventual triumph of Christianity. Reason as the ultimate criterion of religious belief forced him to reject any form of mysticism or, as he once denounced it, "Spiritualism."[17] Specific Christian doctrines never appealed to him; about the knowledge of Christ he once wrote: "Surely if you & I look at the life of Jesus in the same way as that in which we should look at the life of Caesar or Mahomet the belief in the miraculous birth & the disbelief in the existence of Jesus must seem all but equal absurdities."[18] Other incidents like the crucifixion and resurrection he also felt had little historical evidence to support belief.[19] Dicey never missed the consolation of religion, because in his youth he found a substitute that more than compensated for the vagueness of his beliefs.

In place of discredited dogmas, Evangelical fervor manifested itself in an enduring commitment to "useful work" that permeated his activities to the day of his death. Never prone to abstract philosophical musings, Dicey believed "we must find satisfaction in making the best or the most of whatever work one has in hand, and that one's appropriate work is the free development of such faculties as one may happen to possess."[20] He embodied this creed to the extent that he often doubted the success of his own career because he had not obtained the most from his abilities. Reassurance came from an existential joy in work for its own sake; if one worked as diligently as possible, one must be satisfied with that, no matter what the outcome. "I am certain that the only way to happiness," he once wrote, "is to become engrossed in the work you have in hand, & try, if possible, that it shall be good work."[21] The need for

15. Dicey to Bryce, 17 July 1920, Bryce Papers.
16. Ibid., 25 July 1909, ibid.
17. Ibid., 9 January 1914, ibid.
18. Ibid., 10 January 1904, ibid.
19. Ibid., 4 and 8 August 1911, ibid.
20. Dicey to Oliver Wendell Holmes, Jr., 3 April 1900, Oliver Wendell Holmes, Jr., Papers, Harvard Law School Library.
21. Dicey to Charles William Eliot, 17 October 1899, Charles William Eliot Papers, Harvard University Archives.

constant application to his work supplanted the religious faith of his mother.

The other aspect of the Evangelical inheritance that influenced his adult character was his style of belief. Despite his aversion to religious enthusiasm, once Dicey had acquired a particular conviction he recognized no middle ground; to accept a political position, for instance, meant a passionate involvement with the defense of that doctrine. He worked best in sorting out propositions into categories of black and white, for he never accepted the many shades of gray in public affairs. The synthesis of liberal politics with transmuted religious earnestness resulted in a strong dedication to political activity that pervaded his entire life. Politics remained his secular vocation; in it there were clearly demarcated good and bad personalities and philosophies, and no other facet of his life, not even the law, ever superseded it.

Into this atmosphere of strong concern for politics intruded the events of 1848, a year vital to the direction of Dicey's life: "They really turned my whole intellectual interest of my mind towards political and constitutional controversies."[22] Dicey, then just thirteen years old, avidly followed the news of the revolutions sweeping Europe in the columns of the *Times*. Under the tutelage of cousin Sarah Stephen, Albert watched closely the Austrian retreat from Milan and the seeming victory of progress over reaction. Later his hopes rested on the Hungarian revolutionaries; their subsequent failure proved disconcerting to their young adherent, who had taken their success for granted.[23] The impact of 1848 was lasting on the young Dicey: "In many ways I woke up to conscious existence in '48, and I have generally read whenever opportunity offered, accounts of that year."[24] Later his father solidified his enthusiasm for foreign heroes by taking him to a meeting at which Mazzini and Kossuth spoke, this experience intensifying his fascination with politics.

Dicey never failed to credit his parents with a lasting influence on his development: "There has been nothing whatever extraordinary either in my life itself or in the work I have done, but I am

22. Dicey to Bryce, 12 November 1918, Bryce Papers.
23. Ibid., 26 July 1917, ibid.
24. Ibid., 12 November 1918, ibid.

intensely conscious that the sort of way in which I have looked at life, and the matters which have interested me, have been to a certain extent the inevitable result of being brought up at home by very good and intelligent parents who were earnest Whigs and sincere though not violent Evangelicals."[25] Throughout his life he remained loyal to the beliefs first inculcated by his parents. The lives of famous men are often dominated by revolt against parental domination; in Dicey's case maturity reinforced allegiance to youthful values. He exemplified the potent influence of liberalism and Evangelicalism as inherited from his parents, qualified only by an intellectual rigor that gave his Evangelical heritage a distinctive anticlerical flavor. Secure in the values learned at home, Dicey prepared to put them to the test in the outside world.

In 1852, at age seventeen, Dicey left home for the first time to continue his education at King's College School in London. The two years he spent there were marred by recurrent bouts of bronchitis that limited his participation in school life. In later years he won a small measure of fame for eccentricity by his violent prejudice against athletics; his true feeling, fostered no doubt by his own physical limitations, was "that a person loses much in life who cannot take part in physical sports."[26] He did not suffer abuse from his peers because of this lack, but missed the camaraderie sports provided. The curriculum at King's was narrowly classical but very demanding, and Dicey responded well to the strict regimen it imposed. Academic success at King's College School raised the question for his parents whether Albert's health could withstand the demands of a university career.

His father and one brother had attended Trinity College, Cambridge; but, as Albert lacked his father's mathematical talents, no purpose would be served by continuing this family tradition. Instead, Dicey in 1854 matriculated at Balliol College, Oxford. He did not possess a tender conscience at this point, for he signed the Thirty-Nine Articles without hesitation despite his own theological inclinations. Dicey regarded this act as merely acknowledging membership in the Church of England without signifying in any way intellectual assent to any particular creed. Oxford was as for-

25. Dicey to R. S. Rait, 8 March 1922, in Rait, *Memorials,* pp. 286–87.
26. Dicey to Bryce, 23 March 1911, Bryce Papers.

mative for him as the parental and Evangelical influences, so the fundamental importance of university life to Dicey must be examined carefully.

In the first place, Dicey fell under the personal supervision of Benjamin Jowett, to whom he always acknowledged an "incalculable" debt.[27] Having already adopted a self-discipline remarkable in a youth, Dicey now encountered the gospel of work according to Jowett.[28] Jowett argued that religion imposed upon every man the duty to perform his work as well as possible;[29] and Dicey, despite the religious implications, fell completely under Jowett's sway. Dicey regarded himself as "an extraordinary example of Jowett's power of making the very most of such talents as his pupils happen to possess."[30] Jowett impressed on each student the necessity of activity, urging every man to utilize the talents he possessed without fretting about the talents he did not possess.[31] Dicey thought the day he arrived at Balliol among the most fortunate of his life and had so informed Jowett shortly before the death of his former tutor. Jowett in particular reinforced the adherence to a personal philosophy of constant application that Dicey had already received from his parents.

In addition, Jowett set a standard of university teaching to which Dicey aspired but confessed that, rather depressingly, no other tutor could ever approach.[32] As proof of Jowett's kindliness and concern, Dicey offered the following anecdote: "On the morning of my going in for 'Smalls' I went to his room to consult him about the expediency of my chancing the examination. The Greek irregular verbs were then as I fear at all times too much for me & made a plough not unlikely. After we had determined that the risk had best be run J. looked hard at me & said 'Your tie is very badly tied.' This I knew but also knew that I couldn't tie it better. I made an effort to improve it & untied it altogether. J. said nothing but seeing I sup-

27. Dicey to Eliot, 7 April 1904, Eliot Papers.
28. See Melvin Richter, *The Politics of Conscience*, pp. 74–75, for Jowett in action with Dicey's contemporary Thomas Hill Green.
29. Geoffrey Faber, *Jowett*, p. 35.
30. Dicey to James Leigh Strachan-Davidson, 20 May 1909, Miscellaneous MSS, Balliol College.
31. Ibid.
32. Dicey to Evelyn Abbott, 18 April 1897, ibid.

pose the case was desperate said nothing but tied it himself."[33] Dicey admired this personal interest Jowett took in pupils while maintaining the aloofness traditionally associated with Balliol tutors, a point stressed by Jowett's biographer.[34] From Jowett Dicey learned how to teach by personal example; this lesson persisted in spite of Dicey's later conclusion that Jowett's intellectual talents never measured up to his personal gifts of empathy for his charges.[35]

The impact of Jowett did not cease with the end of Dicey's undergraduate career. Jowett proved very helpful when Dicey returned to Oxford in 1882, even on one occasion encouraging his former pupil to stand for Parliament.[36] When Dicey demurred, Jowett dropped the subject immediately and never mentioned it again. For his part, Dicey faithfully sent his books to his mentor in demonstration that he still practiced the precepts of labor learned decades earlier. As the years passed, Jowett insisted to Dicey that the last years should be best and good work still possible, a point Dicey would eventually exemplify. Jowett had inspired him to labor energetically while at Balliol, and the lessons learned there encouraged him in his own declining years. When Jowett died, Dicey summarized their relationship in this manner: "He was one of the best friends I have ever had. Like scores of other Oxford men I owe nearly everything I have done in life to him. His death leaves a tremendous gap here which will long remain unfilled."[37] For all the influence of Jowett, he was not alone in forming the young Dicey.

By 1854 Balliol had already initiated the changes that made the college a producer of so many leaders of late Victorian and Edwardian society. The Balliol ambience stressed academic achievement and individual responsibility. Dicey, for instance, had already devoted himself to serious intellectual effort before coming to Balliol with "an extraordinarily fixed desire to obtain a good degree and a Fellowship."[38] By the combination of personal dedication and the excellent training offered by Balliol, Dicey succeeded in reaching

33. Ibid.
34. Faber, *Jowett*, p. 34.
35. Dicey to Bryce, 18 April 1917, Bryce Papers.
36. Ibid., 12 February 1918, ibid.
37. Dicey to Lord Selborne, 2 October 1893, Lord Selborne Papers, Lambeth Palace Library, London.
38. Dicey to Bryce, 11 September 1918, Bryce Papers.

his goal. In this sense Dicey and Balliol were ideally suited to each other. The less desirable side of this system is reflected in Dicey's later regret that he had regarded literary study only as a means to an end and had never enjoyed literature for its own sake.[39] He had studied too often only to pass examinations, too little for the sake of acquiring a liberal education.

Yet Dicey undoubtedly prospered under the Balliol system: "I gained much intellectual & moral training from our examination system, combined with the infinite care & admirable teaching of the Balliol tutors. The system gave me a fixed & definite scheme of work which I could never have framed for myself, & should not have adhered to if I had framed it. It also kept me working for 4 years more strenuously than I have ever worked, I am ashamed to say, at any other period of my life."[40] The four years Dicey spent so profitably at Balliol enlarged the philosophical framework he had formed prior to arrival. At Oxford in the 1850s he found many other students who shared his political enthusiasms and admired the same academic heroes. The congeniality of his colleagues lessened his shyness, involved him far more in university affairs, and created a sense of confidence in his own abilities.

For Dicey, already the possessor of a deeply ingrained individualism, John Stuart Mill was the foremost English authority of his undergraduate days: "At Oxford we swallowed Mill, rather undigested: he was our chief intellectual food until 1860."[41] His basic conception of liberty, retained throughout his life, Dicey derived from Mill: "I belong to the school of thought & feeling which Mill produced; and I cannot but think that if he were read more now, it would do a great deal of good, and be a salutary corrective. Individuality in its true sense is a source both of greatness and of goodness; and much as we must value all social progress with its accompanying restrictions, we must watch jealously lest these restrictions endanger individuality, and thus destroy that originality which is the very spring of true social progress."[42] Dicey in later life turned against certain implications of Mill's social thought that he con-

39. Ibid.
40. Dicey to Eliot, 28 March 1899, Eliot Papers.
41. Albert Venn Dicey, "Mill 'On Liberty'," p. 17. This lecture, delivered 8 November 1900, was the first in a series on Mill.
42. Dicey, "Mill 'On Liberty'," p. 86. This was the fourth lecture in the series on Mill, and Dicey gave it on 7 March 1901.

sidered a betrayal of Mill's earlier libertarianism. But he never denied his great debt to Mill: "As a young man I owed more to him than to any other English writer," Dicey once wrote, "& on the whole my sense of his goodness has increased rather than been diminished as I have got older. But my confidence in his judgment . . . has been much shaken. His power of exposition . . . seems to me to have deceived both himself and his disciples."[43] The permanent influence of Mill upon Dicey came in the emphasis on logical thought as the final criterion of human judgment. But the more Mill strayed from his original definition of individualism, the less Dicey retained his faith in the demigod of his youth.

Of course, Mill did not stand alone as an influence during Dicey's years as an Oxford undergraduate: "If I were to put down the books which made most impression upon me [at] the end of early youth, I think I should name Tocqueville & Lyall's own Eastern Studies."[44] By Dicey's testimony, the men who impressed him most accelerated tendencies in his own development. Mill intensified the strong belief in reason as the ultimate arbiter of human problems; Tocqueville sparked his curiosity about constitutional theories; and Lyall aroused interest in historical questions. These concerns cultivated in Oxford proved productive long after university days, for Dicey rarely abandoned a topic once it had gained his attention. Indeed, a fault to which Dicey fell prey was his habit of providing all he knew about a given subject in the course of conversation.

For the first two years at Balliol Dicey lived a largely solitary life devoted to his studies. He was sustained by the advice and friendship of Ellen Smith, sister of Balliol tutor Henry Smith. Ellen Smith provided companionship for the young man as well as constant encouragement in his studies. The steadfast attention to work inculcated by Jowett and abetted by his friend resulted in a First Class in Honour Moderations in 1856. This academic success boosted his self-esteem dramatically: "I am inclined to think that evening & the next day to have been nearly the happiest day in my life. I had no right to expect it. It gave delight to my Father & Mother & to the friend [Ellen Smith] I loved most certainly great satisfaction. It was the first real success I had had in my life. My Father died some

43. Dicey to Charles Eliot Norton, 13 June 1905, Charles Eliot Norton Papers, Houghton Library, Harvard University.
44. Dicey to Bryce, 12 June 1913, Bryce Papers.

months before I went in for 'Greats'. Everything I have done of what you may call success since has been too much mixed up with effort or some other sort of pain to come near the joy of this Moderation 'First'."[45] Encouraged by this distinction, he joined with other Balliol men, under the leadership of John Nichol, in forming a society for serious undergraduates to sharpen their intellects.

By far the most important Oxford influence on Dicey, however, came from his role in the founding of the undergraduate Old Mortality Society in 1856.[46] This society has attracted scholarly interest because so many of its members achieved fame in their mature endeavors.[47] Dicey's participation provides a first glimpse of his activities with his peers where he realized the extent of his own ability. The purpose of the Old Mortality was for members to afford "one another such intellectual pastime and recreation as should seem most suitable & agreeable to members of the same."[48] In the years when Dicey played an active role in the society he read essays on a variety of topics.

His first paper consisted of remarks on J. A. Froude's treatment of the first Protestants at Oxford in his *History of England;* the minutes of the society record this debut without comment. On 20 June 1857, Dicey read extracts from Boswell's *Letters,* "displaying that individual's character in anything but an exalted light."[49] The last essay read at the society in the first year was Dicey's on the "Aim of Punishment," which he argued should be the general benefit of the public. This appeal to utilitarian logic found near unanimous concurrence from the other youthful members.

In the following year Dicey first presented a discussion of Herod-

45. Ibid., 31 March 1916, ibid.

46. On the Old Mortality Society in general, see Gerald C. Monsman, "Old Mortality at Oxford," pp. 359–89.

47. The Old Mortality Society flourished from 1856 to 1860 and continued spasmodically after that until about 1865. Besides Nichol and Dicey, an original founder was A. C. Swinburne. Later members included James Bryce, Thomas Hill Green, Walter Pater, and T. Erskine Holland. Membership lists are in the papers of the Old Mortality Society, Ms. Top. Oxon. b. 255, f. 1, Bodleian Library. For all the later success of his fellow members, Dicey considered George Luke the noblest and most promising man in the society. Luke drowned in the Isis in 1862, ending prematurely the potential he had shown at Oxford. See Dicey to Bryce, 18 April 1917, Bryce Papers.

48. Old Mortality Society, Minute Book, Ms. Top. Oxon. d. 242, f. 4, Bodleian Library.

49. Ibid., f. 24.

otus and Thucydides as historians, with emphasis on the religious element that pervaded and ultimately vitiated the work of the former. The minutes commended the clear arrangement of the paper, its distinctive style, and the manner in which it so carefully made points of distinction between the two historians.[50] Dicey next added a critical essay on the writings and character of Charles Kingsley. "With great clearness and precision," he denied Kingsley any originality as a thinker or merit as a novelist.[51] The primary charge against Kingsley was a suffusive clericalism, a failing Dicey could not excuse.[52] Both essays demonstrated the intense dislike of clerical predominance in society he had already adopted.

The final paper before the society dealt with capital punishment, concluding that the present system of penal laws was just in itself and necessary for the prevention of crime. Once again the argument gained the assent of other members while winning admiration for clarity of style.[53] Overall he found the Old Mortality Society congenial, the discussions there memorable and a constant source of intellectual fascination: "I still think that the Essays read there and our discussions on them were remarkable; certainly they were infinitely pleasant, and our evenings are a joy to me to look back upon."[54]

Reading papers for the edification of his friends was not the sole scholarly experience provided by the society, for it also gave an opportunity for writing. Through the Old Mortality Dicey published his first article. In November 1857, John Nichol accepted the management of a failing Oxford magazine on condition that other members join the enterprise with him.[55] *Undergraduate Papers* lasted only three numbers, but in the first issue Dicey contributed a brief comparison of Plato's Republic and the Christian religion.[56] In this maiden effort he displayed the literary traits characteristic of his

50. Ibid., f. 35.
51. Ibid., f. 43.
52. In view of Dicey's confession that his literary studies were motivated by the desire to win academic prizes, it is hardly surprising that his literary judgment was shallow and invariably reflected his own prejudices.
53. Minute Book, Ms. Top. Oxon. d. 242, f. 48.
54. Dicey to Mrs. T. H. Green, 17 September 1882, Thomas Hill Green Papers, Balliol College.
55. George Birkbeck Hill to Annie Scott, 10 November 1857, in Lucy Crump, ed., *Letters of George Birkbeck Hill*, p. 73.
56. Albert Venn Dicey, "The Republic and Christianity," pp. 16–19.

later political polemics. He utilized a dialectical style in which he first presented concisely the conclusions he opposed, then presented his own line of argument, and finally resolved the contradictions in the last paragraphs. He listed initially the superficial similarities of Platonism and Christianity, then proceeded to show the marked differences, and finally concluded that while the Republic remained a mere theory, Christianity had revolutionized the world. The simplistic nature of the youthful argument does not detract from the interest of the expository style he had already developed.

Members of the Old Mortality Society distinguished themselves in other areas, particularly the Oxford Union debates. Dicey spoke frequently at the Union and held the prestigious position of president in the Lent term, 1859. Despite diffidence about his oratorical abilities because of his physical difficulties, through hard work he acquired the art of public speaking and eventually won a formidable reputation. Contemporaries thought highly of his skills at a time when debating prowess was greatly respected.[57] The motions he supported at the Union reflected his preoccupation with politics, international and domestic.

Of the topics the society considered, politics consumed more time than anything else: "I can hardly now quite realise myself the intense interest with which we all kept talking day after day about Louis Napoleon, Italy, and later the war in America."[58] James Bryce, Dicey's close friend and fellow member of the Old Mortality, confirmed this preoccupation with politics when he recalled that political discussions were more prominent at Balliol than elsewhere in the university.[59] Many issues captured the attention of the society, but three international questions took precedence.

The first was the problem of emerging nationalism, especially the question of Italian freedom. The ennobling nature of nationalism appeared self-evident in 1858, with the cause of Italy particularly sacred. Dicey supported intervention in behalf of oppressed nationalities without qualification. Bryce's first essay to the Old Mortality Society had discussed nationalism in glowing terms; few foresaw to what dangerous excesses the principle might be pushed.[60] Dicey

57. H. A. L. Fisher, *James Bryce*, 1: 48.
58. Dicey to Mrs. T. H. Green, 17 September 1882, Green Papers.
59. Bryce to Dicey, 14 November 1913, Bryce Papers.
60. Ibid., 31 December 1918, ibid.

later wrote that he had been "keenly interested" in foreign nationalist movements.[61] National liberty and political unity seemed equivalent, and nationalism attracted the support of the idealism so evident in the society. Only T. H. Green, with his advocacy of cosmopolitan humanitarianism, dissented from the prevailing opinion of his friends. This youthful persuasion never left Dicey, for he considered national assertion a fundamental test of freedom. The cause of nationalism remained with Dicey long after more transient issues had been resolved.

Next came Louis Napoleon, who received one fiery denunciation after another from the Old Mortality. Regarded somewhat contradictorily as both a foolish charlatan and an unscrupulous dictator, the French emperor had his policies subjected to close scrutiny. Dicey later wrote: "I see little reason to think we were wrong in our general estimate of the Emperor; but there is something amusing as I look back upon them, in the youthful vehemence of our denunciations, and in our constantly repeated and constantly disappointed hopes of his downfall."[62] He admitted that as a young man he had completely misjudged the hold Louis Napoleon had upon the French people. This admission did not prevent him from clinging to his initial estimate of the basic evil the emperor had inflicted on France.

Finally, Dicey defended passionately the Northern cause in the American Civil War. This marked one of the few issues upon which he and T. H. Green agreed; he subsequently paid tribute to the strength Green's support gave to his own convictions.[63] The pair had successfully justified Northern actions in Oxford Union debate, specifically on the grounds that slavery was opposed to all true individualism.[64] Dicey later called all these youthful opinions romantic, attributing them to inexperience and idealism. Still, he never retreated from these positions in later life, altering only the reasons for his support.

In domestic politics discussions revolved around the question of reform, particularly a selective extension of the franchise. The viewpoint of the Old Mortality was best expressed by Bryce: "The most marked contrast between those days and the present seems to lie in

61. Dicey to Bryce, 27 July 1917, ibid.
62. A. V. Dicey, in W. Knight, *Memoir of John Nichol*, pp. 140–41.
63. Dicey to Mrs. T. H. Green, 17 September 1882, Green Papers.
64. Bryce to Dicey, 16 February 1909, Bryce Papers.

the fact that we all assumed individualism as obviously & absolutely right. We were not indifferent to the misfortunes of the poor, but looked upon them as inevitable, I did not feel the restless anxiety to remove them, even in defiance of economic laws, which burns in the breast of modern youth. This may have been partly because religion formed the framework of life & thought more largely then than it does now—or at least because the other world seemed nearer & more certain."[65] The real conditions of English life were far removed from the theoretical speculations of university students. Only Green had shown any interest in domestic social movements, and he possessed on this topic, as Dicey acknowledged, "probably somewhat more knowledge than I or perhaps most of us had."[66] Green frequently pointed out the evils of pauperism, a trait Dicey attributed to a power of imagination that caused Green "to realise much more clearly than most of us the actual sufferings of the poor."[67] Thus the Old Mortality neatly combined a steadfast social conservatism with political progressivism.

Dicey fit in well in the Balliol atmosphere of the 1850s: unorthodox in religion and radical in politics.[68] In his adolescent exuberance Dicey proudly accepted the label of radical, a source of considerable embarrassment in later life. His reputation for advanced political views depended primarily upon the anathemas he continuously hurled against the conservatism of Oxford, opposed, as he thought, to the enlightened doctrines of liberalism. He favored the franchise for those who earned it and sympathized with the movement for women's rights. Such opinions, rather extreme in the context of mid-Victorian Oxford, gave him notoriety.

The other major controversy within the Old Mortality Society involved the relationship of politics to religious questions, notably the university tests, disestablishment of the Church of England, and deliverance of the universities from clericalism in general.[69] The crusade to make religious belief irrelevant to university admission attracted many students who shared the society's enthusiasms.[70]

65. Ibid., 14 November 1913, ibid.
66. Dicey to Bryce, 27 July 1917, ibid.
67. Dicey to Mrs. T. H. Green, 17 September 1882, Green Papers.
68. Richter, *Politics of Conscience*, p. 83.
69. Bryce to Dicey, 14 November 1913, Bryce Papers.
70. Lord Annan, "The Intellectual Aristocracy," p. 247.

Interest in specific theological disputes was not in vogue: "I do not remember," Dicey wrote, "any custom which would have prevented me from reading an essay from any topic whatever, religious or non-religious, which I felt interesting. But I do not recollect any direct theological discussion being raised in the essays read at the Old Mortality, though of course we were all frequently discussing enquiries bearing upon signing the Thirty Nine Articles."[71] The mood was secular, and members paid little heed to the legacy of the Tractarian movement.[72] Basic theological problems concerned them not at all, as the society was oblivious to Darwin and the religious questions he had raised. The sole commitment was to freedom of thought, and the membership had no interest in religious controversies as such.

Bryce characterized the Old Mortality Society as a "quite remarkable" body, and Dicey was no less proud of his place in it: "I look with great satisfaction on the fact that the Old Mortality, to which James and I belonged, though we may not have done quite as brilliantly in the world as we expected, has never had any reason to be ashamed of any of its members, & considering we were utterly without any connection, to have produced one Cabinet Minister [Bryce], & I think six Professors [Dicey, Nichol, Bryce, Green, Holland, Nettleship] who perhaps in the aggregate may be taken as equivalent to one C.M., is not bad. Oh, I forgot, we have also the best on the whole of living English poets [Swinburne]."[73] Dicey valued the success of the society all the more because its members had overcome obstacles of every description. He regarded them as living embodiments of individual success through open competition, which proved the validity of his own liberal principles. As Dicey wrote: "We had neither wealth nor rank & suffered at least our fair share of loss from death & disease. Of our books I say nothing; they are only too numerous."[74] Dicey found in the Old Mortality young men of similar background and opinions who strengthened his own values, political beliefs, and ambition.

By the time he took his B.A. degree in 1858, Dicey faced major

71. Dicey to Bryce, 18 April 1917, Bryce Papers.
72. On this point, see Monsman, "Old Mortality at Oxford," p. 379.
73. Bryce to Dicey, 6 May 1909, Bryce Papers; Dicey to Mrs. Bryce, 1 May 1893, ibid.
74. Dicey to Bryce, 16 November 1893, ibid.

difficulties, most prominently the death of his father and subsequent decline in family fortunes. Though the family retained the *Mercury* for another quarter of a century, it was never as prosperous again. He could not share with his father the joy of attaining a First in Greats in the summer of 1858. "By having to put off my schools till the latest time," he once wrote, "it happened that I did not take my degree or rather pass my examination till some months after my father's death & thus lost a good half of the pleasure of success."[75] His father had attached great importance to the result in the hopes that it would secure Albert's future.[76] With degree successfully in hand, Dicey searched for the fellowship that would fulfill his father's expectations.

During the next two years the quest was in vain, as on four occasions Dicey stood for a fellowship without success. His failure stemmed primarily from the difficulty, which plagued him all his life, of writing legibly and rapidly without exhausting himself. Only when Dicey obtained permission to dictate to an amanuensis did he gain a fellowship at Trinity College, Oxford. He had no doubt that Jowett instigated this scheme, although others credited Robinson Ellis, and had prevailed upon the Trinity authorities to cooperate.[77] Through this kindly intervention the fellowship Dicey sought was now his.

Within his circle of friends Dicey's good fortune occasioned much celebration: "Well do I remember," wrote Bryce, "that Trinity Sunday & still better the Trinity Monday when your election gave such delight to the Old Mortality & was the dawning of a happy day for those of us who were going in for Greats & had your lectures for two terms."[78] For the next year Dicey expounded Mill's logic and Aristotle's ethics with the verve born of complete immersion in his new duties.[79] Among several excellent pupils he tutored during this period he always counted Bryce the best.[80] At first his election had caused consternation because of the reputation for advanced views

75. Ibid., 9 March 1896, ibid.

76. Ibid., 14 August 1903, ibid.

77. Dicey to Lionel Jacob, 11 July 1912, Working Men's College MSS, Working Men's College, London. Jacob was vice-president of the Working Men's College.

78. Bryce to Dicey, 29 May 1918, Bryce Papers.

79. Dicey to Lady Farrer, 5 November 1920, in Rait, *Memorials*, p. 270.

80. Dicey to Jacob, 11 July 1912, Working Men's College MSS.

he had acquired. Bryce remembered well "the alarm your selection created among some undergraduates who thought you were certainly a Radical & probably a Positivist or Atheist; & I remember how in a few weeks everyone was happy."[81] Dicey thought this first year of his Trinity fellowship "the best & most effective year I ever spent."[82] His diligence soon reaped its reward in the form of another academic award.

Aside from winning his fellowship, in 1860 Dicey also submitted the Arnold Prize Essay on the Privy Council. Its immediate publication concluded his first Oxford period in a blaze of glory.[83] *The Privy Council* was avowedly a piece of historical research, Dicey's only such work until his last book at age eighty-five. Later scholarship has modified its judgments, but this first major publication contained interesting insights into the problem of the growth of government institutions. For all the promise it showed as a contribution to scholarship, however, it paled beside the 1863 Arnold Prize Essay by Bryce on the Holy Roman Empire, which was an instant classic and remained a permanent memorial to its author.

The significance of *The Privy Council* lay in the clues it provided to Dicey's attitudes at time of publication. For instance, a Whiggish view of history permeated the book, especially the repeated assertion that the development of one institution such as Parliament must necessarily lead to the diminution of power in another institution such as the monarchy. The most striking feature was the strong allegiance to laissez-faire Dicey displayed. He professed surprise that the Privy Council meddled in commerce so frequently, a policy of "which no ruler would now even dream."[84] By way of conclusion Dicey asserted that "the fact that government interference is an evil is now too well established to need the confirmation of further arguments."[85] While *The Privy Council* did not win instant fame for its young author, neither was it a wasted effort. It

81. Bryce to Dicey, 29 May 1918, Bryce Papers.

82. Dicey to Bryce, 19 March 1910, ibid.

83. Albert Venn Dicey, *The Privy Council.* The Whittaker Company published the first edition; Macmillan published the second unrevised edition in 1887. Dicey considered a revised version but in the end he never returned to the topic. See Dicey to the Macmillan Company, 20 May 1881, Macmillan Company Papers, British Museum Additional Manuscripts 55084.

84. Dicey, *The Privy Council,* p. 60.

85. Ibid., p. 109.

introduced Dicey to questions of law and history that occupied the remainder of his life as well as affording him more experience in presenting to the public the fruits of his labor. As Rait wrote, that this early effort could be republished later without damage to his reputation was a credit to Dicey.[86]

When Dicey left Oxford in 1861, he could regard his seven years there with great satisfaction. He had earned a prestigious degree, made friendships that would prove enduring, and published his first book. He had put into practice for the first time the philosophy of work that would guide his career; this discipline became so imbued it made thoughts of retirement painful later in life.[87] His character and opinions had taken final shape with one vital exception, the contribution made by his legal training. In later years Dicey proudly called himself a mid-Victorian reformer, a testimony to the strength of his creed at the end of his student days.

Specifically, Dicey extolled laissez-faire, believed passionately in individual liberty, supported a vigorous foreign policy on behalf of nationalist movements, distrusted the restrictions on society he thought organized religion entailed, and already possessed a keen interest in politics. Dicey's liberalism had a more general content as well: "It meant the gradual, the considered, and therefore the effective, removal of every demonstrated evil which would be curable either by legislation or by the improvement of social habits or sentiments. It was also the rejection no less of the dull conservatism which aimed merely at keeping all things, or at any rate all things not absolutely evil, exactly as they were, than of the revolutionary schemes which, even if unconnected with lawless violence, assumed that even the best institutions existing in the civilized world ought to undergo a fundamental change."[88] Certainly the most remarkable feature of his life was the tenacity with which he clung to the opinions of his student days and the vigor with which he espoused them for the next sixty years. His childhood and Oxford career had molded firmly the values of the mature man. Dicey was to remain remarkably immovable in a world of drastic change.

86. Rait, *Memorials*, p. 35.
87. Dicey to E. L. Godkin, 25 December 1899, E. L. Godkin Papers, Houghton Library, Harvard University.
88. Albert Venn Dicey, "An English Scholar's Appreciation of Godkin," *Nation* 101 (8 July 1915): 52.

CHAPTER TWO

AMBITION DENIED,

1861–1882

UPON LEAVING Oxford Dicey moved to London to reside with his widowed mother and read for the bar at the Inner Temple. His legal education in preparation for the bar added the last important ingredient to the shaping of his mature political and legal philosophy. The final influence on Dicey was his study of and enduring admiration for the writings of John Austin, the founder of English analytical jurisprudence. The effect of Austin on Dicey, rarely stressed by previous writers, was crucial in the formation of his own philosophy of law. Austin affected permanently Dicey's views on the relationship between law and politics, providing Dicey with a unique outlook on the moral basis of political development.

John Austin dominated Victorian jurisprudence as no other figure did. His first major work, *The Province of Jurisprudence Determined*, published in 1832, excited little discussion because few English lawyers admitted the validity of jurisprudence itself, much less paid attention to the correctness of the arguments Austin advanced. After a life of futility and failure to earn any sort of reputation, the posthumous appearance of Austin's *Lectures* brought his work before a wider public and coincided with Dicey's call to the bar in 1863. The analytical system proposed by Austin sparked a general revival of legal theory as a respectable intellectual task for English jurists. Austin proved far more influential from the grave than he had ever been in life. As an ambitious young barrister who prided himself on his intellectual accomplishments, Dicey studied Austinian jurisprudence, which had become the vogue in legal circles, and incorporated it into the value system he had formed.

In three major areas of concern to legal philosophers Austin radically challenged traditional assumptions. Austin's insistence on the necessity for a clear distinction between the law as it existed and the law as it ought to be was the most influential of his assertions.

Austin attacked directly natural law theory, which held that positive law must reflect a standard of morality. This indifference to moral questions was methodological only, for Austin maintained the distinction not from hostility to moral principles, but from the need to avoid confusion of legal and moral questions. The separation of law from morality that Austin demanded inaugurated a new era in jurisprudential theory by supplying a more effective analytical tool for the resolution of legal problems. In the common law jurisdiction Austin became for decades the great legal philosopher against whom all other writers were judged.

Moreover, Austin offered a definition of law as command which many interpreted as voiding any sense of moral obligation inherent in obedience to law. He propounded a theory of sovereignty in which the duty of citizens to obey the law depended ultimately upon the power of the sovereign to command obedience. Sovereignty reposed in that individual who did not habitually give obedience to any superior and habitually received obedience from a majority of citizens. Law as command linked coercion to the certainty of punishment in the case of disobedience. This definition of law suited the criminal law well, but critics soon debated its applicability to civil proceedings.

Finally, Austin reduced the general topic of law to a few simple propositions, then constructed his legal system on the basis of these elementary concepts. Austin conceived his task to be the systemization of English law by delivering it from the chaos of centuries of undisciplined development. Once the validity of ideas such as law, command, and sanction were established beyond dispute, the reconstruction of law on a scientific basis was possible. The rigorous application of logical analysis to legal conceptions and the attempt to free the law from verbal imprecision anticipated the work of English jurists for the next generation. In particular, codification— the scientific pruning of the dead growth of the common law— seemed in the 1860s and 1870s the next great labor for English jurisprudence.

The Austinian influence on Dicey was greatest in the area of analysis, where he embraced enthusiastically the new techniques of jurisprudence. In his later legal and political writings Dicey differed from Austin on several substantive issues even while acknowledging the force of Austin's arguments. Nevertheless, Dicey appropriated from Austin his basic approach to legal problems, that is, the attempt to resolve questions of law by stating fundamental principles derived from thorough analysis of pertinent cases, then building logically a comprehensive body of knowledge about the point in dispute. On the topic of analysis John Stuart Mill regarded Austin's facility for "disciplining other minds in the art of precise thought" as his greatest achievement.[1] Dicey's own work strikingly confirmed Mill's assertion. On one occasion Dicey called Austin "an author whose name can never be mentioned without the profoundest respect by all who value clearness of thought and logical precision of language."[2] Each of Dicey's legal treatises aimed at the Austinian ideal of clarity by utilizing this distinctive method of deducing rules from cases, followed by an exhaustive elaboration of the cases on which the rule was founded. Dicey's devotion to this Austinian methodology allowed him to regard with equanimity attacks on other aspects of Austin's philosophy. When other legal scholars criticized his mentor, Dicey adopted a conciliatory attitude secure in the knowledge that Austin had provided a valid methodology for resolving legal problems even if Austin had sometimes failed in his own endeavors.[3]

Dicey credited Austin with reviving the speculative study of law at a time when "jurisprudence is a word which stinks in the nostrils of a practicing barrister."[4] Austin had accomplished this by encouraging the comparative study of English and Roman law, demonstrating that the two legal systems should be studied in tandem, and showing that each had much to offer the other. For Dicey, after the style of Austin, jurisprudence encompassed primarily the accurate definition of legal concepts. Most important in Dicey's estimation, Austin exhibited "extraordinary powers of logical analysis" which forced upon the reader a number of dogmas with such strength that the impression once made was never obliterated.[5] Dicey spoke the language of the law with a decidedly Austinian accent.

Dicey criticized Austin when warranted, especially his laborious

1. John Stuart Mill, "Austin on Jurisprudence," p. 439.
2. Albert Venn Dicey, "Digby on the History of English Law," p. 374.
3. Albert Venn Dicey, "An Introduction to Jurisprudence," *Nation* 63 (24 September 1896): 234–35.
4. Albert Venn Dicey, "The Study of Jurisprudence," p. 382.
5. Ibid., p. 386.

style. He argued Austin had greater command of thought than of expression: "It is hardly an exaggeration to say that he cannot handle the English language."[6] Dicey also deplored Austin's preoccupation with polemics against the prevailing legal orthodoxies of the early Victorian period, citing Austin's refusal to proceed beyond a few basic themes as proof. From even these faults Dicey profited, for he took great pains in his own work to achieve a readable style. Furthermore, Dicey always treated preceding legal authorities with the greatest respect for their efforts, including a special veneration for Blackstone, who had been a particular target of Austin. Dicey's own legal reputation eventually rested on his clear exposition of basic precepts in language any layman could understand.

Contemporaries attested to the debt Dicey owed Austin, coupling the two men repeatedly. Henry Sidgwick, who had himself evaluated Austin's work at length, wrote apropos *Law of the Constitution:* "I consider your defense of Austin—as to sovereignty in England—the best that can be made: but I should perhaps add that Austin, considering his prolix ostentation of verbal precision, is perhaps the best author for whom such a defense will be accepted as valid."[7] In connection with *Conflict of Laws* Sir Frederick Pollock alluded to Dicey's being "not clear of the damnable heresies of Austin."[8] Just prior to Pollock's comment Dicey himself had written that Austin was in the 1890s "unduly depreciated" and insisted on the influence Austin had exercised on his own development.[9] Dicey took great pride in his allegiance to the Austinian tradition, never renouncing his belief in the source of his own legal assumptions.

Dicey adapted Austinian jurisprudence to the values held when he left Oxford. For example, like other mid-Victorian admirers of Austin, he regarded the separation of law from morality with ambivalent feelings. Many lawyers who accepted the validity of Austin's

6. Ibid.

7. Henry Sidgwick to Dicey, 2 November 1885, General Manuscripts 508(17), Glasgow University Library.

8. Sir Frederick Pollock to Oliver Wendell Holmes, 2 October 1896, in Mark DeWolfe Howe, ed., *Holmes-Pollock Letters*, 1: 71.

9. Dicey to Frederic Harrison, 29 July 1896, Frederic Harrison Papers, Library of Political and Economic Science, London School of Economics. I am indebted for this reference to Professor Martha S. Vogeler of California State University, Fullerton.

system at the same time feared the detachment of moral from legal obligations. Dicey, like Austin, separated the question "what is the law (or the concern of a practical lawyer)" from the question "what ought to be the law (or the concern of the jurist)"; Dicey did not deny "that these enquiries have a connection with each other but I think it greatly conduces to clearness to keep them distinct."[10] This crucial dilemma Dicey resolved by insisting upon the intimate and permanent connection between law and morality while denying their identification. Law and morality should approximate one another, he argued, lest union lead to fanaticism. Law was external, morality internal, or—as Dicey phrased it: "Law is concerned with acts, Morality with character."[11] The utilitarian legal tradition accepted the frequent intersection of law and morals, and to this teaching Dicey adhered.[12] Law must reflect opinion or otherwise mass disobedience would follow, negating law itself. The Diceyan definition of public opinion contained this decisive element whereby opinion supplied the moral backbone to the legal system. Thus Dicey retained the sanction of morality while observing the strict separation of law and morality for juristic purposes.

On the topic of sovereignty Dicey again accepted Austinian premises but altered significantly the inferences to be drawn. Dicey admitted, as Austin urged, that every government must command habitual obedience from its subjects. He agreed as well that sovereignty was indivisible, there being no logical justification for ideas like subsidiary sovereignty. The true test of sovereignty for Dicey, however, was the possession of supreme legislative authority. He conceded that sovereignty depended sometimes upon the use of force as Austin stated, but he believed that it was more contingent on the disposition of citizens to obey. In a few instances fear of punishment caused obedience, but, as Dicey thought, the habit of obedience over centuries was more responsible.[13]

The strong impression Austin made upon Dicey colored his

10. Dicey to Holmes, 19 January 1880, Holmes Papers.

11. This quotation and the other views of Dicey are taken from his lecture "Introduction to English Law" given at the Working Men's College, 7 November 1901.

12. H. L. A. Hart, "Legal Positivism and the Separation of Law and Morals," p. 598.

13. This summary of Dicey's ideas is derived from a lecture delivered 5 December 1901, entitled "Sovereignty."

thought thereafter, recurring in his later political and constitutional works. The steadfast loyalty to liberalism that had marked his undergraduate career, now combined with neo-Austinianism, shaped Dicey's political philosophy, which maintained that sovereignty must be vested in the state but that its only function was the enforcement of individual rights. Whenever he wrote on law, particularly the law of domicile, Dicey retained basic Austinian concepts in methodology and conclusions. These links between Austin and Dicey completed the formation of Dicey's mid-Victorian creed.

Dicey's attachment to Austin appears the more remarkable when it is noted how little other trends in legal scholarship impressed him. The historical investigations of Henry Maine held little attraction, because Dicey believed that Maine's work cast doubt on the efficacy of legislation, a conclusion Dicey preferred to ignore. Dicey respected the erudition of Maine, conceding the significance of Maine's contributions, but historical jurisprudence exercised little influence over Dicey's intellectual development. Dicey exhibited a similar indifference to German jurisprudence, whose image in Dicey's mind persisted as a natural law, theoretical, wildly impractical approach to legal problems. As a result he never appreciated, from a comparative point of view, the value of an alternative to his own legal training such as he found in French and American constitutional history. Austin had provided him with a methodology, but Dicey suffered nonetheless because of the narrow outlook analytic jurisprudence had imposed.

After his call to the bar Dicey settled down to a comfortable existence, thanks to his fellowship, of waiting for briefs. He continued his travels to the Continent, usually accompanied by Bryce; the pair had visited Berlin in September of 1862 during the constitutional crisis that brought Bismarck to power.[14] At this time Dicey also contributed articles on politics to the family newspaper and, in addition, frequently took over editorial duties from his brother Edward. In these writings he stressed the same themes he had pursued as an Oxford undergraduate. His intense ambition would not permit this relaxed life to continue, so he searched for the useful work that might realize his plans.

Despite his later disclaimers, Dicey hoped the bar would provide an entry into the world of politics. These plans misfired on two

14. Bryce to Dicey, 12 December 1919, Bryce Papers.

counts: he did not earn much prominence at the bar, nor did he ever gain the access to the political arena he so ardently desired. As he wrote about his career as a young barrister: "Till I got the Inland Revenue post [1876], the Bar never was anything but a loss to me. I should long ago have starved had I depended on my briefs for food. I had nothing I could really count upon before my marriage but my fellowship."[15] Years later his obituary put it tactfully: Dicey had not possessed the qualities necessary to attract the attention of solicitors.[16] The result was that "after trying to gain fame as a barrister, I at last realised that the expenses of the Bar to most of us exceeded its gains."[17] His dissatisfaction found expression in an article where he attacked the cronyism and restrictive practices employed by the established barrister.[18] As in other areas of society, he could not accept the superiority of entrenched interests who enjoyed their privileges in the absence of competition. That a young barrister should defer to a more experienced colleague on the grounds of professionalism he thought an outrageous situation, contrary to the best thought of the day. Also, Dicey's legal career never acted as the springboard into politics he had hoped: "I don't deceive myself into the delusion that the world lost anything by not achieving these ends," he wrote afterwards. "I think they were legitimate and I am heartily glad that I was never tempted to let failing affect the happiness of my life."[19] As will be seen, this last sentiment was not quite the whole truth.

Dicey joined the Northern Circuit but failed to win distinction. He never adjusted to the hardships of circuit life and was uncharacteristically lukewarm in the performance of his duties. He later confessed to Bryce: "I suppose I ought never to have gone Circuit at all or else have made more of it. However I have no cause to complain for by your intervention I got hold of old [Sir John] Holker. The connection with him was by far the pleasantest & most profitable result."[20] This nagging sense of discontent with his circuit career also prompted this recollection: "Sometimes I wish we could

15. Dicey to Mrs. R. B. Litchfield, ? October 1897, in Rait, *Memorials,* p. 142.
16. The *Times,* 11 April 1922, p. 17.
17. Dicey to Lady Farrer, 5 November 1920, in Rait, *Memorials,* p. 270.
18. Albert Venn Dicey, "Legal Etiquette," pp. 169–79.
19. Dicey to Bryce, 11 September 1918, Bryce Papers.
20. Ibid., 16 July 1889, ibid.

go back again to 64 & 65 when we were with [Sir John] Scott on circuit. One could perhaps make a better thing of life by which I don't mean get more money."[21] Lack of any true success as a barrister helped channel his work toward academic law.

In the first step in this direction, Dicey did not fare well either. In 1866 he undertook the teaching of logic at the Working Men's College in London and soon "brought down a class of 30 to an expiring class of 3."[22] Without the advantages enjoyed by an Oxford tutor and too diffident to seek advice from college officials, he never repeated the experiment at the college. He contemplated substituting a course in law for that of logic but was too shy to make the suggestion to college authorities. This early failure was perhaps a blessing in disguise, for Dicey admitted that at the time he lacked the strength for anything but his duties at the bar.[23] He regretted the enforced departure from the college but had no real alternative in view of his dismal performance.

Through these vicissitudes Dicey followed the course of domestic politics with his customary keen interest. In 1867 the publication of his first article on politics for a national audience signified more than the debut in political writing of a young liberal.[24] The Second Reform Act marked the transition from young radical to mature moderate. Until 1867 his youthful zeal for reform placed him in the radical camp within the Liberal party, led him to espouse advanced views, and caused him to advocate political change in preference to maintenance of the status quo. He had favored reform through a limited extension of the franchise on the assumption that fitness for enfranchisement would be tested; the grant of the vote to the urban working class without careful scrutiny had always struck him as a dangerous innovation.[25] After 1867 his political concerns swung more to the preservation of existing institutions in place of demands for further change. The world of 1854–67 remained ever after for Dicey the zenith of the English political system, and nostalgia for that era was the primary motif of his later politics. As the years passed his tone became more strident in denunciation of move-

21. Ibid., 6 March 1904, ibid.
22. Ibid., 12 June 1913, ibid.
23. Dicey to Jacob, 6 September 1909, Working Men's College MSS.
24. Albert Venn Dicey, "The Balance of Classes," pp. 67–84.
25. Dicey to Bryce, 15 September 1917, Bryce Papers.

ments he disapproved, his identification with the Whig element in the Liberal party stronger, and his estrangement from modern politics more complete.

In the *Essays on Reform* Dicey reaffirmed his faith in individualism by denying that a balance of class interests was preferable to representation of individuals. The greater part of his essay examined the Conservative arguments in support of class representation and the concurrent fear of numbers in the electoral balance; in each case he found them wanting. "Advocates of class representation desire such a political arrangement as would enable a minority," Dicey wrote, "in virtue of their education, wealth, etc. to carry out their views, even though opposed to the sentiments of the majority of the people."[26] In his eyes class representation stood for the class privilege and resistance to change he attributed to Conservatives. "Half the evils of modern England arise from the undue prominence of class distinctions," he added, "and the fundamental fault of class representation is its tendency to intensify differences which it is an object of political Reform to remove."[27] Free trade in political relationships, defined as the competition between individuals for political power, served as the primary antidote for the unrest that had recently disturbed the country. Majority rule was not infallible, he felt, but a nation gained more by the experience of liberty than it lost by the errors. As reform in the direction of individual freedom had blunted middle-class resentment in 1832, so some measure of reform in 1867 would gradually merge the working class into the nation, precluding revolutionary violence. The longer workers were treated as a separate class, the more they would devote their energies to narrow class interests. Two principles underlay his conception of reform: each man was the best manager of his own affairs; citizens ought to be considered individuals first, members of a class second. A majority of the nation should be brought within the bounds of the constitution, although some risks were involved. Dicey looked ahead confidently to the day when artisans would be indistinguishable from other sections of society.

Amidst the welter of debate and shifting political fortunes in 1866–68, little if any specific influence can be ascribed to the essays

26. Dicey, "Balance of Classes," p. 70.
27. Ibid., p. 81.

in general or Dicey's in particular. They were, at best, discussions of reform on a theoretical level without political weight. Dicey later thought his essay had done no harm and that his views had mirrored those of many young liberals in that era. If there was nothing untrue in his essay, still less could it be said he had shown any insight or foresight.[28] It certainly did not gain him notoriety nor provide the entry into politics he sought. His career remained rooted in the mediocrity that threatened more menacingly with each passing year.

Early in 1870 Dicey reversed this trend through publication of his first legal treatise, a study of the intricate rules governing parties to an action.[29] During his apprenticeship for the bar he had shown curiosity about the complex procedures involved in pleading. Pleading depended on the strict application of logical rules and so had appealed to Dicey's passion for orderly arrangement in legal questions. Prior to the Judicature Act of 1873, the rules of pleading overlapped because of unregulated development over the centuries. Its intricacies had given rise to the art of special pleading, already synonymous with unfair argument. This procedural disorder posed a fitting challenge to test his analytical talents. The topic suited admirably his goal of extracting a small number of essential rules from a mass of conflicting opinions.

In the treatise Dicey aimed "to reduce or digest the law of parties into a series of rules, each of which is illustrated and explained by appropriate cases and examples, and confirmed, wherever this is possible, by quotations from judgments or from the pages of writers of acknowledged reputation."[30] The result was 118 rules carefully delineated through a statement of the rule accompanied by supporting cases, then the exceptions to the rules with their relevant cases. From the numerous discordant cases confronting the lawyer, Dicey provided a compendium of the law simply stated, then appended the citations on which he based his conclusions. The reader found the legal principles governing parties to an action explained clearly without the trouble of examining the numerous casebooks on his own.

28. Dicey to Bryce, 19 March 1910, Bryce Papers.
29. Albert Venn Dicey, *A Treatise on the Rules for the Selection of the Parties to an Action.*
30. Ibid., p. iii.

This manner of treatment introduced a major innovation, for prior to 1870 legal treatises were proverbial for their complexity to the uninitiated, lack of literary grace, and methodological disorganization. Though dealing with a diffuse topic, the digest succeeded in presenting the rules of procedure under existing conditions in straightforward fashion. Dicey knew well that his book faced certain obsolescence, because the procedural fusion of common law and equity loomed in the near future. He justified the work on the grounds that, no matter what rules were adapted in the future by a centralized court of law and equity, a thorough knowledge of previous principles would be required.

Parties to an Action held a special place in Dicey's affections, notwithstanding the rapidity with which the book suffered eclipse. In later life he called it "the best legal book I ever wrote,"[31] a surprising verdict in the light of his more famous works to come. His close friend James Bryce had suggested the project to Dicey, who found the subject congenial. For this reason he considered the book "born as it were under a happy star and is full of memories of happy work and sympathy to me."[32] It had cost much effort on his part but it had been a labor of love and so, in his own judgment, represented a better book than any he had written.[33]

As much as he had enjoyed the preparation of the book, he had an even better reason for remembering it with pleasure. The legal profession noticed the book favorably, and this recognition helped establish Dicey's standing as a legal scholar. Lord Bramwell sent a congratulatory note expressing basic agreement with the purpose of the book.[34] Sir John Coleridge, for whom Dicey had started preparing briefs in 1869, wrote: "If it is done half as well as your ordinary work, it will certainly be very good."[35] Dicey also reported to Bryce that Sir John Holker had praised the book, a fact he had heard with great delight from Erskine Holland.[36] *Parties to an Action* does not

31. Dicey to Bryce, 8 December 1917, Bryce Papers.
32. Ibid., n.d. 1870, ibid.
33. Dicey to Lucy Cohen, 5 November 1914, in Lucy Cohen, *Arthur Cohen*, p. 85.
34. Lord Bramwell to Dicey, 13 November 1870, General Manuscripts, 508(1), Glasgow University Library.
35. Sir John Coleridge to Dicey, n.d. 1870, in Rait, *Memorials*, p. 48.
36. Dicey to Bryce, n.d. 1870, Bryce Papers.

measure up to Dicey's classic works; yet, for its time, it was extremely competent, displayed skills esteemed by the legal profession, and brought him some reputation in scholarly circles. The book cannot be said to have exercised any lasting influence on subsequent legal development, although it did synthesize existing knowledge within its own narrow purview. For a maiden effort in legal writing it was well worth the energy Dicey had given it.

Immediately after the publication of the book, Dicey and Bryce began a tour of the United States. This particular journey, because it eventually resulted in Bryce's famous *The American Commonwealth*, ranks beside that of Tocqueville among the important visitations to America by foreign observers.[37] Though it is widely known that this expedition stirred Bryce's curiosity and led to his enduring interest in American affairs, it is less recognized that Dicey's subsequent writings and attitudes also depended in some respects upon the impressions of America gained in 1870. "Certainly of all the external things my journey to the U.S. was to me one of the most important," Dicey wrote, "as it was one of the pleasantest. It had a very close connection with the Law of the Constitution as also one may presume with the American Commonwealth."[38] On another occasion he added to Bryce: "It is curious to think how much in one way or another our journey in 1870 affected both of our lives &, I should say on the whole affected them happily. One may pretty well assume that the American Commonwealth & probably neither the Law of the Constitution nor certainly Law and Opinion would have been produced but for this journey."[39] The American trip of 1870 played as significant a role for Dicey in mapping out his future work as it did for his companion. The reason for this was the effort Dicey made to widen his experience: "Certainly I never made such an attempt to observe things as I did when on that journey."[40] The impact of the United States on Dicey operated on several different levels.

America stimulated his interest in the structure of comparative constitutions, especially the challenge of understanding a written

37. For the details of this trip, see Edmund Ions, *James Bryce and American Democracy 1870–1922*, pp. 37–79.

38. Dicey to Bryce, 4 December 1904, Bryce Papers.

39. Ibid., 12 February 1907, ibid.

40. Ibid., 23 December 1906, ibid.

and conservative document, as Dicey believed the United States constitution to be, after he had been trained in the flexibility of the British constitution. His experience with American federalism sharpened his insight into the British constitutional principles dealing with sovereignty. The impression of federalism originally gained in 1870 influenced his opinion of the merits and demerits of the American government system for the rest of his life. The United States appeared to him a classic example of how public morality acted as the final sanction to a system of positive law. The visit to the United States expanded his imagination about legal institutions and left a permanent imprint upon his work.

Dicey and Bryce did not travel together at all times, permitting Dicey flexibility to visit American cities of his choice. Through his cousin Leslie Stephen, Dicey received introductions to many famous Americans, a number of whom became his lifelong friends. Among the new acquaintances was E. L. Godkin of the *Nation,* an editor of influence whose views on most public issues coincided with Dicey's. Despite later disagreements on political questions, the two men remained friends until Godkin's death three decades later. Two other new friends, Charles William Eliot and Oliver Wendell Holmes, Jr., were closely identified with Harvard University. Dicey loved the New England area and Boston in particular, feeling more comfortable there than in other sections of America. Dicey stayed at Eliot's home, thereupon discovering his host shared such enthusiasms as the improvement of higher education and the movement for women's rights. The friendship with Eliot begun in 1870 matured rapidly and lasted a lifetime. For example, on a visit to England in 1874, Eliot wrote that upon departure Dicey had paused, sighed, and exclaimed, "Oh, Eliot, we are *so* happy together."[41] Eliot had just assumed the presidency of Harvard University, and this friendship inaugurated the close connection between Dicey and Harvard. With Holmes the basis of rapport was the recognition in each other of an acute legal mind. Each man soon developed a deep respect for the ideas and achievements of the other and cooperated in the promotion of the other's career. These three friendships played a major part in aiding Dicey's future professional advancement.

41. Eliot to Bryce, 21 April 1874, ibid. Italics in the original.

Inevitably, American politics attracted his attention, the American experience making a deep impression on Dicey. Among the highlights for the two men was attendance at the state convention of New York Democrats in Rochester. The blatant corruption that permeated state politics shocked the pair, who had difficulty in reconciling the lofty ideals to the sordid practices of American politics:

> We stopped at Rochester, New York to see the state convention
> of the Democratic party there—and certainly learnt something
> from it. They are the biggest set of rogues and scoundrels in
> existence; a gang of robbers in New York City, mostly Irish,
> have gained complete control of the Irish and "rowdy" vote in
> that city, the means of its control in not only the city but the
> state which they treat as so much spoil for themselves and their
> friends. This is the so-called "Tammany Ring" of which you
> have probably heard—which played into the hands of Fisk and
> the Eire railway robbers. . . . The worst feature to us is the indif-
> ference with which corruption, even the gross corruption of the
> New York judges seems to be viewed and the way in which the
> votes of members of state legislators are openly sold.[42]

The elaborate stage management of the convention Dicey thought especially pernicious, for he saw how short of free discussion the convention was, how all decisions had been carefully taken in advance by party managers, and how the system betrayed democracy. This experience intensified the reconsideration of democratic assumptions. Party discipline inhibited individual political freedom by limiting popular control over the government.[43] Bryce later had his opinions altered when attending a constitutional convention in 1890 in Lexington, Kentucky; this gathering "heartened him as much as the party convention at Rochester in 1870 had depressed him."[44] Dicey never deviated from the opinions formed in 1870; he observed a professional party organization in action and never recovered from the shock. The profound impression made upon Dicey by these events can be best seen in the report of a speech he had made just after returning to England: he had already seized upon

42. Bryce to Edward A. Freeman, 26 September 1870, ibid.
43. Rait, *Memorials,* p. 68.
44. Ions, *James Bryce and American Democracy,* p. 148.

36

party discipline as a potentially destructive factor to the English political system as he knew it.[45] Over the next fifty years his detestation of the evils of party management grew more vehement.

Despite the disillusionment caused by this introduction to American politics, Dicey admired far more about the United States than he disapproved. He thought America a living example that popular government was in fact possible. He deemed the absence of sham beneficial or what Bryce termed "a sort of frankness and simplicity about people's intercourse which is refreshing after the stiffness of England."[46] The open society of America with its voluntary tradition appealed to the liberal instincts of Dicey, who felt the opening of professions and absence of a national church constituted impressive social advances. He conceived the United States as a society at once "Democratic and Conservative," one which had excited the warmest enthusiasm in the mass of its citizens. America had approximated the greatest happiness for the greatest number—a fitting Benthamite tribute.[47]

The trip was not all business, for among its lighter moments was the visit of the two men to Niagara Falls where Dicey emerged dripping wet from the "Cave of the Winds" and remarked he had paid two dollars to enter but would gladly have paid four not to have done so.[48] Dicey wanted to publish reflections on the trip immediately but backed out at the last moment, a decision both men later regretted: "I couldn't but reflect as I have done a hundred times what a simpleton I was to arrest the publishing of our impressions of the U.S. in 1870. We certainly had got hold of a good deal worth knowing during our short visit, & tho' I now know we could have taken only a very superficial view of a very small part of the Union, yet, oddly eno', I have never seen reason to think that any of the conclusions we came to, was in itself false."[49] Both men had previously traveled extensively in Europe, but the journey to the New World enlarged their intellectual horizons. For Dicey America presented the ubiquitous example of contrast by which to illustrate principles of the British constitution. On the fiftieth anniversary of

45. Dicey to Bryce, n.d. 1870, Bryce Papers.
46. Bryce to Freeman, 26 September 1870, ibid.
47. Rait, *Memorials*, pp. 71–74.
48. Bryce to Dicey, 28 August 1920, Bryce Papers.
49. Dicey to Bryce, 24 November 1897, ibid.

the venture Dicey summarized his feelings: "I doubt whether two young Oxford men of today could gain what we got from 8 weeks in the U.S."[50] Dicey never lost the fondness for the United States that he had acquired on this "most pleasant excursion."[51] Upon his return to England Dicey had obtained a broader understanding of constitutional development as well as several influential American friends.

Two years later, on 31 August 1872, Dicey took a major personal step in more ways than one by his marriage to Elinor Mary Bonham-Carter, daughter of John Bonham-Carter, M.P. for Portsmouth 1830–41. Not only did this end his bachelor life, but he vacated his fellowship at Trinity College, thereby forfeiting that valued addition to his income. Dicey and his bride had first met as children when their families crossed paths while vacationing on the Continent. Much later they had renewed their acquaintanceship upon meeting again in London. His latent anticlericalism was confirmed by the wedding service, which left him wondering why all marriages were not performed at the Registrar's; during the ceremony he had passed the time by pondering the legal question at what precise moment did the marriage contract become binding.[52] In spite of this minor distraction at its inception, the wedding inaugurated nearly fifty years of perfect companionship.

The pair were ideally suited to each other in temperament and affection. Elinor Dicey was a gifted linguist, an intellectual who shared her husband's ambitions and career.[53] Upon first meeting the new Mrs. Dicey, Charles Eliot wrote that she made an "excellent wife."[54] Throughout her life she supported attempts to improve women's education, taking an active interest in Somerville College, Oxford, to which she donated personal service and financial gifts.[55]

50. Ibid., 23 August 1920, ibid.

51. Ibid., 4 December 1904, ibid.

52. Ibid., n.d. 1872, ibid.

53. Her foremost scholarly contribution was the English translation of Emile Boutmy, *Studies in Constitutional Law,* for which her husband wrote a short introduction.

54. Eliot to Bryce, 21 April 1874, Bryce Papers.

55. On the death of her husband in 1922, Elinor Dicey invited Somerville College to select books from Dicey's personal library. The bequest totaled 300 books, with the titles registered in the Dicey records in the college archives.

Elinor Dicey on Her Wedding Day, 1872
(Courtesy of Victor Bonham-Carter)

She was a life member of the college, serving on its council from 1888 to 1904, and contributed much to its early years.

The couple had no children, and the main impairment to their happiness was the chronic ill health suffered by Mrs. Dicey. Though she rarely fell seriously ill, her health problems severely curtailed their social life, made any activities as a hostess impossible, and prevented her from joining her husband on vacation travels. Dicey wrote in this regard: "Personally in the matter of health, as indeed in many others, I have been far more lucky than I deserve: on the other hand my wife's constant ill-health has terribly lessened the happiness of her life & been a great sorrow for both of us."[56] His correspondence frequently alluded to the physical ailments his wife endured and, though she survived him, she never enjoyed a prolonged respite from the illnesses which plagued her. "Few things weigh upon me," Dicey once mentioned, "more heavily than seeing the existence of one so good & so fitted to be & make others happy is so to speak maimed by ill health. It is a sorrow & would be a mystery did I know of any reason for supposing that the world is created for the happiness of human beings."[57] He sympathized with his wife's infirmities and respected her disabilities: "Ill-health is the cause I think of all the miseries in life which are not caused by wickedness or folly & the worst of ill-health is that it falls on people who so little deserve it."[58] Both husband and wife possessed limited physical strength and soon learned never to strain the resources of the other.

Since the marriage had worsened his financial situation, Dicey now augmented his income by increased journalistic writing. His connection with E. L. Godkin resulted in a large number of book reviews published in the *Nation*, while in England he reviewed extensively in the *Spectator*. The most striking feature of these reviews is the range of theology, history, and literature, as well as the legal and constitutional works, they covered.[59] In the main his reviews showed a signal fidelity to his earlier political opinions. Throughout the 1870s he reaffirmed his belief in Bentham's greatest

56. Dicey to Holmes, 19 April 1896, Holmes Papers.
57. Dicey to Bryce, 2 September 1896, Bryce Papers.
58. Ibid., 14 August 1903, ibid.
59. In the *Nation*, for instance, he published over 250 pieces, most of them in the years 1873–93.

good for the greatest number as the fundamental principle for social progress, criticized any manifestation of religious fanaticism, and watched the political rise of Joseph Chamberlain with grave misgivings, because he feared so strongly the introduction of party discipline into English politics. The longer articles he contributed to English journals covered legal and historical subjects only, for he had not attained either the eminence or the confidence for serious political journalism.[60]

In 1876 the then Attorney General, Sir John Holker, appointed Dicey junior counsel to the commissioners of Inland Revenue, a post he held until 1890. This increased his practice, alleviated his financial problems, but gave him little personal satisfaction. He confided to Bryce, by this time an Oxford professor, that his government work bored him to the point where he spent as much time as possible thinking of Blackstone.[61] His career with Inland Revenue was creditable but without the high achievement he craved. Dicey held briefs in a number of important cases for the government, enjoying success and failure in equal measure. His most famous cases utilized his expertise in the law of domicile.[62]

The first, *Gilbertson* v. *Ferguson,* saw Dicey successfully appeal to the principles underlying the case.[63] The legal point in question was how should dividends paid by a foreign bank be assessed for income tax purposes. Dicey won the case by persuading the judges to look to the principle of who was intended to be charged with income tax and what was the machinery by which these persons were in fact charged. The second, *Colquhoun* v. *Brooks,* failed when Dicey could not make the judges accept his argument that domicile made an individual liable for income tax on all his earnings, not just the part actually received in the United Kingdom.[64] He represented the Crown in these cases because of the reputation he had earned in the field of domicile through the publication in 1879 of his second treatise on a legal topic.

60. These articles by Dicey included: "Development of Common Law," "Legal Education," "Louis Napoleon: 1851 and 1873," and "Judicial Policy of England."

61. Dicey to Bryce, n.d. 1879, Bryce Papers.

62. Rait, *Memorials*, p. 78.

63. Gilbertson v. Ferguson, [1881] 7 Q.B.D. 562.

64. Colquhoun v. Brooks, [1889] 14 App. Cas. 493.

In *The Law of Domicil* Dicey repeated the formula of reducing a complex subject to a series of rules.[65] At the time domicile posed a confusing problem on which little research had been done and still less of value written. Dicey provided this explanation of his purpose: "It is in fact a rather more extensive work than the name would imply dealing with at least two thirds of that unhappily mis-named subject Private International Law. My object has been to state exclusively the rules which are or will be followed by English Courts with regard to the extra-territorial effect of law. I wanted if possible first to show that the subject could be reduced to Rules which might be understood by any intelligent layman & secondly to explain my Rules & prove that they resulted from decided cases or authoritative dicta."[66] In this work Dicey codified domicile into seventy-three rules, based upon statutory enactments, previous cases, or admitted principles. He first stated the rules without comment, then his explanation of the rule, the evidence for it, and in some cases, illustration of why a certain rule had to be considered doubtful because of conflicting opinions. The success of *Parties to an Action* had strengthened his faith in this methodology, and he hoped it would work as well in this instance.[67]

Dicey revealed his loyalty to Austin in this volume by refusing to use the term "private international law" to describe his topic. As he explained, the principles of international law regulated the conduct of nations but were not laws at all.[68] Austin had made enforcement by a sovereign one criterion of law, but in the Europe of 1879 this condition was not satisfied, as no international organization existed to enforce the law. Only those laws which were national, that is, enforceable by a sovereign, met the Austinian requirement for true law. The law of domicile, as Dicey interpreted it, to possess any validity had to be a branch of English law or else it was not law at all. Dicey on domicile stood squarely in the Austinian tradition.

About the subject of domicile Dicey had ambivalent feelings. On one hand it possessed a speculative fascination because of its origin: "I know of no branch of law which is so exclusively of judicial manufacture; and I am coming more and more to the belief that

65. Albert Venn Dicey, *The Law of Domicil.*
66. Dicey to Holmes, 22 July 1897, Holmes Papers.
67. Dicey, *Law of Domicil*, p. v.
68. Ibid., p. iv.

judge-made law is in quality, almost always better than Statute law."[69] On the other hand, Dicey wrote to Bryce in 1879 that "I am sick of the whole topic" and that he was relieved the book was completed, enabling him to be rid of it altogether.[70] Despite this lack of affection for the work, Dicey had persevered in the hopes it might add to his scholarly reputation. For example, he asked Holmes to ensure its review in American legal periodicals so it might reach a wider audience. At the same time, Dicey informed Holmes he hoped to follow in three or four years with "a book covering the whole field of the so-called conflict of laws in which the rules maintained on the subject by our courts may be compared with the principles enforced by tribunals of other countries."[71] Dicey was too optimistic, for seventeen years elapsed before the treatise on conflict of laws appeared. Only his strong dedication to his work sustained him in light of his distaste for the subject.

The Law of Domicil enhanced his scholarly reputation, as it impressed Holmes, who termed the book "most admirably done."[72] Though eventually overshadowed by the *Conflict of Laws*, the treatise on domicile boosted Dicey's fame when most needed. By 1880 he had reached middle age without the success at the bar he had envisioned; his journalistic endeavors had not yet made any appreciable mark on public opinion; and his government career was bogged down in minor legal work. Dicey had not realized to any appreciable extent the promise of his undergraduate days or the goals he had set for himself. This frustrating state of affairs intensified during 1880–82, bringing him to the central decision of his life. In this period, for example, he contemplated competing for a professorship in conflict of laws at Harvard if such a position materialized.[73] Dicey had three options open to him: continue his efforts, hitherto unsuccessful, for prominence at the bar; renew his attempts to enter public life and pursue a political career; find an academic post suited to his physical capabilities where he might continue his research and writing. Dicey reached the crossroads in 1882 when the eminence, or more likely the promise, of the two

69. Dicey to Holmes, 28 September 1881, Holmes Papers.
70. Dicey to Bryce, n.d. 1879, Bryce Papers.
71. Dicey to Holmes, 22 July 1879, Holmes Papers.
72. Holmes to Bryce, 17 August 1879, Bryce Papers.
73. Dicey to Holmes, 19 January 1880, Holmes Papers.

law treatises published during the 1870s won him election as Vinerian Professor of English Law at Oxford. This position, which would almost certainly preclude his other interests, was now his to accept. To this point Dicey's life had consisted of reacting to influences upon him; the Vinerian Chair offered him the opportunity to influence the lives of others. The public career he sought was within his reach.

CHAPTER THREE

THE RESTORATION OF THE

VINERIAN CHAIR, 1882–1909

THE VINERIAN CHAIR, founded at Oxford in 1758, is the oldest professorship of English law in the world. The chair originated in a bequest from Charles Viner, author of a noted abridgment, who left a considerable fortune for that purpose. Sir William Blackstone, author of the *Commentaries* and most influential legal authority in the eighteenth century, inaugurated the professorship, setting an unsurpassed standard of excellence. For a variety of reasons Blackstone resigned in 1766 at the height of his fame, and the chair, so well initiated, passed into the hands of men of lesser attainment, including Blackstone's own son James. During the nineteenth century the position increasingly turned into a sinecure with the incumbents often nonresident in Oxford, failing to distinguish themselves in the world of legal scholarship, and otherwise not doing justice to their duties. The foundation of other chairs of law in 1859 and 1869 focused attention on the deplorable state to which the Vinerian Chair had fallen in the tenure of the sixth Vinerian, John Kenyon, whose long absences from Oxford created scandalous gossip. In 1877 the university awarded the chair to All Souls College, whose governing body determined to revitalize the professorship and restore it to its former eminence. The death of Kenyon in 1880 provided the opportunity for expunging the decay of a century.[1]

Throughout his years in London Dicey had never lost his concern for the problem of legal education nor indeed the condition of Oxford itself. His abortive experience at the Working Men's College did not dampen his enthusiasm for educational reform. In 1869 he had published a long commentary on the university, criticizing the excessive sums granted to absentee Fellows who used them to little

1. For the history of the Vinerian Chair prior to 1882, see H. G. Hanbury, *The Vinerian Chair and Legal Education*, pp. 1–97.

scholarly result, with a consequent paucity of funds for educational purposes in Oxford itself.[2] Dicey argued that men studied specific material in order to be examined, instead of being examined in whatever material they had studied; students learned only for the sake of examinations. Dicey knew well this phenomenon, as it resembled his own scholastic career. Ever the steadfast liberal, he asserted that open competition had caused every advance in Oxford education over the previous fifty years. Dicey maintained that university education needed reform in the direction of equal opportunity for all students in bidding for academic prizes. As far as he could discern, many colleges were still closed corporations dedicated to their own perpetuation instead of education.

In the manifold problems of legal education facing the profession he retained a steady interest. In 1871 Dicey had assisted Bryce in the founding of law schools at Manchester under the auspices of Owen's College and at Liverpool in conjunction with the Incorporated Law Society of that city.[3] In 1872–73 he had lectured on law at Owen's College, but found the constant traveling between London and Manchester too tiring. In addition, Dicey had been a Public Examiner in the Honour School of Jurisprudence at Oxford from 1874 to 1876, discovering for himself the strengths and weaknesses of candidates. By the time of his candidacy for the Vinerian Chair, even after the two decades since his departure from Oxford, he was no stranger to the academic world.

The election of Dicey to the Vinerian Chair was not the foregone conclusion that H. G. Hanbury, the eleventh Vinerian, declared it.[4] Lord Salisbury headed the search committee, which took two years to decide in Dicey's favor.[5] Sir Frederick Pollock, for example, competed for the professorship and, though unsuccessful, soon thereafter obtained the Corpus Professorship of Jurisprudence.[6] Sir William Anson, who became Warden of All Souls in 1881, also

2. Albert Venn Dicey, "Suggestions on Academical Organisation," pp. 407–30.

3. Sir Roundell Palmer, *Speech at the Annual Meeting of the Legal Education Association*, p. 13.

4. Hanbury, *The Vinerian Chair*, p. 100.

5. Dicey to Lord Salisbury, 13 April 1886, 3d Marquess of Salisbury Papers, Hatfield House, Hatfield, Herts.

6. Holmes to Pollock, 25 March 1883, in *Holmes-Pollock Letters*, 1: 20.

stood for the post; the friendship that started in this rivalry lasted till Anson's death.[7] Dicey faced formidable competition, and his success was remarkable. With the offer of the Vinerian Chair in hand, Dicey confronted the climacteric decision that settled his future.

After he had weighed carefully every argument for and against this opportunity, Dicey accepted the professorship and returned to Oxford, where he would spend the rest of his life. This decision proved painful, for it caused the final abandonment of long-cherished plans for a successful career in other areas. Dicey undertook his new duties with no illusions about the problems he faced; about the interim Vinerians since Blackstone he once wrote: "One of them wrote a book on law which no one ever reads; another, and by no means the least distinguished of a very undistinguished body, occupied the Vinerian professorship, and discharged its duties, if at all, by deputy, while he himself held a judgeship in India."[8] He realized that his appointment might lead to a new vitality for the Vinerian Chair or he could continue the sinecure arrangement. The latter alternative he determined to avoid at all costs. To an American friend he wrote that the chair offered a position honorable and congenial: "a post of which I believe I can well reform the duties & which leaves me both means and time to pursue studies which are of interest to me."[9] The positive elements that lured him into acceptance were his enduring concern with legal education, the potential for reform of the Oxford law curriculum, and the possibilities for increasing his own scholarly work.

Powerful forces pulled him in the other direction, for his agreement forced renunciation of two other ambitions he had long harbored. Early in life he had nourished the hope that his undoubted talent for public speaking would provide him the chance to stand for the Commons; but nobody had ever invited him, and, as the years slipped away, his expectations had disappeared with them.[10]

7. Dicey to J. St. Loe Strachey, 14 June 1914, J. St. Loe Strachey Papers, Beaverbrook Library, London.

8. Albert Venn Dicey, "Blackstone," *Nation* 65 (7 and 14 October 1897): 274–76, 295–96.

9. Dicey to Godkin, 29 December 1882, Godkin Papers.

10. Report of Dicey's inaugural speech at the Working Men's College in *Working Men's College Journal* 6 (March 1899): 44.

As he once wrote: "If I had not had my fling, so to speak, at the Bar, I should have been haunted by the visions of imaginary Solicitor Generalships, House of Commons successes, and Judgeships."[11] His enthusiasm for politics never diminished, and, in view of his frequent public speeches and letters to the press, his desire to play a political role never completely vanished, either. Dicey admitted to Bryce that he had once cherished high hopes for a political career but in the end had settled for a professorship.[12] This sense of frustration pervaded his tenure. Though the Vinerian Chair offered a challenge few men could have met successfully, Dicey's ambition was not satisfied, and this supposed failure rankled throughout his term.

The other career to which he aspired but was likewise denied was that of the bench. Dicey's belief that the best elements of English law stemmed from judicial decisions fired his desire for a judgeship, for he thought it a post of enduring influence. He wrote to Holmes that "I believe a seat in our Court of Appeal obtained in a period of life when I still had the power to achieve by labour the credit of performing my work there satisfactorily, would, or ought to have, satisfied my desires."[13] Insuperable difficulties had made this ambition impossible: "I sometimes feel that it would have been a comfort to have known that one had obtained the place which I have often longed for after I knew it was to me unattainable, of a Judgeship. One fatal difficulty, among 20 others, which would in any case have made it hopeless is that unless in the Court of Appeal or in the House of Lords I could never have performed the duties of a Judge of the High court. I could not possibly have taken even the shabbiest notes of a trial."[14] Physical problems precluded ever gaining a place on the bench, but the hope could not be easily stilled. On the occasion of Holmes's appointment as Chief Justice of Massachusetts he wrote:

> Most people I suppose have some latent ambition which is never realised and my own has always been to reach the Bench. In early life I had dreams as most of us have here of getting to the Bench through both the Courts and Parliament. But even

11. Dicey to Lady Farrer, 5 November 1920, in Rait, *Memorials*, p. 270.
12. Dicey to Bryce, 4 January 1885, Bryce Papers.
13. Dicey to Holmes, 19 December 1921, Holmes Papers.
14. Dicey to Bryce, 16 October 1921, Bryce Papers.

before I got my Professorship I knew that there was no real chance of my becoming a Judge & have long ago put the matter aside, as I have also set aside any wish or hope for a Parliamentary career.

Happily I can honestly say that I have never suffered what can be called "disappointment" for I don't think the not having a chance of attaining the position either of an M.P. or a Judge, has ever given me an hour's disquiet. But the feeling that I should very much have liked a seat on the Bench here makes me intensely sympathise with the satisfaction I hope you feel of being C.J. of Massachusetts.[15]

This disclaimer does not ring true, for he complained too often about a subject that allegedly caused him no personal restlessness. The more impressive his legal reputation grew, the more suitable a candidate for the bench he became. Bryce and Holmes agreed that "Dicey would have made a fine reputation as a judge had some Chancellor been bold enough to appoint a man on his reputation as a writer, a thing which can be more easily done in America, tho' it was twice done successfully here in the cases of Blackstone and Blackburn."[16] Unfortunately for Dicey the offer never materialized, with Dicey left to conclude forlornly that "I have not been able to think that my career has been in any way such as I wished for."[17] Thus the acceptance of the Vinerian professorship, though providing many positive opportunities, also contained an element of regret at the abandonment of his other hopes.

Having once taken the position, however, Dicey's sense of obligation to his duties prevailed. He admitted that it imposed upon him a discipline he might otherwise not have accepted, writing to his wife that the professorship had helped develop his powers.[18] He felt deeply the responsibility of the chair and resolved to repay the trust placed in him. When the second edition of *Law of the Constitution* appeared, Dicey sent a copy to Lord Salisbury with the hope that "the work may be a proof that I have at least endeavoured to the best of my ability to discharge the duties of the office to which

15. Dicey to Holmes, 3 April 1900, Holmes Papers.
16. Bryce to Holmes, 15 March 1918, Bryce Papers.
17. Dicey to Holmes, 19 December 1921, Holmes Papers.
18. Dicey to Mrs. Dicey, 16 November 1886, in Rait, *Memorials*, p. 100.

I was appointed."[19] Perhaps the best example of his application may be seen in the effort he devoted to his treatise on the conflict of laws. This topic had long since ceased to intrigue him, but he eventually completed the book. "My motive for not dropping the book more than half done when I came to Oxford was I think a worthy one," he wrote, "I felt I could not hold the Professorship with credit unless on some important branch of law I could claim to be an authority."[20] Despite the problems associated with this publication, Dicey had persevered because he owed the chair his best labor. The initial project Dicey planned as Vinerian professor was a history of England from a legal point of view: "It might well have taken the whole of my remaining life first to realise what I meant and then carry out my conception, and no doubt the work would even now be a fragment."[21] This work put aside, *Conflict of Laws* prevented him from joining fully the public life of Oxford. In the end this sacrifice had been worthwhile: "My motive was this, and I think it was a good one: I had a strong feeling that if I stood in Blackstone's shoes and could not repeat his feat of summing up the law of England, which was certainly beyond my powers, I ought to get at any rate, if possible, the reputation of being a leading authority on some one branch of English law. Then too when I was elected here the Conflict of Laws seemed to me all but done. In this I was mistaken. But I think that to a certain extent it gave me, falsely perhaps, a certain legal reputation which I wanted much to attain."[22] The commitment to the Vinerian Chair may best be summarized in his remark that "I don't want to go down to posterity with Kenyon."[23] Whatever the reservations Dicey privately may have held concerning the professorship, once the position was his he strove mightily to restore its prestige.

If Dicey had little affection for some branches of English law, for the law in general he possessed great love. He considered the common law "the most original creation of the English genius."[24] He

19. Dicey to Salisbury, 13 April 1886, Salisbury Papers.
20. Dicey to Bryce, 24 August 1920, Bryce Papers.
21. Ibid., 3 May 1918, ibid.
22. Ibid., 16 October 1921, ibid.
23. Ibid., 20 October 1894, ibid.
24. Albert Venn Dicey, "Digby on the History of English Law," *Nation* 21 (9 December 1875): 373.

predicted that English law "will be the lasting monument of England's greatness."[25] Yet about legal education Dicey believed that the system did not do justice to the body of law itself. Legal education exemplified the sprawling nature of its subject, so Dicey wished to bring order out of the chaos he detested in legal matters. His dissatisfaction with the state of legal education was long standing, therefore reform of law instruction at Oxford became a major objective as Vinerian professor.

His first writing on this subject, in 1871, established the framework for his later efforts at reform.[26] Dicey thought the training of barristers so poor as to be embarrassing; though many voices proclaimed that the common law should be studied scientifically, no professors of law ever explained its principles in logical fashion. As a result, the barrister received an education that was fragmentary and incomplete; no man reading for the bar obtained a carefully planned course of legal study. Reading in chambers he thought especially useless, an expensive sham practiced on the apprentice. This method of instruction imposed an immense burden of useless work upon the student, for the aspiring lawyer had at the outset to extract principles of law from a mass of detail with which he was not familiar. Further, it destroyed the value of watching the law in action, because the student had no prior background against which to judge the different activities he viewed. Finally, the education at the Inns of Court was far too narrow, and subsequent practice, rather than expanding the lawyer's horizons, usually caused him to specialize even more. The law as an integral part of liberal education gained no support from this educational system. At this early date Dicey diagnosed the ills carefully but as yet, other than a vague reference to the benefits of professorial teaching, had not worked out in detail an operable alternative. In the 1870s he confined himself to practical efforts at amelioration through his participation in the Legal Education Association.

By the time of his inaugural lecture in 1883, Dicey had evolved his basic approach to the reform of law teaching. He emphasized professorial teaching as the main contribution law faculties should make to legal education. Professorial teaching "gives prominence to

25. Albert Venn Dicey, "Professor Maitland," *Nation* 91 (29 September 1910): 293.
26. Dicey, "Legal Education," pp. 115–27.

principles as a decision gives prominence to exceptions and I am quite convinced that Professorial lectures & writings very rapidly tell on the Judges."[27] This conception embodied the technique already utilized in his own first two law treatises. Professorial teaching should impart the principles of law as a complement to the practical job training of reading in chambers. Gaining recognition for the professorial method against centuries of tradition posed a formidable task, so Dicey began with his first official act as Vinerian professor.

In his inaugural lecture, *Can English Law Be Taught at the Universities?*, Dicey answered his question affirmatively, outlining the area where he would make the greatest contribution to his university.[28] After an indictment of contemporary educational customs in terms similar to that of 1871, he indicated that the situation had worsened because the Judicature Act of 1873 had eliminated pleaders, the only element of the profession, Dicey felt, who had dealt with principles of law. The tragedy here, as he had written in 1871, was that "the only professors of law which the English bar has ever possessed will therefore have ceased to exist just when professorial teaching has been felt to be a necessary element in the education of a barrister."[29] The apprentice lawyer, in the decade since 1873, had lost the only real guides to the principles of English law. Into this void must step the professors who would set forth the law as a coherent unity, reduce the mass of legal rules to an orderly series of principles, and provide a scientific basis for education. Professors could best accomplish this goal by stimulating the renovation of legal literature.

Professorial teaching, in Dicey's estimation, supplied four ingredients to a legal education which the Inns of Court, by their very nature, could not furnish. At the universities a student learned the law as a whole, plus the relation of one branch of the law to another within the legal system. Next, the professors should inculcate the habit of analyzing and classifying legal concepts, a duty Dicey thought essential as a result of his own Austinian heritage. In addition, the universities stressed the law as a series of rules and

27. Dicey to Holmes, 28 September 1881, Holmes Papers.
28. Albert Venn Dicey, *Can English Law Be Taught at the Universities?* The lecture was delivered at All Souls on 21 April 1883.
29. Dicey, "Legal Education," p. 123.

exceptions, carefully demarcating the limits of ascertained principles. Finally, the professors must create a desperately needed legal literature. Dicey believed only the professors could provide the treatises that demonstrated the rationality of law, treated it in a clear style, and postulated its fundamental principles.

During his twenty-seven-year tenure in the Vinerian Chair, Dicey made every effort within his power to follow his own prescription. It was no coincidence that Dicey published his three great law books during this period. Indeed, the 1880s have been singled out as a decade when Oxford law professors published a remarkable number of books, "some of them exerting great influence and possessing lasting value."[30] Despite the emphasis on writing, Dicey never excluded teaching responsibilities, supporting every effort to extend the teaching activities of All Souls into other areas.[31] His facility for public speaking of which he was so proud added an extra dimension to his lectures and won them fame within Oxford, but professorial lecturing did not fulfill his inaugural hopes, as he came to recognize all too well.

Professorial teaching upgraded law instruction at Oxford by 1909, but the standards reached did not measure up to Dicey's expectations. Over the years he realized that the art of good lecturing was not equivalent to the art of good teaching, especially in the Oxford context. The real problem lay in merging the professorial and tutorial methods of instruction; each professor should not only lecture but also tutor in the college from which he derived part of his stipend.[32] The professorial lecture should kindle enthusiasm, Dicey argued, and convince the student that the elementary principles of law were ascertainable. The lecturer must aim at eliciting the sympathy of his pupil and show him that the study of English law was no less interesting than any other branch of learning. Even the best lecturer, however well he succeeded in these objects, might yet fail to convey all the information he possessed.[33]

Dicey ultimately conceded that tutorial instruction at Oxford pro-

30. F. H. Lawson, *The Oxford Law School, 1850–1965*, p. 85.
31. Sir Charles Oman, in Rait, *Memorials*, p. 96.
32. Dicey to Bryce, 27 May 1902, Bryce Papers.
33. Albert Venn Dicey, "Law-Teaching, Oral and Written," in H. H. Henson, ed., *A Memoir of the Right Honourable Sir William Anson*, pp. 84–101.

vided advantages set lectures could not: "The professorial system tends towards the production of good lectures, probably to be embodied in books, the tutorial system tends toward the teaching of individual pupils so that they may carry away in their thoughts the truths, or at any rate the doctrines, which the tutor wishes to impress upon him."[34] The best spirit of the Oxford tutor, so he believed, lay in his affection for his men. The passion of the professor was to benefit his class, the passion of the tutor to benefit his particular men. In the end Dicey confessed he had never discovered how to combine the merits of tutorialism with the virtues of professorial teaching.[35]

Eventually Dicey acknowledged that legal training might come in different guises, for after his lectures at Harvard University in 1898 he thought the Harvard Law School taught the basic principles of English law better than any other institution.[36] The set lectures at Harvard accompanied by the catechetical style of class discussion pioneered by C. C. Langdell represented a major improvement in law instruction. So impressive was the Harvard Law School that he concluded it was "by far the greatest institution in existence for the teaching of English Law."[37] Dicey never lost faith in the lecture approach but admitted that by itself it had not proven as successful as he desired. He concluded eventually that some form of amalgamation between the Oxford and Harvard methods would constitute the "perfection of teaching" he sought.[38] Successful professorial teaching remained an ideal but one not capable of easy realization.

The pressures of the Vinerian Chair conflicted with duties Dicey believed he owed to other segments of society, and he never resolved the dilemma of apportioning his time accordingly. He saw clearly his obligations to his students but, at the same time, recognized that he had incurred responsibilities toward his university. He also felt very strongly that his position imposed upon him the duty of contributing to the public life of the nation. Dicey did not approve of a university acting as a forum for contemporary discussions, so

34. Ibid., p. 88.
35. Dicey to Bryce, 12 June 1913, Bryce Papers.
36. Albert Venn Dicey, "The Teaching of English Law at Harvard," pp. 742–58.
37. Dicey to Eliot, 7 April 1904, Eliot Papers.
38. Dicey to Norton, 29 January 1899, Norton Papers.

for this reason he had frequently declined invitations to debate politics at the Oxford Union. His desired political career in abeyance because of the academic appointment, Dicey still aspired to play a role in national affairs. He relegated his duties to Oxford to a secondary place so that he might devote his time to the other two areas, his professorship and the nation, which seemed to him to have greater priority. As Dicey wrote of himself: "I think no man can accuse me of having in any way shunned the public expression of my political convictions."[39] This attitude was the best described by long-time friend and sometime member of the House of Commons Arthur Elliot:

> All his letters to me show the strength of his feeling that he owed to the public the duty of making known his political opinions, after he had carefully thought them out. He was one of the most modest of men; but he knew that his legal and constitutional writings were very highly valued amongst those interested in such things, and he rightly recognised that with honest students of politics his opinions counted. Thinking that the country ought to be, and was largely, governed by public opinion, it went against his conscience to keep silence; whilst he saw men, as he thought, misguided, errors of policy committed, and conduct on the part of statesmen, which he considered lowered the moral standard of British political life allowed to pass uncensured.[40]

This conception of his Vinerian obligations satisfied two of his deepest impulses: the first, the sincere conviction, which grew steadily over the years, that national policy was mistaken; the second, and not nearly as lofty, that his outspoken political rhetoric compensated for the lack of involvement in high politics.

Therefore, within the Oxford community, Dicey had neither the time nor the ambition for more than a limited part in university affairs. Among the triumvirate of demands upon his time—his research, the Oxford world, and national politics—his university role gave way by design to the other two areas. Upon his return to Oxford a number of friends urged Dicey to stand for university

39. Dicey to Jacob, 23 February 1910, Working Men's College MSS.
40. Statement by Arthur Elliot, n.d., affixed to collection of his letters to Dicey, Arthur Elliot Papers, National Library of Scotland, Edinburgh.

office. He declined to do so for two reasons: "The one was that I had had no training as a Professor, and found the labour of getting up adequate legal knowledge and putting it into the form of effective lectures very great. The other was that I thought, and I think truly, that a successor of Blackstone should show that of one branch of English Law at least he could speak with authority."[41] Dicey spent so much time on the *Conflict of Laws* and then political Unionism that his Oxford opportunities passed him by. In his one bid for university prominence he missed election to the Hebdomadel Council by two votes.[42] Too late he saw what his self-imposed isolation had wrought. This failure confirmed to Dicey that his policy of abstention was best: "I live entirely out of the world of University government. Being what I am I believe it is the best course, but it has its inevitable disadvantages."[43] Dicey never believed himself part of Oxford, with this fact adding to his sense of failure about his own work.

This conscious lack of participation in university proceedings notwithstanding, Dicey made several contributions to Oxford in which he took pride. The first concerned his role, along with other noted academic lawyers at Oxford such as Bryce, Anson, Pollock, and Holland, in the establishment of the *Law Quarterly Review*. His cooperation in this venture stemmed from a long-standing disappointment in existing legal periodicals.[44] In order to raise the standards of academic law, he joined eagerly in "the adventure of a new periodical aiming at the promotion of legal science without neglect of practice, and devoted chiefly to the Common Law but not disregarding comparative study."[45] Dicey wrote frequently for the *Law Quarterly Review* and should be numbered among its founders, even though Pollock singled out Holland as the true driving force behind the scheme. That the *Review* set up its editorial offices in London did not dampen his enthusiasm for the project. The success of the journal remained a concern to him even after its reputation was assured.

The advancement of education for women had early attracted Dicey's attention, and throughout his Oxford tenure he supported

41. Dicey to R. S. Rait, 7 March 1922, in Rait, *Memorials,* p. 285.
42. Dicey to Bryce, 20 March 1896, Bryce Papers.
43. Ibid., 11 May 1897, ibid.
44. Dicey to Holmes, 19 January 1880, Holmes Papers.
45. Sir Frederick Pollock, "Our Jubilee," p. 6.

efforts to obtain degrees for women. He thought the refusal of degrees to women all too typical of the narrow spirit he detested in Oxford. More important, he believed education essential to the individual self-realization he prized so highly. In the acrimonious national debate during 1896 and 1897, Dicey played an active role. The failure to obtain degrees for women at that time did not dismay him, for he was confident of ultimate success. He followed closely the success of women in their examinations, taking pride in their accomplishments. At the finish of the immediate controversy in 1896 he wrote: "My own impression is that we moved a little too soon in the matter of the B.A. I am not however sure of this. It is quite possible that the first attempt whensoever made must have been a failure. That thro' Parliament if not thro' the University the degree will be gained within the next 10 years is my full expectation."[46] Dicey underestimated the length of time required by some fifteen years, but never slackened in efforts to improve educational opportunities for women.

In one instance only did Dicey succeed in having a university reform accepted by Oxford authorities. Upon return from Harvard in 1898 he was so taken with the students encountered there that he fought to make graduates of foreign and colonial universities eligible for the Oxford B.C.L. degree.[47] He recruited Bryce to his plans for altering the university statutes by the promise that a new influx of overseas students would improve dramatically the Oxford Law School.[48] One year after lecturing at Harvard, as evidence of his concern, he contrasted the lively American audience with the twenty apathetic young men who had attended his class that day in Oxford.[49] Dicey met less resistance than he anticipated, overcoming Oxford insularity without difficulty. By his unstinting praise of the Harvard Law School he disarmed opposition to the reform, ensuring the appropriate changes in university regulations.[50] The Oxford Law School still did not compete favorably with the classics in attracting

46. Dicey to Mrs. Edward Caird, 22 July 1896, Miscellaneous MSS., Balliol College. Edward Caird, a colleague of Dicey in the Old Mortality Society, had succeeded Jowett as Master of Balliol.
47. Mrs. Dicey to Mrs. E. L. Godkin, n.d. but presumably early 1899, Godkin Papers.
48. Dicey to Bryce, 18 May 1899, Bryce Papers.
49. Dicey to Eliot, 17 October 1899, Eliot Papers.
50. Dicey to Norton, 20 March 1900, Norton Papers.

the best English students. Dicey predicted that the importation of ten American students every year of the caliber he had found at Harvard could not help but improve conditions at Oxford.[51] Soon thereafter his contentions received striking confirmation.

With the foundation of the Rhodes scholarships Dicey made certain that these visitors should likewise read for the B.C.L. if they so chose.[52] The effect of these changes, for which he was directly responsible, did him great credit. The Rhodes scholars rapidly raised standards, forming the backbone of the Law School.[53] Dicey himself, never too sanguine about his own plans, concluded the Rhodes scholars had introduced to Oxford "a body of men who form a new and good element in our university life."[54] The opening of Oxford to new blood from abroad stands as a permanent testament to his breadth of view on the value of diversity in legal education.

In spite of the reputation he earned as Vinerian professor, Dicey possessed no real affection for Oxford nor any true sense of accomplishment during his tenure. Skepticism about the commitment of the university to his educational ideals plagued him after his return in 1882. In this respect he never completely lost his youthful suspicion that Oxford represented aristocratic privilege. Only radical reform could cure that defect: "I sometimes think Oxford will never prosper till she has been plundered."[55] He was never satisfied that sufficient university resources were channeled to the Law School.

Beyond this complaint, his main doubt about his Oxford years was the belief that his efforts at reform had not fulfilled expectations. Because he set his own standards so high and attached such great importance to the teaching of English law, some feeling of inadequacy was inevitable. Bryce, in his 1893 valedictory address, reflected sadly that his own hopes for the improvement of legal education had fallen short of attainment.[56] After twenty years in the

51. Dicey to Eliot, 21 September 1900, Eliot Papers.
52. Ibid., 18 October 1904, ibid.
53. Lawson, *The Oxford Law School*, pp. 110–11.
54. Albert Venn Dicey, "The Extension of Law Teaching at Oxford," p. 1.
55. Dicey to Bryce, 13 June 1891, Bryce Papers.
56. Brian Abel-Smith and Robert Stevens, *Lawyers and the Courts*, pp. 166–67.

Vinerian Chair, Dicey echoed this sentiment that the Oxford Law School had not advanced as far as he had hoped.[57] The real difficulty lay not in Dicey's success or lack thereof but in the priorities of the university, which by tradition emphasized studies far removed from the law. Bryce, in reflecting upon the disappointment of his own academic career, testified that the best university students had no interest in preparing for the academic life. Nor, Dicey agreed, did the Law School fare any better: "The dreary point is that the quality of the men is extraordinarily poor."[58] The result, Bryce wrote to Dicey long afterwards, was that "your experience was doubtless better but law at Oxford was always a small side channel away from the main stream."[59] Dicey struggled valiantly for high standards in the Oxford Law School, but never knew that sense of achievement that his efforts had surely merited.

This enduring dissatisfaction accounted for the affinity of Dicey for the Harvard Law School, so paradoxical in one closely identified with Oxford. Harvard enjoyed all that Oxford could not provide: greater financial resources and a superior faculty, plus a spirit that permeated the entire institution and gave the Law School a special vitality.[60] Dicey admired the pride of place Harvard accorded the teaching of law, never reconciling himself to the secondary rank it possessed in Oxford. The oft-repeated preference of Dicey for teaching at Harvard must be understood in this context; he rarely made his friends understand his desire to be associated with an institution where the law was alive.[61] Among the projects he promoted was the regular exchange of faculty and pupils between the two schools: "As far as the Law Schools in each place go, about which alone I can really judge, the gain to us would be great & undoubted, because your school has, under favourable circumstances attained a development which from unfavourable circumstances, we have not been able to reach. And I think that there would be some gain on your side also. In truth I am haunted by an idea that could the required arrangements be made, the Law School of each University might supply something which is lacking to the other. But this is a mere

57. Dicey to Eliot, 7 April 1904, Eliot Papers.
58. Dicey to Bryce, 24 November 1897, Bryce Papers.
59. Bryce to Dicey, 29 May 1918, ibid.
60. Dicey, "Teaching of English Law," p. 743.
61. Dicey to Bryce, 16 January 1910, Bryce Papers.

dream which in my time will never be realised."[62] Though it might plausibly be argued that no individual could possibly have brought about the full realization of Dicey's goals, nevertheless the belief that he had not accomplished all he had set for himself tormented him and contributed to the sense of failure he had about his Oxford career. Dicey was his own sternest judge, accepting no excuses for shortcomings real or imaginary.

There was personal as well as professional disappointment with Oxford life. Though he had made many friends in Oxford during his undergraduate days, he found it difficult to repeat this process after 1882 when he was "too old to make new ones."[63] Mrs. Dicey provided the best summary of the Diceyan ambivalence about Oxford when she wrote: "I often feel how solitary we are now in Oxford & wish we were back in London but it is too late for that. Well as the Professorship suited Albert—he gave himself up so completely to that & writing his books that he made no new *real* friends here, & we both miss that tho' everyone has always been most friendly to us. We were both rather too old to strike roots in a new place."[64]

Deep concern for the reputation of the professorship first prompted Dicey to consider retirement in 1907 after a quarter of a century of service, but at that time his friends prevailed upon him to remain. Doubts about continuing persisted until he made the final decision in late 1908.[65] No amount of argument could deter him, so that in 1909 he took the "melancholy step" of giving up his position.[66] Increasing deafness and the advance of years had left him no alternative. As he put it: "I am rather more than 74. I am sure that it is better the Vinerian Professorship should pass into younger hands."[67] And he explained in greater detail to his wife:

> Lastly, I am anxious, beyond what I can express, to keep up my good repute as a professor and to set a good example of profes-

62. Dicey to William James, 20 November 1898, William James Papers, Houghton Library, Harvard University.

63. Dicey to Caird, 20 November 1893, Miscellaneous MSS., Balliol College.

64. Mrs. Dicey to Bryce, 18 May 1917, Bryce Papers. Italics in the original.

65. Dicey to Eliot, 22 November 1908, Eliot Papers.

66. Ibid., 28 May 1909, ibid.

67. Dicey to Strachan-Davidson, 20 May 1909, Miscellaneous MSS., Balliol College.

sional conduct. I have been far less successful as a teacher than I had hoped to be. This comparative failure has sprung in part from my own fault or, at any rate, deficiencies. But I have tried more consistently than for most good objects to keep up the repute of my chair. I should feel that my life has been a failure did I not partially succeed. I have seen too many professors who have damaged their own reputation and done harm to the University by holding their posts too long.[68]

Dicey regarded retirement with apprehension, thinking it would ruin whatever life remained to him, because for fifty-five years, since his matriculation at Oxford, compulsion of some kind had driven him to work with more or less steady activity.[69] In any case, this fear was entirely misplaced, for All Souls elected him to a fellowship which continued his teaching, and by 1909 public affairs offered sufficient excitement to occupy his time. Still, Dicey was saddened even while admitting the necessity of formal retirement: "It is an unpleasant thing to have to decide when to cut one's own throat. For my own fame, I doubt not my resignation is a wise step, and I doubt not that it is in the long run best for the chair."[70] To ease the pain of the change, Dicey determined to keep busy: "I am quite prepared to go on working here if, as I expect, I continue to live here. I hope my friends may approve of what I have done. Resignation, turn it as one may, is always a somewhat melancholy affair."[71] He salvaged the best from what had promised to be a terrible personal decision.

For the topic of his valedictory address as Vinerian professor, Dicey selected Blackstone's *Commentaries.* As a consistent neo-Austinian he had never accepted Blackstone's natural rights arguments, but this disagreement did not blind him to the merits of his predecessor in the Vinerian Chair. "The *Commentaries* live by their style. Blackstone possessed power of expression, clearness of aim, literary judgment or tact";[72] these qualities had earned Blackstone

---

68. Dicey to Mrs. Dicey, summer 1909, in Rait, *Memorials,* p. 201.

69. Dicey to Eliot, 28 May 1909, Eliot Papers.

70. Dicey to Bryce, 13 June 1909, in Rait, *Memorials,* pp. 202–3.

71. Dicey to Goldwin Smith, 26 May 1909, Goldwin Smith Papers, Cornell University Library, Ithaca, New York.

72. Albert Venn Dicey, "Blackstone's Commentaries," p. 661. Dicey gave the farewell lecture on 12 June 1909.

his deserved fame. As he once wrote to Bryce, he emphasized that Blackstone, "being a considerable lawyer and a consummate man of letters, for the first time made English law part of the literature of England."[73] This conviction that legal writing must be wedded to literary style had influenced his own work and accounted for the constant revisions before Dicey would allow publication.

Praise of Blackstone was not the sole purpose of his lecture. To *National Review* editor Leo Maxse he indicated: "The statement it contains as to the revolution produced in legal literature during the last 50 years, is novel and important."[74] To this revolution Dicey himself had made no small contribution. Above all, the farewell lecture should "impress upon ordinary readers" the great reform in legal writing the previous decades had witnessed.[75] Dicey was thus especially pleased to have the Blackstone piece appear in a popular journal, for he had thought originally the subject would hold little interest for the layman.[76] He acquainted his audience with the significant number of classic textbooks that had first appeared in the period of his professorship.

Dicey retired from the Vinerian Chair after a career that obtained many commendations from contemporaries and has earned the praise of subsequent scholars. The next Vinerian professor, W. M. Geldart, of whom Dicey wrote that he was "quite the best lawyer we have had in Oxford for a long time,"[77] paid tribute to Dicey's accomplishments: "To a style no less weighty, no less forcible, clearer and more terse than Blackstone's, to a learning no less thorough and detailed, he has added a critical insight and analytical power, of which Blackstone could not boast."[78] In an anonymous testimonial of 1917, the author asserted it was "in no small measure due to him that the Oxford School of Law has grown up from a small and rather neglected body to be one of the most important and flourishing in the University. He has supported all movements

73. Dicey to Bryce, 13 June 1909, in Rait, *Memorials*, p. 202.
74. Dicey to Leo Maxse, 25 September 1909, Leo Maxse Papers, West Sussex County Record Office, Chichester.
75. Ibid., 12 October 1909, ibid.
76. Ibid., 14 October 1909, ibid.
77. Dicey to Bryce, 16 January 1910, Bryce Papers.
78. W. M. Geldart, *Legal Personality*, p. 4.

for its reform and advancement."[79] H. G. Hanbury termed the election of Dicey to the chair the second foundation, likening it to the original appointment of the great Blackstone. Hanbury concluded his assessment of Dicey by calling him "one who revived a tradition, always a more difficult feat than to create a tradition. When he came to the Chair, its position seemed wellnigh hopeless; his mere advent infused into it the most priceless ingredient of Pandora's box. Under his occupation it went from strength to strength, and had, when he resigned, become an institution which was respected and renowned throughout the world."[80] More recently F. H. Lawson has maintained that Dicey "remains a great figure and a great man, one of the glories of the Oxford Law School and of English law in general."[81] This universal praise for his professorial career must be set against Dicey's own assessment.

The estimation of his performance as Vinerian professor demonstrated the diffidence that characterized Dicey's legal labors. In 1894, for example, Dicey wrote to Bryce of his certainty that an individual must always feel he has fallen short of what he ought to accomplish, adding "no one can say how deeply I feel this myself."[82] He never dispelled this pervasive feeling of failure despite all the outward signs of success he acquired: "When I spoke to you of the real & deep disappointment at the result or non-result of my work here, I ought to have added that for this I blame no one unless it be myself & even for myself I have not so much blame as regrets for mistakes. Errors themselves are mainly blameable not in themselves but as the fruit of defects of character. Of the regrets for failure please speak to no one."[83] Dicey did not value academic success on the same level with political or judicial influence, thus condemning himself to constant recriminations for his own alleged lack of accomplishment. That others did not share this pessimistic

79. Anon., "Professor Dicey: Portrait and Sketch," pp. 1–2. Dicey suspected Bryce of writing this tribute, but Bryce denied any role. Dicey also received denials from Holland and Pollock. C. P. Ilbert then became the leading candidate; see Dicey to Bryce, 31 January 1917, Bryce Papers.

80. Hanbury, *The Vinerian Chair*, p. 163.

81. Lawson, *The Oxford Law School*, p. 71.

82. Dicey to Bryce, 11 October 1894, Bryce Papers. This revealing letter ended with the uncharacteristic admonition: BURN THIS.

83. Ibid., 6 March 1904, ibid.

view was patent. One final example must suffice; upon the retirement of Dicey in 1909 Lord Curzon, then Chancellor of Oxford University, sent the following appreciation: "I may be permitted to send a brief line of sincere and grateful recognition of the preeminent contribution that you have made for a period of more than a quarter of a century to the life, the learning, and the public distinction of Oxford. Your name and works have shed a lustre upon the University, which no successor can hope to reproduce, and in your retirement we hope that she may still be able to rely upon the voice and head of one of the most learned and broad-minded of her sons."[84] This praise from Curzon came as a most pleasant surprise, for Dicey confessed he had underrated the esteem and friendliness of his colleagues.[85] Only at the end of his professorship did Dicey realize the good impression his work had made over the years.

Whose appraisal was nearer the truth: the self-depreciation of Dicey or the plaudits by his contemporaries and later scholars? Despite the doubts Dicey entertained, his influence as Vinerian professor proved lasting. Measured against the standard of other Vinerians, he came closest to emulating Blackstone: "In the justice of his appreciation of men and things, in the shrewdness of his diagnosis of the trend of contemporary events, and in the never-failing charm of his literary style, he was the equal of Blackstone."[86] Dicey set a new standard of excellence for academic lawyers and helped make that profession a worthy calling. He rescued academic law from indifference, transformed it into a field attractive to the best undergraduate minds, and opened up new areas of influence for academic lawyers. He carried out to the best of his ability a major function of an Oxford professor: publication of significant works in his area of competence. These books, as will be seen, encouraged the habit of judges looking to academic lawyers for support and sometimes guidance. And finally, he raised the Oxford Law School to a higher level of professionalism and established a tradition that still endures. For all these services Dicey merited the accolades that posterity has bestowed.

Previous writers on Dicey have naturally focused their attention

84. Lord Curzon to Dicey, 28 May 1909, General Manuscripts 508(55), Glasgow University Library.
85. Rait, *Memorials*, p. 204.
86. Hanbury, *The Vinerian Chair*, p. 104.

on his academic role because there Dicey gained his greatest fame. After Dicey's death when Holmes wrote of him: "What a dear, naif, ingenuous creature he was, and how modest as to his own powers,"[87] he referred solely to Dicey's career as academic lawyer. About these powers, as his Vinerian experience showed, Dicey was modest to the point of diffidence. But in other areas of vital concern to him, especially politics, he had no hesitation in making outrageously dogmatic statements. This side of Dicey has never been explored: the vehemence of his opinions was in inverse proportion to his qualifications on any given subject. On legal and constitutional questions, where even the judiciary acknowledged his authority, he offered suggestions with great reluctance. This hesitancy never touched his political pronouncements, for the deeper he became embroiled in controversies the more opinionated he grew. Thus the fame of Dicey as Vinerian professor stemmed in large part from his having to deal with those subjects for which he was best qualified. Nevertheless, his work in the Vinerian Chair will ensure the admiration of his name wherever English law is taught; no other aspect of his life can tarnish that success. Dicey provided his own epitaph: "I have done little good to the world, but I have tried my best by the Professorship."[88]

87. Holmes to Pollock, 20 February 1925, *Holmes-Pollock Letters*, 2: 156.
88. Dicey to Mrs. Dicey, 12 April 1908, in Rait, *Memorials*, p. 197.

CHAPTER FOUR

THE CONSTITUTIONAL EXPERT:

LAW OF THE CONSTITUTION

SOON AFTER ACCEPTING the Vinerian Chair Dicey repaid the trust reposed in him by the publication in 1885 of *Law of the Constitution*, his most influential treatise, which catapulted him into the front rank of constitutional authorities.[1] Considerable attention will be devoted to a review of Dicey's doctrines, for, as has often happened to works of classic stature, the book is now more often cited than actually read in its entirety. As H. G. Hanbury noted, Dicey has suffered the same fate as John Austin: "His critics have misquoted him and criticized their own misquotations."[2] Whenever possible in the next two chapters Dicey will speak for himself in explanation of his major conclusions.

Dicey employed in *Law of the Constitution* the methodology followed in his previous legal volumes, a rigorous analysis of the available evidence leading to the formulation of fundamental constitutional principles. F. H. Lawson, a sympathetic critic of Dicey, has emphasized the difficulty of this task, a problem of which Dicey was well aware.[3] The chaotic state of scholarship about constitutional matters offended the intellectual tidiness Dicey preferred. He had long expressed dissatisfaction with contemporary writings on constitutional law and so, like Austin, wished to reduce the subject to a few basic conceptions of undoubted validity. The purpose of the book was, as Dicey wrote, "to state what are the laws which form

1. Albert Venn Dicey, *Introduction to the Study of the Law of the Constitution.* Dicey prepared the first seven editions of the text, or through 1908; in 1915 he simply added a long introduction to the eighth edition in place of a major revision. The tenth edition, which will be used here for quotation, appeared in 1959 with an extensive introductory essay by E. C. S. Wade.

2. H. G. Hanbury, *The Vinerian Chair and Legal Education,* p. 137.

3. F. H. Lawson, "Dicey Revisited," p. 113.

part of the constitution, to arrange them in their order, to explain their meaning, and to exhibit where possible their logical connection."[4] From the mass of cases, judicial opinions, and statutes bearing upon constitutional arrangements, Dicey extracted three principles he felt expressed the axiomatic characteristics of British development: the sovereignty of Parliament, the rule of law, and the conventions of the constitution.

Constitutional speculations had intrigued Dicey since his undergraduate days, and that, plus his travels to America and on the Continent, turned him toward the comparative method utilized extensively throughout *Law of the Constitution.* That the basic ideas of the book germinated for a long period seems an inescapable conclusion. As early as 1868 Dicey had rehearsed his definition of liberty, which he eventually expanded into chapter V of the book.[5] The phrase "rule of law" he used for the first time in 1875 to describe a salient feature of the constitution, exactly the same sense he would give it a decade later.[6] This formulation of the rule of law owed much to its expression by W. E. Hearn in 1867, an intellectual debt Dicey openly acknowledged.[7] The slow evolution of his ideas, as these examples demonstrate, prepared him for his opportunity when the Vinerian professorship beckoned.

In June of 1884 Dicey offered the completed manuscript for publication to the Macmillan Company.[8] The actual writing of the book had taken place during the previous two years, originating in his professorial lectures. This procedure enabled him to alter the organization of his thoughts until he was satisfied he had found the right arrangement. In the anxiety to see the book in print, Dicey offered Macmillan any profits from the sale of the original edition of 750. A small first edition would sell out quickly, Dicey calculated, and thus necessitate the rapid issuance of a second edition.[9]

4. *Law of the Constitution,* p. 32.

5. Albert Venn Dicey, "The Legal Boundaries of Liberty," pp. 1–13.

6. Albert Venn Dicey, "Stubbs' Constitutional History of Great Britain," *Nation* 20 (4 March 1875): 154.

7. H. W. Arndt, "The Origin of Dicey's Concept of the Rule of Law," pp. 117–23.

8. Dicey to Macmillan Company, 9 June 1884, Macmillan Company Papers, B.M. Add. Mss. 55084.

9. Ibid., 1 July 1884, ibid.

While the book was in press in 1885, he urged his publisher to have the book in Oxford shops before the autumn return of students and faculty. In this careful supervision he was not disappointed, because within six months he informed Bryce that the first edition had indeed sold out.[10] Shortly thereafter Dicey wrote to the Macmillan Company about a second edition and, with the book a clear success, suggested equitable financial plans for both parties.[11] The subsequent editions, with their steady sale, solidified Dicey's financial position so that money was never again a worrisome problem.

The scrutiny exercised over publication details does not contradict the diffidence Dicey expressed about his scholarly endeavors. Before its appearance he had no illusions about the value of *Law of the Constitution:* "It contains some things (very few I own) which it were absurd to call original but which I think have been hardly said expressly before."[12] At the same time, in the event of his sudden death, he asked Bryce, with the assistance of Holland, to sort out his papers and publish whatever seemed worthwhile. If that unhappy situation should arise, Dicey wrote, "I should like the world to know that I have done my best to work, though the result of my labours is neither great nor remarkable."[13] Once again his strong ambition clashed with the fear of failure he so often experienced.

The anxieties he entertained about the reception of the book were not justified. His Oxford associates lost no time in proclaiming its merits; Bryce, for example, forwarded a copy of Dicey's work to Gladstone with this endorsement:

> I have ventured to send to you, yesterday, a copy of Mr. Dicey's book, the Law of the Constitution, which some of us here are disposed to think the most valuable contribution made to the scientific study of the British Constitution since the publication of Mr. Bagehot's brilliant essay. Mr. Dicey, who now holds the professorship here first held by Blackstone, much wished to

10. Dicey to Bryce, 11 February 1886, Bryce Papers.
11. Dicey to Macmillan Company, 14 February 1886, Macmillan Company Papers, B.M. Add. Mss. 55084. The second edition numbered 1250 copies with Dicey receiving 4/ of the 12/6 price.
12. Dicey to Bryce, 9 December 1884, Bryce Papers.
13. Ibid.

offer his work for your acceptance, but his personal knowledge of you is so slight—he once met you dining at my house in 1877—that he has asked me to be the means of transmitting it to you as the highest authority on constitutional questions.[14]

From first publication the book earned critical praise and throughout Dicey's lifetime enjoyed consistent popularity with the general public and in academic circles. Its freedom from jargon realized Dicey's aim of a treatise the average layman might understand. Its extraordinary influence stems in part from the fact that it appealed to expert and ordinary citizen alike.

Before examining the three constitutional principles Dicey delineated, one other question concerning *Law of the Constitution* must be answered. To what degree did Dicey's political views determine his conclusion on constitutional matters? The most trenchant of Dicey's critics, Sir Ivor Jennings, has argued that Dicey's conception of the constitution, the belief that rights of individuals had led to constitutional principles, came directly from his Whig political beliefs: "Dicey saw the constitution of 1885 through Whig principles."[15] No doubt the Diceyan constitution reflected the strong political opinions he held. The real question, which Jennings ignored, was whether the constitution of 1885 did in fact depend upon Whig principles. Dicey himself wrote that the "four writers whom I read with perpetual profit & enjoyment on all constitutional matters are Burke, Paley, Macauley, & Bagehot."[16] Dicey's interpretation of the constitution depended upon recognized works of authority in the first instance, and it was grossly unfair to Dicey to imply that *Law of the Constitution* simply indulged his politics. Emphasis on private rights at the expense of public rights was characteristic of nineteenth-century constitutional thought, so Dicey hardly broke new ground as he often admitted. The growing importance of public law was a fact concealed from Dicey, or at least underrated by him in 1885.

The crucial element for the interpretation of *Law of the Constitution* lies in the tradition of Austinian legal analysis: formal dissection of a legal problem in order to discover basic axioms. E. C. S.

14. Bryce to William E. Gladstone, 31 October 1884, Bryce Papers.
15. Sir Ivor Jennings, "In Praise of Dicey," p. 128.
16. Dicey to Godkin, 26 June 1900, Godkin Papers.

Wade made this point tentatively, arguing that Dicey followed in the footsteps of Austin by subjecting constitutional law to scientific study.[17] As Austin had tried to determine the province of jurisprudence, so Dicey attempted to mark the boundaries of constitutional law. It may readily be conceded that political views influenced the language of the book as Jennings argued, but the primary component was the legalistic attitude that sought the truth by discovering fundamental principles of the constitution. His Austinian heritage, not his Whig views, in essence shaped the conclusions of *Law of the Constitution.*

Demarcating the province of his study led Dicey into immediate difficulties with historians and political scientists. The claim that constitutional law embraced "all rules which directly or indirectly affect the distribution or the exercise of the sovereign power in the state" reflected the Austinian preoccupation with law as primarily a problem of sovereignty.[18] He subdivided this description by specifying rules that were true laws, that is, statutes or common law; and the rules that were not laws in the strict sense, that is, conventions. Many critics, especially Jennings, have found this formulation severely restrictive if not outright erroneous.[19] Law as only those rules enforceable in a law court (itself a reminder of Dicey's indebtedness to Austin) excised a substantial number of activities usually regarded as constitutional in nature. This distinction was imperative, for Dicey needed limits to his inquiry lest, flooded by evidence, he could not uncover the few axioms he sought. Indeed, after decades of hostility toward the Diceyan conceptualization of the problem, some scholars have praised his careful discrimination amidst the veritable explosion of materials associated with changes in government functions during the twentieth century.[20] By concentrating on three major constitutional ideas, the book gained a force

17. E. C. S. Wade, "Introduction," in *Law of the Constitution,* p. clxxxviii.

18. *Law of the Constitution,* p. 23.

19. Sir Ivor Jennings, *The Law and the Constitution,* pp. 33–41. He argued Dicey had overemphasized private rights at the expense of other areas of constitutional law.

20. Geoffrey Marshall, *Constitutional Theory,* pp. 7–12. Marshall did not defend Dicey's delimitation of constitutional law completely, arguing that a modification, not elimination, of Dicey's work in this area was in order.

and unity of thought superior to that of more exhaustive treatises. These three principles must now be examined.

Dicey asserted the sovereignty of Parliament in no uncertain terms, calling it from a legal point of view "the dominant characteristic of our political institutions."[21] The purpose of this section was: "To explain the nature of Parliamentary sovereignty and to show that its existence is a legal fact, fully recognised by the law of England; . . . to prove that none of the alleged legal limitations on the sovereignty of Parliament have any existence; . . . to state and meet certain speculative difficulties which hinder the ready admission of the doctrine that Parliament is, under the British constitution, an absolutely sovereign legislature."[22] Parliamentary sovereignty he defined as "the right to make or unmake any law whatever; and, further, that no person or body is recognized by the law of England as having a right to override or set aside the legislation of Parliament."[23] Dicey defined law as "any rule which will be enforced by the courts,"[24] a statement starkly Austinian in its language. With sovereignty and law specified for the reader, he then proceeded to an elucidation of the doctrine itself.

Dicey described the unlimited legislative authority of Parliament as the positive side of parliamentary supremacy. He relied in the first instance upon the testimony of previous constitutional authorities, Coke and Blackstone. The other supporting evidence was legislative: sweeping statutes such as the Act of Settlement, the Acts of Union, and the Septennial Act of 1716. Dicey also stressed the tradition of indemnity acts, which made legal various acts illegal at the time of commission. In 1885 he could not produce one case in proving his argument. This omission has been well described: "Dicey announced that it was the law that Parliament was omnicompetent, explained what this meant, and never devoted so much as a line to fulfilling the promise he made to demonstrate that this was so."[25] His critics have often used this point against him, that only history but not the law itself was on his side.

21. *Law of the Constitution*, p. 39.
22. Ibid.
23. Ibid., pp. 39–40.
24. Ibid., p. 40.
25. A. W. B. Simpson, "The Common Law and Legal Theory," in A. W. B. Simpson, ed., *Oxford Essays in Jurisprudence*, p. 96.

In the negative sense Dicey defined parliamentary sovereignty as the absence of any competing legislative authority. He cited Austin, then his close friend Holland, to substantiate his claim that sovereignty must be indivisible, that the essence of true sovereignty was freedom from any limitation, and that pluralistic sovereignty was a contradiction in terms. Invoking the authority of Austin once again, Dicey accepted the proposition that sovereignty must reside in every civilized state.[26] Having put forward his own case, Dicey then turned to three specific objections to the doctrine of parliamentary supremacy.

The first of these arguments, that acts of Parliament were invalid if they transgressed principles of morality or rules of international law, he disposed of with little trouble. The thrust of Austinian jurisprudence had aimed at the divorce of positive law from moral considerations, so Dicey simply indicated that a plea for the invalidity of a law because it was immoral had never succeeded in any English court. The law was binding on the individual no matter what reservations he had about its moral content. The nature of parliamentary sovereignty was such that any law, whatever its alleged moral turpitude, formed a valid law enforceable by the courts.

In countering the second argument Dicey denied that Parliament had no right to touch the royal prerogative. This was primarily an objection already decided by history, for the events of the seventeenth century had answered this question for succeeding generations. In 1885 constitutional evolution dictated that the executive exercise whatever powers remained to the Crown. More to the point, Parliament possessed the authority to regulate or even abolish Crown prerogatives if it chose. Control of the Crown was a major factor in assuring the supremacy of Parliament.

Finally, Dicey examined the problem of whether the legislative authority of one Parliament might be restricted by the enactments of a predecessor or, in other words, whether Parliament could bind the acts of a successor. Changes in the Acts of Union, such as Irish disestablishment or alterations in the religious tests for Scottish universities, showed the futility of attempts to legislate for all time. Attempts by one sovereign body to fetter an equally sovereign body

26. *Law of the Constitution*, p. 61.

had always failed.[27] In 1885 Dicey had concluded that parliamentary sovereignty was an undoubted legal fact, complete in both its positive and negative aspects. Parliament might legislate on any topic it pleased, no other institution within the British constitution rivaled it, and no court had the authority to rule its acts *ultra vires*. The doctrine of parliamentary sovereignty formed "the very keystone of the law of the constitution."[28]

Dicey, given his deep interest in politics, recognized as Austin had not that this strictly legal analysis of sovereignty did not completely satisfy. The sovereignty of Parliament had political implications as well. Therefore he made the famous distinction between legal and political sovereignty in order to account for the obvious fact that the electors played the predominant role in the political system. He had to reconcile the theory of parliamentary sovereignty with the restraint on that power exercised by the voters.

Dicey accomplished this by his assertion that there were both external and internal limitations on the actual use of authority and that these limits were consistent with his definition of sovereignty.[29] The external limit to sovereign power lay in the possibility that citizens would disobey any law repugnant to a great majority. While Parliament might in theory do anything, political circumstances dictated what in reality might be accomplished. Widespread resistance would nullify legislation which, though legally valid, was beyond parliamentary power to enforce. Popular opposition limited the sovereignty of Parliament on every side; a law incapable of enforcement simply meant no law at all. The internal boundary grew out of the nature of sovereignty itself, for even the worst despot ruled in accordance with the conditions of his own time, including the moral feelings of the society he headed. A British parliament composed of gentlemen would not pass morally reprehensible laws.

27. It should be noted that the courts, where Dicey enjoyed a great vogue in the early twentieth century, have shaken his authority on this issue. The 1953 case of MacCormick v. Lord Advocate raised the possibility of entrenched clauses whose provisions could not be abrogated, at least by ordinary act of Parliament. See Geoffrey Marshall, *Parliamentary Sovereignty and the Commonwealth*, pp. 72–75.

28. *Law of the Constitution*, p. 70.

29. Ibid., pp. 76–85.

Representative government prevented a disastrous cleavage between the wishes of the sovereign and the desires of subjects. It opened lines of communication that harmonized possible conflicts between the two parties. The distinction between the electorate and Parliament has drawn criticism, because it obscures the fact that the sovereign and the electorate are really one in Great Britain.[30] Dicey insisted that representative government produced the best means of reconciling actual limitations on sovereignty with the legal doctrine of parliamentary supremacy.

Dicey next compared the characteristics of a sovereign parliament with the traits of nonsovereign legislative bodies. Parliamentary sovereignty consisted of: "First, the power of the legislature to alter any law, fundamental or otherwise, as freely and in the same manner as other laws; secondly, the absence of any legal distinction between constitutional and other laws; thirdly, the non-existence of any judicial or other authority having the right to nullify an Act of Parliament, or to treat it as void or unconstitutional."[31] Adopting the terminology of Bryce, Dicey labeled these qualities of the British constitution examples of its "flexibility," by which he meant it could be altered at any moment.[32] In each case he stressed the uniqueness of English constitutional development, because its ease of change had rendered unnecessary any reduction to written form. In the description of colonial legislatures as nonsovereign bodies, Dicey emphasized the legal sovereignty of the Imperial Parliament. The recognition of this legal fact paved the way for the political policy of granting to colonies freedom of legislation. Careful supervision of colonial legislatures was superfluous, for the retention of the Crown's veto symbolized the possession of ultimate legal sovereignty. As imperial policy favored noninterference, colonial parliaments rarely experienced encroachment by the Imperial Parliament, because no reason to demonstrate the realities of legal sovereignty existed. At home and abroad parliamentary sovereignty was undoubted.

30. Geoffrey Marshall and Graeme C. Moodie, *Some Problems of the Constitution*, pp. 17–18.

31. *Law of the Constitution*, p. 91.

32. Dicey used "flexible" and "rigid" to emphasize whether constitutional change occurred through regular or extraordinary methods. See Dicey to Bryce, 9 December 1884, Bryce Papers.

During Dicey's lifetime this exposition of the sovereignty of Parliament swept away all opposition. As A. W. B. Simpson has written: "The basic book and the best written book, is Dicey, and it is around Dicey that nearly all lawyers study constitutional law. This has been so for a long time now. . . . The oracle spoke, and came to be accepted."[33] Rarely has a single book on the constitution reaped such acclaim and dominated the field so thoroughly. To call it an instant classic does not do it sufficient justice in regard to the authority it acquired in Dicey's lifetime. The facts of British political life appeared to demonstrate the truth of his dogmas at every turn. Even on an emotional issue like Home Rule, both friend and foe accepted the major premises of his argument, deducing different conclusions from Dicey's constitutional principles.

Only after his death did the first searching reexaminations of the Dicey version of parliamentary supremacy begin. The major attack on his conclusions came from Jennings, who found a very doubtful validity in Dicey's explanation.[34] In particular Jennings criticized the distinction between legal and political sovereignty on the grounds that legal sovereignty was fictitious. Jennings argued it was not supreme power at all but merely a legal idea by which lawyers expressed the relations between Parliament and the courts. To the discussion of sovereignty Jennings introduced the notion of rules plus their role within any legal system. Any parliament could indeed bind a successor by altering the rules of procedure for legislation itself.[35] Injection of rule theory into the debate reflected the growing concern of jurists in the twentieth century for analysis of legal systems by investigating the rules governing a system. Nevertheless, Jennings fared badly in this area, compared to the success of his criticisms of Dicey's other major principles. Few other scholars disavowed the Diceyan orthodoxy on which they had been raised.

Since World War II a veritable onslaught of criticism has befallen Dicey, with the result that revision and qualification of his sovereignty doctrine has proceeded in many directions. Following the lead of Jennings, other critics have synthesized the Diceyan theory of unlimited parliamentary supremacy with the theory that the exercise of that power may in fact be restrained by laws concerning

33. Simpson, "Common Law and Legal Theory," p. 96.
34. Jennings, *Law and the Constitution*, pp. 144–92.
35. Ibid., pp. 152–53.

the manner of its use. R. F. V. Heuston summarized this "New View" of parliamentary sovereignty in this fashion:

> (1) Sovereignty is a legal concept: the rules which identify the sovereign and prescribe its composition and functions are logically prior to it; (2) there is a distinction between rules which govern, on the one hand, (a) the composition, and (b) the procedure, and, on the other hand, (c) the area of power, of a sovereign legislature; (3) the courts have jurisdiction to question the validity of an alleged Act of Parliament on grounds 2(a) and 2(b), but not on grounds 2(c); (4) this jurisdiction is exercisable either before or after the Royal Assent has been signified—in the former case by way of injunction, in the latter by way of declaratory judgment.[36]

This concept of sovereignty hinged on the dissimilarity between the area of power and that of procedure, a point Dicey clearly never considered.[37] Rules governing the use of power were no less rules of law, the new interpretation held, and therefore might be altered only on their own terms.

Dicey has not lacked for modern partisans on behalf of his orthodox (that is, older) explanation of parliamentary authority. H. W. R. Wade has defended Dicey's explanation in his argument why courts enforce without question all acts of Parliament.[38] The answer lies in the uniqueness of the rule by which the courts so enforce, a rule itself unalterable by Parliament: "The rule of judicial obedience is in one sense a rule of common law, but in another sense—which applies to no other rule of common law—it is the ultimate *political* fact upon which the whole system of legislation rests."[39] The rule of total enforcement is a historical fact that will change only when political revolution causes such a transformation. Wade admitted that Dicey's deceptively simple statement of parliamentary sovereignty masked pitfalls for the intellectually unwary. This neo-Diceyan view of Wade's has been endorsed by other authorities, so it would be wrong to regard the defense of Dicey as merely the minority report of judicial deviants.[40]

36. R. F. V. Heuston, *Essays in Constitutional Law*, pp. 6–7.
37. A. L. Goodhart, "The Rule of Law and Absolute Sovereignty," p. 951.
38. H. W. R. Wade, "The Legal Basis of Sovereignty," pp. 172–97.
39. Ibid., p. 188. Italics in the original.
40. E. C. S. Wade and A. W. Bradley, *Constitutional Law*, p. 60.

The attempt to reconcile the two divergent theories of sovereignty has led to the concept of entrenchment or statutory procedure by which an act of Parliament might contain special provisions affecting the repeal of the statute itself. Geoffrey Marshall has urged that parliamentary sovereignty be rephrased: "Parliament cannot place any blanket *prohibition* on its future action but can place procedural restrictions on such action."[41] While it may no longer be said that Dicey stands above criticism, it is true that he has not been completely discredited either. Modern arguments about sovereignty usually start where Dicey left off.

In view of the continued debate about the veracity of Dicey's conclusions, how does this affect the estimate of Dicey? One resolution lies in the opposite directions taken by Dicey and his critics. Dicey started from a mass of constitutional data and extracted a formula capable of precise statement. The purpose of critics has been a technical commentary on his work. In other words, Dicey worked from the complex to the simple as Austinian jurisprudence directed him; his critics have moved from the simple to the complex. Little wonder that their conclusions have been at variance. The focus on rule theory by modern scholars has led to more sophisticated formulations of parliamentary sovereignty, but whether it has resulted in a truer description must still be termed an open question. Measured against his own purpose, Dicey succeeded admirably, for he popularized a doctrine acceptable to the general public for generations. It also has proven satisfactory to the judiciary if not to some academic lawyers.

The second solution to Dicey's role in the sovereignty discussion depends upon the definition of the problem itself. As Marshall has stated: "The problem is complicated by its containing a factual uncertainty about the English legal system wrapped up in a theoretical problem about legal systems in general."[42] If sovereignty is primarily a legal question, then surely Dicey's critics are correct. But if, as Dicey saw, both the legal and political consequences of sovereignty must be explained, then certainly his book contained basic truths about law and politics that subsequent jurists have confronted reluctantly. Even the most ardent defender of Dicey would concede that his ideas of parliamentary supremacy in impe-

41. Marshall, *Constitutional Theory*, p. 52. Italics in the original.
42. Ibid., p. 44.

rial affairs have vanished along with the Empire they served. Nevertheless, the notion that parliamentary sovereignty is fundamental to the British constitution, no matter how extended the debate on its exact nature, seems assured of continuing support from scholars in all disciplines.

The question of what influence Dicey's teaching has exercised is much easier to answer. Even Jennings admitted that Dicey succeeded in becoming the recognized authority on the subject.[43] No other scholar has taken his place. His facility of expression has kept his doctrines alive. Dicey has dominated the discussion even more than his mentor Austin. In every sense of the term Dicey provided the classic exegesis of sovereignty; he has framed the boundaries within which all later debate has taken place. The contribution of Dicey in this area may be paraphrased from the verdict of F. H. Lawson: an enormous amount of the best thought since Dicey has been devoted to the critical appraisal of his work.[44] Modern revision has not eroded the solid foundations Dicey provided for his doctrine.

The second characteristic of the British constitution Dicey expounded was the rule of law. By this phrase he meant three different aspects of the same principle. In the first sense, Dicey believed in the "absolute supremacy or predominance of regular law as opposed to the influence of arbitrary power, and excludes the existence of arbitrariness, of prerogative, or even of wide discretionary authority on the part of the government. Englishmen are ruled by the law, and by the law alone; a man may with us be punished for a breach of law, but he can be punished for nothing else." The second meaning Dicey gave the rule of law involved "equality before the law, or the equal subjection of all classes to the ordinary law of the land administered by the ordinary law courts; the 'rule of law' in this sense excludes the idea of any exemption of officials or others from the duty of obedience to the law which governs other citizens or from the jurisdiction of the ordinary tribunals." Finally, he used the phrase to show "the law of the constitution, the rules which in foreign countries naturally form part of a constitutional code, are not the source but the consequence of the rights of individuals, as defined and enforced by the courts; that, in short, the principles of

43. Jennings, *Law and the Constitution,* p. 320.
44. Lawson, *The Oxford Law School,* p. 72.

private law have with us been by the action of the courts and Parliament so extended as to determine the position of the Crown and of its servants; thus the constitution is the result of the ordinary law of the land."[45] Each of these separate meanings requires further explanation.

In the first sense, as originally written in 1885, Dicey emphasized the superior position Great Britain enjoyed in having no distinction between private and public law, a luxury unknown to other European countries. The supremacy of ordinary law, maintained by unity of jurisdiction, stood in sharp relief to other legal systems. His fear of discretionary executive authority, expressed in unequivocal language, formed the most important corollary to this first element in the rule of law. Dicey equated discretion with arbitrariness, claiming "discretionary authority on the part of the government must mean insecurity for legal freedom on the part of its subjects."[46] Discretionary authority need not be oppressive; caprice, whether despotic or not, entailed the rule of lawless government.

In the second instance, Dicey clarified his original statement by adding that not only was no man above the law, but also that every man, whatever his rank or status, was subject to ordinary law. Every government official shared the same responsibility for his acts as did every ordinary citizen; English law recognized no alternative law systems administered by special tribunals. Though some officials incurred by virtue of their office legal liabilities from which other citizens were exempt, they could not because of that fact avoid the legal obligations borne by all citizens.

Finally, Dicey invested rule of law with a meaning he called the predominance of the legal spirit. He referred to the process by which the constitution had evolved through the centuries, with the principles thereof resulting from individual judicial decisions passed from generation to generation. In foreign countries rights of the citizenry proceeded from the general principles of the constitution, usually accompanied by idealistic language about the nature of the rights guaranteed. The English constitution contained no abstract statement of rights but did reflect the grounding of the constitution in legal precedent. The primary example Dicey offered was the

45. The three quotations are from *Law of the Constitution,* pp. 202–3.
46. Ibid., p. 188.

Habeas Corpus Act, which declared no principle and defined no right but was worth a hundred constitutional assurances.

The exposition of the rule of law through the use of English examples alone did not satisfy Dicey. He illustrated the rule of law particularly by contrasting it with the system of administrative law prevailing in France. The comparative study of constitutions intrigued Dicey, but certainly his comparison of the English rule of law with French *droit administratif*, as will be seen in the next chapter, was less than fortunate. In defense it must be remembered that he pioneered a method of legal analysis now taken for granted: "One reason why the law of the constitution is imperfectly understood is, that we too rarely put it side by side with the constitutional provisions of other countries. Here, as elsewhere, comparison is essential to recognition."[47] The errors committed by Dicey in pursuing this comparative method and the deserved criticism he has received on that account should be balanced by admiration for the attempt in the first place.

Having defined the rule of law to his own satisfaction, Dicey then devoted the next seven chapters of the book to its elaboration in practice through examination of major constitutional areas. The first of these concerned the right to personal freedom, where Dicey contrasted the seventh article of the Belgian constitution, with its idea that personal liberty was a special privilege granted to citizens above the ordinary law, with the English doctrine that personal freedom was the outcome of the ordinary law of the land as enforced by the courts.[48] Deprivation of liberty occurred in England only when an accusation of crime was lodged, with the accused having the right to trial. When convicted, the citizen then suffered the punishment prescribed by law for his crime. This led Dicey to two subsidiary conclusions. No official who had illegally interfered with the liberty of a citizen might plead that he had merely followed the orders of a superior, for each bureaucrat was individually responsible for his acts. Furthermore, the courts provided a remedy for such illegal interference, whether of short or long duration. Once again Dicey cited the Habeas Corpus Act as a procedural safeguard vindicating the right to personal freedom. The state could punish, he added, but it could hardly prevent the commission of crimes. Unless

47. Ibid., p. 205.
48. Ibid., pp. 206–37.

specific evidence to the contrary existed, every citizen possessed a presumptive right to personal freedom without interference from public or private authorities.

In regard to freedom of discussion, Dicey suggested that English law recognized no abstract claim on behalf of the right to liberty of thought or to freedom of speech.[49] Freedom of discussion in England amounted to nothing more than writing or saying anything a jury thought expedient. The state restricted its activities to punishment of distinct breaches of the law like libel or slander, thereby ensuring the absence of prior censorship. In this area as well the government could act only after the commission of a crime. Any violations of the law by word or act were punishable in the ordinary courts through customary legal procedures. Once again Dicey emphasized that liberty of the press and the right of free discussion resulted from the predominance of the ordinary law. The lack of discretionary government authority in this field illustrated another facet of the rule of law in England.

Dicey made the same arguments about the right of public meeting, insisting that no general right of assembly had ever been recognized by the courts.[50] The right of public meeting flowed from the fact that what was legal for one citizen remained legal for ten thousand citizens in a group. Any legal public activity did not become unlawful simply because it could excite illegal opposition and lead indirectly to a breach of the peace. Magistrates had no right to forbid a public meeting because other individuals might commit crimes in reaction to it. In the famous case of *Duncan* v. *Jones,* Lord Hewart cited the Diceyan doctrine with approval while reiterating that any meeting held for the purpose of unlawful activities might be prevented if reasonable cause existed for the authorities to believe this might be the case.[51] Dicey knew that this freedom was not absolute, but his main objective was a demonstration of the "process by which the decisions of the courts as to the rights of individuals have in effect made the right of public meeting a part of the law of the constitution."[52]

In the next two chapters Dicey applied the rule of law to the

49. Ibid., pp. 238–69.
50. Ibid., pp. 270–83.
51. Duncan v. Jones (1936) 1 K.B. 218, cited in D. L. Keir and F. H. Lawson, *Cases in Constitutional Law,* pp. 203–7.
52. *Law of the Constitution,* p. 283.

topics of martial law and the army.[53] Orderly government at times required a resort to martial law, Dicey admitted. His previous exposition of the rule of law had made clear the need to limit the province of martial law. He feared that a declaration of martial law could become an alternative, arbitrary legal system fatal to the rule of law. So he concluded that under martial law force might be employed to restore order, but the meting out of indiscriminate punishment was not permissible. The authority of a civilian court prevailed over that of a military court in any conflict of jurisdiction. Dicey asserted that obedience to the command of a superior constituted no defense to criminal charges brought against a soldier. In this context he no doubt underrated the difficulties of any soldier deciding for himself what was a lawful order; Dicey's point emphasized that a soldier retained the obligations of an ordinary citizen. Status as a member of the army did not exempt the soldier from those responsibilities.

Dicey chose the revenue as an example of the rule of law, showing briefly that all sums expended by the government required the sanction of an act of Parliament.[54] The efficient audit system ensured that every penny spent was in accordance with law. Here his own experience with Inland Revenue served him well in giving him insight into the legal problems involved. He pursued this line by defining the responsibility of ministers not in the ordinary political sense, but in the technical sense that every minister was legally responsible for every act he undertook on behalf of the Crown. Through this mechanism even the Crown obeyed the law of the land. Legal liability supported parliamentary responsibility, assuring that Cabinet officials respected the law as well. On the basis of his examination of these several aspects of the constitution, Dicey concluded that the rule of law formed a fundamental principle of constitutional law.

Subsequent evaluation of the Diceyan rule of law has been in direct contrast to the fate of his doctrine about parliamentary sovereignty. That, it will be recalled, swept all before it during his lifetime, coming under attack only since World War II. The rule of law attracted scholarly criticism even before his death; Harold Laski wrote in 1917 that the rule of law was "today so theoretical and so

53. Ibid., pp. 284–311.
54. Ibid., pp. 312–24.

beset on all hands by exceptions as to be hardly applicable at all."[55] In addition, the example of totalitarian regimes between the world wars refocused attention on the ways in which legal systems might be subverted for illegal purposes. Since 1945 the modern tendency to invest the rule of law with widely different meanings has been the greatest problem in evaluating Dicey's original contribution.

Once again Ivor Jennings has played a major role in the criticism of this Diceyan doctrine.[56] Jennings found a basic fault in Dicey's not having elicited a principle of law, but merely enshrining his own political philosophy under the guise of the rule of law. Jennings concluded that the rule of law was "rather an unruly horse." If it was just a synonym for law and order, then it was certainly not unique and might become a euphemism for the very arbitrary principles the rule of law opposed. Otherwise the phrase was either too subjective or too latitudinarian in scope. In any case, Jennings argued, the rule of law simply did not signify what Dicey had hoped about the supremacy of the law.

Ironically, the criticisms of Dicey made by Jennings work just as effectively when turned on Jennings himself. That Dicey defined liberty only in the negative sense of freedom from government interference cannot be denied; his whole life testified to the strength of his belief in that ideal.[57] For Dicey the rule of law embodied a traditional concept signifying freedom from arbitrary government activity in every sphere of life. Jennings reflected a positive liberalism favorable to government intervention as a cure for social problems, so Jennings articulated his own political philosophy when he criticized Dicey. Thus many exceptions to the rule of law Jennings mentioned were really the exceptions that proved the rule, not examples destructive of the rule of law itself.[58] The real question was whether Dicey's phrase illuminated a principle capable of reinterpretation in a different era. On the rule of law Jennings has not shaken the Diceyan rule of law to the extent that he successfully questioned parliamentary sovereignty.

55. Harold Laski to Holmes, 28 November 1917, in Mark DeWolfe Howe, ed., *Holmes-Laski Letters*, 1: 113.

56. Jennings, *Law and the Constitution*, pp. 54–62, 305–17.

57. For an analysis of negative and positive freedom in the English context, see David Nicholls, "Positive Liberty, 1880–1914," pp. 114–28.

58. H. W. R. Wade, " 'Quasi-Judicial' and Its Background," p. 225.

Since 1945 constitutional lawyers have adapted the rule of law to the circumstances of modern society. Many writers have now admitted that Dicey's vision of absolute equality before the law was erroneous even in 1885 because of Crown immunity from the usual processes of law.[59] Since then, immunities granted to groups like trade unions plus the clarification of special powers conferred on the police have illustrated the existence of special rights and duties in the constitution. But the enduring value of the Diceyan rule of law lies not so much in the narrow sense he used to denote a principle of the constitution; as a more general statement of rights, it now expresses the aspirations for justice of millions around the world who have never heard Dicey's name. Critics now see the rule of law as a protection against the arbitrariness of state action possible with the growth of government intervention in many daily activities of its citizens. This use of the concept applies to any legal system, whatever its ideological foundations.

Indeed, if the rule of law still faces criticism, it is because modern authorities have invested it with a variety of meanings beyond Dicey's dreams. R. M. Jackson has therefore concluded that "the Rule of Law ought now to be regarded as a fine sonorous phrase, to be put alongside the Brotherhood of Man, Human Rights and all the other slogans of mankind on the march."[60] Others, while sympathizing with this aim of global jurisdiction for the rule of law, have suggested that a new statement be submitted, not the rule of law with its meaning substantially altered.[61] The attempt at universal validity for the concept, in some quarters, weakened the rule of law through imprecision.

Conversely, some recent critics have welcomed this development, believing that an expanded concept might benefit all legal systems. A typical argument is that the rule of law articulates a "basic idea which can serve to unite lawyers of many differing systems, all of which aim at protecting the individual from arbitrary government."[62] Or, viewed from a different perspective, the actions

59. D. C. M. Yardley, *Introduction to British Constitutional Law*, p. 61. The exemption was not removed until the Crown Proceedings Act of 1947.
60. R. M. Jackson, *The Machinery of Justice in England*, p. 341.
61. O. D. Schreiner, *The Contribution of English Law to South African Law, and the Rule of Law in South Africa*, p. 84.
62. Wade and Bradley, *Constitutional Law*, p. 74.

of the state "must be based on and traceable back to an ultimate source of legal authority."[63] In the final analysis, what Dicey intended as a static dogma immutable for the ages has acquired a dynamism that has aided its adaptation to many different societies. Liberty of the individual, freedom from arbitrary government activity, and recourse to the courts are enduring ideals Dicey extolled even if they derived ultimately from his own parochial political philosophy. A. L. Goodhart for instance, in praising *rule under the law*, listed three requirements for its existence, all of which are implicit or explicit in Dicey's doctrine.[64] The simplicity of expression Dicey achieved has made his formulation essential for any later reappraisal of the phrase.

Perhaps the most ironic development of all was the suggestion by J. F. Garner that the rule of law has become the new natural law, a normative ideal toward which all legal systems should strive.[65] That Dicey, with his deep intellectual obligation to Austin, should be in this position, one Austin would have rejected, signifies analytic jurisprudence come full circle. Garner admitted that the rule of law could never invalidate the positive law of a country, a proper Austinian attitude, but the role of the Diceyan rule of law as an ideal for legal systems still seems secure. In that guise it exerts more influence in the modern world than it ever did in Dicey's lifetime.

Few would now criticize the fundamental premises of the rule of law—that a citizen enjoys his liberty in due observance of the law, that he may be deprived of that freedom only for offenses known to the law, and only by the procedures specified for that purpose. These essential elements have remained central to the constitution in spite of the changes since 1885. Dicey was surely wrong in his Whiggish belief that discretionary government authority necessarily led to a diminution of individual freedom. Discretionary power, when restrained by law, need not be arbitrary. Since the publication of *Law of the Constitution*, British history has demonstrated how increasing demands for state services may harmonize with ideals of freedom from a different political philosophy. Gradual blending of public and private rights has permitted vast expansion of the govern-

63. Norman S. Marsh, "The Rule of Law as a Supra-National Concept," in A. G. Guest, ed., *Oxford Essays in Jurisprudence*, p. 248.

64. Goodhart, "Rule of Law," pp. 947, 961.

65. J. F. Garner, *Administrative Law*, p. 17.

The Orchard, 80 Banbury Road, Oxford
(Courtesy of Victor Bonham-Carter)

ment into new areas, while at the same time this process has been leavened by the enduring regard for the individual that the rule of law expounds. Once again Dicey provided a practical principle to guide the growth of this increasingly important area, and also left an ideal that jurists still find worth contemplating.[66] Though he had not posterity in mind, the Diceyan rule of law stated a constitutional maxim succeeding generations have found valuable.

The influence of the rule of law must be seen on two levels: the practical and the theoretical. Lawyers have accepted the doctrine as a basic component of the constitution ever since 1885. The rule of law "has had such a profound influence" that its importance cannot be too strongly emphasized.[67] No individual since Blackstone has had such an impact as Dicey on the development of constitutional law. The rule of law has exercised such direct influence because it

66. Yardley, *Introduction to British Constitutional Law*, p. 62.
67. O. Hood Phillips, *Constitutional and Administrative Law*, p. 41.

"gives expression to a concept which is generally accepted by people irrespective of personal political views."[68] The succinct explanation of the doctrine in plain language made Dicey the standard authority for public opinion. As a theoretical ideal the rule of law has played a significant role in constitutional speculations.[69] Dicey delineated a standard of justice that transcended his own era and has lived on as a norm for other legal systems. As Lawson concluded: "You cannot escape Dicey. And what a feather it is in his cap to have coined the phrase 'the Rule of Law'!"[70]

When Dicey turned to an explanation of conventions of the constitution, he recognized that he faced problems largely of his own making. He had already stated that only law in the strict sense should be considered by the constitutional lawyer, and yet he now proposed a study of constitutional morality, a strange area indeed for a disciple of Austin. In this treatment he aimed "to define the relation between the legal and the conventional elements in the constitution, and to point out the way in which a just appreciation of this connection throws light upon several subordinate questions of constitutional law."[71] Dicey faced the problem of reconciling his definition of constitutional law with the alleged importance of conventions.

The crucial issue for Dicey was accounting for obedience to conventions. Enforcement of laws loomed large in the calculations of Austinian jurisprudence. This posed the problem of obligation in conventions: why should they be obeyed?[72] Dicey admitted conventions were not laws, because no law court would enforce them. Without a sanction he believed conventions had no rationale at all. The fear of impeachment provided one sanction, but this weapon had long since passed into obscurity. The force of public opinion as ultimate sanction Dicey also rejected on Austinian grounds. Likening this argument to the assertion that moral force, not military force, buttressed international law, he could not accept that this truly portrayed the situation.

He escaped from this dilemma by concluding that in fact the force

68. J. Harvey and L. Bather, *The British Constitution*, p. 405.
69. Jackson, *Machinery of Justice*, p. 339.
70. Lawson, *The Oxford Law School*, p. 72. "Coined" is too strong; "popularized" is a more accurate description. See note 7 of this chapter.
71. *Law of the Constitution*, p. 418.
72. J. D. B. Mitchell, *Constitutional Law*, p. 28.

of law constrained obedience to constitutional conventions. In this manner conventions, which by definition should not have been included in constitutional law, now came within the purview of his explanation. Dicey based this conclusion on the belief that violation of a constitutional convention would ultimately result in transgression of the law. This solution followed from his conviction that law courts were central to the constitution; conventions, though not law in the immediate sense, derived ultimately from positive law. Strict rules regulating conventions were impossible, because each convention in its own way tried to secure "obedience by all persons to the deliberately expressed will of the House of Commons in the first instance, and ultimately to the will of the nation as expressed through Parliament."[73] Thus constitutional conventions assured the permanent political sovereignty of the electorate.

The Diceyan analysis of conventions of the constitution was not original. He often acknowledged that in *Law of the Constitution* he had simply stated the obvious for the benefit of his readers. Hood Phillips has detailed a lengthy list of legal progenitors amounting to a tradition antedating Dicey.[74] Foremost among the influences on Dicey was historian Edward A. Freeman.[75] Dicey and Freeman were friends from Oxford, and their relationship did not suffer during the two decades Dicey spent in London. He never hid his admiration for Freeman's historical works, even after their political paths had parted.[76] From the work of Freeman, Stubbs, and other historians, Dicey obtained the historical background he felt sufficient to prove his point about legal sanctions underlying conventions. The combination of historical and legal knowledge provided Dicey an edge over his predecessors, as Hood Phillips concluded; Dicey supplied a "clearer and more precise formulation" of the problem, because he had "a more practical grasp of how the law works."[77] Again Dicey

---

73. *Law of the Constitution,* p. 456.

74. O. Hood Phillips, "Constitutional Conventions: Dicey's Predecessors," pp. 137–48.

75. Sir William S. Holdsworth, "The Conventions of the Eighteenth Century Constitution," p. 161.

76. See the review by Dicey, "Freeman's Growth of the Constitution of Great Britain," *Nation* 15 (12 and 19 September 1872): 169, 188; also the memorial article by Dicey, "Professor Edward A. Freeman," pp. 86–88.

77. Hood Phillips, "Constitutional Conventions," p. 148.

had succeeded in abstracting a general statement of principle from the writings of at least a dozen previous authorities, thus putting his own stamp on it through concise expression.

Once again Jennings has proved the most thorough critic of Dicey's conclusions, even while admitting that the account of conventions made "a magnificent contribution to English public law."[78] The gist of Jennings' dissatisfaction lay in the distinction Dicey postulated between legal and nonlegal rules. Jennings had no trouble in citing acknowledged conventions whose violation entailed no breach of law.[79] He emphasized the fallacy Dicey inherited from Austin that the essence of law lay in its enforcement, maintaining on the contrary that courts never enforce a law but rather give a decision or make an order. Dicey had only himself to blame for ambiguity on this point, because he had first defined conventions as rules which were not laws, then later insisted that obedience to them resulted from fear of breaking the law if they were not obeyed.[80] Dicey was trapped by the Austinian preconceptions he brought to the subject.

Jennings' concentration on this aspect of Dicey's doctrine—the separation but ultimate interconnection of law and convention—has not found favor with later critics.[81] The argument by Jennings that the real sanction for conventions and subsequent obedience to them arose from fear of the political consequences of disobedience rather than legal results possessed some validity. But if conventions were politically sanctioned only, then a large majority of any party presumably could run roughshod over any convention, violating it with impunity. The obligation factor in constitutional conventions remained unsolved. In this case Dicey's insistence on careful distinctions among law, conventions, and politics made analysis of the problem simpler. The fullest discussion of the Dicey and Jennings positions made clear that neither was completely compelling.[82] If anything, however, Geoffrey Marshall and Graeme C. Moodie supported Dicey with one modification. They defined conventions as

78. Jennings, "In Praise of Dicey," p. 130.
79. Jennings, *Law and the Constitution*, p. 148.
80. *Law of the Constitution*, pp. 24, 445–46.
81. Marshall, *Constitutional Theory*, pp. 10–12.
82. Marshall and Moodie, *Some Problems of the Constitution*, pp. 35–41.

"the ways in which certain legal powers must be exercised if the powers are to be tolerated by those affected."[83] They added, contrary to Dicey, that violation of a convention would not likely lead to a breach of law, but rather a change in the law or even in the constitutional structure itself. The political consequences of which Jennings had written would have effect much more quickly than a judicial proceeding. This synthesis of the variant interpretations of constitutional conventions validates above all the contention of Dicey that these understandings were of major importance to constitutional law.

Whatever reservations modern authorities have about the acceptability of the Diceyan explanation of conventions, they agree that he gave the "classic exposition" of the topic.[84] The association of Dicey with conventions remains unbroken. In view of the preceding criticisms, his doctrine should not be regarded as erroneous, only incomplete. His definition still covers many of the parliamentary understandings in existence since 1885, but does not fit entirely some modern conventions. The basic distinction between law and convention still solves more problems than it creates.[85] Though Dicey recognized the political nature of conventions, his Austinian assumptions led him to stress legal values at the expense of political factors. E. C. S. Wade, in citing this section as the most valuable portion of the book, concluded that Dicey's shortcomings do "not lessen the debt which is owed to Dicey for his brilliant exposition of the nature of conventions."[86]

Comparisons of the influence of Dicey in the areas of parliamentary sovereignty, the rule of law, and conventions of the constitution are somewhat invidious, for he vitally affected the understanding of constitutional law in all three. *Law of the Constitution* spilled over with suggestive discussions of important topics beyond his three major principles, so its influence has not been limited to these doctrines alone. The book has sparked continuing debate in other constitutional areas as well. It is to these other issues raised by *Law of the Constitution* that attention must now be turned.

83. Ibid., p. 40.
84. Kenneth C. Wheare, *Modern Constitutions*, p. 122.
85. Mitchell, *Constitutional Law*, p. 29.
86. E. C. S. Wade, "Introduction," *Law of the Constitution*, p. cxci.

CHAPTER FIVE

THE POLITICAL EXPERT:

LAW OF THE CONSTITUTION

ICEY'S CONCLUSIONS about the nature of French *droit administratif* and the absence of any corresponding system of administrative law in England have provoked a storm of controversy ever since the book first appeared. Constitutional scholars have questioned every aspect of his work on this subject. Dicey never made a more fertile error, for he has dominated the study of English administrative law for better or worse as has no other individual. He included this discussion under the heading of the rule of law, but so widespread has criticism become of his teaching that specific treatment is required.

In his consideration of *droit administratif* Dicey followed his customary method of abstracting fundamental concepts from his evidence, then drawing his conclusions from an elaboration of those ideas. He defined *droit administratif* as "that portion of French law which determines, (i) the position and liabilities of all State officials, (ii) the civil rights and liabilities of private individuals in their dealings with officials as representatives of the State, and (iii) the procedure by which these rights and liabilities are enforced."[1] Next, he explained the two leading principles upon which French administrative law rested. He took specific note of these ideas because, as Dicey judged, they were completely alien to modern Englishmen. The first principle held that the government and every servant thereof possessed special rights against private citizens, with the extent of those rights differing from those governing the relations between ordinary citizens. The second involved the separation of powers, Dicey arguing that the government and its officials were to a great extent free from the jurisdiction of the ordinary courts.[2] Each

1. *Law of the Constitution*, p. 333.
2. Ibid., pp. 336–38.

branch of government must not encroach upon the functions of the other parts, an idea Dicey attributed to Montesquieu's misapprehension of the way the English constitution worked.

Dicey distinguished further four characteristics of *droit administratif,* each calling for special emphasis. First came the distinction in French law between ordinary and administrative law, which meant to Dicey that laws supervising the government and its officials in relation to ordinary citizens bore little resemblance to the law as it applied to private citizens. Next, he made the point that ordinary courts had no concern with disputes between a citizen and the state, for these matters came under the jurisdiction of an administrative tribunal. In addition, French law limited judicial authority by the doctrine that administrative bodies should not suffer interference from the ordinary courts. Lastly and the most sinister feature of all in French law, Dicey invested *droit administratif* with the despotic characteristic of protecting any government official from the ordinary courts, whatever sort of illegal act he had perpetrated. Illegality in the performance of government duties whether or not in obedience to superiors escaped the control of ordinary courts.[3]

That Dicey might form such a picture of French administrative law was consistent with his legal and political philosophy. Because he considered enforcement a primary criterion in the validity of law, Dicey thought a system of law dependent upon arbitrary tribunals of little value in the protection of private rights. Since he had always regarded liberty as essentially freedom from government interference, *droit administratif* seemed an open invitation to government to meddle in the private affairs of citizens. On both counts the French system made a perfect foil for the rule of law in England. Comparison of the two legal systems enabled Dicey to stress the positive value of English law.

Droit administratif, he claimed, rested upon ideas absolutely foreign to English law; in this context he repeated his objection to having the relations between citizens and the state governed by different principles from those governing individuals. The liberties of the English constitution arose from the ordinary law of the land, not a special law code. Because of the definition he gave to the rule

3. Ibid., pp. 339–46.

of law, Dicey took great pains to deny that *droit administratif*, either intentionally or not, had become part of English law. Extensions of quasi-judicial authority to government officials on the grounds of convenience did not betray the essential principles of English law: "There exists in England no true *droit administratif*."[4] The rule of law in England protected individual liberty against government oppression better than in any other country.

That French administrative law had real merit Dicey readily admitted. He complained that few English lawyers possessed any appreciation of its value for comparative purposes. He acknowledged that by 1908 its modern development had given to the French citizen protection from administrative authorities instead of serving as a blanket invitation to despotism. Among its features Dicey was impressed by the modern development of easy, inexpensive access to administrative courts in France, though he also added that judgment was sometimes subject to long delay. Much of this improvement in legal procedure, it should be noted, Dicey attributed again to judicial activism. Despite this recognition of its merits, he concluded that even in 1908 *droit administratif* was still inconsistent with the liberties afforded by the common law.[5]

The most remarkable aspect of Dicey's concern with administrative law was the almost invincible ignorance he displayed about the evolution of domestic administrative jurisdiction during his own lifetime. Though the exact dates and extent of this process cannot be described with precision, it is clear that Dicey possessed little knowledge of this vast growth throughout the nineteenth century. Having gained a perception early in life of an England governed without undue complexity, Dicey adhered to this notion with his characteristic inflexibility. Given such misunderstanding of a topic in his own country, it is not surprising that he experienced trouble in understanding the bases of the French system.

Dicey proved twice unlucky in that both past and future events undermined his conclusions. Initially, he was misled by reading Tocqueville, a bad choice for the historical background of *droit administratif*.[6] As will become increasingly clear, Dicey's ability in

4. Ibid., p. 390.
5. Ibid., pp. 404–5.
6. See M. A. Sieghart, *Government by Decree*, pp. 69–70; and Seymour Drescher, *Tocqueville and England*, pp. 87–88.

historical research in no way matched his intellectual achievements in other fields. Future developments also proved him wrong, because the trend of twentieth-century social development, with its rapid expansion of government services, made his complacent belief in the absence of English administrative law appear ludicrous. However well intentioned his writing on this subject, modern constitutional scholars have shown striking unanimity in their condemnation of Dicey.

The litany of charges against Dicey stretches out endlessly. Every allegation cannot be listed, but certain criticisms have become standard. Scholars have pointed out he harbored an obsessive fear that administrative courts in France existed for the sole purpose of exempting officials from the control of ordinary law and, in effect, made them a law unto themselves.[7] Furthermore, Dicey concerned himself unduly with remedies against administrative excesses, thus fostering a narrow understanding of administrative law in general which does not do justice to the topic at all. He emphasized the problems of delegated legislation at the expense of other aspects of administrative law; specifically, he worried about duties and liabilities while ignoring powers and organization.[8] In addition he misunderstood the French Conseil d'Etat, which resulted in a fundamental misapprehension of the role of administrative courts.[9] Even before the appearance of the first edition, Dicey called *droit administratif* "that very curious topic" and indicated to Bryce it would simplify his task of explaining what was meant by the rule of law.[10] Finally, he argued that administrative law and his own rule of law were mutually exclusive.[11] In the end therefore, his critics have maintained, he distorted *droit administratif* beyond recognition.

Besides a thorough misinterpretation of French law, Dicey also committed at least two notable errors about English law. In the first instance he stressed the importance of an Englishman's right to sue any official personally in an ordinary court of law. He gave no indication of the difficulties this procedure created nor in any way

7. H. W. R. Wade, *Administrative Law*, p. 7.
8. J. A. G. Griffith and H. Street, *Principles of Administrative Law*, p. 4.
9. S. A. de Smith, *Judicial Review of Administrative Action*, p. 5.
10. Dicey to Bryce, 3 January 1885, Bryce Papers.
11. D. C. M. Yardley, *Introduction to British Constitutional Law*, p. 60.

acknowledged that French law served the needs of suitors better.[12] And then, after having emphasized the evils of immunity from the ordinary process of law existing in France, he ignored the immunity of the Crown from liability in tort. In 1885 this effectively prevented almost all suits against the Crown except by special proceeding. His misleading conclusions questioned the very existence of administrative law in England just when the need for its study began.[13] On both sides of the English Channel Dicey left the study of administrative law in a chaotic state, creating confusion instead of the few basic principles he sought.

On one thing only his critics all agreed; whatever the precise nature of his errors, his mistakes have dominated the study of administrative law in England ever since. W. A. Robson blamed Dicey for the four-decade delusion that the country possessed no administrative law at all.[14] Another commentator added that the formal study of the subject has never fully recovered from the Diceyan denial of its existence.[15] In other words, the influence of Dicey "long threw a chilly shadow over administrative law."[16] Finally, Dicey persuaded English lawyers to regard administrative law "as a misfortune inflicted upon the beknighted folk across the Channel."[17] This almost universal denunciation of Dicey, if nothing else, demonstrated the unique influence he has exercised on this increasingly important branch of English law. He has become the authority upon whom each newcomer practices his critical skills.

The most dramatic example of this impact on subsequent interpretations emerged from the *Report on Ministers' Powers* in 1932, just a decade after Dicey's death, when the avowed purpose of the committee was: "to report what safeguards are desirable or necessary to secure the constitutional principles of the sovereignty of Parliament and the supremacy of the Law."[18] Not only the ideas but the language of Dicey spiced the report; *Law of the Constitution*

---

12. Sir Cecil T. Carr, *Concerning English Administrative Law*, p. 23.

13. Alan Harding, *A Social History of English Law*, p. 385.

14. W. A. Robson, *Justice and Administrative Law*, p. 28.

15. Griffith and Street, *Principles of Administrative Law*, p. 3.

16. H. W. R. Wade, *Administrative Law*, p. 7.

17. De Smith, *Judicial Review*, p. 5.

18. *Report of the Committee on Ministers' Powers* (April 1932), Cmd. 4060, p. v.

permeated every page. The Donoughmore Committee, as it was known, cited Dicey favorably so often that Sir Cecil Carr remarked that the committee investigated whether Britain had gone off the Dicey standard in regard to administrative law and, if so, what was the quickest way to return.[19] The committee accepted Dicey as gospel, inquiring whether his constitutional teachings were being betrayed by delegated legislation heretics. In particular, the committee embraced Dicey's antithesis between *droit administratif* and English law: "In our opinion Professor Dicey's conclusion is no less true today than it was in 1915."[20] Recommendation XI of the report exhorted that no system of administrative law in any guise should be established in England.[21] As many critics have noted, this imperative was especially unfortunate, for administrative law was already a fact of constitutional life. The shade of Dicey might have read the report secure in the knowledge that his doctrines still prevailed.

As strongly as the majority of the committee felt, dissenting voices made their feelings plain. Committee member Harold Laski has left a detailed picture of Sir William Holdsworth examining each witness from the civil service with the ill-concealed suspicion of secret plots in violation of the rule of law by unconstitutional grasping for power. Lord Hewart's 1929 book *The New Despotism* had popularized the theory that English liberties had fallen prey to a bureaucratic army whose only interest was power beyond the restraint of law. Laski denounced such theories as manifestly unfair to the civil service, patiently explained that delegated legislation meant no such loss of freedom, but his views could not counteract the strength of Dicey's authority.[22] No more striking testament to Dicey's influence exists than this absolute devotion to the rule of law demonstrated by the Donoughmore Committee. "Overall it represented the high point of the impact of Dicey on English legal thought,"[23] a conclusion difficult to challenge. After 1932, as the evidence of his miscalculations mounted, criticism replaced praise for his work.

19. Carr, *Concerning English Administrative Law*, p. 26.
20. *Report of the Committee on Ministers' Powers*, p. 111.
21. Ibid., p. 118.
22. Harold Laski, *Reflections on the Constitution*, pp. 42–45.
23. Brian Abel-Smith and Robert Stevens, *Lawyers and the Courts*, p. 120.

Amidst the general scorn accorded the Diceyan conclusions since the Donoughmore Committee, two notable exceptions have appeared. C. J. Hamson dealt sympathetically with Dicey's concentration on the assumed universal jurisdiction in the hands of the English judiciary and its French antithesis, the independence of the executive.[24] In Dicey's preoccupation with judicial authority the influence of Austin may again be discerned. Just as sovereignty was indivisible, so jurisdiction, to be effective, must be complete. The conclusion that English judges should continue exercising full jurisdiction in ordinary courts was therefore natural to him. Hamson, even while extolling the merits of the French system, took an understanding attitude toward Diceyan errors about French law. Hamson termed Dicey's mistakes extraneous when compared with the insight that divided jurisdiction formed the key element of *droit administratif*. Hamson shared this enthusiasm for universal jurisdiction, although it had faltered by 1954, and the French system then guaranteed greater protection to the ordinary citizen. He deplored the "fashionable derision" of Dicey, approving the Diceyan rule of law not as an immutable principle from the past, but as a goal toward which the English constitution still must strive.[25]

The other defender was F. H. Lawson, who traced the evolution of Dicey's views on *droit administratif* in order to suggest that he was closer to the truth than his critics had realized.[26] Lawson outlined how Dicey had carefully revised his conclusions between the first edition of 1885 and the seventh edition of 1908, indicating that he kept abreast of French legal development and altered his judgments when necessary. By 1908 Dicey conceded, according to Lawson, that a century of practice had evolved a system of true law from its earlier arbitrariness. Much of the credit for this development Dicey gave to the effect of precedent and judicial legislation. French judges had effectively shaped the direction of the law toward a more equitable system of justice by the use of judicial devices ordinarily associated with common law jurisdictions. French administrative law had changed during the nineteenth century as equity had developed in Stuart England. It possessed in 1908 fixed principles administered by courts in regular fashion. Dicey believed that the legal

24. C. J. Hamson, *Executive Discretion and Judicial Control*, pp. 5–6.
25. Ibid.
26. F. H. Lawson, "Dicey Revisited," p. 112.

system expressed the spirit of French institutions, prospering because Frenchmen thought it beneficial. Lawson argued, like Hamson, that Dicey had grasped the essential characteristics even if erring in matters of detail. Dicey had not been unfair to *droit administratif* as so many of his critics had charged. He had understood that English courts attempted to deter administrative excess in advance, whereas French courts offered remedies against administrative actions already taken.

A key element in this defense was a 1901 Dicey article on *droit administratif* that showed how attuned he was to changes occurring in France.[27] Dicey incorporated this article into the seventh edition (1908), the last he personally supervised. Lawson stressed Dicey's merits as a comparative lawyer, arguing that Dicey possessed a subtle appreciation of how French law had changed under modern conditions, demonstrating a more flexible outlook than many of his critics. By putting Dicey's changing opinions in historical perspective, Lawson believed they deserved a greater credence than most modern authorities had acknowledged.

Dicey's apparent change of heart toward a more sympathetic interpretation of the French system has atoned somewhat, in the view of many critics, for the original misstatements about *droit administratif*. Recantation is the word often used to describe this recognition by Dicey of his own errors. The evidence from his correspondence does not support such a conclusion, for, in fact, Dicey never lost his visceral suspicion of French administrative law, nor did he ever regret his conclusion that *droit administratif* could never protect individual liberties as effectively as the common law. As with most components of his legal-political creed, he was remarkably tenacious in his opinions, often in spite of evidence to the contrary.

Certainly any admiration for *droit administratif*, however sincere, never recovered from the effects of the Dreyfus affair. This confirmed all his worse suspicions about the superiority of public rights in relation to an ordinary citizen. The travesty of justice inflicted upon Dreyfus reinforced his belief that the private rights of an individual could not prevail within the French system of law.

27. Albert Venn Dicey, "*Droit Administratif* in Modern French Law," pp. 302–18.

Dreyfus was the victim of the "grossest act of deliberate injustice which has been committed during the century."[28] Dicey had no doubt in 1899 that Dreyfus would again be convicted, harboring little hope that the Court of Cassation would quash the verdict. The closer Dicey followed events in France, the more distressed he became at the possibility of a clerical, monarchist reaction.[29] His own fear of clericalism in any form made this possibility more sinister to him than to most Englishmen. The Dreyfus affair convinced Dicey that the French legal structure could not resist political passion of the type Dreyfus aroused. Therefore in the 1901 article on *droit administratif,* even when noting its gradual changes, Dicey nevertheless repeated that such a system had "obtained no foothold in England."[30]

As Lawson rightly pointed out, at the time of the seventh edition, the subject once again claimed his attention. In a long letter to his publisher Dicey commented on the revisions he had made in this section of the book. At this time he admitted that *droit administratif* had changed since 1860, when his original impressions had formed. He now recognized that decades of case law had transformed it into a more or less regular judicial system. Yet even with these concessions he insisted that to Englishmen it was still a "peculiar" system. More significantly, Dicey added "that I have to a certain extent—I think to only a *slight* extent—exaggerated the arbitrary or governmental character of *Droit Administratif* as it now exists in the year 1907."[31] Dicey's repudiation of his original assertions was more apparent than real.

Some months later Dicey again alluded to the nature of *droit administratif* and his work on the subject. Here he confessed to "grave errors in my original description" but excused his mistakes by pleading that the system had changed drastically during the previous two decades.[32] This time he referred to *droit administratif* as "very curious," still insisting that the principles of law involved,

28. Dicey to Strachey, 16 August 1899, Strachey Papers.
29. Ibid., 22 August 1899, ibid.
30. Dicey, *"Droit Administratif,"* p. 305.
31. Dicey to Macmillan Company, 18 December 1907, Macmillan Company Papers, B.M. Add. MSS. 55085. The emphasis is mine.
32. Dicey to A. Lawrence Lowell, 30 September 1908, A. Lawrence Lowell Papers, Harvard University Archives.

however admirable the French system had become, were opposed to or at least different from English ideas about the rule of law. Dicey maintained that *droit administratif* still permitted control of the judiciary by the executive in violation of the independence of the judiciary as he understood it. Lawson credited Dicey with giving great prominence to the development of the Conseil d'Etat as an independent court;[33] but to Lowell Dicey vigorously stipulated that the Conseil d'Etat could not be so treated. Furthermore, Dicey charged that the social legislation of the Asquith government destroyed the rule of law and introduced administrative law to England without even the merits it had in France.[34] That the rule of law and *droit administratif* were mutually exclusive Dicey never doubted.

The final opportunity to examine Dicey's views occurred in 1915 when he published a short commentary on *Local Government Board* v. *Arlidge,* a landmark decision in the evolution of English administrative law.[35] In this case the Law Lords, with Lord Chancellor Haldane delivering the opinion, rejected the proposition that government departments in their exercise of judicial or quasi-judicial authority must follow the procedure of an English court. Government authorities must act with fairness and justice, but the ultimate judge of procedural safeguards was Parliament, to whom the minister was responsible. This decision effectively minimized the role of the courts in supervising administrative acts, and "it is now easy to see that the House of Lords missed a great opportunity."[36] The reaction of Dicey to this case has been often cited by those who allege the reversal of his views.

Once again the public Dicey was far more circumspect in his opinions than the private Dicey. He admitted in the *Law Quarterly Review* that the decision had great legal merit, for the management of government business could not be compared to the conduct of a trial. It was often a great convenience to allow a government department latitude in determining how to expedite its affairs. Efficiency must count for something lest all government work become

33. Lawson, "Dicey Revisited," p. 119.
34. Dicey to Maxse, 27 June 1909, Maxse Papers.
35. Albert Venn Dicey, "The Development of Administrative Law in England," pp. 148–53.
36. H. W. R. Wade, *Towards Administrative Justice*, p. 61.

weighted down by procedural rules. Even the private Dicey concurred on this point: "This may not be an unreasonable decision. A good deal in my opinion is to be said for it."[37]

The real question for Dicey was whether this decision introduced a form of *droit administratif* into England. He remained optimistic about the ability of the ordinary law courts to control the administration.[38] He put up the brave front that his concept of rule of law prevailed, because the ordinary courts still dealt with breaches of the law, this fact fatal to the existence of true *droit administratif*. As he expressed it:

> A Government department must exercise any power which it possesses, and above all any judicial power, in the spirit of judicial fairness and equity, though it is not bound to adopt the rules appropriate to the procedure of the law courts. This duty of compliance with the rules of fair dealing is insisted upon by the House of Lords in *Local Government Board* v. *Arlidge,* and it is probably that in some form or other the English courts will always find the means for correcting the injustice, if demonstrated, of any exercise by a Government department of judicial or quasi-judicial authority.[39]

This faith in the continuing judicial control of government authorities should be interpreted as a hope for the future, not a statement of fact.

In private Dicey gave Lowell a very different opinion. The Arlidge decision, he wrote, "distinctly recognises the fundamental principle of administrative law, namely that an administrative tribunal is not bound to act as if it were a law court."[40] This declaration rings true, for Dicey always applied the rule of law strictly, regarding any

---

37. Dicey to Lowell, 15 January 1915, Lowell Papers.

38. Geoffrey Marshall and Graeme C. Moodie, *Some Problems of the Constitution,* p. 112.

39. Dicey, "Development of Administrative Law," p. 151.

40. Dicey to Lowell, 15 January 1915, Lowell Papers. This opinion of Dicey is doubly interesting, for Lawson attributed to Dicey the belief that it was "the essence of French administrative law that it should apply different principles to government and to ordinary private intercourse." See Lawson, "Dicey Revisited," p. 116. Dicey clearly felt otherwise about what constituted the fundamental principle.

breach as catastrophic. On one hand Dicey showed no signs of sincere recantation and is open to censure for his stubborn refusal to
admit the validity of French administrative law as a legal system.
On the other hand his sentiments about the Arlidge case demonstrated his recognition of administrative law in England, exonerat-
ing him of the charge that he never discerned this obvious fact. The
most incisive part of Dicey's *Law Quarterly Review* commentary
noted that the decision marked a great fissure in the unity of jurisdiction to which he was dedicated.[41] Anticipating the far-reaching
consequences of the case, Dicey foresaw that judicial reticence
might dismantle the rule of law as he had originally conceived it.

From the foregoing discussion the conclusion must be that, however much he altered the language of *Law of the Constitution*,
Dicey never truly appreciated the merits of *droit administratif.* The
distrust first predicated in 1885 suffered little qualification despite
textual changes made by 1908. Dicey did not possess a flexible intellect, and once satisfied that he had found the truth, he rarely found
occasion to reverse his position. He never admitted any weakness
in his basic assertions nor did the alleged mitigation of his errors
extend to more than points of detail.

Though Dicey's efforts at comparative law may be praised as the
fumbling approach of a pioneer of genius,[42] this does not excuse the
obstinacy with which he clung to his views even as contradictory
evidence mounted. In his public writings Dicey grudgingly
acknowledged the merits of *droit administratif;* privately he still
maintained that no other legal system matched that of England. The
essential unfairness of his attitude may best be seen in his assumption of the inferiority of French law. He never admitted that his
initial impressions about its arbitrary character were groundless,
nor did his fears about *droit administratif* in England ever material-
ize. When the recognition of administrative law in England became
inevitable, Dicey maintained the distinction between the two systems by a differentiation of spirit preserving the dichotomy for
years to come. The Diceyan conclusions about *droit administratif*
do not measure up intellectually to the elucidation of his major
principles.

41. Dicey, "Development of Administrative Law," p. 151.
42. Lawson, "Dicey Revisited," p. 121.

Another topic Dicey examined in *Law of the Constitution* through the comparative method was federalism, contrasting it with his doctrine of parliamentary sovereignty.[43] Dicey also published his first article in the *Law Quarterly Review* on the subject of federalism.[44] Arguments in both book and article were identical, though the chapter in *Law of the Constitution* contained a more thorough elaboration of the evidence.[45] He used the United States as his model, basing his conclusions on his travels in and study of that country. This essay into comparative political analysis improved little over his work on *droit administratif*.

Federalism satisfied two apparently irreconcilable political aims: the harmonizing of national sovereignty with the perpetuation of state sovereignty. The principle guiding this phenomenon specified that matters of common concern should be the province of the national government; all other matters should be reserved to the states. Three major characteristics resulted from this basic premise: the supremacy of the constitution, the division of power among equal bodies of government, and the authority of courts to rule on constitutional matters. In each case the British constitution provided an opposed doctrine, and so the analysis of federalism illuminated neatly the principle of parliamentary sovereignty.

Dicey drew important conclusions from the comparison of the two systems of government. Throughout his lifetime he never changed his belief that federal government meant weak government.[46] From a legal standpoint he could not accept the proposition, absurd to an Austinian, that sovereignty might be truly divided within a state. No doubt his travels in the United States in 1870 influenced him as well, particularly just after the issue of states rights versus national rights had been decided in the American Civil War. As he wrote: "I believe the States are still in a true sense the sovereign power, without however any right of secession."[47] The passive role of the American government at that time also contributed to his notion of the inherent weakness of federalism. No Amer-

43. *Law of the Constitution*, pp. 138–80.
44. Albert Venn Dicey, "Federal Government," pp. 80–99.
45. Like so many subsequent academics, Dicey saw the advantage of publishing a book chapter separately as an article.
46. *Law of the Constitution*, p. 171.
47. Dicey to Freeman, 26 February 1891, Bryce Papers.

ican political development altered his basic conviction that a federal government could not possess a sovereign in the same sense that parliamentary supremacy embodied sovereignty in Great Britain. The most direct effect of this belief in the essential weakness of federalism was in his vehement opposition toward any form of Irish Home Rule based on the federal model. Both legal and political attitudes combined to prejudice him against a solution to the Irish Question along federalist lines.

Dicey also claimed that federalism tended to produce reactionary conservatism, so he prized the flexibility of the British constitution over the rigidity of its American counterpart.[48] Concern with the outward symbols of government led him astray, for he believed amendment of the American constitution the most significant of constitutional activities. Preoccupation with external aspects of constitutional development never allowed him to conceive the possibility of fundamental change in the American system through judicial interpretation or legislative innovation. In 1885 political currents in the United States were already undermining the validity of his conclusion about the weakness of federalism.

Evaluation of *Law of the Constitution* would be incomplete without reference to the lengthy introduction to the eighth edition published in 1915. This served to amplify topics first raised by the book, but not intrinsic to its three major principles. As he was then approaching eighty years of age, Dicey found the task of continuous revision onerous. Rather than revise the text any further, he wrote a separate essay for this edition.[49] Lawson saw no relevance in this introduction, feeling it had little significance.[50] This conclusion is difficult to understand, because Dicey used the introduction to discuss two political topics for which he had no room in the text. One was the referendum, which Dicey passionately wished to become a part of constitutional practice; the other was the party system, which he had long felt a sinister menace to English political life, an aspect of the constitution he was zealous to abolish. Dicey injudi-

48. *Law of the Constitution*, p. 173.
49. Dicey had long since regretted his agreement to revise the book; he cited approvingly the example of Sir Henry Maine who had published his books and never touched them again. See Dicey to Macmillan Company, 18 December 1907, Macmillan Company Papers, B.M. Add. Mss. 55085.
50. Lawson, "Dicey Revisited," pp. 112–13.

ciously vented his political hostilities; the essay was a political tract with little pretense to the objectivity of the original edition.[51]

The 1915 introduction to *Law of the Constitution* tested the three principles Dicey had first proclaimed in 1885. He still considered the sovereignty of Parliament the cornerstone of the constitution. However, the Parliament Act of 1911 had greatly increased the share of sovereignty possessed by the House of Commons and diminished that of the House of Lords.[52] The potential for tyranny of an unrestrained Commons he felt a major threat to future constitutional development. The rule of law had fared even worse. Dicey perceived a decline in reverence for the rule of law caused by the grant of quasi-judicial authority to government officials, by the distrust of judges and the law itself by large sections of the population, and by the habit of lawlessness of some groups on behalf of social and political goals. In his discussion of constitutional conventions Dicey inserted his pleas for the referendum and against the party system.

Until 1886 Dicey failed to see the political potential of the referendum, terming it one of the weaker institutions of Swiss democracy.[53] The bitterness of the 1886 Home Rule debate sent him searching for a political formula capable of resolving divisive issues. The referendum thus appeared in a new light when Dicey published an article on Switzerland in 1890.[54] Conversion to the merits of the referendum caused him to initiate a public debate on the subject, but this effort failed miserably as it aroused little public interest.[55] By 1894 a Home Rule bill had advanced as far as the House of Lords, so the referendum attained greater value in Dicey's estimation as a block to such radical legislation. Therefore he renewed his public efforts on its behalf, though again with little success.[56] The other contributors to the *National Review* symposium on the referendum

51. Even Jennings, the most consistent critic of Dicey, conceded that the Vinerian professor tried to be objective about constitutional matters in the first edition, though, as Jennings saw it, the attempt failed. See Jennings, "In Praise of Dicey," pp. 128–29.

52. "Introduction," *Law of the Constitution,* 8th ed., p. xxiv.

53. Rait, *Memorials,* p. 122.

54. Albert Venn Dicey, "Democracy in Switzerland," pp. 113–45.

55. Albert Venn Dicey, "Ought the Referendum to Be Introduced into England?," pp. 489–511.

56. Albert Venn Dicey, "The Referendum," pp. 65–72.

either rejected the idea outright or else damned it with such faint praise that it gained no popular backing. The decade 1895–1905 saw the government safely in Unionist hands, so Dicey allowed the referendum to fall into abeyance. The advent of the Liberals in 1905, followed by their tremendous electoral victory of 1906, revived its utility. As the political situation heated up in the years succeeding, Dicey published one other article on the topic in his bid for its incorporation into political life.[57] By 1910 Dicey believed the referendum to be the people's veto, attaching great significance to it as a panacea for issues like Home Rule.

After his initial public efforts failed, Dicey lobbied privately on behalf of the referendum. In 1892 he outlined arguments in favor of it to Lord Salisbury in an effort to interest the Tory leader in the idea:

> Constitutional devices can rarely do much positive good; they may however, I conceive, avert some evil arising from unnoticed though very real alterations in the working of the Constitution. For reasons some of which appear in the article I send your Lordship, I have long been convinced that the Referendum (which after all is nothing more nor less than a national veto) must sooner or later be introduced into the constitution in order to guard the rights of the nation against the usurpation of national authority by any party which happens to have a Parliamentary majority. The principle of the Referendum has two great merits. It is at once honestly democratic in theory & conservative in practice. It is, again, a principle which, as I have tried to point out in my article, the House of Lords could in effect introduce into any measure such as a Home Rule Bill which involved a fundamental change in our institutions.[58]

From the outset Dicey conceived the referendum as a negative force prohibiting the radical legislation of which he disapproved. He never expected that it might become a national affirmation on behalf of a given issue. As the years passed he grew progressively disenchanted with the "socialistic" direction of politics; because of this the ref-

57. Albert Venn Dicey, "The Referendum and Its Critics," pp. 538–62.
58. Dicey to Salisbury, 11 November 1892, Salisbury Papers.

erendum loomed more important to him as a brake upon contemporary developments.

In 1894 he made at least one notable convert to the referendum in J. St. Loe Strachey, editor of the *Spectator*. At the beginning of the year he wrote to his friend:

> I am sure we are right in agitating for the Referendum. Wherever I go I find it popular. Personally I think that I should have preferred real Parliamentary government as it existed up to 1868. But I have not the remotest doubt that under the present condition of things sham Parliamentary government means a very vicious form of government by party, and from this I believe the referendum may partially save us. It has the great merit of being the only check on party management which is in perfect harmony with democratic sentiment. . . . The only course which can be safely taken is to appeal in every shape from factions to the nation.[59]

Shortly thereafter Dicey elaborated his views to Leo Maxse in connection with his forthcoming article in *National Review:*

> I should like for example to pass an Act enacting that, as Strachey suggests, a referendum might be required by a resolution of either House, in respect of any Act e.g. affecting:—
> (1) The rights of the Crown
> (2) The Constitution of Parliament
> (3) The Acts of Union & other large constitutional topics which might easily be enumerated.
> It is true that an Act of Parliament might repeal or override the Referendum Act itself, but this though a plausible, is not a valid objection. The Referendum Act would practically be secured by the odium which any Ministry or party would incur by depriving the people of their right to be appealed to. I am quite certain that, once established, the Referendum would never be got rid of by anything short of a revolution. This is its great merit. It makes the democracy itself a check on party tyranny.[60]

In Dicey's opinion the virtues of the referendum were inversely proportional to the evils of the party system. The greater the threat

59. Dicey to Strachey, 29 January 1894, Strachey Papers.
60. Dicey to Maxse, 2 February 1894, Maxse Papers.

of the latter, the more valuable a constitutional safeguard the former became. As he wrote to Strachey: "I value the Referendum first because of its doing away with the strictly speaking absurd system which at present exists, of acting on the presumption that electors can best answer the question raised, e.g. by Home Rule, when it is put to them together with a totally different question of Prohibition, and generally that it is wise to mix up systematically, questions of persons with questions of principle, & secondly, though in a certain sense mainly because the referendum is an emphatic assertion of the principle that the nation stands above parties."[61]

As the years passed Dicey valued the referendum even more highly, for he believed it might also thwart any legislation aimed at social reform. In 1904, for instance, he wrote to Bryce that "a Referendum is, as things now stand, the only mode available which (as far as political mechanism can do anything) for proving an effective check on rash legislation as regards fundamental institutions such as the Poor Law."[62] Not until the dramatic political events of 1909 did Dicey resurrect his pet project. After the Lloyd George budget had precipitated a clash between the Lords and Commons, Dicey thought the referendum the only solution to the dispute. Dicey wrote Maxse that he had entertained this conviction for years because it was "clearly democratic & certainly Conservative."[63] It took the political crisis of 1909–10 to focus general attention upon the referendum, a result Dicey enjoyed:

> It is surprising after one has advocated a change for 20 years, to see a chance of its being carried out. It is singular & not perhaps very fortunate that in accordance with English habits, a reform good in itself, should be proposed by men who probably do not believe in it, & who want to meet a party difficulty. Still I hail it with satisfaction. Once let the precedent be established, & two results will ensue: (1) We shall have a new & strong arm against the excesses of a party which has obtained a parliamentary majority out of proportion to its real power. (2) The weapon can be used with immense effect against Home Rule. (3) To give the House of Lords a right of appeal to the people will in the

61. Dicey to Strachey, 6 May 1895, Strachey Papers.
62. Dicey to Bryce, ? April 1904, Bryce Papers.
63. Dicey to Maxse, 26 June 1909, Maxse Papers.

long run increase the power of rational Conservatism, for which I care much without increasing the power of the conservative party, for which I care nothing.[64]

The only reservation about its introduction was Dicey's belief that a political battle between Lords and Commons was not sufficient to justify the innovation.

Though pessimistic about the possibilities, Dicey continued his campaign on behalf of the referendum. In the 1910 *Quarterly Review* article he again stressed two major benefits: the referendum alone clearly expressed the will of the nation, and only the referendum might check the ever-increasing power of the party system.[65] For this very reason, he charged, the Liberal government would never accept the proposal: "It is fatal to the party system wh. they worship."[66] Dicey's pleas for the referendum went unanswered until late 1910, when Unionist leaders pledged themselves in principle to the referendum.[67] This decision prompted an exchange of congratulatory letters between Dicey and Strachey in the belief that their long campaign had succeeded. Strachey acknowledged Dicey as the Englishman who had initially advocated the referendum and deserved the credit for its triumph.[68] For his part Dicey thought perseverance had paid off: "That it will come into existence is now morally certain."[69] Unfortunately for Dicey Unionist leaders never regarded the referendum as more than a tactical electoral expedient. Any real chance for its introduction was stillborn. The referendum accentuated the rift between tariff reform and free trade Unionists, so the Unionist leadership quickly passed on to other matters.

The rapid transformation from victory to defeat crushed Dicey, though he certainly might have anticipated such a result. In the next years he continued his efforts but the old enthusiasm had gone. His one chance for direct constitutional influence had slipped away. Bryce consoled him by gently pointing out that Dicey might be

64. Ibid., 12 October 1909, ibid.
65. Dicey, "The Referendum," pp. 558–59.
66. Dicey to Strachey, 2 June 1910, Strachey Papers.
67. For a detailed account of the referendum in politics at this time, see Neal Blewett, *The Peers, the Parties and the People,* pp. 171–91.
68. Strachey to Dicey, 24 November 1910, Strachey Papers.
69. Dicey to Strachey, 1 December 1910, ibid.

mistaken in his basic assumption that the referendum was inherently conservative.[70] It might well serve, he added, revolutionary purposes if the people united behind a movement or ideology. Throughout the long period of his efforts the idea of appealing to the people had not gained much support among Tory leaders. The rule of mere numbers had never been a political idea to which Conservatives had warmed. Furthermore, the referendum as a check upon party power cannot have commended itself too strongly to leaders locked in party warfare themselves. If Dicey failed to convince others of its merits, still he had earned the distinction of being the only man of his generation who had consistently supported it. Whatever standing the referendum had attained as a possible solution to vexing political questions may be attributed directly to Dicey.

The party system made the referendum necessary, and so the two concepts were really part of the same problem to Dicey. On modern party discipline and organization, his grievances were long standing. His correspondence contained numerous tirades about the abuses of party spirit, reflecting his distrust of its development. Dicey accepted grudgingly the necessity of party, for he possessed little interest and less knowledge about the mechanics of political life, caring only for the formal elements of constitutional theory. By 1915 the evaluation of party as a constitutional phenomenon failed, because Dicey could not separate his own strong feelings on the subject from his role as commentator.

At one time or another Dicey attributed every political evil imaginable to the party system. A succinct expression of these accumulated complaints appeared in 1909, a moment when Dicey believed the iniquities of party verged on triumph.[71] Party conflict had destroyed the consensus essential to a viable two-party system. The pressure of party concerns forced government officials into regarding themselves as party leaders rather than servants of the nation. Politics had degenerated into a mere game, not the discharge of high national duty Dicey envisioned it. Party politicians confused the electorate through oversimplification of issues; electors, the political sovereign of the nation, never had the opportunity to decide a specific issue.

70. Bryce to Dicey, 26 December 1910, Bryce Papers.
71. Albert Venn Dicey, "English Party Government," pp. 604–27.

These conclusions merged with his opinion that Liberal leader Herbert Henry Asquith made political decisions motivated solely by the desire to secure his position as party boss. The greater the success Asquith enjoyed, the more pessimistic Dicey became about arresting the pernicious influence of party: "The best I can hope for is that the country may be got to see the advisability of restricting rather than extending the area of party influence."[72] But he did not anticipate living long enough to see any radical alteration in the working of the party system.[73] Politics demanded a direct accountability of politicians to the electorate. As he wrote on one occasion: "The only power to which even the party spirit & the vanity of M.P.'s must yield is authority of the electors."[74] Increased devolution of government authority, already the object of his distrust because it transgressed the rule of law, was suspect because "it is the last touch of the Party system, for the Party leaders at once try to increase their power and diminish their responsibility."[75] Dicey conceived of himself as a last barrier before the England he loved succumbed to the modern barbarians: "I am rather anxious to save up carefully such strength as I have, as I am doing all I can to fight the constitutional innovations proposed by the Government. Who can say for certain whether one is right or wrong, though, like others, I have great confidence in my negative opinions."[76] Dicey was right to suggest that he proved more formidable in attack than he ever did in making a positive case for his political creed; the role of opposition suited his talents best.

To illustrate the decline of modern politics as a result of party growth Dicey at one point offered a periodization of party government. From 1760 to 1832 the grosser forms of political corruption had disappeared in England. From the First Reform Act to 1882, party government worked best, based on individual judgment in politics and dedicated to the liberty of all citizens. After 1882, public life had declined in character, with politicians as a group much less trustworthy. It was no coincidence Dicey remembered his youth as a golden age or that the political decline coincided with the emer-

72. Dicey to Smith, 26 May 1909, Smith Papers.
73. Ibid., 19 April 1910, ibid.
74. Ibid., 4 August 1909, ibid.
75. Dicey to Lowell, 15 January 1915, Lowell Papers.
76. Dicey to Jacob, 14 December 1910, Working Men's College MSS.

gence of the Irish Question. Nostalgia for the mid-Victorian days prevented an unemotional assessment of the political developments through which he had lived. Dicey attributed this decay to two major causes: the advent of democracy had inevitably enfranchised the less-educated elements of the community, with a consequent indifference to questions of constitutional principle; and since 1882 the power of the party system had increased immensely, subordinating national goals to the needs of partisanship. The net result, Dicey concluded, was that "I am grown too old & living in an age to which I hardly belong."[77] This recognition did not deter the flood of anathemas from North Oxford on political questions. On both topics, the referendum and the party system, Dicey tried all his powers of persuasion and denunciation respectively, but in neither case did he enjoy any measurable success in influencing the immediate political scene.

Before final evaluation of *Law of the Constitution*, Dicey's sentiments about the book must be noted. On one occasion he called it "for effectiveness the best thing I have ever done & which cost me less labour than any other book."[78] It should be noted here that, as Dicey grew older and his writing took more effort, he increasingly rated his books by the work they required rather than the reputation they achieved. So another time he referred to it as "born under a lucky star, & has owing greatly to the start James [Bryce] got for it done far better than anything else I ever wrote or am likely to write."[79] This referred to Bryce's strong promotion of the book, which brought it to the attention of politicians and the general public as well as the academic community. Dicey's fondness for the book reflected his recognition that it had established his reputation as a constitutional scholar.

Law of the Constitution does not now enjoy a wide audience, for it is, as Lawson has written, more phantom than reality.[80] In Dicey's own lifetime the book exercised vast influence upon the judiciary, its citation in important cases indicating the prestige it had acquired. On students of constitutional law the impact was just as impressive. His student Harold Laski wrote: "But it was Dicey who

77. Dicey to Bryce, 23 July 1911, Bryce Papers.
78. Ibid., 16 May 1902, ibid.
79. Dicey to Mrs. Bryce, 21 November 1902, ibid.

captivated me most—a kind of mellow wisdom that was really masterly. I didn't always agree and I sometimes doubted accuracy, but I never stopped admiring—a very big achievement."[81] After his death Dicey has influenced research on constitutional law if only by his errors. If his portrayal of the constitution was not completely accurate, it has affected powerfully the way others have pictured it. Discussion of parliamentary sovereignty must still consider his theories; the rule of law has become synonymous with the aspiration for justice by mankind; and whatever their precise definition, constitutional conventions form a standard part of constitutional law. Compared with other constitutional tomes, the book had a distinctive flair. It was free of jargon, written in forceful language, and could be understood by both lawyer and layman. *Law of the Constitution* has remained the most influential constitutional textbook of the last century.

80. Lawson, "Dicey Revisited," p. 109.
81. Laski to Holmes, 12 January 1921, in *Holmes-Laski Letters,* 1: 307.

CHAPTER SIX

DICEY AND IRELAND:

THE MAKING OF A UNIONIST

THE PUBLICATION OF *Law of the Constitution* at the same time as the emergence of Home Rule offered Dicey at age fifty the opportunity for a place in the political world. The Irish Question came to dominate Dicey's life, and his views gradually hardened into bitter opposition to every form of Home Rule. One basis of his resistance lay in the belief that this devolution, no matter in what guise it was presented by proponents, infringed the sovereignty of Parliament and portended the dissolution of the United Kingdom. As an avid spectator of the English political scene, Dicey had followed Irish problems in a general way since the disestablishment of the Irish Church in 1869 and in particular since Charles Parnell had forced the Irish situation upon England by tactics of parliamentary obstruction. Until Dicey's death Ireland remained his political passion; previous writers have usually noted his strong Unionist views without pursuing the matter in any depth.

Only Trowbridge Ford and Christopher Harvie have examined the origins of Dicey's hostility to Home Rule.[1] Harvie has criticized thoroughly Ford's conclusions, especially the attribution to Dicey of articles and opinions he did not write and express.[2] Yet, to a

1. Trowbridge H. Ford, "Dicey's Conversion to Unionism," pp. 552–82; and Christopher Harvie, "Ideology and Home Rule: James Bryce, A. V. Dicey and Ireland, 1880–1887," pp. 298–314.

2. In this regard Harvie used the *Haskell Index* to the *Nation*, published by the New York Public Library, where all contributions by Dicey, signed and unsigned, are listed. Mr. James J. Storrow, publisher of the *Nation*, informed the author that he was "quite sure nothing by Dicey has been omitted" (Mr. Storrow to the author, 15 October 1974). If further proof be needed for the authority of the *Haskell Index*, the following should suffice. In a letter to Bryce, 20 March 1896, Bryce Papers, Dicey wrote: "By the way in a back number of the *Nation* written I should think some six months ago, & signed Observer, you will find all in substance, I have to say about

surprising degree, Harvie came to opinions similar to those of Ford in finding that Dicey "only narrowly endorsed" Unionism and until 1886 he was "fundamentally sympathetic" to Irish nationalism.[3] Too great reliance on Dicey's activities in the 1880s has led these two authors to misinterpret the evolution of Dicey's views about the Irish Question. His opposition to Home Rule, or any alteration of the Union for that matter, had its roots in a youthful commitment to nationalism that placed greatest emphasis on the moral consequences of political unification. In addition, in the years before 1886, Dicey supplied ample evidence of the basic consistency of his political position.

Between 1880 and 1885 the best description of Dicey's attitude is sympathetic negativism. Throughout this period he rejected any proposal that smacked of fundamental constitutional change in relations with Ireland.[4] Home Rule or national independence for Ireland *never* claimed his allegiance. But he did recognize that the Irish people had suffered greatly as a result of English rule. His concern for the population of Ireland manifested itself when he pleaded for a more tolerant view of Catholic Ireland on the part of his fellow Englishmen.[5] He had no love for the Gladstonian attempt to rule Ireland by coercion, as this did not meet traditional English standards of justice. For example, he denounced the seizure of Parnell in 1881 even while acknowledging that the move had succeeded in its object.[6] The basic theme for Dicey in this period was finding a remedy for Irish grievances not at odds with the constitutional framework of Great Britain. Home Rule never seemed a suitable solution to his problem.

The answer for Dicey lay in the strict enforcement of the ordinary

---

Unionist policy in Ireland." Was this unsigned contribution of 17 October 1895 listed in the *Haskell Index?* On page 136 this item is correctly attributed to Dicey, establishing that his anonymous writings were included. In addition, the author concurs with Harvie's judgment about "monumentally inaccurate articles by Trowbridge H. Ford"; see Christopher Harvie, *The Lights of Liberalism,* p. 321, note 1.

3. Harvie, "Ideology and Home Rule," pp. 502, 507.

4. See Albert Venn Dicey, "What Is the State of English Opinion about Ireland?," *Nation* 34 (2 February 1882): 97.

5. Albert Venn Dicey, "Edmund Burke on Affairs with Ireland," *Nation* 33 (18 August 1881): 135.

6. Dicey to Bryce, 8 November 1881, Bryce Papers.

law of the land, with one major reservation. He argued that Ireland could not be ruled by arbitrary English government, because such a plan had all the defects of despotism.[7] Rigid enforcement of the law alone could not succeed, because Irish juries refused to convict obviously guilty individuals. The true resolution of Irish troubles called for governing Ireland exactly as other parts of the United Kingdom, through the regular process of the law, except for a modification in criminal procedure allowing abolition of trial by jury in some cases or perhaps only in some districts. England must not renounce values simply for the sake of keeping order in Ireland.

The corollary to this Diceyan policy recommended treatment of Ireland exactly like that of Scotland.[8] The union with Ireland was not at fault, only the way in which England had implemented it. The Irish Union lacked the coherence which had made the Scottish Union so successful. England had demonstrated a callous disregard for Irish institutions not in keeping with the solicitude shown toward Scotland. The 1707 union had preserved the best in Scottish national life, whereas the Irish Union had accomplished the reverse. What of the solutions put forward by the Irish themselves? Dicey wrote that the independence of Ireland was "as every sane man must admit that it is, an impossibility."[9] Thus, the union with Ireland should be maintained despite pleas to the contrary from some sections of Irish opinion.

In 1882, in his *Contemporary Review* article, Dicey rejected specifically the idea that Home Rule provided a constructive answer to the Irish Question. The problem, as he wrote to Bryce, was obtaining fair treatment for the Irish within the structure of the Union: "I think a bona fide attempt to treat the Irish members as the persons entitled to decide on Irish legislation may turn out the best way out of our difficulties."[10] This power should be exercised within the framework of the Union, not by the establishment of a separate legislative body at Dublin. Meanwhile the defects of Glad-

7. Albert Venn Dicey, "How Is the Law to Be Enforced in Ireland?," pp. 538–41.

8. Albert Venn Dicey, "Two Acts of Union," pp. 177–78.

9. Albert Venn Dicey, "Home Rule from an English Point of View," p. 85.

10. Dicey to Bryce, 1 November 1882, Bryce Papers. Quotations in this paragraph are from this letter.

stonian policy hampered potential solutions, for Gladstone could not decide whether Ireland was a part of or distinct from the United Kingdom.

Because Dicey envisioned the transformation of Ireland into another Scotland, he deplored a worsening of relations between England and Ireland. Various violent incidents in Ireland had roused the righteous as well as unrighteous indignation of Englishmen, complicating the path of English policy. Furthermore, Gladstone assumed a greater political capacity on the part of the Irish than Dicey thought appropriate. Therefore schemes for extension of local government were Liberal plans he could not endorse: "Good administration is in many cases better than local self-government." Finally, the Gladstonian policy of coercion conflicted with English national character. Arbitrary government in whatever guise most Englishmen found repugnant. Criticism of Gladstone did not mean endorsement of Home Rule; on the contrary, it usually signified his fear that the prime minister had gone too far in abdicating authority in Ireland. Such considerations affected Dicey greatly in 1881 and 1882: "The subject is hardly ever long out of my mind."

Near the end of 1882 Dicey again wrote at length about the Irish Question. He recognized the difficulty of his own position, caught as he was between the widespread prejudice of Englishmen against Ireland and the hostility of Irishmen toward the Union. As he expressed it: "I hardly know any subject more painful, for on the one hand the tone of English feeling & of English language is in my judgment often thoroughly bad & in fact absolutely painful for any humane or thoughtful person to notice whilst on the other hand this wretched state of sentiment seems to me to be like most widespread sentiments; the natural & almost inevitable outcome of circumstances & character."[11] Dicey believed national character among the Irish might yet change, as illustrated by the eventual acceptance of the 1707 union by Scotland. So Irish aspirations could still be satisfied within the United Kingdom if the English met their legitimate demands. As for the English:

> There are two points which do not excuse but a little palliate the general tone about Ireland. *First,* though it is possible I may not judge fairly, there seems to me to be prevalent among

11. Dicey to Godkin, 29 December 1882, Godkin Papers.

Irishmen an "unreasonableness" of sentiment which if natural enough does their cause great injury. They seem to me often to think it a grievance that they cannot at once have all the advantages of British citizenship & of Irish independence. *Secondly*, it is certainly the case that one class of Irishmen will often speak of another in language quite as revolting as Englishmen ever employ about Ireland.[12]

At this point Dicey still hoped the Union might survive the strain placed upon it by radical opinion in Ireland.

In 1883 and 1884 Dicey relegated Ireland to a secondary place in his thoughts when the tumult in Ireland subsided after the dramatic events of the previous two years. He now had other tasks that demanded much of his time. Duties as the new Vinerian professor took his attention, in particular the preparation of his inaugural lecture in 1883. After that he commenced writing *Law of the Constitution*, taking the better part of a year, from the middle of 1883 into 1884. In addition, Dicey spent considerable time in tandem with Oscar Browning as an examiner in constitutional history in the University of London.[13] This same decline in interest, at the very time Ford alleged Dicey's conversion to Unionism, may also be demonstrated by the drop in his contributions to the *Nation*. Dicey felt the pressure on his time, cutting back on these writings rather dramatically.[14] On his own, Dicey had good reason for paying less attention to Irish affairs.

The most important element of all in this drop sprang from events in Ireland. Parnell used the two years to consolidate his grip on the Irish National League; not until after the Reform Act of 1884 was any dramatic initiative available to him. During this period the Irish Question seemed remote and academic. Dicey could afford the luxury of detachment, for his views carried no political weight at this

12. Ibid.

13. The Dicey-Browning correspondence dealt almost exclusively with the time-consuming arrangments for these duties. Though examined in the offices of the Historical Manuscripts Commission, London, this collection will eventually be located in the Hastings Public Library.

14. In 1881–82 Dicey had published some 37 items in the *Nation*; in 1883–84 this had dropped to just 15 reviews and articles. See the *Haskell Index*, p. 135.

time. He did not change his opinion that Home Rule would never resolve Irish problems, but the issue did not seem crucial, because no English party espoused the cause.[15] Dicey shared the comfortable view of most Englishmen that Home Rule posed no immediate threat to English politics.

By 1885, with *Law of the Constitution* in press, Dicey again had more time for politics. The Irish Question assumed a new dimension in that year when Parnell shifted his support to the Conservatives, making possible a minority Salisbury government. Dicey at this point still opposed Home Rule, but not yet with that rampant emotionalism which marked his later years. At the beginning of the year he wrote that "the notion is gradually dawning on the public that the alternative for good or bad is alternately between union and separation (complete independence)."[16] He repeated his contention that all special coercion must cease, only the ordinary law strictly enforced could have any real effect. If that did not work, then with the greatest regret he would advocate separation. Dicey suggested that momentous constitutional changes such as Home Rule should be considered only by a special ad hoc Parliament where all plans might be debated independent of party motives. He thought such an assembly would suit his own talents as well as not unduly tax his physical resources.

These sentiments indicated the direction in which Dicey had gradually moved. Ireland must face a future where the only alternatives were national independence or strict maintenance of the Union; a compromise arrangement like Home Rule simply would not work. Dicey placed great confidence in the redemptive value of the Union and, if properly maintained and administered, proclaimed it might still secure the future of Ireland. The confused political gropings in 1885 contributed to his growing sense that some denouement of the Home Rule controversy must be forthcoming. Like many of his contemporaries, however, he did not anticipate the conversion of Gladstone to Home Rule.

Dicey had criticized the Irish policy of Gladstone since 1880, but the Irish issue was only one of the grievances he held against the Liberal leader. In October of 1885 Edward Dicey published an article

15. Albert Venn Dicey, "Notes on the Relation between Home Rule and English Politics," *Nation* 37 (26 July 1883): 72–74.

16. Dicey to Bryce, 3 January 1885, Bryce Papers.

charging a failure by Gladstone in implementing the fundamental principles of liberalism: freedom of the individual, integrity of the United Kingdom, and maintenance of the Empire. In particular, Gladstone's flirtation with Irish support was "fraught with the greatest danger to the United Kingdom."[17] For his brother Albert, who shared the same political enthusiasms, the situation promised nothing but trouble. In the *Nation* Dicey discussed the lack of alarm most Englishmen expressed in the face of the crisis he believed impending.[18] To Godkin he amplified these views: "You can have no idea of the odd state of the political world here; we are all like people fighting in the dark. That among well to do or educated Liberals there is a great deal of dissatisfaction I am quite certain, but that this dissatisfaction will produce any great effect at the elections is most uncertain."[19] Dicey predicted the Liberals would win the forthcoming election, but that the Irish and social questions would prove too difficult for a Liberal cabinet. Once Gladstone stepped down as Liberal leader, he added, the Liberal party would disintegrate, followed by a reconstruction of parties. The revolt of the Liberal Unionists fulfilled at least part of this prophecy, but not on the scale Dicey predicted. Though he foresaw intense political turmoil, he still hoped for a solution to the Irish Question without damaging the Union.

In December 1885 Gladstone's conversion to Home Rule reverberated throughout the political world. Dicey was not completely surprised, for through Bryce he had access to the political gossip of the day. At the beginning of December Bryce had written to Gladstone about the failure of what Bryce regarded as a moderate Irish policy: "All the Ulster Liberals whose opinions I have enquired are not only strenuous supporters of the Union, but opposed to any Central Council for Ireland, which would, they think, deliver their

17. Edward Dicey, "The Plea of a Malcontent Liberal," p. 465. Donald Southgate, in *The Passing of the Whigs 1832–1886*, p. 367, erroneously attributed this article to Albert Dicey. The opinions expressed probably did not vary greatly from those of A. V.; the brothers shared the same political principles even though they were not particularly close.

18. Albert Venn Dicey, "A Phase of English Opinion," *Nation* 41 (15 October 1885): 319–21; "Why Englishmen Are Not Alarmed at the Political Crisis," *Nation* 41 (22 October 1885): 340–41.

19. Dicey to Godkin, 16 October 1885, Godkin Papers.

province into the hands of the Nationalists and the priests. The furthest point they are willing we should go to is the establishment of county boards."[20] Bryce thought some major policy revisions essential, doubtless informing Dicey that important decisions were imminent. The impact of Gladstone's choice on Dicey was immediate and decisive. The Irish Question, now with an English party pledged to its solution through Home Rule, imposed a final choice between the Union and Home Rule. For five years Dicey had avoided this confrontation by formulating acceptable compromises, but moderation was no longer an alternative.

By Christmas 1885 Dicey had adopted the attitude of absolute hostility to Home Rule that increasingly dominated his life, gradually becoming so extreme that it tarnished his reputation for probity so laboriously acquired in other areas. Events in England had forced his hand, not matters in Ireland, for which he had little interest. The potential for Home Rule became realizable only when Gladstone dedicated himself to its triumph. This in turn had forced Dicey to make a final decision about where his loyalties lay. Two pieces of evidence pinpoint the final commitment of Dicey to the rejection of Home Rule in all forms. Arthur Elliot, himself a prominent Unionist, wrote to Dicey long after this period: "I am sure that every year that has passed since XMAS 1885 has given additional evidence in support of the Unionist views which you have expounded so much more completely than anyone else. For thirty-three years the Irish Home Rule policy presents a record of persistent failure. Gladstone did a bad turn for his country by that mad and immoral surrender to Parnell. I am sure none of us need regret the stand we made then and since against attempts, which however they might be disguised, were essentially steps destructive to the Nationhood of the United Kingdom."[21] For his part Dicey recalled in later life that only those living in 1885 could "realise the suddenness and astonishment of Gladstone's conversion to Home Rule to the English public."[22] The threat to the Union was now more serious, so he must support maintenance of the Union against any attack.

The path Dicey followed to outspoken Unionism was straight-

20. Bryce to Gladstone, 1 December 1885, Bryce Papers.
21. Elliot to Dicey, 23 June 1918, Elliot Papers.
22. Dicey to Elliot, 1 April 1912, ibid.

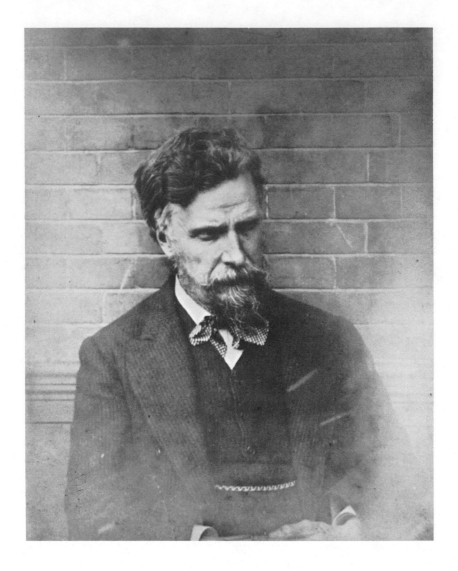

The Unionist Advocate, 1886
(Courtesy of Victor Bonham-Carter)

forward and consistent, not the dramatic change of heart detailed by Ford and Harvie. It was a slow evolutionary process dictated primarily by political circumstances beyond Dicey's ability to influence or, in some cases, to fathom. Dicey underwent no emotional conversion to Unionism, but merely remained faithful to political beliefs held since his youth. Arthur Elliot wrote that until 1886 both he and Dicey "believed ourselves to be strong liberals."[23] Thus Dicey ended an ardent Unionist, but he was always so. Given his political background and record of opposition to Home Rule, his Unionism was a foregone conclusion.

Why was Dicey so convinced a Unionist? He had belonged to the Whig element of the Liberal party, and ever since 1867 he had grown more dismayed at the course of English politics, especially the assaults on individualism he perceived in social legislation of the period. Dicey trusted as well in the historic mission of the British Empire, believing it a positive force for good in a deteriorating world. Above all else, the key to understanding Dicey on Ireland lies in his total commitment to the Union as a symbol of the greatness of the United Kingdom. The Union had completed the transformation of Great Britain into a world power dominant in the nineteenth century. It should have caused the prosperity of Ireland, but the failure in this case did not shake his faith in the theoretical value of Unionism. Liberal Unionism, whatever other politics it eventually encompassed, depended in the first instance on maintenance of the Union. Dicey never wavered in his belief that Home Rule would ruin England and Ireland, wreaking havoc far beyond any evils perpetuated by the Union. England must give Ireland justice but only without disturbing the Union.

The integrity of the Union became for Dicey the touchstone for all his other political opinions. From his undergraduate days he had praised nationalism as an integrative factor in European history, citing the moral and political regeneration of countries long divided, such as Italy. Home Rule confronted him with a nationalist movement whose ultimate goal was separation from an existing political entity and whose hallmark was rancor. No matter how long he studied the Irish Question, Dicey never acknowledged Irish nationalism, for Home Rule negated every aspect of nationalism he had

23. Statement by Elliot, n.d., affixed to Dicey-Elliot correspondence, ibid.

ever admired. It violated every principle of patriotism by threatening the national safety of Great Britain. The Union stood for peace and prosperity, for the glory of Great Britain, and the secure future of the country; Home Rule meant disintegration, economic ruin, and a perilous future. Therefore Dicey dedicated himself completely to the preservation of the Union, and the issue claimed a significant portion of his energy in 1886 and after.

Most of 1886 Dicey devoted to aiding the Unionist cause into whose ranks he had become a volunteer. The first result was a short article on Home Rule as colonial independence in which he listed the fallacies inherent in this form of Home Rule.[24] He admitted the manifold problems of Ireland should not be attributed to any one man or policy, and certainly not to the Union, but he thought it certain that Gladstonian policy would never confer the benefits Home Rulers implied. No doubts on this point now troubled Dicey; as he wrote to Bryce: "It is perhaps odd I should press this but I feel it more strongly than I can tell you & more strongly than perhaps people would believe of me."[25]

In May Dicey informed Bryce that he had joined the Liberal Committee for the Maintenance of the Union: "I did not feel I could honestly do otherwise as on the particular point they are fighting I agree with them."[26] The break with the Liberal party did not come easily, for his traditional liberalism had led him to support the Liberal party consistently even though he had often criticized the leadership. He was keenly aware that once he had denounced the Gladstonian party, little chance for return would be left. To Bryce he added: "Fate seems to destine me for the member of oppositions & judging by the general results of my aiding friends at elections my advocacy of a cause is not of very good omen. It is certainly provoking that after having sympathised in the main with all the Liberal attempts to put matters right in Ireland, & hating as I do the common English tone about the Irish I am unable to agree with the present Irish policy of the Government."[27] A residual distrust of the Tories persisted, making Dicey uncomfortable about his future political allegiance. In Dicey's estimation Bryce, who had followed Gladstone into advocacy of Home Rule, would find the Parnellites

24. Albert Venn Dicey, "Ireland and Victoria," pp. 169–77.
25. Dicey to Bryce, 10 April 1886, Bryce Papers.
26. Ibid., 18 May 1886, ibid.
27. Ibid.

strange political bedfellows: "I am afraid we shall both be led into rather strange & very uncongenial political company. Meanwhile I shall to the best of my ability oppose at the next election every form of Home Rule policy."[28]

Home Rule marked a parting of political paths for these two close friends. Their correspondence continued in as friendly a vein as before, but they rarely referred to Ireland, as if the topic might prove too painful. To the end of his life Dicey considered Bryce the most faithful of friends.[29] Bryce shared many of Dicey's social and economic dogmas, but Ireland separated them ever after. Bryce doubtless had Dicey in mind when he wrote: "The Whig or Hartingtonian section may be abandoned as irreconcilable. The Radical or so-called Chamberlainite section are, most of them, capable of being recovered. They don't care much for C. personally, and will not follow him unless they happen to agree with him."[30] Dicey himself had little use for Chamberlain on account of his advanced social politics, thinking the favorable attitude toward the Union his only commendable doctrine. Long after 1886 Bryce confessed to Dicey his reasons for joining the Home Rule movement:

> The first was that 5 years in the House of Commons had convinced me that the British Parliament could not *under our party system,* which makes men do anything to turn out their opponents, successfully govern Ireland. This was the ground Lord Spencer took as the most upright and fairest-minded man that I have ever known in public life. My second reason was that it seemed to me that after the democratization of England in 1885, it was more than probable that the logic of democratic principles & the force of democratic sentiment would end by giving the Irish majority what they wanted, whether or not it was good for Ireland, &, I may add, whether or not it involved risks to England.[31]

The gulf between the two men on the Irish Question never narrowed no matter how often they agreed on other matters.

Throughout 1886 political controversy over Home Rule flour-

28. Ibid.
29. Dicey to Lady Farrer, 5 November 1920, in Rait, *Memorials*, p. 270.
30. Bryce to Sir Henry Primrose, 24 May 1886, Bryce Papers. Primrose was private secretary to Gladstone.
31. Bryce to Dicey, 27 November 1921, ibid. Italics in the original.

ished as never before. Dicey finished *England's Case against Home Rule* in June 1886, offering it to Macmillan's for publication. *Law of the Constitution* had sold well, establishing Dicey's name with the general public. Dicey had received an honorary degree from Edinburgh University on 21 April and felt this recognition fitted him to place before the country a controversial work on Ireland.[32] The discussion of Home Rule had so animated public opinion by June that when he approached Macmillan's about the book, he was confident it would sell very well.[33] Macmillan's shied away from the subject, this rejection forcing Dicey to turn to John Murray. As a result of this initial setback he lost valuable time in getting the book before the public. It did not appear until the middle of November, when the rejection of the Gladstonian Home Rule bill and subsequent election of 1886 were already history. By then the heat had already abated temporarily from the Home Rule issue.

England's Case against Home Rule was the best book Dicey ever produced on the Irish Question in terms of originality and moderation of tone.[34] It appeared before passion warped his judgment, and he could rightly pose as a "scientific constitutionalist" in examining this proposed piece of legislation. All later works on Home Rule were variations on themes first stated in 1886, embroidered with modern statistics. If repetition alone could sustain his arguments, Dicey would have overcome all resistance. He never felt compelled to alter his essential position as the years passed.

To his credit Dicey disclosed at the outset the assumptions underlying the book, and, though startling in retrospect, they informed the reader exactly where Dicey stood. He freely admitted, for example, that he possessed no special acquaintance with Ireland or Irish history. His concern with Home Rule extended only to "the advantages and disadvantages from an English point of view, on the one hand of maintaining the Union, and on the other of separation from Ireland."[35] He openly acknowledged that he aimed the book at the audience already hostile to Home Rule. He made no attempt to persuade opponents like Home Rulers or Irish Separatists; to the

32. Dicey to Macmillan Company, 13 April 1886, Macmillan Company Papers, B.M. Add. Mss. 55084.
33. Ibid., 14 June 1886, ibid.
34. Albert Venn Dicey, *England's Case against Home Rule.*
35. Ibid., p. 2.

Unionist faithful alone he preached in order to furnish arguments justifying their continued opposition to Home Rule.

The method he employed for this political purpose was similar to that of his earlier works on constitutional subjects. Dicey first isolated the arguments for and against Home Rule, explaining them as clearly as possible and citing the evidence in favor of each. Then he discredited the Home Rule position to the best of his ability, enhancing his own conclusions in the process. This scholastic style of reasoning, so successful when applied to masses of undigested legal material, resulted in severely reductionist conclusions when treating a complex political issue. Dicey saw the problems of oversimplification this procedure involved, but conceived his task to be to rise above the false rhetoric of parliamentary debate.

What Dicey intended was no less than destruction of a centrist position in the Home Rule controversy. He conceded that Irish Nationalists held honorable political views, crediting them with honesty in avowing their objectives. Home Rulers he suspected of favoring independence but hiding behind the innocuous facade of Home Rule. Maintenance of the Union or national independence for Ireland were the only alternatives to Dicey, for Home Rule promised worse evils than either of these. Since he assumed, like most Englishmen, that Irish independence was impossible, opposition to Home Rule was the only course of action possible.

Dicey drew three general conclusions that he felt vitiated Irish demands. First, Home Rule would reverse the expansion of the British Empire and endanger the political unity of the country. Next, the demand for Home Rule amounted to a constitutional revolution within the United Kingdom, an event he deemed disastrous because it would end the historic trend toward unity for Great Britain. Finally, he emphasized repeatedly that Home Rule would never satisfy the demands of the Nationalists. The Home Ruler asked for a renegotiation of the political partnership, not for the dissolution demanded by the Nationalist. Dicey contended that Home Rule made no sense, that the Union with Ireland was an either/or proposition without room for compromise. The choice for England was not between Home Rule and the Union, but between independence for Ireland and the Union. Home Rule must fail because it could never meet the expectations of either Unionist or Separatist.

For Dicey Home Rule meant "the endowment of Ireland with

representative institutions and responsible government."[36] It would create an Irish Parliament free from the control of Westminster and make the Irish executive responsible to the Irish people. Home Rule as an extension of local self-government, advocated by many English politicians, could not resolve Irish problems, for the Irish themselves had expressed little interest in this scheme. Dicey hammered away at the constitutional difficulties Home Rule entailed in case of disputes between the Irish and British parliaments. Home Rule as local self-government could not satisfy the demand for independence, because there were many spheres where Ireland could not act unfettered by British policy. Proponents of Home Rule had passed it off to Englishmen as little more than an increase in local self-government; in Ireland they made it appear nothing less than national independence. Such divergent interpretations boded ill for future relations between the two countries if Home Rule were enacted.

Dicey then turned to the strength of Home Rule sentiment in England. Gladstone dominated this feeling as evidenced by the little attention Home Rule had attracted in England prior to his conversion to the cause. Beyond the strength from people who unwaveringly followed Gladstone, much public support derived from misplaced faith in the infallibility of democratic theory. Popular opinion in the past had produced both good and bad results, so by itself public opinion provided no guarantee of truth. In addition, he argued that Home Rule received support from those Englishmen who felt five hundred English gentlemen should be free of the continuous pressure exerted by a small band of Parnellites: "Cowardice masks itself under the show of compromise, and men of eminent respectability yield to the terror of being bored concessions which their forefathers would have refused to the threat of armed rebellion."[37] Moderation, at least in his political writings, did not appeal to Dicey. Sentiment alone encouraged the Home Rule movement in England rather than any intellectual conviction that it was sound policy.

The criticisms advanced by Dicey provide a good sampling of his approach to the problem. By this time Dicey accepted that his inter-

36. Ibid., p. 20.
37. Ibid., p. 45.

est in politics depended substantially on what he opposed, not the positive aims of his own creed. Therefore when he explained anti–Home Rule arguments, he felt that the book gained in cogency and ease of expression.[38] In the first place, Ireland was geographically too close to England for autonomy, posing a future security problem if independent. Next, the tendency of modern civilization was in the direction of powerful states; the United Kingdom should therefore remain intact. Further, the argument that three million Irishmen desired something did not thereby entitle them to it. England and Ireland had always stood at different stages of civilization, he maintained, and therefore Irish demands were not presumptively valid. In addition if, as he conceded, the English presence in Ireland had caused great evils, this fact was still unfavorable to Home Rule. The proper policy was an effort by the British government to remedy Irish grievances, especially those connected with the land question. If the basic problem was economic, as Dicey believed, then the Union alone could resolve it, for the superior resources of Great Britain must salvage the Irish economy. If the true trouble was indeed political, that is, prompted by feelings of nationality, then the correct conclusion was not Home Rule but complete separation. To the argument that England suffered from the parliamentary obstruction of the Parnellites, Dicey replied that this problem did not merit a constitutional revolution as remedy, even as a painful toothache did not suggest suicide as remedy. Pleas for Home Rule therefore failed on two major counts: it would not cure the complaints of Ireland, and Home Rule reasoning led more logically to separation than Home Rule itself.

The union with Ireland had increased immensely the power of the central government of the United Kingdom as shown by the abject failure of Irish revolution in 1848 after the near success of 1798. Power granted to Dublin must detract from the authority of London, weakening the entire country. Secondly, Irish prosperity was possible only through economic reforms sponsored by the Union. Finally, the Union alone curbed religious and political violence in Ireland. In this context Dicey played his own Orange card by insisting that Home Rule would betray Irishmen who had performed the duties and claimed to retain the rights of British citizens. "To main-

---

38. Dicey to Mrs. Dicey, 10 November 1886, in Rait, *Memorials*, p. 99.

tain the Union is to maintain the effort to perform the obligations of the country, and to compel all citizens of the country to perform the duties imposed by law."[39] If England could no longer enforce justice in Ireland, again separation, not Home Rule, was the appropriate policy for England to follow.

Against national independence for Ireland Dicey presented four objections. Separation would reverse centuries of English statesmanship, confessing weakness which might provoke the aggression of enemies. Abdication of power by states foreshadowed death as in the case of individuals. Furthermore, the independence of Ireland meant the loss to Great Britain of both men and money, for Ireland had always contributed heavily to the Empire in these areas. An independent Ireland exposed the western coast of Britain to potential danger, though he did admit that a greater sense of national unity in Great Britain might arise without Ireland. The most serious objection was the indelible disgrace to the United Kingdom for abandoning Ulstermen whose loyalty was above reproach. In any event separation promised great humiliation for England with some offsetting compensations. Home Rule possessed all the evils but none of the rewards that national independence presaged.

Dicey next dissected the four major forms of Home Rule as set forth by proponents. Home Rule as federalism he had already attacked in 1882; Home Rule as colonial independence he had denounced earlier in 1886. Home Rule as the revival of the 1782 Grattan constitution Dicey considered a dead historical issue, so that its resurrection was impossible. He aimed the bulk of his onslaught at Home Rule under the Gladstonian constitution. Parliamentary sovereignty bore the brunt of attack, because Dicey contended that Home Rule destroyed this fundamental principle of the British constitution. His Austinian outlook forced him to reject any limit on the exercise of sovereignty. Under the Gladstonian constitution, with a separate Parliament in Dublin, the sovereignty of the British Parliament was rendered legally doubtful and reduced morally to nothing. Home Rule would not secure justice for all Irishmen, especially unpopular minorities; they would remain at the mercy of an executive controlled by Land Leaguers. Perhaps most important of all, Home Rule could never be a lasting settlement of

39. *England's Case*, p. 140.

constitutional relations. Neither side would be satisfied by a half-way measure like Home Rule. Irritation would fester until another political crisis resulted, with the entire controversy repeated.

The conclusion of the book reiterated the main points put forward earlier, especially the assertion that Irish discontent sprang from economic causes. Bad administration and an alien body of law governing tenure of land contributed to the economic problems Ireland suffered. The rhetoric of nationalism had no substance, therefore England had no obligation to heed its message. When the British Parliament cured these economic ills, unrest in Ireland would vanish. Consequently there was no need for "dangerous speculation on possible remedies." Preservation of the Union formed the only sound policy to pursue, for the Union embodied two principles contributing to the greatness of the United Kingdom: maintenance of the supremacy of the whole state and the use of that supremacy to secure for every citizen the rights of liberty and property conferred by law. Retention of the Union presented the only just and expedient plan for England to follow.

The legalistic turn of mind that had served Dicey so well in his earlier books now proved irrelevant to this controversial political question. Though the book possessed the virtues of clarity and precision, seeming to organize the issues above the emotionalism of politics, there is no mistaking the air of unreality, as if Home Rule were just another constitutional question, discussable as any other ordinary piece of proposed legislation. Nor did Dicey keep his own Unionist prejudices out of the work, though he had pledged to do so. Furthermore, by the simple expedient of denying outright the existence of Irish nationalism, Dicey limited the debate to issues favorable to his own contentions. His conclusions rested on the probability of future consequences if Home Rule passed. This argument was the more remarkable, for just three years earlier Dicey had rejected, in reference to 1832, the contention that reform would lead inevitably to revolution.[40] For the evidence to sustain his gloomy prophecies Dicey turned to history. Yet he rejected outright the relevance of historical arguments to the Irish problem, relevance depending upon whether history supported his case or not. Most of

40. Albert Venn Dicey, "The Reform Act of 1832 and Its Critics," pp. 116–31.

the constitutional reasoning he advanced amounted to nothing more than assertions without proof about the future. His opponents quickly noted that what may be asserted without proof may also be denied without proof. As E. A. Freeman wrote to Bryce: "Since I came here, I have read Dicey—he does not seem to be so strong as usual. I generally admire him most when I must go against him; he is wonderfully clever in putting his case. But I really do not think he is up to his usual rank. Still it has made an impression and should be answered."[41] Because the book attracted widespread interest, Home Rulers hastened to counter its effect.

Public reaction to *England's Case* followed lines laid down by the Home Rule controversy itself. Unionists hailed its appearance as the definitive statement on the defects of Home Rule. The reputation earned by *Law of the Constitution* ensured a wide audience for Dicey. The prestige of an acknowledged constitutional authority now buttressed the Unionist cause, and they moved quickly to exploit the advantage. For their part Home Rulers, while not persuaded by the book, praised the dispassionate treatment of the Irish Question. John Morley, for example, wrote: "I must at once say that I am full of admiration. First at the exhaustive completeness with which you have handled the matter, and second at the faultless temper and high tone of your treatment. I don't know another instance where the subject of passionate and burning controversy has been so honestly dealt with."[42] As for Liberal Unionists, Joseph Chamberlain, who had destroyed the Home Rule bill earlier in 1886, gave guarded approval to the book: "I am convinced that the opposition to Mr. Gladstone's proposals must be vigourously maintained. I am, however, in favour of a large extension of the principles of Local Government throughout the United Kingdom although I feel that the conspiracy against law in Ireland may delay its application to that country."[43] Within the ranks of convinced Unionists John Venn wrote Dicey that *England's Case* should be read by "all who love their country & desire the prosperity of Ireland. I cannot imagine a greater calamity to both England & Ireland than 'Home

41. Freeman to Bryce, 22 May 1887, Bryce Papers.
42. John Morley to Dicey, 18 November 1886, General Manuscripts 508(28), Glasgow University Library.
43. Joseph Chamberlain to Dicey, 20 December 1886, General Manuscripts 508(39), ibid.

Rule' would be. Home Rule would certainly be ruin to Ireland, & an irreparable evil to England!"[44] The book claimed the attention of all parties to the Home Rule dispute, establishing Dicey as the foremost critic of Home Rule outside Parliament.

England's Case against Home Rule introduced Dicey to the heady world of high politics with its exciting political contacts. Dicey fit neatly into that category of apocalyptic Unionist described by Cooke and Vincent as "chiefly underemployed journalists, academics, and members of the upper classes whom for one reason or another life had excluded from a political role."[45] He was an example of the "political virgin" who needed the crisis to justify his existence on the periphery of politics, but never succeeded in breaking the closed system of "Unionist opinion."[46] Now the primary academic apologist for Unionism, Dicey wasted little time in pursuing his new avocation.

He sent a copy of the book to Lord Salisbury with the notation that though "its conclusions indirectly support the Irish policy of Her Majesty's Government, [it] is written by a Liberal without any reference to the comparatively minor questions which divide English parties."[47] Dicey repeated to Salisbury that his sole purpose was the examination of Home Rule from an exclusively English point of view. Salisbury sent a perfunctory acknowledgment, a reply disconcerting to Dicey in view of the support he had rendered. The impersonal touch demonstrated to Dicey why the Unionist leader commanded respect, but nothing like the extravagant loyalty Gladstone aroused in his followers.[48]

The first edition sold out in a month, so by December 1886 Dicey enjoyed the pleasant task of preparing a second edition. He sent the new edition to Lord Selborne, former Liberal Lord Chancellor but now an avowed Unionist. Dicey thanked Selborne for the "very kind manner in which you mentioned my book at the Unionists Conference."[49] In the second edition Dicey had incorporated the legal

44. John Venn to Dicey, 27 December 1886, General Manuscripts 508(19), ibid.
45. A. B. Cooke and John Vincent, *The Governing Passion*, p. 19.
46. Ibid., pp. 19–20.
47. Dicey to Salisbury, 12 November 1886, Salisbury Papers.
48. Dicey to Mrs. Dicey, 16 November 1886, in Rait, *Memorials*, p. 100.
49. Dicey to Selborne, 20 December 1886, Selborne Papers.

opinion of Selborne in support of his assertion that Home Rule destroyed parliamentary sovereignty. As he explained to Selborne: "I confess that I was so startled by Mr. Gladstone's assertion that the Government Bill did not involve the repeal of the Act of Union, that knowing he must have made this statement under legal advice, I feared I must in some way have misunderstood the legal effect of the Bill. Under these circumstances your speech which makes me hope that you agree in the main with my view of the law has greatly reassured me, & I have ventured to refer to it in a note as apparently confirming my view."[50] The second edition did not satisfy the demand, so a third edition appeared in 1887; Dicey would not enjoy such success ever again with his political works.

In the aftermath of *England's Case* different facets of Dicey's attitude toward Home Rule emerged in correspondence with three individuals. In writing to Goldwin Smith, then residing in North America after a stint as Regius Professor at Oxford, Dicey expressed deep pessimism about the outcome of the Home Rule issue. From 1886 on Dicey played a Cassandra role, emphasizing the evils certain to result from a dissolution of the Union. This foreboding increased as time passed, illustrating the absolute devotion to the Union crucial to understanding the political paths he followed. Dark assessments of the future soon dominated his correspondence, so that he became a self-appointed guardian of the Union. He regarded himself as particularly suited for this part because, unlike politicians who had many transitory party concerns to affect their conduct, he had the freedom to disregard petty politics and concentrate on the fundamental constitutional principles underlying political problems. Even in 1886 he predicted to Smith an unceasing Home Rule battle: "I heartily wish you were in England to write for us, but as you are not, we must each do the best we can to fight this battle out. We are I suspect only at the beginning of a contest & between ourselves, my hopes of successful maintenance of the Union are not too strong."[51] Smith shared these sentiments, opposing Home Rule just as vehemently as Dicey. For Smith Gladstone represented the "Prince of Demagogues," and he explained further: "No doubt, in spite of the victory of last summer, the outlook is still dark. A great party is desperately committed to Home Rule.

50. Ibid.
51. Dicey to Smith, 15 November 1886, Smith Papers.

The Irish rebellion is nothing. It is the work of a set of adventurers of the regular Irish type, without an ounce of military sense at their command, and would be put down with the greatest of ease, if there were a government in England and the spirit of the nation were high."[52] Dicey doubted if the country would ever bestir itself sufficiently to settle the Irish Question once and for all by a complete rejection of Home Rule in all its nefarious forms. Until that decisive event occurred, Dicey lived in perpetual fear that Home Rule might pass on the momentum of a small majority in the Commons.

An exchange of letters with Gladstone illuminated the specific differences between Dicey and the Liberal leader. The publication of *England's Case* had been doubly damaging to the Gladstonian cause, because Gladstone himself had months earlier invoked the name of Dicey in support of Home Rule. In trying to demonstrate the compatibility of parliamentary sovereignty with Home Rule, Gladstone had said in the House of Commons when introducing the bill: "I do not know how many gentlemen who hear me have read the valuable work of Professor Dicey on the *Law of the Constitution*. No work that I have ever read brings out in a more distinct and emphatic manner the peculiarity of the British Constitution in one point, to which, perhaps, we seldom have occasion to refer— namely, the absolute supremacy of Parliament. We have a Parliament to the power of which there are no limits whatever, except such as human nature in a divinely ordained condition of things imposes."[53] That Dicey should have denounced Home Rule embarrassed Gladstone; Unionists rejoiced at the irony of Gladstone's constitutional authority proving to be an antagonist.

The primary difference between the two men involved a dispute about the role Irish history should play in resolving the Home Rule dispute. Dicey deplored arguments from history except when useful as proof of future disaster to come. Dicey had sent a copy of *England's Case* to Gladstone with the hope, though Gladstone probably could not agree with much of the book, that he would recognize it as "an attempt to discuss a most important matter in a calm and serious spirit."[54] In reply Gladstone paid handsome tribute to the

52. Smith to Dicey, 8 December 1886, General Manuscripts 508(15), Glasgow University Library.

53. 8 April 1886, *Parliamentary Debates*, Third Series, 304, p. 1048.

54. Dicey to Gladstone, 8 November 1886, William E. Gladstone Papers, B.M. Add. Mss. 44499.

logic, knowledge, perspicacity, and perfect integrity of aim in the book, admitting there were many parts of the book he could agree with. But Gladstone demurred when the relationship of the Irish past to Home Rule arose; for him "the historical argument has the most important judicial bearings on our argument as to the Act of Union."[55] Gladstone compared Dicey's knowledge of Irish history unfavorably with his own, a point Dicey privately conceded.[56] Gladstone prided himself on his acquaintance with Irish history, which he thought greater than any other politician. Because he placed such a premium on the historical argument, Gladstone placed the organization of a series of essays on Irish history in the hands of James Bryce. For this aid to the Home Rule cause, Bryce suggested a "Special Service grant of money . . . might properly and usefully be given for such historical investigations as you contemplated."[57] Bryce found this task more difficult than he had anticipated, as it took until December 1886 before a sufficient number of contributors could be enlisted.[58] As with Dicey's own book, the Bryce volume appeared too late to alter hardened political attitudes.[59]

Most revealing about this brief Dicey-Gladstone correspondence was Dicey's insistence that, as a Unionist, the relation between Irish history and modern politics had no value for the Irish Question.[60] Only the recent past, since 1879, had relevance for Dicey; he discounted the importance of events before that date. This conclusion demonstrated the unhistorical attitude Dicey brought to the Home Rule dispute. As will be seen, Home Rule was not the only area where Dicey's contempt for history caused problems. Nor did Dicey agree with Gladstone's commitment to popular judgment: "I cannot honestly say that your letter has greatly shaken my opinion of the value of the appeal to popular judgment on questions requiring for their solution much reflection & knowledge."[61] In this Dicey again showed his basic misunderstanding of the emotional basis of

55. Gladstone to Dicey, 12 November 1886, ibid.
56. Dicey to Mrs. Dicey, ? December 1886, in Rait, *Memorials*, p. 101.
57. Bryce to Gladstone, 26 July 1886, Bryce Papers.
58. Ibid., 22 December 1886, ibid.
59. James Bryce, ed., *Two Centuries of Irish History*. Among the contributors were Bryce, E. L. Godkin, and John Morley.
60. Dicey to Gladstone, 17 November 1886, Gladstone Papers, B.M. Add. Mss. 44499.
61. Ibid.

the Home Rule controversy. Reason was perhaps preferable to passion, but this admonition hardly reflected practical politics. In any event Gladstone had the last word, calling Dicey's book: "the most considerable & fair argument by far that has appeared on that side but not one to abash us."[62]

Above all his correspondence with Lord Hartington, future Duke of Devonshire, revealed most completely his thoughts on the Home Rule crisis. Originally Dicey had sent a copy of his book to Hartington, leader of the Whig faction within the Liberal party and the most prominent Liberal Unionist. He hoped Hartington might regard the book as "a well meant, however feeble an effort to support the policy of the Liberal Unionists" and thanked him for the part Hartington had played "in vindicating the principles of true Liberalism."[63] Hartington replied politely but no more. At the end of 1886 Liberal Unionists held an ambiguous political position, with Dicey reflecting this uncertainty. So he attempted to dispel the mood with this long entreaty to Hartington:

> The present crisis, in the judgment of hundreds, both Liberals and Conservatives, reduces ordinary party questions to insignificance. The one duty, we feel, of every patriotic Englishman is to support the rule of law throughout the whole United Kingdom, to maintain the Union, and, with this object, to prevent the return to office of Mr. Gladstone and his followers. This is vital, everything else is for the moment of trivial importance. We look to your lordship to see that the Separatists do not return to power. Their victory would mean something much worse than even the calamity of the establishment of a Parliament in Ireland. It would mean under present circumstances, the supremacy of Mr. Parnell, the utter demoralisation of politics, and the ruin of the United Kingdom. What may be the best means to avert a Separatist triumph, it is for you to judge. It would be presumptuous for anyone, not engaged in political life, to say whether the Liberal Unionists ought to unite with the Conservatives, or whether the Unionist leaders should assume Office. What it is not presumptuous to say is that at the

62. Gladstone to Bryce, 30 November 1886, Bryce Papers.
63. Dicey to Lord Hartington, 12 November 1886, Devonshire Papers, Chatsworth, Derbyshire.

present moment the difference between Liberals & Conservatives is, in the eyes of men outside the House of Commons, as nothing compared with the difference between Unionists and Separatists. This is a point on which the feeling of persons outside political life is different, I fancy, from that of Members of Parliament. This difference I insist upon, because if you should chance not to perceive it, you would, in my opinion, misjudge the whole situation. Your lordship is quite possibly hardly aware of the greatness of the position you occupy. You are the only leader in whose honesty, common-sense, & patriotism, men of the most different parties absolutely confide. What we do not feel so sure of—you must allow me to speak plainly—is that you have all the confidence in yourself which is required by this crisis. What I venture to assert with absolute assurance, is that if at this moment you rise above party, and appeal to the nation as a whole, you will find yourself supported by honest men of all classes, and of all political ways of thinking. What we need is a statesman who can show that he cares for the nation, & for the nation only, and what we believe is that you are such a statesman. This conviction in common with every other Liberal Unionist, and also with thousands of Conservatives, I share to the fullest extent. This is my excuse for addressing your lordship and imploring you to trust in yourself, and in the support of the nation. You can save the nation from the most terrible calamity which could befall it—the return to power of men who do not believe in the unity of the whole nation—the disruption of the United Kingdom and the ruin of all confidence in public men. You can avert this calamity, and I urge you to subordinate every other consideration to the necessity of averting it. My name will at least show you that I have given some thought to politics, and that strong as my language may sound, the strength springs from the strength of my conviction, since I am not habitually a violent writer.[64]

To this request Hartington proved indifferent. In reply he referred to the basic difficulty inherent in Dicey's attempt to treat Home Rule only as a constitutional problem. In a mild rebuke Hartington, while

64. Ibid., 23 December 1886, ibid.

conceding the value of *England's Case,* charged Dicey with attaching insufficient weight to practical political considerations.[65] By this fault Dicey, who had basked in the glow of success his book had earned,[66] consigned himself forever to following politics from afar. Despite his best efforts to influence major Unionist leaders, they exploited his arguments only when it suited their purposes, leaving Dicey in academic solitude.

Unionist adherents cited *England's Case* frequently, although few pretended to understand the subtleties of the constitutional arguments. The book suffered from the discussion of contemporary politics in a dry academic style. Dicey obviously cared passionately about the Union, but the self-imposed role of constitutional commentator restricted the infusion of that emotion into the work. When the later Home Rule books abandoned the pose of indifference, they degenerated into strident tirades of little value. Yet a detached attitude had not made the impression he had hoped. Even with good sales Dicey had no illusions about its effect, writing to his wife: "One check on vanity is that though the book is a success, the day when a book could have real effect on politics is gone. . . . The voters don't read books and the book-reading classes are, I suspect, ceasing to have political interest." [67] He recognized with sadness that the work had failed in its major objectives: to establish his reputation as a political authority and to convince the country that Home Rule should be rejected.

The influence of this initial essay in political controversy lay in the brief advantage it gave Liberal Unionists when they employed constitutional arguments against Home Rule. Justin McCarthy, a principal political lieutenant of Parnell, feared the book's impact so much that he wrote a rebuttal, *The Case for Home Rule.* As McCarthy put it: "A volume ushered into the world with so much ceremony, accepted as a sort of gospel by a certain party, and affecting to be so sweepingly destructive of a great cause, demands a patient consideration."[68] McCarthy countered Dicey's arguments

65. Hartington to Dicey, 3 January 1887, General Manuscripts 508(63), Glasgow University Library.
66. Dicey to Mrs. Dicey, 2 December 1886, in Rait, *Memorials,* pp. 101–02.
67. Ibid., ? December 1886, in ibid., p. 101.
68. Justin McCarthy, *The Case for Home Rule,* p. x.

point by point, so a complete summary is not possible. A fair verdict would be that the Irishman answered effectively most of Dicey's assertions, particularly his discounting of Irish history: "All that history teaches is to be ignored, to be wiped away, and a quarrel as old as the hills is to be investigated as if it were a mushroom controversy born of conditions that only came into existence the week before last."[69] Of course McCarthy brought his own prejudices to the fray, for he was no disinterested observer. He concluded that "it does not need much study of Mr. Dicey's pages to discover that most of his arguments are fantastic and misleading, and that even where the arguments themselves are sound, the deductions from them are quite inaccurate."[70] For his part Dicey never deigned to admit the existence of the McCarthy book; with his own mind clear Dicey had no interest in differing viewpoints. The battle lines for the future were clearly staked, for the Unionist warrior Dicey had found the political crusade to which he could devote himself unhesitatingly.

69. Ibid., p. 9.
70. Ibid., p. 172.

CHAPTER SEVEN

THE LIFE OF A UNIONIST,

1887-1898

FOR THE NEXT period of Dicey's life, from 1887 through the outbreak of the Boer War, the Irish Question governed his life, although to posterity his work in other areas seemingly outweighed his political activities in importance. A fundamental contention of this book is that Dicey's concern for the Union controlled the allotment of his time after 1886 and that this obsession with Ireland, usually noted briefly in works on Dicey, detracted from the number of his contributions on legal and constitutional matters. This emphasis on Irish affairs reflects what Dicey himself worried about and wrote on in the years after 1886. His reputation rested now on two books, *Law of the Constitution* and *England's Case against Home Rule*, but, significantly, Dicey exploited his role as political commentator far more than his position as interpreter of the constitution. Dicey devoted more attention to his political polemics than to any other area of work.

On 30 March 1887 Dicey spoke at the inaugural dinner of the Liberal Union Club, Hartington presiding, at which the organ of Unionism, *The Liberal Unionist*, made its debut.[1] He reported the contents of his speech to Bryce, in the process elaborating his views on Ireland as they developed after 1886: "It expressed a conviction which I hold with the utmost seriousness & which strengthens upon me day by day namely that the Liberal Unionists and I must add the Unionists generally do in the rough and in the only way in which political parties ever can do so, represent the best moral feeling & the national feeling of the country. . . . All I want to do is to make perfectly clear that in spite of lightness & I dare say flippancy of my way of talking I entertain a much more serious conviction than you or at any rate your sister, might at first sight

---

1. Michael Hurst, *Joseph Chamberlain and Liberal Reunion*, p. 341.

believe."[2] Continued hardening of his attitude may be seen in his refusal to attend a dinner where he would have to deliver a toast to the Liberal party. He could not in good conscience perform this duty.[3] The fissure between Gladstonians and Liberal Unionists widened as time elapsed.

For the remainder of the year Dicey placed his pen at the disposal of the Unionist cause. In a pamphlet published in July he enumerated the duties of Unionists for the foreseeable future: to look plain facts in the face, to consolidate the whole Unionist party, and to preach to the electors the vital importance of maintaining national unity.[4] He believed the Home Rulers and Separatists had rallied from their defeat of the previous year. In spite of this he remained optimistic about the moral strength of the Unionist position. The maintenance of the Union, Dicey argued, concerned the maintenance of law, the maintenance of political morality, the maintenance of national existence. The cause of national unity superseded every other consideration, dwarfing into insignificance the petty distinctions between parties that loomed so large in the eyes of party zealots whose respect for party outweighed the good of the nation. Unionists must enlist ordinary citizens to address the electors, for they could not rely on already overburdened Unionist politicians. Unless Unionists matched the enthusiasm of their foes, their faith in the national unity of the United Kingdom could never triumph over the temporary infatuation of Gladstonians and the genuine fervor of Irish Nationalists. Even when the political scene appeared favorable to their cause, Unionists could not relax their vigilance about Home Rule.

Some months later he published in book form letters to the *Spectator* he had written about errors in Unionist strategy.[5] Many of the arguments were already familiar, such as the necessity for sinking party differences in order to repel "the assaults of revolutionists whose efforts menace the integrity and power of the United Kingdom." In two areas Dicey introduced new arguments for Unionists to ponder. In the first place, he wrote, Home Rule posed

2. Dicey to Bryce, 4 April 1887, Bryce Papers.
3. Ibid., 11 June 1887, ibid.
4. Albert Venn Dicey, "The Duties of Unionists," in *The Case for the Union.*
5. Albert Venn Dicey, *Letters on Unionist Delusions.*

a political conflict so fundamental that it could never be resolved by compromise. Unionists believed the United Kingdom formed a nation; Home Rulers believed the claims of Irish nationality were morally superior to the rights of the United Kingdom. Between these viewpoints no middle ground was possible. The violent demand for revolutionary innovation should not be mistaken for constitutional agitation on behalf of peaceful reform. In the second place, he defended Lord Hartington and other Liberal Unionist leaders for their alliance with the Conservatives on the grounds that party allegiance must not interfere with loyalty to the nation. To every Unionist, leader or follower, political policy should be subordinated to the securing of national unity. Gladstonian Liberals had sold out to the Parnellites, therefore only resolute defense of the nation without any compromise could save the Union.

On one hand, that Dicey possessed little if any actual political influence was patent; his university status earned him inclusion in Unionist functions, though few Unionist leaders paid him any attention, a situation he professed to favor.[6] He never emerged from the political shadows. On the other hand, Unionism represented for him a more rigid set of political beliefs than any of the more influential ideologies of the nineteenth century. Dicey had jettisoned the liberalism expressed by the Liberal party for the sake of Unionism as soon as a conflict between the two became apparent. Without the responsibility of power Dicey indulged without restraint his penchant for violent political rhetoric. His attitude reflected that doubt about compromise common to the political dilettante. On a personal level his oft-mentioned generosity to political adversaries continued, but in his writings woe to those who laid profane hands upon the Union. The divisive nature of the Irish Question from 1886 forward is often overlooked because Home Rule had failed and the Unionists held power almost exclusively for the next two decades. That situation did nothing to allay Dicey's fears for the Union. That Dicey was not unique in the ferocity of his opinions may be seen in the comment of Bryce to a friend at the end of 1887: "Things are less pleasant in England for those who join in politics than they have been within living memory, so bitter has feeling

6. Dicey to Mrs. Dicey, 16 May 1888, in Rait, *Memorials*, pp. 129–30. This account of a political dinner at the Duke of Bedford's London home pointed out the limited role Dicey played at such gatherings.

become, especially that of the so-called Unionist or Dissentient Liberals against the Home Rulers of the same party and especially against Mr. Gladstone. There is a social boycott on the part of the former, who, with the Tories, include five-sixths of 'society' in London. . . . We hear no longer argument on either side but recrimination."[7] Though the Irish issue waxed and waned from 1886 to 1914 in response to many political variables, it injected a permanent antagonism to English politics, betraying the stability and gamesmanship often attributed to late Victorian and Edwardian politics.

As if in an affort to validate his friend's observation, in April 1888 Dicey rejoined the battle for the Union, for the first time attacking the motivation as well as the policies of his opponents. In the process he abandoned the false objectivity of a constitutionalist.[8] The cause of Unionism, he now argued, depended upon the plainest rules of morality, for Unionists were not only the wise but the moral party. Home Rule did not truly represent the wishes of Ireland, because the Irish minority, who were the wealth, vigor, and honesty of the land, detested the policy in every particular. Home Rulers had turned into the New Jacobins bent on the destruction of law and property, therefore Unionists must fight for the supremacy throughout the whole state of common honesty and fairness. Did the debut of this new theme have any effect? The scanty evidence suggests not, for he always preached to the converted, having no illusions about changing the minds of confirmed Home Rulers. For example, E. A. Freeman wrote to Bryce about the latest Dicey effort: "I have just read Dicey in Cont. Rev. I don't see that what he says touches me. I believe in Home Rule for Ireland, as I believe in it for Jersey."[9] Realization that his polemics had no real effect on public opinion led Dicey to attempt a different approach.

Beginning in April 1888 and extending over the next two years, Dicey sent letter after letter to Arthur Balfour, nephew of Lord Salisbury and then chief secretary for Ireland. This correspondence originated in a suggestion by Dicey that Unionist policy should not include an increase in penalties on convictions under the Crimes Act, as this would cause discredit to the Unionist government.[10] It

7. Bryce to Mrs. S. Whitman, 17 December 1887, Bryce Papers.
8. Albert Venn Dicey, "New Jacobinism and Old Morality," pp. 475–502.
9. Freeman to Bryce, 6 April 1888, Bryce Papers.
10. Dicey to Arthur Balfour, 27 April 1888, Arthur Balfour Papers, B.M. Add. Mss. 49792.

would give the appearance of revenge, a spirit not worthy of Unionism. His advice reiterated that only the ordinary law enforced strictly in the ordinary way could pacify Ireland to any extent. Balfour's rejoinder in favor of increased penalties did not convince Dicey entirely, but he was sufficiently impressed by Balfour's start in office to place his hopes for Ireland in the hands of Balfour, the only politician capable of administering the Crimes Act effectively. He also pressed upon Balfour that Unionist policy should not include pledges of local self-government extended to Ireland, a policy advocated by Unionist stalwart Joseph Chamberlain, but which Dicey had always opposed resolutely lest local government fall into the hands of Home Rulers.[11]

The summer of 1888 brought Ireland back to the forefront of English politics, presenting Dicey with specific issues to contemplate: the special commission to examine the nature of Parnellism and the various charges brought against Parnell for conspiring with other Irish leaders to violate the law in Ireland.[12] Included was the publication by the *Times* in 1887 of a facsimile letter suggesting Parnell's approval of the Phoenix Park murders in 1882. When Parnell requested a select committee to consider these affairs, he received a prompt refusal from the Unionist government. Instead, the special commission was appointed despite misgivings by some Unionists, including Dicey, and the bitter opposition of Home Rulers to the judges selected.

Dicey wrote to Balfour that he disapproved the special commission, because it deviated from his cherished principle that every man had the right to trial in the ordinary courts of the land, having no right to demand any other sort of trial.[13] He feared that the national issue of Home Rule might be reduced to the personal issue of Parnell's integrity. In addition to the letter, Dicey enclosed a long memorandum on the special commission which stressed repeatedly the necessity of constituting a *legal tribunal* to carry on a *legal inquiry* and act exactly like a regular court.[14] Witnesses must be under oath, subject to cross-examination, and liable to the penalties

11. Ibid., 3 May 1888, ibid.
12. For the special commission, see L. P. Curtis, Jr., *Coercion and Conciliation in Ireland 1880–1892*, pp. 277–300; F. S. L. Lyons, *Charles Stewart Parnell*, pp. 393–432.
13. Dicey to Balfour, 13 July 1888, Balfour Papers, B.M. Add. Mss. 49792.
14. The emphasis on the legal nature of the proceedings was Dicey's.

for perjury. Dicey recognized that meeting his suggestions would require firmness on the part of Unionist leaders, but he thought them essential if the commission should influence the public. Some weeks later he pressed upon Balfour that the inquiry into Parnell's conduct be as sweeping as possible, especially the conniving of Parnell and his associates at boycotts in Ireland.[15] Dicey, like most Unionists, hoped the commission might discredit Parnell once and for all, but he had a foreboding that it might backfire if not handled properly. If the conditions he thought necessary could not be obtained, no commission at all might be wiser: "Whether it is advisable to have a Commission at all costs is to me a very arguable question."[16]

When the special commission opened its proceedings, his apprehension about the outcome had not abated. These fears found expression in a short note appearing in the *Spectator,* where Dicey argued that even if the letter attributed to Parnell by Richard Piggott proved a forgery, this fact alone would not favor Home Rule.[17] Dicey then turned his attention to the charges brought by Gladstonians about the enforcement of the Crimes Act. Balfour assured him that he did all in his power to answer allegations of wrongdoing, welcoming suggestions on Unionist policy from Dicey as well as the opportunity to explain his own views.[18] In reply Dicey proposed that the government publish a plain statement of facts about the Crimes Act in order that Unionist speakers might contradict Gladstonian misrepresentations as quickly as possible.[19] In his own speeches he often wished to denounce assertions he believed false, but had not the means to assemble the facts in support of his position. The proposed report should be made public even if some cases told against the government: "The one essential thing for the

15. Dicey to Balfour, 1 August 1888, Balfour Papers, B.M. Add. Mss. 49792.

16. Ibid.

17. "A Word of Warning from Professor Dicey," pp. 1187–88. Dicey may well have discussed this point with others, because Bryce wrote in the same vein that the merits or demerits of Parnell made no difference to Home Rule. Bryce argued that if the letter was authentic, this should not discredit Home Rule. Bryce to Freeman, 5 August 1888, Bryce Papers.

18. Balfour to Dicey, 10 September 1888, Balfour Papers, B.M. Add. Mss. 49792.

19. Dicey to Balfour, 18 September 1888, ibid.

Unionist cause is that the truth should be known to the electors."[20]

The truth became all too apparent early in 1889 when Piggott broke down in the witness box, confessing to the forgery of the Parnell letter. Unionist charges against Parnell collapsed. The promised destruction of the Irish leader turned into a wave of popularity in England he had never before experienced. Sympathy for Home Rule increased dramatically, even though, as Bryce noted, no logical connection between the failure of the *Times* case and the validity of Home Rule arguments existed.[21] A most uncharacteristic silence settled upon Dicey, as if, like most other Unionists, he needed a respite to decide the best means of extricating Unionism from the ruins of the special commission. At one time Dicey suspected that Irish partisans of Parnell might assassinate the commission judges in order to abort the proceedings;[22] now the Unionists stood convicted of conspiracy in the eyes of the public. Dicey and other Unionist adherents had no alternative but ride out the storm in silence. They waited for the publication of the commission report in the hope that some political advantage might yet be salvaged from its pages.

The state of Unionism was not the only source of discomfort to Dicey. On the eve of the release of the special commission report, Gladstone took advantage of his position as honorary fellow of All Souls and spent ten days in residence in early 1890. Historian Charles Oman recalled that Dicey, "the most furious and eloquent of Liberal-Unionists," resolved to absent himself from the college as long as the destroyer of the Liberal party was present.[23] Anson, the warden of All Souls, prevailed upon Dicey to attend the reception at the outset of Gladstone's stay if only for the sake of the college's reputation for hospitality. To this plea Dicey responded. At the reception Gladstone immediately made every effort to draw his critic into conversation, tactfully posed a question of constitutional law on which he would accept Dicey's opinion alone, and

20. Ibid.

21. Bryce to Freeman, 8 March 1889, Bryce Papers.

22. Dicey to Balfour, 18 and 23 November 1888, Balfour Papers, B.M. Add. Mss. 49792.

23. This paragraph is based on the recollection by Sir Charles Oman in *Things I Have Seen*, pp. 78–82.

reduced Dicey to a surprising state of wordlessness by his solicitude. The contrast between the two men was instructive, for Gladstone, constantly open to new ideas, envied those with a creed they could maintain to the last.[24] Dicey exemplified strict adherence to personal beliefs, and so could not comprehend Gladstone's capacity for intellectual and political development. This confrontation with the object of so many of his vehement denunciations demonstrated anew Dicey's unsuitability for a political career. He needed the presence essential to the success of many Victorian politicians, and, equally as damaging, his oratory was effective only in set pieces. He never mastered the art of spontaneous repartee often demanded at political meetings. He lacked dismally the qualities necessary for success in the often hectic style of English politics.

The report of the special commission appeared on 13 February 1890, presenting Dicey with the occasion for yet another foray into political controversy. From that point through June he prepared *The Verdict,* an attempt to extract some Unionist benefit from the Parnell material in the report.[25] A complete reading of the report prompted him to undertake the project, so impressed was he by the political ammunition he thought it contained. Dicey wrote to Lord Selborne of his firm conviction "that it has placed in the hands of Unionists a most powerful weapon if only they know how to use it. The perversions of the Gladstonians do not greatly trouble me."[26] The new book must emphasize the less-publicized conclusions of the report, because the vindication of Parnell had overshadowed all other aspects. As Dicey now believed:

> Everything alleged by Unionists, except the direct personal charges against Parnell, seems to me in substance made out. I do not see how any man can now honestly deny that Boycotting is a totally different thing from exclusive dealing, or that the Irish party are collectively responsible for an attempt to carry through a change of law by intimidation & violence. We now know for certain that they are revolutionists & not constitu-

24. D. A. Hamer, *Liberal Politics in the Age of Gladstone and Rosebery,* p. 70.

25. Albert Venn Dicey, *The Verdict: A Tract on the Political Significance of the Report of the Parnell Commission.*

26. Dicey to Selborne, 27 February 1890, Selborne Papers.

tional reformers. . . . My intense interest in the cause of Unionism which seems to me to be the cause both of patriotism & of plain justice is my only excuse for having written so much.[27]

To Selborne Dicey revealed also the main tactical point of *The Verdict:* the importance attached to the Scottish verdict of not proven. Gladstonians had interpreted this as an acquittal, so he sought Selborne's approval to interpret the phrase as signifying that the evidence for guilt was incomplete. In no way did it imply a judgment of innocent. To ignore this distinction, Dicey thought, missed the crucial value of the report.[28] Upon receipt of Selborne's endorsement of his interpretation, Dicey proceeded with the book: "The more I study the Report the more I am struck with the force of its direct, & still more of its implied, censures on the conduct of the Respondents."[29] Dicey worked quickly in the belief that Home Rule had truly been delivered into the hands of the Unionists.

The Verdict appeared in July 1890. The most charitable estimate of the book is that Dicey used all his forensic skills to make the best of a bad political brief. The *Times* had rendered, he wrote, "a signal service to the State for which they have as yet received, even from Unionists, nothing like due gratitude."[30] It was a political judgment so partisan that the book deserved little attention and received less. The book proved in vain, for the Parnell letter had been the focal point of the inquiry. Parnell's vindication with increased prestige withstood easily Dicey's emphasis on other parts of the report.[31] Most of the events Dicey described had occurred in the early 1880s, already ancient history to public opinion. To all but the most embittered Unionist *The Verdict* proved a sorry effort.

Why, after opposing the special commission at its inception, did Dicey commit his prestige to such a hopeless task as making Unionist propaganda out of a situation that had already turned into a Unionist fiasco? L. P. Curtis wrote that "to explain Unionist conduct one must look beyond the Irish Sea, for the men who sponsored the commission were inordinately concerned with the integrity and

27. Ibid.
28. Ibid., 14 March 1890, ibid.
29. Ibid., 17 March 1890, ibid.
30. *The Verdict*, p. viii.
31. Conor Cruise O'Brien, *Parnell and His Party 1880–1890*, p. 233.

future of the British empire."[32] This statement applies to Dicey except that his primary concern was Unionist, not imperial; the integrity he brooded over encompassed only the United Kingdom, not the overseas empire. Ultimately, imperial matters commanded his allegiance, but the consistency of his political attitudes after 1886 lay in the absolute devotion he gave to the maintenance of the United Kingdom itself. He would risk anything, even his reputation, for its sake. The Union symbolized British greatness to Dicey, so the more immediate the threat, the more radical political action he entertained to safeguard it. His defense of the Parnell commission to the bitter end was the logical conclusion of his strong Unionism.

In the aftermath of the Parnell debacle Dicey's fears for Unionist chances at the next election increased. Trying to find an issue around which Unionists could coalesce, he proposed to Balfour that priority be given to the Land Purchase bill then under consideration. Dicey had just ended one of his infrequent trips to Ireland, reporting that "every word I heard in Ireland confirmed my belief that the maintenance of the law, and a sweeping measure of purchase constitute the only true policy for Unionists."[33] This stance was consistent with his opinion that economic benefits would eventually destroy Home Rule agitation. He felt that a dramatic gesture on land purchase would not only benefit Ireland, but also alleviate the electoral difficulties Unionists faced. As he wrote: "If the Purchase bill is passed even a defeat at the general election will be a great, but I believe reparable, misfortune. If the Bill is not passed defeat at the election is to my mind certain & defeat will then mean discredit from which as a Unionist party we shall never recover."[34] This apocalyptic view of Unionist fortunes soon proved false, for salvation lay close at hand.

In mid-November 1890 the Parnell divorce case brought the Irish leader to the tragic finish of his political career. The bitter debate over his leadership of the Irish parliamentary party and his loss of this battle cost him his political influence. The divorce destroyed the fund of public sympathy Parnell had enjoyed since the Piggott forgery was exposed. Dicey recognized that the split in Home Rule

32. Curtis, *Coercion and Conciliation*, p. 299.
33. Dicey to Balfour, 3 October 1890, Balfour Papers, B.M. Add. Mss. 49792.
34. Ibid.

ranks worked to the advantage of Unionists, suspecting that Parnell was unlikely to step down as Irish leader without a battle. On the very day the decision against Parnell and Mrs. O'Shea became public, Dicey wagered that Parnell would not retire from the leadership of the Irish party within three months.[35] Dicey followed the events of November-December 1890 avidly, and, in a letter to the *Times* entitled "The Cant of Cynicism," Dicey pointed out that public men had insisted so strongly on Parnell's adultery that they forgot he was a traitor and liar as well. Unionists must not sympathize with the desperate efforts of a traitor to avoid the ruin he so richly deserved. "We Unionists are at this moment in an impregnable position, which can be sacrificed by nothing but our own folly," he wrote and added later, "to argue further against Home Rule is hardly necessary; Parnellite practice is supplying the confutation to Gladstonian theory."[36] Later in December Dicey advised Balfour that the Conservatives should remain in office as long as possible in order that the Parnell divorce could have maximum impact: "I believe that nothing but time to think matters well over will enable the honest but very dull electors to understand the effect of recent events."[37] Balfour preferred the loftier tone that the government should not seek immediate political advantage, assuring Dicey the government contemplated no general election in the near future.[38] Dicey rejoiced in the fact that the year which had begun so badly for Unionism closed on a note of triumph.

Two other notable events of 1890 affected Dicey on Ireland. In that year he took silk, thereby adding the dignity of Queen's Counsel to the legal laurels he had already earned.[39] Also, he resigned from his position with the Inland Revenue, providing more time to devote to other affairs, though he still held government briefs after that on special cases. The direct effect of this increase in leisure

35. See the bet made 17 November 1890, recorded in Sir Charles Oman, ed., *The Text of the Second Betting Book of All Souls College 1873–1919*, p. 111.

36. *Times*, 9 December 1890, p. 8.

37. Dicey to Balfour, 29 December 1890, Balfour Papers, B.M. Add. Mss. 49792.

38. Balfour to Dicey, 1 January 1891, ibid.

39. The seal and letter of appointment as Q.C. are still preserved among the Dicey materials in the Muniments Room of the Working Men's College.

may be seen in the notebook Dicey began in 1891 as a permanent record of Irish politics.[40] This notebook, better than any single piece of evidence, showed his obsession with Ireland. By this time a recognized authority on constitutional law, the possessor of a reputation already unsurpassed in the Anglo-American legal world, Dicey devoted his time to a digest of Home Rule speeches, shifts in public opinion, and the course of legislation affecting Ireland. Rarely did legal topics find their way into the notebook, usually a laconic note about a case in the area of conflict of laws.[41] The notebook was fullest for 1892, when the excitement of the July election caused him to follow politics with the keenest interest. Early in 1891, because of his ardent commitment to the Unionist cause, the *Spectator* bestowed on Dicey the accolade of "the keeper of the Liberal Unionist Conscience."[42] This conscience, of Unionists generally and Dicey in particular, so the *Spectator* insisted, was the old-fashioned kind, concerned with positive engagements, plain responsibilities, and even-handed justice.

After a relatively long (for him) abstention from Home Rule controversy in 1891, the election of 1892 brought Dicey to the Irish wars again. In March he urged zealous Unionists to spare no legitimate effort to win the general election, because so many other Unionists failed to grasp the momentous character of the impending conflict.[43] The true governors of Ireland, in the event of a Home Rule victory, would be the men found guilty (privately by Dicey) of criminal conspiracy. Unionists should not cooperate with Irish politicians for the sake of temporary political gain. For the survival of Unionism compromise meant death. Dicey admitted to Bryce on the eve of the election that these arguments had become standard: "I cannot pretend to have developed many new aspects lately of the Home Rule question. It is coming by degrees, as all things must, to a question rather of power than of argument. Ballots are better than bullets, but after all, it comes at last to a fight. The oddity of all

40. This notebook is among the Dicey memorabilia in the archives of Somerville College, Oxford, and will be referred to as: Dicey Notebook. I am indebted to College librarian Pauline Adams for placing this document at my disposal.

41. Dicey Notebook, f. 13.

42. "The Liberal Unionist Conscience," p. 193.

43. Albert Venn Dicey, "The Defence of the Union," pp. 314–41.

historical contests is that they almost invariably produce something essentially different from that which either party contemplates. Of course I speak of the results produced in many years, e.g. a century."[44] The closer the election, the more Dicey emphasized the emotional aspects of the Home Rule situation.[45] The protest of Irish Protestantism became the protest of all the liberality, the enlightenment, and the loyalty of Ireland. Union, justice, and equal rights had made them the most loyal citizens of the United Kingdom. Protestant Ulster demonstrated the beneficent effects of the Act of Union, a process Dicey still hoped might be repeated in the Catholic south.

In the aftermath of the 1892 election Unionist defeat spurred Dicey to greater efforts to shadow the Irish policy of the new government. When he congratulated Bryce upon appointment to the chancellorship of the Duchy of Lancaster, Dicey pointed to the first mistake of the Liberals: "It is not my business to improve the arrangements of the present Ministry, but it is my private opinion that it has been a great mistake not to send you to Ireland instead of Morley."[46] Dicey soon carefully recorded the outbreaks of violence in Ireland attendant upon the change of governments, which he attributed to the substitution of Liberal permissiveness for Unionist adherence to strict enforcement of the law.[47] He also kept close watch on Morley's performance as chief secretary for Ireland lest some error in policy escape his attention.[48] With a new Home Rule bill in the offing, Dicey made copious notes on any speech or article referring to Home Rule.[49] He continued his frequent appearances in the Unionist cause, which led Bryce to depict him as "thundering away against Home Rule on platforms."[50]

In the Home Rule bill of 1893 the greatest change from the bill defeated in 1886 was the inclusion of Irish members at Westminster, from which they had been excluded earlier. Dicey delighted in quoting the Gladstone and Morley of 1886 in support of exclusion against the Gladstone and Morley of 1893 in favor of inclusion.

44. Dicey to Bryce, 22 June 1892, Bryce Papers.
45. Albert Venn Dicey, "The Protest of Irish Protestantism," pp. 1–15.
46. Dicey to Bryce, 18 August 1892, Bryce Papers.
47. Dicey Notebook, ff. 49–52.
48. Ibid., f. 58.
49. Ibid., ff. 59–81.
50. Bryce to Holmes, 6 April 1893, Bryce Papers.

Once the bill was before the House of Commons Dicey explained to Joseph Chamberlain: "I am studying the Bill with care. Among its many assailable points that which I should mainly attack is the retention of the Irish members. It vitiates everything. Nor is there any real inconsistency between this & the attack made in '86 on their exclusion. There are insuperable evils in each plan. Of the two I think the evils of retention the greatest."[51] His concern lest the Home Rule bill should pass into law led to the publication of *A Leap in the Dark* in the summer of 1893.[52] This latest volume testified eloquently to Dicey's admission that new arguments about Home Rule were scarce. He once again attempted to prove that Home Rule created a new constitution for the whole United Kingdom, that this new constitution would injure both England and Ireland, and that it would initiate a constitutional revolution, because Home Rule subverted the bases of the existing constitution. The victory of Gladstone and Home Rule assured the triumph of Parnellism and conspiracy, of Dublin over Belfast, of protection over free trade, and of constitutional injustice over equality before the law. Dicey recognized the threat of civil war inherent in such strong opposition, but neatly sidestepped the issue by declining to discuss the ethical limits to the exercise of constitutionally unlimited sovereignty, or at what point this opposition justified armed resistance. In 1893 circumstances spared Dicey the necessity of putting his conscience to the test, but future Home Rule crises would not afford him a similar luxury. Home Rule, Dicey argued, permitted no concession or compromise by Unionists; if all else failed they must rely on the House of Lords to reject the bill in order that it be submitted to the people for approval. He had anticipated this possibility as early as 1891 when he suggested that the Lords had the duty to throw out any Home Rule bill until it had received the deliberate judgment of the nation.[53] Events followed the Diceyan

51. Dicey to Joseph Chamberlain, 1 May 1893, Joseph Chamberlain Papers, JC 5/23/1, Birmington University Library.
52. Albert Venn Dicey, *A Leap in the Dark: A Criticism of the Principles of Home Rule as Illustrated by the Bill of 1893*.
53. *Times*, 8 October 1891. Dicey made the statement while addressing a Unionist meeting at Accrington. Ironically, the report of his speech appeared the same day as a long report on the death of Parnell two days earlier in Brighton.

scenario closely; the Home Rule bill passed through the Commons after heroic exertions by Gladstone, then met an overwhelming defeat in the House of Lords by a vote of 419–41 in September 1893.

This outcome pleased Dicey, though so intense was his fear of Home Rule that he never felt completely safe from its threat no matter what the political situation. As he wrote to Selborne in October 1893: "On the whole I am myself in better hopes as regards the success of the Unionist cause than I have been for some time. I think I can see signs that honest Gladstonians are becoming alarmed, . . . I think that the Unionists can be relied upon to stand firmly together, a matter about which immediately after the general election I had some doubts.[54] Despite this upturn in Unionist fortunes, in a revealing speech delivered in Dublin at the end of the year, Dicey still preached the gospel of Unionism in danger.[55] Gladstone's retirement, he urged, would not end the evils of Gladstonianism; the battle against Home Rule must be fought with eternal vigilance and a firm belief in the righteousness of Unionism. Unionists must not relax their guard now that the immediate danger was past. In his peroration Dicey made this appeal: "We must exert ourselves with redoubled energy; we must make this public concern as much our interest as if it were our private affair. Then I say again, 'Pray heartily, fight heartily.' You will say that I have wandered into a kind of religion rather than politics. I cannot separate the two. Fervour of feeling is essential to vigour of action. You will never triumph unless you make a kind of religion of your politics, or turn your politics into a kind of religion. Then, having done all you can in a just cause, you can appeal to the just aid of Heaven."[56] This strain demonstrated anew the passionate faith Dicey had in the virtues of the Union as well as why his speeches invariably found such an enthusiastic response among the true believers. Dicey never doubted God was a Unionist.

Throughout 1894 the weaknesses of the Liberal government under Lord Rosebery became patent, with Home Rule receding into the background, especially since the Liberals could not agree on Irish policy. This decline did not appease Dicey, who rejected the

54. Dicey to Selborne, 2 October 1893, Selborne Papers.
55. Albert Venn Dicey, "The Unionist Outlook," pp. 463–84.
56. Ibid., pp. 483–84.

notion that the Union was safe. In a long letter to Leo Maxse he revealed his thoughts on the current state of Unionist policy:

> It is I think 3 or 4 years since I said at some public meeting that the one point on which Unionists and Separatists were agreed was that we wished to hear no more of Home Rule. But though I clearly perceive this I believe it would be a fatal error to drop the Irish Question. Will you let me explain, as the matter is of some consequence, my ground for this conviction & therefore for my dissent from your view?
>
> The attack on national unity is to me very like an invasion being an attack on the life of the nation, & I feel as I should about an invasion, that the one paramount duty of every man is to repel it. Every other object ought to be subordinate to this end. Unionism is the very life of the Unionist party. Once let the necessity of repelling the Separatists fall out of view and our whole position becomes in my judgment a weak one. It is quite true there are hosts of other reasons why I now oppose the Gladstonians but my two main grounds are first their attempt to carry Home Rule, & secondly their refusal to submit the question of Home Rule, or in other words the H. Rule Bill of 1893, to the arbitrament of the nation. An appeal to the people is the one thing at which we ought to aim & is the only way of getting rid of the sort of nightmare which oppresses us all.
>
> To let the Irish Question drop is to play into the hands of the Gladstonians, & this in at least two ways.
>
> First they will be glad enough to have their fiasco of 1893 forgotten. Nothing would suit them better than to go on for 2 or 3 years longer doing everything they could to gain popularity & availing themselves of every chance of sowing division among the Unionists. This is their one chance. It is quite possible that if we drop the Irish subject the next general election may, like the last, turn upon a set of confused and different issues, and that the Government may again get a majority who without being much of Home Rulers may be prepared to vote for Home Rule.
>
> Secondly—The dropping [of] the Irish Question on which all Unionists are agreed is certain to involve us in controversies on which we are disagreed. I have no great enthusiasm for the Welsh, or indeed for any other, Church, but were I in Parlia-

ment I should be fully prepared to say that till the question of the Union was settled I would not even consider the question of Welsh Disestablishment and from his speeches—I speak from no other knowledge—I should suppose this to be very nearly Chamberlain's own position. But if the Irish Question be dropped how on earth can we refuse to consider questions like that of disestablishment? And this is merely one example, which happens to occur to me out of a score on which the Unionists would if they let themselves be involved in new controversies, be divided.

If indeed the Gladstonians were deserting H. Rule there might be some reason for letting the Irish Question drop though even then I should think the policy of doing so extremely dubious. But they have not, & the truth is they cannot, throw over H. Rule. When Lord Rosebery tried to provide them with a way of escape by his reference to the "predominant partner" they refused to follow his lead.

The difficulties, let me add, (to prevent misapprehension) which I have in my mind would not exist if a Unionist Government with a strong majority were returned to power. Such a Government should make it its first business to secure the Union, which might and ought to be done by a distribution of seats in accordance with numbers, & such a Government would also undoubtedly take in hand important measures of improvement on which the mass of the party could agree. But this is a matter of the future. Our present duty is to rout the Separatists. It can no more be done by dropping the Irish Question than the American Union could have been restored by raising the Siege of Richmond.

Were it possible without risking divisions I should be glad that the Unionist leaders stated openly their intention to carry out some measures to which a Unionist Government will certainly have to give its attention, such as the extension of the Land Purchase System in Ireland, the reform of the House of Lords etc.[57]

These fears proved ludicrous in view of the multifarious problems the Rosebery government encountered during 1894 and 1895. Even

57. Dicey to Maxse, 6 September 1894, Maxse Papers.

Dicey recognized that a Home Rule victory was impossible, so he turned his attention increasingly toward his work in conflict of laws.

The return of a Unionist government in 1895 intensified his feeling of security, therefore by the end of the year he placed Home Rule in the background for the first time in a decade. At the beginning of the year he had published an article defending the role of the House of Lords in the 1893 defeat of Home Rule.[58] The Lords had preserved the supreme authority of the nation against a small, transitory majority in the Commons. This situation suggested three Unionist policies: (1) no measure diminishing the authority of the House of Lords as protector of the rights of the nation could be tolerated; (2) Unionists, whether Conservative or Liberal, must be prepared when the unity of the nation was secure, to reform the Upper House;[59] (3) Unionists must safeguard the supremacy of the nation by protecting fundamental institutions such as the Union from revolutionary proposals advanced by a faction. These restraints should be embodied in a redistribution of representation between Ireland and England, then introduction of the referendum. In a congratulatory note to Joseph Chamberlain he again lobbied for legislation to resolve finally the Irish Question:

> I am not sanguine enough to hope that the Home Rule agitation
> is entirely disposed of; the Opposition show even less loyalty
> than I expected—and I didn't expect much—in accepting the
> national verdict. But I do hold that the immediate danger of a
> Home Rule success has passed away and that the Unionists
> now hold in their hands the means for making the Union abso-
> lutely secure. The two measures I personally most desire are
> the settlement of the Irish Land Question by a final & generous
> scheme of purchase, and such a redistribution of seats on a
> thoroughly democratic basis as may take from Ireland her inor-

58. Albert Venn Dicey, "Unionists and the House of Lords," pp. 690–704.

59. Dicey advocated a reduction of the House of Lords to 150 or 200 members and the House of Commons to 400 members. He hoped this might raise the level of character and increase the efficiency of both houses. In order to reform the Lords, he was prepared to accept life peerages or even make the upper house elective.

dinate, and give to England her proper share of representation.
. . . All I really wish to do is to congratulate you on a success
which I fully believe has been the saving of the nation.[60]

In what amounted to a farewell article, Dicey published in the
Nation a repetition of his feelings about Unionist policy.[61] From
1896 to 1903 the Irish Question subsided sufficiently for Dicey to
complete at last projects postponed for a decade by his Unionist
endeavors.

Among its other effects the Home Rule controversy precipitated
a crisis in Dicey's commitment to democracy, shook his earlier faith
in its efficacy, and eventually caused him to denounce democracy
in the name of the nation. His previous belief in the judgment of the
electorate, already disturbed by the reckless suffrage increases of
1867 and 1884, yielded to profound doubts when it became apparent
that millions of Englishmen persisted in voting for Home Rule.
Since that issue constituted the touchstone of all his politics, a
theory that endangered the Union had to be revised to counter that
possibility. For this reason democracy acquired a different meaning
after the emergence of Home Rule than it had possessed earlier.

In his youth Dicey had thought himself an advanced Liberal, enthusiastically supporting proposals for an extension of the franchise.
Throughout the 1870s the major reservation about democracy in
action involved the disturbing restrictions on individual liberty in
strict party discipline. Dicey remembered fondly the independent
M.P. of 1832–67, believing him the epitome of English political
individualism. In 1880 Dicey had written that English democracy
rested on a love of order, a Conservative spirit, and a belief in the
doctrines of ordinary morality as the guide to public life.[62] After the
Home Rule crisis of 1886, however, his belief in the permanence of
these virtues fell off sharply. The greater the loss of his original faith
in democracy, the more he romanticized the past. The Whigs of the
mid-Victorian period appeared in retrospect the parliamentary group

60. Dicey to Chamberlain, 29 August 1895, Chamberlain Papers, JC
5/23/2.
61. Albert Venn Dicey, "The Policy of Unionism," *Nation* 61 (17 October 1895): 272–74.
62. Albert Venn Dicey, "Democracy in England in 1880," *Nation* 30
(3 June 1880): 414–15.

he admired most. By 1888 he was already lamenting the declining prestige of Parliament, contrasting parliamentary government (which he praised) with government by Parliament (which he vigorously denounced).[63]

At this point the referendum rescued him from the dilemma of his pessimistic appraisal of democracy by providing a political mechanism he believed both democratic and conservative. Where democracy is king, Dicey wrote, the referendum is the royal veto.[64] Thus he remained loyal to the principles of democracy, and because he assumed that the referendum would always check revolutionary change, he thought the referendum would provide democratic politics with needed stability. In 1890 and 1891 Dicey published a series of articles in the *Nation* where he reassessed his earlier democratic creed.[65] Here Dicey repented his faith in the virtues of majority rule because modern politics made it so difficult to obtain an unequivocal assertion of the national will. Furthermore, democracy and progress were no longer synonymous, for democracy resulted in socialist experimentation and unnecessary restrictions upon individual freedom that democracy should have opposed. This disillusionment he expressed to Bryce: "I am afraid that the longer one lives the more convinced one becomes that no reform, however great, can from the nature of things produce all the benefits which naturally are expected from it. . . . I have no doubt, let me add, that there is gradual improvement in the world, but its gradualness is to me by far its most marked feature."[66] As his fears for the future increased, the voice of the people merited attention only when supporting causes Dicey approved; when democracy sustained harmful policies, then democracy forfeited its validity.

The events of 1892–93, when Gladstone used a small majority in the House of Commons to carry the Home Rule bill, added a new dimension to his anxiety about the onrush of democracy. He expressed this in the formula: The Nation versus The House of Commons. On this theme Dicey wrote at length to Leo Maxse:

63. Albert Venn Dicey, "Parliamentary Government and Government by Parliament," *Nation* 46 (7 June 1888): 464–65.

64. Dicey, "Democracy in Switzerland," pp. 136–37.

65. Albert Venn Dicey, "Democratic Assumptions," *Nation* 51 (20 November 1890): 397–99; 52 (15 January, 18 June 1891): 46–47, 497–98; 53 (16 and 30 July 1891): 46–47, 83–84.

66. Dicey to Bryce, 21 August 1895, Bryce Papers.

It is I think of immense importance that people should realise that a small & transitory political majority, though it necessarily exercises the powers, has not the authority of the nation. On this point my mind is becoming more and more clear. One oddity of so-called Liberal opinion is this: that Liberals resist the authority of the majority where they ought to obey it & adulate a majority where they ought not to treat its authority as unlimited.

In Executive matters I hold that the Government of the day ought even though put into office by but a small majority, to be whilst it continues the Government, in general supported by good citizens. My reason is this, viz:—that in Executive matters the majority must of necessity be treated as the organ of the nation, otherwise the action of the nation is at every turn weakened. A party which is not in a position to carry on the administration ought not to hamper the action of the Ministers of the day. Moreover matters of administration are transitory. On the other hand on matters of constitutional change I do not think a small majority has any moral right to act with vigour. The presumption is in favour of the existing state of affairs, because on the whole it may be assumed to be the permanent will of the nation. Add to this that a constitutional change once made is, or ought to be, final, and therefore ought not to be made by any body of men who do not clearly represent the final will of the nation. Till modern times this has been the practice, though not the theory, of English constitutional government, and it is, as I have pointed out, recognised as a democratic principle in every true democracy.

Now observe what our Gladstonian opposition has done. Throughout the whole existence of the Unionist Government it hampered administration. Men who could not themselves govern tried, often by means verging on illegality to make government in Ireland impossible. The same men have now a slender majority & they act on the supposition that this gives them a moral claim to dissolve the Union.

I do not maintain that the Gladstonians are the only party who have acted factiously in opposing the action of the National Executive. The House of Lords in 1880 or 1881— I forget which—made a grave moral and political mistake in throwing out Forster's Compensation for Disturbance Bill, retired, or dissolved rather than consent to carry on the administration of affairs without the powers they deem necessary. Just in the same way I think the late Unionist Parliament had refused to pass the Crimes Act. However this may be, there is a peculiar & odious inconsistency in the Gladstonian position. When the verdict of a Parliamentary majority is decisively against them on matters of administration they show no respect to its authority. When they have a feeble majority in their own favour they treat it in matters of legislation, as possessed of political omnipotence.[67]

Soon after he amplified his new democratic theory to E. L. Godkin: "What I do wish impressed on the public is that democracy in England at least is certain to come & ought in wisdom to be accepted; but that every one ought to resist the tendency to confuse the conviction that the majority do & will rule with the idea that therefore what the majority wills must be wise and right."[68] The wisdom of democratic sentiment lay in the degree to which its judgments corresponded to Dicey's views.

The more Dicey pondered the implications of popular government, the more pessimistic he grew about the future of parliamentary government. Despite the universal belief in the virtues of parliamentary democracy then prevalent, he saw little reason to forecast its permanent success. He believed that the prestige of Parliament had declined since the days of his youth, and, in writing to Bryce, he assigned four reasons for its demise: (1) Parliament had already achieved many of the ends it had aimed at during the nineteenth century; (2) due to the growth of social unrest, the evils of absolutism no longer seemed so obvious to public opinion; (3) parliamentary government was not suited for "social improvements or innovations based on constructive legislation"; (4) and therefore, parliamentary government had turned into government by Parliament, an inefficient and unpopular form of administration. Dicey deplored this loss of confidence, because "institutions change or perish not because something better is discovered but because the faith which supported them has died."[69] By the time these specula-

67. Dicey to Maxse, 1 January 1895, Maxse Papers.
68. Dicey to Godkin, 5 November 1896, Godkin Papers.
69. Dicey to Bryce, 28 September 1895, Bryce Papers.

tions appeared in print, Dicey had adduced additional factors to account for the decline of Parliament.[70] The spread of constitutional government around the globe had diluted its prestige as well as caused disenchantment when it did not provide the panacea so many had anticipated. Furthermore, Parliament had contracted two diseases for which there seemed no remedies: the tyranny of minorities and the failure of Parliament to represent the will of the nation. Finally, a point Dicey frequently emphasized, modern society demanded of Parliament tasks for which it was ill suited, especially legislation demanding government intervention in social and economic affairs. Parliamentary democracy no longer seemed the wave of the future he had once believed it.

In the context of his preoccupation with Irish affairs, the publication of Dicey's greatest legal work, *Conflict of Laws,* seemed of secondary importance to him.[71] Yet this classic textbook remains the foremost contribution on which his reputation as a legal scholar rests. It marked the most ambitious effort to fulfill his hope that a branch of English law might be synthesized into a statement at once legally accurate and literate and interesting to laymen. In view of the role *Conflict of Laws* played in expanding his reputation, it is surprising to what extent Dicey forced himself to complete the volume. Only his tremendous sense of obligation to his work drove him to finish the book at all. He exhibited an eloquent testament to faith in "useful work" by his determination to terminate the project even after his enthusiasm had waned.

The 1879 *Law of Domicil* had previewed his more extensive, later work; over the years Dicey had published several articles showing his continued interest in private international law.[72] He planned originally to follow *Law of the Constitution* with *Conflict of Laws,* making his mark rapidly as Vinerian professor. But he never mustered a sustained passion for this self-imposed burden, so the book

70. Albert Venn Dicey, "Will the Form of Parliamentary Government Be Permanent?," pp. 67–79.

71. Albert Venn Dicey, *A Digest of the Law of England with Reference to the Conflict of Laws.*

72. Albert Venn Dicey, "Conflict of Laws and Bills of Exchange," pp. 497–512; "Note," pp. 102–4; "On Private International Law as a Branch of the Law of England," pp. 1–21 and 113–27; "The Criteria of Jurisdiction," pp. 21–39.

had evolved slowly with politics often delaying progress. As he grew older this unfinished work weighed heavier on his conscience, strengthening his resolve to finish the project. As early as the summer of 1892 he wrote to Bryce that "I am now sticking tight to my law book and intend to do so until it is somehow ended."[73] Good intentions were not enough, for he fought the Home Rule bill of 1893 in preference to his legal work. Only after its defeat did he return to his trying task: "I have been toiling painfully in every sense of the word at the revision of the M.S.S. of my book. I long more than I can express to have it done, & principally because I need a kind of rest I can't get till I put the whole topic out of my mind."[74] In reply to Bryce's sympathy, he added: "I quite agree with you that I had better never attempt again to write another book of the kind. The kind of work is very difficult, & there are many who can do it better than I can, whereas speculations about constitutions, & I think general statements of legal principles, suit such powers as I have. However there is something gained by having studied minutely one branch of law."[75] One year later he still struggled manfully toward completion but seemingly to little avail: "I wish less of my time had been given to this horrible conflict of laws. There are lucky inspirations such as was *Law of the Constitution* & unlucky inspirations such as was this book."[76] In spite of these negative feelings, Dicey plodded ahead.

Not until November 1894 could he report any substantial progress: "I am at last making way with my book. . . . I quite feel with you that such books do not really repay the trouble & time they cost."[77] He had encountered two major difficulties in preparing the book: his goal of clarity in arrangement caused problems of organization; then he worried about his gift for accurate legal expression, which, if it failed, might negate his aim of producing an authoritative textbook covering the entire body of law. In both instances he surmounted the obstacles but only through effort of the most laborious type.

As usual with his scholarly endeavors, Dicey's appraisal of the book was very pessimistic, sure that the work would never repay

73. Dicey to Bryce, summer 1892, in Rait, *Memorials*, p. 125.
74. Ibid., 17 September 1893, Bryce Papers.
75. Ibid., 7 November 1893, ibid.
76. Ibid., 20 October 1894, ibid.
77. Ibid., 15 November 1894, ibid.

the effort he had expended. "Neither Parties nor the Law of the Constitution cost me half as much effort," he wrote, "yet they are much better books in their way than this one."[78] Because this branch of law depended so heavily on judicial decisions instead of statutes, a familiarity with case law was essential, yet he complained to Bryce that "I have not a good memory for cases; no one has read so many & remembers so few."[79] At the end of the year Dicey still toiled at his task, complaining all the while.[80] He eventually finished the book, though only his special sense of duty gave him the perseverance.

Even after he completed *Conflict of Laws* in 1896, this satisfied Dicey only in the way that it removed a tremendous load from his shoulders. When finally done he explained to Oliver Wendell Holmes the genesis of the book: "It began as a sort of expansion of my Domicil & now alas has misdeveloped into a huge unwieldy 'Digest'. . . . The book was born under an unlucky star & was again & again put aside that I might denounce Home Rule in its various forms & as a last torment has been now for nearly a year printing at New York or Boston."[81] Among the troubles he experienced at this late date, apart from printer's errors, was some difficulty in obtaining the American copyright.

Dicey termed the work a rather wearisome performance, dull and uninspired. He feared he had produced a hybrid attractive to neither the practical lawyer nor the academic theorist. In a letter to Bryce he wrote: "It is a dreary effect of working long at a subject that one gets all too late to know how it might have been treated better and with less labour. . . . What a queer thing life is."[82] In the end the most fervent emotion upon publication was relief: "Thank heaven the Book is done but the doing of it has taken too much out of my life in time and energy."[83] Even afterwards, with the book a professional success, Dicey took a dim view of his work, noting that the importance of digests had declined, which made his book less useful than if it had appeared as scheduled in the 1880s.[84]

78. Ibid., 28 February 1895, ibid.
79. Ibid., 28 September 1895, ibid.
80. Dicey to Strachey, 23 December 1895, Strachey Papers.
81. Dicey to Holmes, 19 April 1896, Holmes Papers.
82. Dicey to Bryce, 24 July 1896, in Rait, *Memorials*, p. 140.
83. Dicey to Godkin, 5 November 1896, Godkin Papers.
84. Dicey to Bryce, 4 June 1900, in Rait, *Memorials*, p. 186.

What compulsion drove Dicey to immerse himself in a legal specialty for which he had little sympathy cannot be answered with precision, but three considerations appear to account for his tenacious adherence to the book. In the first place, conflict of laws was a field of recent origin and therefore did not require a knowledge of legal history, in which Dicey possessed little expertise. It consisted almost entirely of judicial decisions, so this enabled him to work in legal materials congenial to him. Second of all, Dicey admired the work of his predecessors in the field. The earliest authors, Story and Savigny, he thought the only ones worth reading on the subject.[85] Within English law Dicey valued the contribution of John Westlake, whose book *Private International Law* first appeared in 1858, one of the few English legal textbooks Dicey respected written before 1880. He freely acknowledged his debt to Westlake's pioneering effort. Professional regard had combined with sincere personal esteem to entice Dicey into following Westlake's footsteps: "There is no man living for whom I have a greater respect."[86] Upon the death of Westlake in 1913 Dicey wrote: "I have lost one of the most honest and the most trustworthy of friends and counsellors."[87] Dicey praised also the constancy of political opinion Westlake demonstrated: "Westlake knew nothing of the hesitation and half-heartedness which is often the bane of modern life. He was utterly free, for instance, from the weakness of some Unionists who were always hankering for some compromise with Home Rule. He remained to the day of his death the Unionist of 1886."[88] In the third place, Dicey had the prestige of the Vinerian Chair to consider, and so his desire to build its legal reputation sufficed even when his heart was not committed. Each played its part in sustaining his interest.

For the format of the book Dicey employed again that of the earlier law books, attempting to extract from case law the principles recognized by English judges, then arranging them systematically into rules and exceptions, accompanied by explanations when required. This concern for legal principles reflected his belief that

85. Dicey to Holmes, 2 June 1898, Holmes Papers.
86. Dicey to Jacob, 15 November 1911, Working Men's College MSS.
87. Dicey to Strachey, 15 April 1913, Strachey Papers.
88. Albert Venn Dicey, "His Book and His Character," in *Memories of John Westlake*, p. 40.

ignorance about them was the main defect of English law and law-yers.[89] In another context Dicey described his goal: "If an author of ingenuity has reduced some branch of the law to a consistent scheme of logically consistent rules, he supplies exactly the principles of which a Court is in need."[90] The first edition contained 188 rules, many of which subsequent legal development has superseded. No real purpose would be served by a summary of these rules, since many are now invalid. The real interest of the original edition lies now in Dicey's introduction, where he discussed the legal philosophy he brought to the work.

Nowhere else did Dicey reveal so completely his dependence on Austinian jurisprudence for a conceptual framework than in the contrast of his own "positive method" with that of authors who utilized the "theoretical method."[91] He charged that the theorists passed imperceptibly from what the law was to what the law ought to be. This progression constituted the basic fallacy Austin had de-nounced in his own analytic jurisprudence. Dicey rejected outright the assumption, which he attributed primarily to German jurists, that there must exist self-evident principles of right, superior to legal rules, which all judges should recognize as valid. The conflict of laws must start with laws defined strictly in the sense that they derived their authority from the support of the sovereign in whose territory they were enforced. The "positivist" school discovered what were the laws, not what they ought to be. No maxim should be treated as law unless it belonged to the municipal law of a given country. This desire to purge law of international implications may be linked as well to the ardent nationalism Dicey held in the political world; the Union not only fulfilled his political hopes but in this case permeated his legal philosophy. Supranational elements in law had no validity whatever for him.

Dicey recognized the main defect of the "positive method" to be the simplistic treatment accorded common principles governing the extraterritorial acknowledgment of rights. Yet he determined to ex-cise the doctrine of comity from conflict of laws for two reasons: first, it encouraged the idea that foreign laws were valid only at the

89. Rait, *Memorials*, p. 125.
90. Albert Venn Dicey, *Lectures on the Relation between Law and Public Opinion in England during the Nineteenth Century*, p. 363.
91. *Conflict of Laws*, pp. 15–20.

discretion of judges; second, it confused the content of law with the reasons for adopting specific rules of law.[92] Despite its admitted shortcomings, "the positive method is the mode of treating the rules of private international law which ought to be adopted by anyone who endeavors to deal with them as a branch of the law of England."[93] His book embodied this distinctive jurisprudence, succeeding beyond his dreams.

The reaction to *Conflict of Laws* was immediate and overwhelmingly favorable, the book quickly taking its place among the classic works of English law. Sir Frederick Pollock wrote to him: "I think it will be the work of authority (so far as any new book can be authoritative) for our time at any rate, and fully justifies the great amount you have put into it. The Introduction pleases me greatly: I only wish you could have developed it more. In particular I rejoice in your summary abolition of that confusing term *comity*."[94] Pollock was no ardent Austinian, but he valued the service Dicey performed in clarifying the basic concepts essential for advance in the field: "I wish Dicey had more sense of history: he is not clear of the damnable heresies of Austin. But it will be a most useful book."[95] Geldart, Dicey's successor as Vinerian professor, provided the best account of the influence Dicey exerted: "He has not only reduced to order one of the most intricate and technical branches of our law, and illuminated it with an unrivalled wealth of comment and illustration, but he has exerted a potent influence on its development."[96]

As with other basic textbooks, Dicey on conflicts has acquired a life of its own beyond the years of the original author. The initial Dicey text has been revised and edited under the direction of J. H. C. Morris to keep it abreast of modern legal developments, ensuring its continued authority.[97] The influence of Dicey on this branch of law is difficult to exaggerate. In England the effect of his

92. J.-G. Castel, *Conflict of Laws*, p. 28.

93. *Conflict of Laws*, p. 20.

94. Pollock to Dicey, 16 September 1896, General Manuscripts 508(3), Glasgow University Library. Italics in the original.

95. Pollock to Holmes, 2 October 1896, in *Holmes-Pollock Letters*, 1: 71.

96. W. M. Geldart, *Legal Personality*, pp. 4–5.

97. J. H. C. Morris, general editor, *Dicey and Morris on the Conflict of Laws*.

writing on judicial decisions has been "considerable."[98] Through his French colleague Antoine Pillet, himself a noted authority whom Dicey described as a genius,[99] the codification of law by Dicey made general principles of English law available to civil lawyers without examining a large number of cases. In the United States his book made a "profound impression," with American practice copying many of Dicey's principles.[100] Current textbooks, even when rejecting or correcting Dicey's rules, prove his enduring influence. As R. H. Graveson has concluded:

> This was a remarkable book in at least three respects: First, its appearance as a general and comprehensive treatment of a relatively new subject expressed in the dogmatic form of a digest of principles and rules had the greatest influence on the course of judicial decision, for it satisfied urgent needs of its time, those for rationalisation of the system and proposals for its development. Secondly, the book is notable for its original aim of applying equally to the American as to the English conflict of laws. It is an example of the community of the common law. . . .
> Thirdly, Dicey in a page and a half states six general principles under which he brings the entire *Digest* of some eight hundred pages.[101]

This achievement was the more remarkable when set against his lack of enthusiasm for the work itself.

The publication of *Conflict of Laws* freed Dicey to seek another topic of scholarly attention, and with the political scene dominated by a Unionist government, he had ample opportunity. Soon thereafter he delivered the lectures that formed the basis of his book on law and opinion in nineteenth-century England. His conclusions have stirred controversy ever since.

98. R. H. Graveson, *The Conflict of Laws,* p. 30.
99. Dicey to Holmes, 2 June 1898, Holmes Papers.
100. Hessel E. Yntema, "Dicey: An American Commentary," p. 2.
101. R. H. Graveson, "Philosophical Aspects of the English Conflict of Laws," pp. 342–43.

CHAPTER EIGHT

THE LAWYER AS HISTORIAN:

LAW AND OPINION

IMMEDIATELY AFTER the success of *Conflict of Laws*, with that intellectual curiosity that was evident throughout his life, Dicey cast about for a suitable scholarly topic to pursue. Because the Harvard lectures followed so closely, historians have erroneously assumed that the topic of law and public opinion always fascinated Dicey, and that the 1898 lectures climaxed a long period of interest in this subject. In fact the opposite was true. In 1897 Dicey had decided to make the comparative study of constitutions the next book he would write.[1] He took special interest in delineating the "spirit of constitutions" as illustrated by such criteria as: (1) the relation of the courts and executive or courts and the legislature, (2) the conception of administrative law, (3) relations between church and state, (4) and perhaps the definition of individual freedom as opposed to the idea of the state. He confessed to Bryce that the project had not started well because of his inability to define exactly what made up the spirit of a constitution. His provisional definition—that the spirit of any constitution best expressed itself in the tacit assumptions of a specific era that were not the assumptions made by another generation—did not fully satisfy. For a lawyer who prided himself on clarity of expression, the inability to define the essence of his new project troubled his analytic sense. Research into constitutional topics never really began, making Dicey susceptible to suggestions about more malleable topics.

To the intellectually becalmed Dicey, President Charles Eliot of Harvard suggested in the fall of 1897 that he present a lecture series under the auspices of the Harvard Law School.[2] On numerous occasions since 1870 Dicey had mentioned a return journey to the United States, but the continuing poor health of his wife made it

1. Dicey to Bryce, 16 March 1897, Bryce Papers.
2. Ibid., 24 November 1897, ibid.

impossible for the couple to consider the undertaking. Dicey secured the necessary leave from his academic duties, and although Mrs. Dicey could not accompany him, he began planning seriously his visit to Harvard. At the outset of 1898 his formal acceptance of Eliot's offer completed arrangements.[3] As the trip grew closer, he looked forward to the chance to renew old friendships.

The role of Eliot in the genesis of these lectures was more than ceremonial, for he suggested to Dicey that they might cover the connection between law and public opinion in the nineteenth century. Dicey appreciated this advice, for he had considered fleetingly the development of English law for that period as his next project.[4] The final choice of topic came at Eliot's behest, with Dicey recognizing a good subject when he saw one. Proof of Dicey's gratitude may be seen in the elaborate care he took in wording the dedication to Eliot of the subsequent book.[5] This was a small price for the aid Eliot had given to the conception of the work.

Dicey started his preparations promptly, but the elementary state of the lectures may be gauged from Dicey's query to Holmes whether Harvard possessed the Law Reports, the primary source for legal research.[6] The time available to Dicey before he delivered the lectures was very limited. He gave the lectures in October and November 1898, often preparing the final version shortly before he gave them. The book based on the Harvard lectures did not appear until 1905. There can be little doubt that the original talks embodied Dicey's conclusions, not to say prejudices, while the intervening seven years afforded him the opportunity to search for the evidence to support his assertions. He admitted that he wrote the lectures while in New England,[7] a process hardly conducive to sophisticated research. Thus, he was completely honest when he wrote in the Preface to *Law and Opinion* that the book was not a work of research.[8] The conclusions came first, then came the research.

Public opinion was not a topic completely foreign to him, for over

3. The invitation from Eliot to Dicey was dated 7 January 1898; Dicey replied on 7 February 1898, Eliot Papers.
4. Dicey to Eliot, 24 June 1898, Eliot Papers.
5. Dicey to Bryce, 18 July 1904, Bryce Papers.
6. Dicey to Holmes, 2 June 1898, Holmes Papers.
7. Dicey to Mrs. Dicey, 2 November 1898, in Rait, *Memorials*, p. 160.
8. *Law and Opinion*, p. viii.

the years he had written occasional pieces on the subject. Perhaps the best example was a four-part article Dicey published in the *Nation* in 1884.[9] In this he vented his distrust of the emotional nature of public opinion, which was an obstacle, as he surmised, to the rational decision-making of the educated classes who should dominate English society. The interesting aspect of this article was Dicey's recognition, at this early date, that in the eyes of many the state was a proper instrument to redistribute wealth. Therefore, he argued that this fundamental idea of socialism, as he conceived it, had touched the conscience of the wealthy. Ideas that in 1848 every educated man of common sense had rejected now in 1884 had revolutionized English opinion. Dicey perceived that the policy of minimizing state interference had ceased to be a tenet of either the Liberal or Conservative party. These observations were important, because they previewed a major thesis of *Law and Opinion* more than twenty years before its publication, lending weight to the argument that the 1898 lectures embodied Dicey's preconceived notions. Since the book examined the history of opinion, any consideration must evaluate his qualifications to write history.

The problem of Dicey's ability as historian merits close scrutiny, for it will play an important part in the interpretation of *Law and Opinion*. His work for the *Nation* in the 1870s included reviews of such historians as Froude, Freeman, Buckle, and Motley, so to this period attention must be turned first. For Dicey, already committed to the Austinian task of deducing fundamental principles upon which to base a body of knowledge, history's purpose was to uncover historical laws. In denouncing Froude and Freeman he wrote:

> These writers have neither of them any interest in or any comprehension of the view of history which considers the growth of society to depend upon fixed laws or principles. This view, no doubt, has been the subject of gross exaggeration, and it is, to say the least, extremely doubtful whether a single principle has yet been ascertained which can even metaphorically be termed a historical law. Yet erroneous and premature as have been most of the theories already started, no man can

9. Albert Venn Dicey, "The Social Movement in England," *Nation* 38 (10 January 1884): 29–30. This first part was most important.

believe that really great historians will not always attempt to deduce from past events the general principles on which their course has depended. Characteristically enough, both the writers under review utterly neglect the generalizations of political economy, which certainly throw light on some of the most perplexed enquiries as to human progress.[10]

On the same theme, in an attempt to preserve the reputation of Buckle, Dicey praised him for the effort "to make history something more than a chaotic mass of anecdotes" and the concern that "human actions must be at last made the subject of general rules, principles, or laws."[11] This desire for scientific certitude in history appeared as well in his division of labor with Oscar Browning, when both examined in constitutional history at the University of London in 1883. Allowing Browning free rein in historical questions, Dicey took the law for his province, posing "questions each of which admits of a definite answer," as if legal questions alone had that quality and historical questions did not.[12] His belief in the inability of history to provide unassailable truths made the discipline repugnant to his mind.

On another occasion Dicey discussed his understanding of what he termed the classical and modern theories of history. The classical theory he defined as an art in which the primary function of the historian was the narration of events to illustrate the historical laws he had discovered.[13] A great piece of historical writing, he wrote, is a work of art "deriving at least half its merits from the beauties of its style and the careful arrangement of its parts." Later, Dicey added that "the first of all traits by which historical talent is marked is the capacity for narrative."[14] He subscribed to this theory in preference to the modern practice, which he defined as the historian immersing his reader in a mass of documents and letting the mate-

10. Albert Venn Dicey, "Two Historical Essayists," *Nation* 13 (14 December 1871): 387.

11. Albert Venn Dicey, "Mr. Buckle," *Nation* 16 (17 April 1873): 271.

12. Dicey to Browning, 17 November 1883, Browning Papers.

13. Albert Venn Dicey, "Motley's Life of Barneveld," *Nation* 18 (7 May 1874): 301.

14. Albert Venn Dicey, "Seeley's Life and Times of Stein," *Nation* 29 (4 September 1879): 159.

rial speak for itself.[15] The necessity of filling the text with original documents sacrificed lucidity. For the historian accuracy was essential; but research, in the Rankean sense of strict fidelity to the sources, was not. He believed that clear organization of known facts had fulfilled the task of the historian. Because history was essentially artistic in nature, and certainly not as scientific as the law, the best historical writing was impressionistic and did not attain the certitude possible in legal studies.

These theories about historical study, first stated when he was a young man, remained his throughout his life. In supporting the candidacy of Samuel Rawson Gardiner for the chair at Oxford vacated by the death of Freeman, Dicey added his reservations: "Gardiner's two defects as an historian are want of literary power as a narrator, & I think want of insight into the possible wickedness of human nature."[16] He also criticized the alleged parochial concerns of historians; about Freeman, for instance, he wrote:

> His utter absence of interest in matters even in his own line which did not come within his scope was very curious. He was quite capable, for example, of understanding law; but he never seemed to me to see that the law of a country, & especially of a country like England, was part of its history. All of us have very marked limitations of interest. I am quite aware that these limitations in my own case, for example, are excessive. But there was something peculiar & very hard to define in the way in which Freeman turned aside from certain aspects even of history. I think, for example, he would have admitted the importance of economical conditions, but I don't think he felt any real interest in economic questions as they bear upon history.[17]

And as a final statement on the value of historical research Dicey wrote in admiration of Goldwin Smith's *United Kingdom:*

> I am glad to see a practical protest against the idea that an historian is mainly a glorified antiquarian whose one vocation is to hunt up new facts and who is neither justified in using the results obtained by his predecessors, nor bound to show a power

15. Dicey, "Motley's Life of Barneveld," p. 301.
16. Dicey to Bryce, 23 March 1892, Bryce Papers.
17. Ibid., 22 June 1892, ibid.

of grasping facts as a whole and narrating them with clearness. . . . I ought to add that in my own mind, whatever exaggerations one may be guilty of in public controversy, I don't for a moment underrate research. It is, of course, absolutely necessary to the progress of knowledge. All I really maintain is that research is not everything. It is equally necessary for a good historian to be able to grasp results of other people's labours and to express these results with clearness and force.[18]

Those elements of the historian's craft he praised—organization, expression, and generalization—and those he despised—antiquarianism and narrowness of vision—balanced one another. Dicey accepted the utility of history to the extent that it reinforced his personal values; when it failed to do so, he rejected history as any guide to the past. The law had trained him to regard human experience as divisible into two categories: guilty or innocent, true or false. History demanded that many gray areas of life must be recognized in which neat categorization was impossible. Dicey found intellectual solace in giving himself over entirely to positions he had taken. The inability of history to suit his either/or demands represented one aspect of his disillusionment with the discipline.

Dicey never abandoned the search for the magic formula of a few substantial rules underlying human history that might satisfy his craving for absolute certitude. In a piece on Blackstone he praised the commentator for supplying only the amount of historical background necessary for understanding, not succumbing to the temptation of inundating the reader with documents. As Dicey put it: "He always remembered that he was a teacher of law, and neither a legal dogmatist nor a legal antiquarian."[19] The greatness of Blackstone as a teacher of law lay in his abstraction of principles, then their forceful exposition, a methodology Dicey emulated as much as possible. Therefore, he concluded that history should kindle interest in "the principles by which these events have been regulated and of the general conclusions which they suggest."[20] Once the laws of history had been ascertained, the historian should arrange the past into a coherent pattern for the benefit of his readers.

18. Ibid., 11 January 1900, in Rait, *Memorials*, p. 181.
19. Albert Venn Dicey, "Blackstone," *Nation* 65 (14 October 1897): 295.
20. Albert Venn Dicey, "How Ought History to Be Taught at a University," *Nation* 82 (10 May 1906): 389.

Since history provided equivocal answers to the enduring questions of existence, as Dicey believed the law did not, the value of history for him sank in proportion to its ambivalence.

The strongest statement by Dicey on the utility of history came in an unpublished lecture of 1890 given at the Liverpool Institute.[21] Proponents of history, he maintained, cited the prophetic value of history in the sense that by its study one solves the problems of the future. Worldly common sense, however, suggested that "history is no better than an old Almanack." Were men restricted to the conclusions either of learned pedantry or of cynical scepticism? For the answer to this question, Dicey quoted Burke: "The principles of true politics are those of morality enlarged."[22] Dicey proposed therefore to distinguish in what sense history might be acceptable as a guide to politics. His preoccupation with history exclusively as politics was itself revealing.

Dicey spent the lecture demonstrating that, in most cases, history had no value at all. He rejected emphatically the idea that history presented a set of precedents to which politicians might turn for guidance as lawyers looked to cases. The latter formed an exact science, whereas the former did not. To perceive the resemblance between past and future, he argued, the individual needed insight into the contemporary scene; but this insight, when it existed, was itself the best introduction to politics. It could not be acquired by a study of the past, though it might be strengthened thereby. Analogies between past and present were shallow, therefore the more misleading for their superficiality.[23] This judgment led Dicey to dismiss the contribution of history to human affairs. Dicey decided that "the more profoundly you studied history, the less inclined you were to use it either as a collection of precedents or a basis for prediction."[24] Because no rules governed history, it suffered in comparison to other exact sciences: "We cannot use History as setting certain laws."[25] He sought its help to reinforce his own beliefs, and when that aid was not forthcoming, Dicey ignored it.

21. Albert Venn Dicey, "History and Politics," General Manuscripts 192, Glasgow University Library.
22. Ibid., p. 2.
23. Ibid., p. 4.
24. Ibid., p. 13.
25. Albert Venn Dicey, "History," p. 193.

This disdain for history invites comparison with the attitude of fellow lawyer and contemporary, Frederic Maitland. In 1896, after the publication of *Conflict of Laws*, Dicey received the following apologia from Maitland:

> The only direct utility of legal history (I say nothing of its thrilling interest) lies in the lesson that each generation has an enormous power of shaping its own law. I don't think that the study of legal history would make men fatalists; I doubt it would make them conservatives: I am sure that it would free them from superstitions and teach them that they have free hands. I get more and more wrapped up in the middle ages but the only utilitarian justification that I ever urge, . . . is that if history is to do its liberating work it must be as true to fact as it can possibly make itself, and true to fact it will not be if it begins to think what lessons it can teach.[26]

Since Dicey believed the only function of history to be the teaching of conservative lessons for the present, it was not surprising that Dicey should disregard this plea. After a testimonial to the vigor of Maitland's lectures, Dicey wrote of the man now recognized as the greatest of English legal historians: "His results might easily be stated with greater clearness & his antiquarian researches have little more to do with law than with theology—perhaps not so much."[27] This characteristic lack of interest in what the law had been, so common to Victorian lawyers, and the fixation with what the law was at the moment illustrated the chasm between the two men. In fairness, Dicey eventually conceded the superior gifts of Maitland, eulogizing him in this fashion: "I never met with a learned man who less oppressed one with his learning: I do not know anyone who can pretend to fill his special place."[28] In 1909 Dicey asked the *Spectator* to let him review Maitland's *Equity* for the purpose of "expressing my intense admiration for the man & his work."[29] Maitland, the lawyer turned historian, made the transition bril-

---

26. Maitland to Dicey, fall 1896, General Manuscripts 508(14), Glasgow University Library.

27. Dicey to Bryce, 24 November 1897, Bryce Papers.

28. Ibid., 23 December 1906, ibid.

29. Dicey to Strachey, 29 September 1909, Strachey Papers.

liantly; Dicey, with his unsophisticated understanding of history, never duplicated that feat.

Only once did Dicey attempt to resolve a historical problem using the tools of the historian. He tried to show that Pitt's prophecy of Napoleon's ultimate defeat after the fall of Ulm lacked historical proof.[30] This essay proved a dismal failure, as a number of discussants agreed that Dicey had not convincingly argued in behalf of his position. Even on this specific point Dicey had not undertaken intensive research. The result was disastrous; as one of his critics wrote: "Now, if Professor Dicey had investigated this story in accordance with true historical methods, he would scarcely have been content to base all these suppositions upon the files of the *Times* newspaper and upon a printed diary."[31] The thorough drubbing he received confirmed Dicey in the opinion that the historical method resulted in trivial pedantry. He did not repeat the experiment.

After this experience Dicey never deceived himself that he had mastered the historian's skills. For instance, he admitted to Bryce: "I do not possess the gifts required for historical research, still less have I ever pursued it."[32] In reference to *Law and Opinion*, he commented upon Maitland's praise of the book: "I was constantly touched by his appreciation of a work such as Law & Opinion which was in such a different line from his own labours & must have seemed to him, *rightly eno' so deficient in research.*"[33] *Law and Opinion* was therefore, by the testimony of the author himself, not the result of historical research in any sense. In addition Dicey never believed himself a repository of historical information. After the death of Freeman, he recalled: "It often amused me to see his absolute refusal to recognize the fact that my own historical knowledge is vague, &, on most periods very slight."[34] There is no evidence Dicey ever made an attempt to remedy that deficiency.

The net result of his attitude toward history was a hostility to what he called the historical method, which emerged in *Law and Opinion*. The last section of the text contained an attack on the historical spirit and its destructive consequences for the England of

30. Albert Venn Dicey, "Was Pitt a Prophet?," pp. 305–14.
31. *Contemporary Review*, 70 (October 1896): 588.
32. Dicey to Bryce, 14 June 1916, Bryce Papers.
33. Ibid., 23 December 1906, ibid. Italics added by the author.
34. Ibid., 23 March 1892, ibid.

1905.[35] Dicey argued that historical research had dampened the ardor for reform, consequently the zeal for human improvement had diminished. He specified the effect of Sir Henry Maine's work, which had undermined the faith in legislation so central to Benthamism. Further, Maine had been, through his historical approach, the foremost critic of Austin's analytic jurisprudence, and so Dicey had another reason to oppose the impact of Maine's writings. The historical method had combined also with the idea of nationalism to the detriment of good government. The narrow nationalism prevalent on the Continent in 1905, so opposed to the faith of the Old Mortality Society, had produced racial divisions instead of an atmosphere congenial to utilitarian law reform: "Here, in short, the historical spirit unites disastrously with the apotheosis of instinct."[36] This realization, in view of the hopes he had once entertained for the moral improvement promised by nationalism, pained him deeply. The blame was easy to assign: "The historical spirit, therefore, in giving prominence to the idea of nationality has told against the authority of utilitarian liberalism."[37] History had encouraged the disintegration of his ideals, and he could not bear that loss, so for that reason he consigned history to the darkness.

If Dicey could not accept the historical method, what did he put in its place? He made a radical distinction between the study of law and the study of history, writing that "it is scarcely possible to treat law at the same moment from the position of an historian and from the position of an analytical jurist."[38] The investigation of law demanded a dichotomy between the purposes of history and jurisprudence. Only Maitland had transcended the chasm between the two disciplines: "In Maitland we observe for once the union of talents which it is generally felt can hardly co-exist—the logic of law and the spirit of historical investigation."[39] In writing *Law and Opinion*, whatever else he may have intended, Dicey planned the book to be unlike the historical works he so often denounced. The unhis-

35. *Law and Opinion*, pp. 455–62.
36. Ibid., p. 461.
37. Ibid., p. 462.
38. Albert Venn Dicey, "Digby on the History of English Law," *Nation* 21 (9 December 1875): 374.
39. Albert Venn Dicey, "Professor Maitland," *Nation* 91 (29 September 1910): 293.

torical assumptions of Dicey have been noted but not pursued by other writers.[40] Dicey followed the customary (for him) procedure of approaching his topic from the legal standpoint so long dominated by his allegiance to the legal philosophy of John Austin. Of the methodology he had made his own he wrote: "The analytical method . . . has no connection with historical inquiry or research, which it practically discourages or excludes."[41] *Law and Opinion* was the work of a lawyer operating on premises central to Austinian jurisprudence. The implications of this fact must be considered after examination of two other characteristics of the book.

The first deals with the Diceyan definition of public opinion. By 1905, as has been seen in the last chapter, the youthful belief in democracy had turned to doubt and a pessimistic estimate of its future. Public opinion did not mean *vox populi;* he alluded frequently to the poor, honest, but ignorant British elector who could not be entrusted with the task of disentangling complex issues, then making rational decisions. When he defined public opinion, Dicey did so in Austinian terms, suggesting that the public opinion governing a country was that of the sovereign, whether the sovereign was a monarch, aristocracy, or mass of the people.[42] With the ordinary citizen dismissed as a contributor to the enlightened opinion Dicey valued, true public opinion derived from the majority "of those citizens who have at any given moment taken an effective part in public life."[43] They supplied the moral backing essential to the functioning of the legal system. As W. L. Burn wrote: "At bottom he assumed an England (perhaps an upper middle-class England) which was in control of the situation; which would be able to take its time and gradually absorb or transmute or reject the ideas presented to it."[44] This Austinian heritage has attracted little attention, overshadowed as it is by Dicey's debt to Bentham, which is evident throughout the book.

40. See Oliver MacDonagh, "The Nineteenth Century Revolution in Government," p. 55; and J. A. G. Griffith, "The Law of Property (Land)," in Morris Ginsberg, ed., *Law and Opinion in England in the 20th Century,* p. 118.

41. *Law and Opinion,* p. 411.

42. Ibid., p. 10.

43. Ibid.

44. W. L. Burn, "The Conservative Tradition and Its Reformulations," in Ginsberg, ed., *Law and Opinion in the 20th Century,* p. 46.

Dicey never tired of proudly proclaiming himself an "unrepentant Benthamite" who persevered in the faith of his youth through all vicissitudes. He divided his loyalty to Bentham into three separate areas. In the field of law, where he possessed greatest expertise, appreciation of the Benthamite contribution knew no bounds: "The history of modern English law is the history of a gigantic revolution produced by the ideas of one man."[45] In this area Dicey was at his best, capable of such breadth of view that he admired equally Bentham the legal reformer and Blackstone the object of Bentham's scorn. About Bentham the legislator Dicey wrote that "the peculiarity of Bentham's genius lies in the fact that he perceived that legislation was an art, and brought to the art of legislation that kind of inventive talent and resource which is generally applied to the prosecution of scientific discovery, or to the improvement of mechanical inventions."[46] As a faithful observer of public affairs since 1850, Dicey could legitimately claim some competency in assessing the impact of Benthamite ideas. When it came to the connection of Bentham with laissez-faire, there is no evidence Dicey ever made a serious study of economics.[47] Belief in laissez-faire and free trade did not result from reflection on his part. Discussion of economic problems rarely rose above the level of the platitudes he had recited since undergraduate days. The essential point is that in *Law and Opinion* when Dicey discussed Benthamism as law reform, he had a valid claim to the attention of readers; with Benthamism as legislative technique, he possessed some grounds for putting forward his views; with Benthamism as laissez-faire, he had no competence at all.

In his private correspondence Dicey invariably discussed Bentham as law reformer, proof that Bentham attracted him mainly for his contributions in this area. During the writing of *Law and Opinion* Dicey wrote: "No merely 'chirpy old gentleman' ever produced anything like the effect of Bentham. Nor do I think it matters much that his philosophy is open to obvious criticism & his theory of life imperfect & narrow. What he really did was to take the received &

45. Albert Venn Dicey, "Modern English Law," *Nation* 23 (2 November 1876): 273.
46. Albert Venn Dicey, "Bentham," *Nation* 27 (5 December 1878): 352.
47. Albert Venn Dicey, "Sidgwick's Methods of Ethics," *Nation* 22 (9 and 16 March 1876): 162–63, 180–81.

in the rough sound views as to human welfare prevalent in England
& insist that law should be systematically and in that sense scientifically made subservient to the production of such welfare or
rather the production of the conditions which produce it."[48] The
roots of Dicey's affection for Bentham lay in esteem for his law
reform activities. It is worth noting as well that dissatisfaction with
Bentham's philosophy did not alienate Dicey. After the publication
of the book, Dicey penned this magisterial judgment about the importance of Bentham:

> How far was a man who gives his name to a movement in
> reality of great influence on the course of the movement? My
> answer in the case of Bentham is this. If he had never existed,
> many of the changes he & his school advocated would (ere this)
> have taken place. This holds I fancy of the intellectual or moral
> leader of every great movement, even of Xianity itself. Then too
> it is the inevitable tendency of all of us to identify a general
> movement of thought with some man who gave his name to it.
> From what I have read, as an ignoramus, & from what I have
> heard definitely said by Huxley, I infer that Bacon did a good
> deal to preach belief in science but did in reality little to pro-
> mote it.
>
> But when these & the like reflections are taken into account,
> I deliberately think that at the present day, we are more likely
> to underrate than to overrate the influence of Bentham. A man
> is sometimes best understood from his failures. . . . The point
> on which I want in this matter to insist is that Bentham pos-
> sessed two very rare qualities. He had the gifts of an inventory.
> He persuaded his generation or rather the best men of it that
> laws could be systematically reformed on distinct principles
> with a view to the public good & further e.g. as to procedure
> thought out the steps by which this could be done. Suppose
> even that his views of public good were erroneous or, as I should
> suppose imperfect, consider how few have been the cases in
> which the preachers of law reform have thought out even a
> tolerable system. If a man of Bentham's talent could at the
> present day think out a systematic scheme of Socialistic reform
> or innovation. Suppose he had made himself a master of the

48. Dicey to Norton, 19 March 1901, Norton Papers.

existing law of England. Suppose he had preached his doctrine for 50 or 60 years. Suppose he had at last now when the world is clearly tending towards socialism created a small school of ardent disciples & gained the attention of leading politicians. His influence might, in my judgment be disastrous but would I think be enormous. And all that I have supposed is, I think, true of Bentham. . . .

Of course I entirely admit that B's work was carried on by men only indirectly influenced by him. Still I believe that his influence really was far greater than we now imagine.[49]

Here again the postulating of Bentham's influence depended upon the work as law reformer. Dicey's knowledge of the other aspects of Bentham's work suffered by comparison, it being no more than the general acquaintance of an educated Victorian gentleman.

Given this background on Dicey's view of history, public opinion, and Benthamism, the text of *Law and Opinion* proceeded logically from Dicey's intellectual and political assumptions. In the first place, the book did not result from extensive research about nineteenth-century England; it was, as Dicey wrote, a work of "inference or reflection."[50] He determined to uncover certain basic ideas by which the connection between law and public opinion might be explained. Furthermore, these primary concepts, in order to force themselves upon the reader, had to be expressed in precise aphorisms. The best example of the care Dicey took in this matter may be seen in his testing the reaction of Bryce to the following phrases: "Toryism was a reminiscence—Benthamism is a doctrine—collectivism is a hope."[51] By the time the book appeared, the attempt to summarize his division of nineteenth-century opinion had turned into: "Blackstonian Toryism was the historical reminiscence of paternal government; Benthamism is a doctrine of law reform; collectivism is a hope of social regeneration."[52] *Law and Opinion* abounded with such attempts at depicting eras in simplistic phrases, appealing in style but more misleading than informative. Finally, Dicey relied on the dogmas acquired in youth to explain the economic influence of Benthamism. Whether laissez-faire was essential

49. Dicey to Bryce, 18 August 1908, Bryce Papers.
50. *Law and Opinion*, p. viii.
51. Dicey to Bryce, 10 January 1904, Bryce Papers.
52. *Law and Opinion*, p. 69.

to Benthamism is not as important as the fact that Dicey, reared on this prevailing opinion, identified them,[53] making that a central part of his argument. This appraisal of Bentham may well be "highly idiosyncratic,"[54] but why Dicey accepted this formula should be clear; it flowed directly from the triple distinction he made in Benthamism. Dicey had embraced the same value system for half a century.

If Dicey had an imperfect grasp of what he approved, he never gave any evidence at all that he had studied in systematic fashion that which he opposed, socialism, Marxism, or any other of the philosophies he lumped together as collectivism. He readily admitted that E. L. Godkin had warned him in 1898 that he had explored insufficiently the phenomenon of collectivism; when the book appeared he conceded this ignorance had been lessened but not removed by subsequent examination.[55] He defined collectivism in such a way as to make it the antithesis of the individualism he valued so highly. Dicey showed no sensitivity to shades of opinion on the Left, as witnessed by his equation of socialism with tariff reform, whose proponents included many virulent opponents of socialism. Detailed research was not required, for he wanted the lowest common denominator among the different groups and ideas he treated.

Perhaps the incident best illustrating the social philosophy underlying *Law and Opinion* occurred in 1910 when Dicey indulged in a rare moment of introspection. He had heard from a friend who knew the poor at first hand that women who worked hard all their lives could not by age sixty save enough to retire comfortably. Thereupon he wrote to Strachey:

> If my friend is right, even as regards the mass of working women, whether ladies or servants, there seems to me a much stronger case for state aid than I hitherto believed existed. If the view on the other hand, which I have hitherto entertained, that

53. See R. L. Crouch, "Laissez-Faire in Nineteenth Century Britain," pp. 199–215, for a strong argument that a man of Dicey's background had reasonable grounds for assuming the existence of laissez-faire in mid-Victorian England.

54. S. E. Finer, "The Transmission of Benthamite Ideas 1820–1850," in Gillian Sutherland, ed., *Studies in the Growth of Nineteenth-Century Government*, p. 12.

55. Dicey to Mrs. E. L. Godkin, 9 July 1905, Godkin Papers.

men and women who have to support themselves, can by proper conduct, lay by sufficient to ensure the independence according to the scale of living to which they are accustomed for old age, then it seems to me that if you look at the matter very broadly, pauperism ought to be treated as prima facie something like a crime, i.e. the failure to perform one's full duty to the state.[56]

To the literature since the 1880s detailing the extent of poverty in England, Dicey was oblivious. The social ethics of 1860 persisted in Dicey even after the passage of a half century. Strachey wrote in reply that he had no answer, suggesting that few Englishmen retained the habit of thrift and those who did would always provide for the future.[57] Thus reassured that the old values endured, Dicey continued as serene as before in the belief that the state had no business meddling in the private affairs of its citizens.

As with many of his books, the writing required a large expenditure of energy, a problem his advancing age compounded. Dicey repeated the Harvard lectures several times at Oxford, striving for the precision he wanted. Not until 1903 did he feel confident to approach a publisher about *Law and Opinion*.[58] He had complained previously about the difficulties of reducing the lectures to written form and had not been optimistic about completing the task.[59] Even after the first chapters were at Macmillan's, his troubles did not cease. He always found the task of revision painful, especially now that it seemed fruitless: "But the result is not satisfactory; there is too much repetition; the sentences hang loosely together & they are often misarranged & I have almost an incapacity for correction."[60] Nevertheless, the book gradually took shape. Dicey remained on edge even with the manuscript safely in Macmillan's hands, lest another author publish a book similar in design to *Law and Opinion*.[61]

Typically, Dicey dreaded publication of the book. He called the

56. Dicey to Strachey, 14 March 1910, Strachey Papers.
57. Strachey to Dicey, 15 March 1910, ibid.
58. Dicey to the Macmillan Company, 3 April 1903, Macmillan Company Papers, B.M. Add. Mss. 55084.
59. Dicey to Norton, 19 March 1901, Norton Papers.
60. Dicey to Bryce, 10 January 1904, Bryce Papers.
61. Dicey to the Macmillan Company, 9 March 1905, Macmillan Company Papers, B.M. Add. Mss. 55084.

book superficial, admitting the subject needed additional research.[62] Later he compared it unfavorably to *Law of the Constitution*, terming it "not very meritorious."[63] This apprehension for the success of his serious works was not false modesty, but simply another manifestation of the curious way in which he combined diffidence in scholarship with arrogance in his political polemics. In this instance the concern was unnecessary, because, whether deserved or not, the book has attracted praise from first appearance in 1905.

It is impossible to summarize each argument Dicey advanced in *Law and Opinion*. Certain of his theses have sparked more controversy than others, so emphasis on the more influential assertions is necessary. In lecture IV Dicey reached the heart of his subject when he put forward the famous tripartite division of the nineteenth century into: old Toryism or legislative quiescence (1800–30), Benthamism or Individualism (1825–70), and Collectivism (1865–1900). The core of the book lay in the next four lectures, where he explained each category and its major characteristics. Interestingly enough, he devoted two lectures to what he detested, collectivism, and only one to the object of his affection, Benthamism. These dates, as Dicey admitted, were imprecise, but he pleaded the impossibility of fixing exact dates when a body of opinion began exerting influence.[64] Critics have often noted this indifference to precise dating of his classifications,[65] but this tendency must be understood in the context of his search for basic truths. Details simply did not mean as much to him as they have to readers.

Dicey thought that the period of old Toryism was dominated by a Blackstonian optimism that led in legal affairs to a satisfied acquiescence in the status quo. The French Revolution had caused a patriotic hostility to reform, giving rise to a reactionary Toryism exemplified by Lord Chancellor Eldon. The confluence of reaction with a contented spirit acknowledging no possibility of improvement in the British constitution postponed law reform for a generation. Many legal fictions survived into this period, lending an air of unreality to constitutional arrangements. Gradually this passion for

62. Dicey to Eliot, 25 October 1904, Eliot Papers.
63. Dicey to Bryce, 6 June 1905, in Rait, *Memorials*, pp. 189–90.
64. *Law and Opinion*, p. 66.
65. See, for example, Henry Parris, "The Nineteenth-Century Revolution in Government," pp. 24–25.

stability passed into a recognition of the need for legislative activity: "The English people had at last come to perceive the intolerable incongruity between a rapidly changing social condition and the practical unchangeableness of the law."[66] Though he credited alterations in society for the decline of old Toryism, the death blow to legislative passivity came from Benthamism with its coherent plan of law reform. The triumph of Benthamism closed the era of legislative stagnation.

With Bentham Dicey went straight to the point: "Bentham was primarily neither a utilitarian moralist nor a philanthropist: he was a legal philosopher and a reformer of the law."[67] Dicey attributed the strength of legislative utilitarianism to the belief that the end of human existence was the attainment of happiness, secured by scientific legislation. Laissez-faire, he noted, was not logically an integral part of utilitarianism, but it was the most vital part of Benthamism, supplying to law reform "its power and its character."[68] The application of laissez-faire theory attacked every restriction on human liberty that could not be justified by the principle of utility. In his retrospect on the early and mid-Victorian era, Dicey concluded that Benthamism had swept all before it. When required to explain this dominance, however, he offered such vague reasons as: utilitarianism was "in the air," or it fell in with the natural conservatism of Englishmen, or that Benthamism equaled individualism and this found its natural home in England. These answers, as critics have noted, were meaningless.[69] On the appeal of Bentham Dicey wrote: "The creed owed its power in part to the large element of truth, now much underrated, which it contained, in part to its self-consistency and to the clearness and precision of its dogmas, and in part also to the unbounded faith of its adherents."[70] Many examples followed where Benthamism had protected individual legal rights by removing archaic restrictions.

In lectures VII and VIII Dicey examined collectivism, and he had no trouble in pointing out areas where state interference had increased during the century. Collectivism undermined the principles

66. *Law and Opinion*, p. 111.
67. Ibid., p. 127.
68. Ibid., p. 147.
69. See Finer, "Transmission of Benthamite Ideas," p. 12.
70. *Law and Opinion*, p. 411.

of individualism in several ways. Tory philanthropy, because it remedied suffering through state action, led to intervention in the factory system on humanitarian grounds. The movement for factory reform led to a parliamentary clash between individualism and collectivism, and "on that field Benthamite liberalism suffered its earliest and severest defeat."[71] The working classes had abandoned Chartism, concentrating on trade unionism in the pursuit of collectivism. They now pressed for legal changes to facilitate the union of all workers in pursuit of their vision of society. New theories like Christian socialism challenged Benthamism, heralding an approaching revolution in public opinion. Even the development of the modern corporation hindered individualism, for it restricted freedom by lessening the importance of the person. The existence of large corporations had "transformed the abstract principle that all property, and especially property in land, belongs in a sense to the nation, into a practical maxim on which Parliament acts every year with the approval of the country."[72] Finally, the reform acts of 1867 and 1884 had empowered the working classes who, in a vague and indefinite manner, desired laws promoting socialism. State intervention possessed the advantage that its good results were clearly recognizable, whereas its evils were less visible. As Dicey summed up: "Few are those who realise the undeniable truth that State help kills self-help."[73]

In the analysis of collectivism Dicey stressed that it rested upon two assumptions: it denied that laissez-faire was a sound principle of legislation, and it believed in the benefits of government action in social and economic matters. In many spheres of human activity collectivists had promoted legislation to increase the responsibility of the state for the welfare of the individual. Dicey understood fully that the flow of current affairs was against him in 1905. So pervasive had collectivist ideas become that even modern individualists were socialists on some issues. The heresy flourished unchecked, with some collectivist strength, paradoxically enough, from Benthamism.

In lecture IX Dicey credited Benthamism with three major contributions to the success of socialism by 1905. He perceived that some aspects of Benthamism had fostered the very collectivism it so

71. Ibid., p. 236.
72. Ibid., p. 247.
73. Ibid., p. 256.

heartily opposed. The principle of utility when applied to the laboring classes had revolutionized social relationships, because government had previously concentrated on the prosperity of the wealthy classes. Parliamentary sovereignty provided collectivists with the legislative instrument to carry through their plans. Finally, Benthamism had made legislative activity customary, ensuring the constant extension of government activity. Utilitarianism contained despotic tendencies not noticed by its devotees of the mid-Victorian period. This prompted Dicey, who at page 170 had quoted with approval Bentham's denunciations of natural rights theory, at page 308 to reverse his ground, praising innate-rights theory as a limitation upon the despotism of the majority. Benthamites, he concluded sadly, "had forged the arms most needed by socialists."[74]

Unlike *Law of the Constitution*, which has enjoyed continuous attention because one or more of its three doctrines has seemed relevant, *Law and Opinion* caused an initial burst of enthusiasm, then faded into obscurity only to be revived after World War II, when historians sought the origins of the emerging welfare state. The book received widest praise from the generation nearest in time to the events Dicey discussed. Harold Laski, for example, gave the book highest accolades in the 1920s.[75] After the interlude of neglect Dicey assumed a greater stature for his pioneering effort: "a work of great originality, energy and imagination. It virtually uncovered and specified for the first time the developments which it attempted to explain."[76] With historians showing increased concern for the growth of government activity, Dicey became a focal point in the continuing scholarly debate about the "nineteenth-century revolution in government." *Law and Opinion* has caused more discussion since 1958 than it did in the immediate aftermath of publication.

A rehearsal for this controversy occurred in 1948, when J. B. Brebner argued that Dicey had misled two generations of historians about Bentham as an advocate of laissez-faire; in fact, Brebner posited, Bentham had propagated the collectivism Dicey hated.[77] Brebner managed this feat by ignoring Dicey's specific recognition of the

74. Ibid., p. 309.

75. Laski to Holmes, 28 July 1925, in *Holmes-Laski Letters*, 1: 771.

76. Oliver MacDonagh, *A Pattern of Government Growth, 1800–1860*, p. 324.

77. J. B. Brebner, "Laissez-Faire and State Intervention in Nineteenth-Century Britain," pp. 59–73.

collectivist debt to Bentham contained in his ninth lecture. Before long several scholars attacked Brebner's assertions and, very sensibly, concluded that in some contexts the principle of utility implied laissez-faire, while in others it supported government intervention. Dicey had admitted the ambiguous legacy of utilitarianism on this point throughout *Law and Opinion.* The book is open to criticism in many places, but Dicey on the individualist and collectivist legacy of Bentham is not one of them. Dicey's original conclusions about the connotations of utilitarianism have survived such ill-advised attacks as Brebner's.

In 1958 and 1960 articles by Oliver MacDonagh and Henry Parris in the *Historical Journal* sparked a reassessment of government development in the nineteenth century.[78] This has consisted primarily of detailed studies of individual government departments or the enforcement of legislation dealing with a particular abuse, usually to determine whether the conclusions harmonize with the MacDonagh thesis of pragmatic government growth or the Parris thesis on the enduring importance of Benthamite ideas. This process has resulted in many articles, several books, and ultimately those hallmarks of academic importance: bibliographical articles and a symposium.[79] Throughout this controversy Dicey has been the foil, the author against whom scholarly points might be made before revealing the results of new research. This phenomenon may be seen, for instance, in the statement that "while Dicey's interpretation is dead, its ghost continues to animate much of the discussion of Victorian administrative history, and his categories of discussion, with a special emphasis upon a polarised tension between 'individualism' and 'collectivism', are retained."[80] The purpose here is not analysis of the many facets of the "revolution in government" debate, nor the rescue of Dicey from his critics. However, there is a need for

78. MacDonagh, "Nineteenth-Century Revolution in Government," pp. 52–67; Parris, "Nineteenth-Century Revolution in Government," pp. 17–37.

79. I have not thought it necessary to specify the many works this description covers. Those who have followed the "revolution in government" controversy are familiar with the historiography. Those who have not would not be interested in a lengthy list of works.

80. William C. Lubenow, *The Politics of Government Growth, 1833–1848,* p. 9.

reassessment of *Law and Opinion* as it fits into the research field of Victorian administrative history; it is time to exorcise the ghost.

First of all, the "revolution in government" debate has involved increasingly technical studies of administration. It is difficult to see why this should have proceeded from *Law and Opinion*, because Dicey had not the slightest interest in administrative matters. Most scholars in this controversy have studied the passage and later history of a law: Did the statute work or how was it amended? Mac-Donagh rightly pointed out Dicey's various omissions: no public servants, no departmental reports, and no parliamentary investigations.[81] This oversight was deliberate, for he cared only for the circumstances prior to the enactment of a law. Nothing bored him more than a description of how a government department functioned. If Dicey had misled administrative historians, it is fair to say that the delusion has been perpetuated by the failure to study the man as well as the book. Administrative history must avoid *Law and Opinion*, for Dicey neither dealt with Benthamism as a problem in the history of ideas nor treated the long process of government growth as a pragmatic evolution.

Secondly, MacDonagh contended that Dicey avoided a Whig interpretation of the nineteenth century, an assertion vigorously denied by Parris: "Dicey's career as a political partisan is of the greatest relevance to an understanding of his thought."[82] Parris was correct but may be criticized for not following adequately his own insight, because he never related Dicey's political opinions to the content of *Law and Opinion*. If the central fallacy of the Whig theory of history is judging the past by contemporary standards, then Dicey stands convicted. He divided his account of Victorian public opinion on the sole criterion of the attitude displayed toward state intervention. The book contained Dicey's political testament, no more and no less. The values of 1905 intruded constantly upon the account of the Victorian era. Edwardian political battles vitiated the interpretation of Victorian history.

Law and Opinion is the work of Dicey most cited by historians, but this is unfortunate because, as the examination of his presuppositions indicated, a work of history is precisely what the book is

81. MacDonagh, "Nineteenth-Century Revolution in Government," pp. 55–56.

82. Parris, "Nineteenth-Century Revolution in Government," p. 18.

not. Yet historians have persisted in looking to the book as an accurate guide to the events it described. MacDonagh touched the crux of the matter, though in an erroneous sense, when he called it a work of imagination. Unfortunately Dicey, who possessed precious little of that commodity, did not obtain a deeper insight into his subject. Instead he constructed, deftly and with great care, an explanation conjured up from his own recollections.[83] *Law and Opinion* depicted the Victorian world as Dicey remembered it, indeed as he hoped it had been, because that portrait was crucial to his 1905 politics. Whatever the book might be, historians should not accept it as a work whose goal was historical reconstruction.

Does this mean the volume should be dismissed as without value? It still repays study by historians as a guide to aspects of late Victorian and Edwardian thought. The discussion of individualism versus collectivism has interest in the context of 1905, not the 1830s or even 1870s.[84] As a work of scholarship, because Dicey had strayed from his area of expertise, the book does not merit the praise often bestowed upon it;[85] as a revealing part of Edwardiana, it has intrinsic value, ensuring it a permanent place among the important books of that period. *Law and Opinion* should no longer suffer abuse from historians, because Dicey never intended that the book should serve as the definitive account of an administrative revolution.

Impressive proof of Dicey's contemporary political concerns appeared in the introduction to the second edition of *Law and Opinion* in 1914. He chose this method of updating the book in preference to a full revision of the text, as this suited his health better. He did this for *Law of the Constitution* as well, accounting for the long introductions to the two books in the editions of 1914 and 1915 respectively.[86] "I am quite certain that this course is the best one for me" was his verdict on this way of avoiding a tiring

83. Ibid., pp. 24–26. Parris suspected this was one answer to why Dicey had gone so far wrong, but again provided little evidence to support what were well-founded suspicions.

84. Norbert C. Soldon, "Individualist Periodicals," pp. 17–26.

85. Parris, "Nineteenth-Century Revolution in Government," has a convenient list of references at pp. 17–18.

86. Dicey to Sir Frederick Macmillan, 1 July 1912, Macmillan Company Papers, B.M. Add. Mss. 55085.

revision.[87] In June 1913 Dicey started the introduction, which took longer to complete than he had anticipated.[88] The result was a political diatribe that had not the slightest veneer of objectivity or scholarship. The most quoted portion of the 1914 introduction recorded Dicey's sad reflection that "by 1900 the doctrine of *laissez-faire*, in spite of the large element of truth which it contains, had more or less lost its hold upon the English people."[89] One after another the statutes passed by the Campbell-Bannerman and Asquith governments were subjected to the test of Diceyan laissez-faire and found wanting. Dicey denounced public opinion for its failure to adhere to the old values.

As Dicey conceived it, the 1914 introduction served as a final political statement: "I have lived on into a generation which is not my own & my last words are the voice of 1886 heard in 1913."[90] The fears of socialism were more intense as Dicey realized that each passing year repudiated more of the inheritance to which he was so emotionally attached. On another occasion he called the introduction "little else than the last thoughts of an old mid-Victorian who has survived into an age to which he does not belong, and which probably he does not understand. . . . Still I am glad to have had an opportunity of saying pretty much my last words on this topic."[91] Of course it should be added Dicey made little effort to understand current affairs, except by a stubborn fidelity to the causes of his youth.

Law and Opinion supplied the crowning touch in his own lifetime to his public standing. Earlier diffidence about the book notwithstanding, Dicey thought it "the best thing I have ever written & much more mature than *Law of the Constitution.*"[92] This proved the truth of the maxim that no man should be judge in his own cause. But Dicey was not alone in his high estimation of *Law and Opinion;* upon receipt of the second edition, Eliot called it "a first-

87. Dicey to Bryce, 30 November 1912, Bryce Papers.

88. Dicey to Macmillan, 20 June 1913, Macmillan Company Papers, B.M. Add. Mss. 55085.

89. *Law and Opinion*, 2nd ed., p. xxxi.

90. Dicey to Bryce, 21 January 1913, Bryce Papers.

91. Dicey to Lowell, 27 May 1914, Lowell Papers.

92. Dicey to Macmillan, 1 July 1912, Macmillan Company Papers, B.M. Add. Mss. 55085.

rate piece of work, well brought down to 1913."[93] The final irony, in light of the nostalgic adherence to laissez-faire throughout the book, was the grudging admission by Dicey, after the experience of World War I, that state intervention might effect reforms he had thought previously the exclusive province of laissez-faire.[94] At age eighty-three he managed a slight escape from the intellectual prison that had entrapped him all his life. This small concession came too late to affect *Law and Opinion;* it already stood as a monument to Dicey's mid-Victorian heritage.

93. Eliot to Bryce, 28 July 1914, Bryce Papers.
94. Dicey to Eliot, 14 November 1918, Eliot Papers.

CHAPTER NINE

THE DECLINE OF ENGLAND,

1899–1914

WHILE DICEY LECTURED at Harvard in the fall of 1898, he accepted a new appointment in England, one increasing his personal sense of accomplishment during years beset with bitter dissappointment: the principalship of the Working Men's College in London. He had left the college after his unsuccessful stint as lecturer there in 1866, but contact with the college had persisted by virtue of his friendship with college official Richard Litchfield and his wife Henrietta. Litchfield prevailed upon Dicey to accept the position of principal, taking office when he returned from the United States.[1] Dicey had sympathized with the goals of the college, for he believed it the best educational institution to make working men productive and independent members of society. He admired the tradition of voluntary faculty service, the inexpensive education available, and the spirit of camaraderie between teachers and students. The college, he wrote approvingly, "is grounded on the invaluable combination of self-help and mutual aid."[2] Dicey never regretted incurring this obligation, for the college amply repaid his generosity in personal satisfaction.

Prior to his appointment, the principalship had been primarily honorary, the real work of supervising the college handled by the vice-principal and bursar. Dicey could not accept this arrangement, immediately taking a personal interest in the life of the college. At the outset of his tenure Dicey undertook a course of six lectures on the rights of English citizens as well as making a sizable donation to the college's building fund. He never faltered, even in the face of increasing age, in carrying through his determination to play an

1. J. F. C. Harrison, *A History of the Working Men's College 1854–1954*, p. 153.
2. Albert Venn Dicey, "The College as It Is Now," in J. Llewelyn Davies, ed., *The Working Men's College 1854–1904*, pp. 253–54.

active role in college affairs: "I do not think that a figurehead is really beneficial in the long run to any institution. I am certain that from top to bottom in the working of the Working Men's College there should be life and energy."[3] Dicey lectured frequently at Crowndale Road, giving the benefit of his erudition to an audience who would have had no opportunity otherwise to hear an Oxford professor on a regular basis. He presided over the move of the college to its present location, never tired of writing fund solicitations on behalf of the school, and constantly beseeched his academic colleagues to present guest lectures there. All this work he performed with pleasure: "I can hardly express with sufficient strength my sense of the pleasantness & benefit to myself of my connection with W.M.C. & especially of our friendship."[4] His leadership proved advantageous to the college as well as himself.

Inevitably, after the resignation of the Vinerian Chair in 1909, Dicey faced leaving the Working Men's College as well. In early 1911 he broached the possibility of retirement to college authorities on the grounds that at his age he could not become more vigorous and did not wish to harm the future of the college by overstaying his welcome. "Resignation," he wrote, "has always a touch of sadness. This is inevitable, but surely there is a time to retire as a time to come forward, and there are few thoughts in my later life which are so pleasant to me as the memories of my connection with the W.M.C. I can without exaggeration say that they are purely happy. Very few are the occurrences in life of which one can say as much."[5] This first attempt at resignation failed, for Dicey and his wife reconsidered after entreaties from college officials, and it was postponed temporarily. Dicey took this opportunity to advise, while the college searched for a successor, that the new principal ought to "do as least as much as I have been able to do for the W.M.C. & if possible more."[6] The retirement of Sir Charles Lucas from the Colonial Office ended the search sooner than anticipated; Lucas had served as vice-principal of the college from 1897 to 1903, thus making an ideal candidate. Dicey urged that Lucas should be approached, as he

3. Dicey to Sir Charles P. Lucas, n.d. 1912, in Rait, *Memorials,* pp. 176–77.
4. Dicey to Jacob, 3 June 1910, Working Men's College MSS.
5. Ibid., 31 January 1911, ibid.
6. Ibid., 13 February 1911, ibid.

was in every way qualified for the principalship.[7] At the close of his valedictory address he summed up his relationship with the college: "I have no belief that what I gave you was particularly good, but I always tried to give you my best."[8]

Dicey retained a great affection for the Working Men's College, for his role in its welfare had given him a new interest in life: "That was Mrs. Dicey's view, and the interest was no doubt deeper and happier for the knowledge that she shared it with him to the full. The College became the child of his later years. It was never out of his mind."[9] On the occasion of a contribution to the Maintenance Fund of the college, Dicey added: "My connexion with the institution is to me one of the most happy circumstances in my life."[10] From the college Dicey acquired new friends and a new purpose in life at a time when he needed such renewal.

If Dicey found great satisfaction in service to the college, the school profited even more from his guidance. In a testimonial dated 2 November 1912, college authorities attested to his achievement: "When you entered upon your office, the future was uncertain: you leave it amid every sign of assured and stable success."[11] His successor, Lucas, testified to the value of his personal attention to college affairs: "Not only for his addresses, shrewd intellect, but also a personality which threw itself into life and made itself one in sympathy with us."[12] Dicey's concern with the fortunes of the college was not just a sidelight to more important activities, for no matter what work he started, Dicey strove for the best performance possible. The ethic of strict application to work would accept no less. Frustrations of which he complained in other areas of his work never entered his relationship with the college; he took pride in his accomplishments, never complaining about the time he had devoted to the improvement of the college.

As far as the public issues Dicey followed were concerned, the last years of the nineteenth century found him agitated about the

7. Ibid., 5 November 1911, ibid.
8. Sir Charles P. Lucas, "Albert Venn Dicey," p. 225.
9. Sir Charles Lucas, in Rait, *Memorials*, p. 179.
10. Dicey to Jacob, 25 November 1916, Working Men's College MSS.
11. This broadside is among the Dicey materials in the Working Men's College MSS.
12. Lucas, "Dicey," p. 224.

problem of war: in one case potential, in another actual. In 1895 he had worried about the prospect of war between the United States and Great Britain over the Venezuela question. His affection for America was undiminished, so war between the two countries distressed him: "My whole mind is taken up with this terrible prospect of war with the U.S. Cleveland has contrived to commit the greatest crime of the century; and the Americans are proving, if proof is needed, that a democracy can be as tyrannical & self-willed as a King."[13] Dicey desired a treaty embodying the principles of the Monroe Doctrine in order that such a quarrel would not be repeated in the future. War between these two countries, so closely tied by bonds of language and culture, he considered unthinkable. No matter what the provocation, the United Kingdom must ensure that every step short of war would be used to resolve problems, because: "If once it begins it will soon become a war perhaps against all the world for the maintenance of the British Empire & to end it prematurely would be as great a sin as to begin it without absolute necessity."[14] In this instance war was averted, but Dicey had so feared the possibility that he took steps to forestall recurrence of Anglo-American misunderstanding.

In April 1897 he published an article calling for common citizenship between the United States and Great Britain.[15] He did not intend political unity, as neither country would consent to an abrogation of its sovereignty, but, strictly speaking, a common citizenship without further implications. The immediate consequences of this plan would, he admitted, be small, although he put faith in the indirect moral benefits likely to ensue. Common citizenship would intensify the sentiment of solidarity throughout the entire English race. The prevalence of common legal conceptions revealed to any intelligent observer the essential unity of the English-speaking people. A "reunion" of the English people would preserve the good results and undo the evils of separation. Dicey elaborated this concept in private, arguing that an *entente cordiale* if not actual alliance was imperative. Only this "may save Anglo-Saxon principles of law & liberty & nothing else will."[16] He pursued this theme with

13. Dicey to Strachey, 23 December 1895, Strachey Papers.
14. Ibid.
15. Albert Venn Dicey, "A Common Citizenship for the English Race," pp. 457–76.
16. Dicey to Bryce, 12 May 1898, Bryce Papers.

American friends, repeating his belief that the solution to global problems lay in the rule of Anglo-Saxon nations and ideals.[17] Community of interest should lead to a common policy lest the two natural allies drift into needless antagonism.

Unfortunately for Dicey, as with so many of his public calls to action, this particular plan, as he himself put it, "fell flat."[18] He admitted that the proposal for common citizenship was premature, yet contended that the English race was destined in a century or two to dominate the civilized world. He held out hope that his dream of national reunion might one day aid this process. His stay in the United States in 1898 did nothing to minimize his belief in the unity of the two countries: "My two visits have been so happy that I will not tempt fortune to spoil my recollection of the place by the failure of a third."[19] This intense desire for Anglo-American cooperation caused him to approve American expansion in the belief that domination by Anglo-Saxon nations was inevitable.[20] The purpose of this leadership was not power for its own sake, but the imparting of the blessings of English civilization: "But I am more and more convinced that to spread English ideas of law & justice is the one vocation of the English people as it will probably be our one permanent achievement."[21] Dicey was not blind to American faults, for after a decade of close surveillance of Anglo-American relations, he wrote: "Both branches of the English people seem to me to act somewhat better in foreign affairs than do Continental States. But to make up for this both branches of the English people persuade themselves that they pursue in international affairs far more disinterested principles than they in reality act up to."[22] That conclusion never shook his allegiance to the community of interest between the two nations. Dicey continued to foster better understanding on both sides of the Atlantic.

The Boer War presented him with a different set of problems. Dicey supported the war from the outset, as he had not the slightest doubt about the necessity of British participation.[23] The superior

17. Dicey to Eliot, 20 September 1898, Eliot Papers.
18. Albert Venn Dicey, "England and America," p. 441.
19. Dicey to Bryce, 29 December 1898, Bryce Papers.
20. Dicey to Norton, 19 March 1901, Norton Papers.
21. Dicey to Holmes, 3 April 1900, Holmes Papers.
22. Dicey to Bryce, 23 March 1911, Bryce Papers.
23. Dicey to Eliot, 19 December 1899, Eliot Papers.

value system of the British made the subjugation of the Boers morally justified. The war had produced a feeling of unanimity rare in England, with such backing essential lest European intervention lead to a full assault on the British Empire. Even in the beginning when the news was grave, he remained confident of ultimate success.[24] As with other causes he maintained, once he had committed himself to a definite policy, he would not tolerate dissenting arguments.

At the inception of the Boer War, for instance, Dicey began recording every bit of information he could find on "Irish Nationalists and the Transvaal War."[25] Since the Irish Question was the touchstone by which he judged all other issues, the war proved no exception. He assembled reports that Irish Nationalists opposed the war so that he might stigmatize them as traitors to the United Kingdom, unworthy of consideration by English statesmen. The response of Ulster in support of the war he regarded as justification for favoring its claims above those of the Nationalists.

His support for the war was strongest when the prospects for final victory looked dimmest. For example, Dicey took exception to a phrase in the *Spectator* that implied Britain must set a time limit to the effort against the Boers. He protested to Strachey that "this limiting the period during which we mean to fight for the maintenance of the Empire is, in my judgment a fatal error. Of course no human contest can be continued for an indefinite time. But a nation which means to win must be prepared to fight for a perfectly indefinite time."[26] He feared that enemies of Great Britain would interpret the expression as a confession of weakness. The Boer War swept away other political problems; only the Indian Mutiny, Dicey recalled, compared to it for impact on the country.[27] When British strength finally tipped the balance against the Boers, Dicey discovered an unexpected bonus of the war in the restoration of a confident national spirit. The more certain victory became, the greater his belief in its justice: "I believe the war myself to be as just as it is necessary & to bear a curious resemblance to the conflict with

24. Dicey to Godkin, 25 December 1899, Godkin Papers.
25. Dicey Notebook, f. 93.
26. Dicey to Strachey, 9 January 1900, Strachey Papers.
27. Dicey to Mrs. E. L. Godkin, 18 March 1900, Godkin Papers; Dicey to Norton, 20 March 1900, Norton Papers.

Secession."[28] However strained this analogy, the Boer War remained justified in his eyes.[29]

The long anticlimax to the Boer War did not alter that opinion, for once joined, the war for Empire must be fought to the bitter end. When stories of the suffering caused by British policy circulated in the press, Dicey dismissed them as unfair and dangerous: "There seems to be considerable risk that humane feeling about the sufferings of women & children may lead people to do a good deal of injustice to the Army, the Government, & the nation."[30] He took a hard line on peace negotiations, believing that the Boers must be crushed before terms could be discussed. Any other appraisal of the Boers was "very like the Gladstonian cant that the Parnellites were ready to be loyal to the United Kingdom."[31] The failure to achieve complete superiority left Dicey dejected, because this cheated Great Britain of the victory so richly deserved. The great moral struggle for Empire, as he saw it, petered out amidst recrimination and conditional victory. This disappointment soon gave way to an even greater crisis.

In May 1903 Joseph Chamberlain launched his campaign for tariff reform. The divisive effect of tariff reform on the solidarity of the Unionist party began, in Dicey's estimation, a series of catastrophic events in England not halted until the start of World War I. This process meant the corruption of England, reducing Dicey to the role of Cassandra lamenting the decline of the England he loved. Home Rule, tariff reform, and the growth of socialism threatened those values he held most dear. As the prospect for success of each increased, Dicey gloomily contemplated the future. The debasement of England was an integrated process for Dicey, although composed of many constituent elements. Any absolute separation of political questions must therefore be artificial. However, since the Irish Question formed the ultimate problem against which other issues paled into insignificance, the consideration of Home Rule must be postponed. Dicey found enough to worry him even without the Irish controversy.

The advent of tariff reform caused yet another major shift in his

28. Dicey to Holmes, 3 April 1900, Holmes Papers.
29. Dicey to Eliot, 17 April 1900, Eliot Papers.
30. Dicey to Strachey, 26 June 1901, Strachey Papers.
31. Ibid., 15 March 1902, ibid.

estimate of Joseph Chamberlain. Prior to 1886 Dicey had distrusted his advocacy of social reform programs as well as his disciplined political machine. After 1886 Dicey had revised his opinion in the light of Chamberlain's defense of the Union, resulting in a sympathetic judgment of his talents. As late as 1901, with the Boer War floundering in mismanagement and defeat, Dicey still had reservations, though these were now outweighed by Chamberlain's virtues: "Chamberlain has to my mind many defects as a statesman. He is rash and I have no sympathy with the sort of ideas of which his desire for an Old Age Pension scheme is an example; but I am privately coming more and more to the conclusion that he is nearly the only strong man and able administrator we have."[32] The tariff reform movement once again brought Chamberlain into Dicey's disfavor.

No single event demonstrated more clearly the central place of the Union in Dicey's political beliefs than the rapidity with which he discerned the potential disaster to Unionism posed by tariff reform and the subsequent subordination even of his free trade faith to the maintenance of the Union. Soon after Chamberlain initiated the tariff reform campaign, Dicey joined the Unionist Free Food League. The real problem, he argued, was that even a small rift in Unionist ranks might produce an electoral shift sufficient to oust the Unionist government.[33] He hoped any split in the party would be small, but this proved illusory.[34] In an article for *Contemporary Review* Dicey made his position clear: he was still a free trader and could not accept tariff reform, the new fiscal policy had split Unionist followers, and it had given the Liberals an issue around which they could rally.[35] To many Unionists besides himself, Dicey wrote, the maintenance of the Union outweighed strict adherence to free trade. The Union was again in danger, for with the Unionist party in disarray, Home Rule might revive with an even greater chance of success. This risk was too dangerous to compensate for the theoretical advantages, as yet unproven, of tariff reform. The alternatives facing Unionism he detailed in a letter to Strachey:

32. Ibid., 1 July 1901, ibid.
33. Dicey to Maxse, 11 August 1903, Maxse Papers.
34. For an account of the progressively worsening fortunes of Unionist free traders, see Richard A. Rempel, *Unionists Divided*.
35. Albert Venn Dicey, "To Unionists and Imperialists," pp. 305–17.

Now, as in 1886, I am convinced that the most important thing is to preserve the Union with Ireland and at any cost to maintain in Ireland the supremacy of the law. Economical legislation is, compared with this object, a matter of great, but of secondary, importance. The evil of keeping the present Government in office or of returning a Unionist majority at the next general election is the encouragement which will thereby be given to a policy of Protection. The evils, on the other hand, which flow from turning out the present Ministry and putting the leaders of the Opposition into office are these:

(1) The encouragement of the agitation for Home Rule. . . .
(2) The sacrifice of the best chance that the Land Act may prove a success. . . .
(3) The cessation of any strenuous effort to enforce in Ireland obedience to the law.
(4) The reversal of our policy in South Africa. . . .
(5) Concessions to the conspiracy of the Passive Resisters. . . .

In the dogma that Home Rule is dead I have no belief whatever. The matter is one to which I have given sixteen years careful consideration, and on this point I feel some confidence in my own judgment.

I am of course perfectly aware, not having forgotten 1885, that concessions to Irish Nationalism may come from Unionists. This is a peril on which we must constantly keep our eyes fixed. The best way to avoid it appears to me, as at present advised, to be, to keep in office a Unionist Government as long as we can, and to return, if it be possible, a Unionist majority to the next Parliament, and as a Free Trader I desire that among the majority there should be as many Free Trade Unionists as possible.

I have purposely, however, avoided the merely economic question. It is not one on which I am specially competent to judge, and it seems to me that where honest experts are disagreed persons who are not experts must think and speak with a certain amount of diffidence.[36]

From this point forward, though he did not abandon free trade, he consistently urged compromise on the economic issue upon the warring factions as the safest guarantee of the union.

36. Dicey to Strachey, 28 October 1903, in Rait, *Memorials,* pp. 116–17.

For the next two years Dicey watched with mounting dismay the weariness of the Balfour government. The real problem lay in the fact that neither of the two parties represented the bulk of the electorate.[37] The Unionist government did not satisfy the belief in free trade to which Dicey assumed the nation adhered; the Liberal opposition did not represent the national faith in the maintenance of the Union. The result was political confusion: the remedy was that rarity in politics, plain speaking. Only the Unionist free traders had made their position clear, the Cabinet and opposition had kept silent about their future plans. Open and honest policies alone could save the situation if the political deadlock might be eliminated. Dicey misjudged badly the inroads tariff reform had made upon the Unionist party, overestimating the strength of Unionist free traders. The Unionist debacle at the election of 1906 showed how essential compromise on economic issues was to the strength of Unionism. The advent of the Campbell-Bannerman government prompted a greater effort by Dicey to secure conciliation within Unionist ranks.

Free trade Unionists confronted the dilemma of which issue to emphasize: free trade vs. protection or the Union vs. Home Rule. Dicey had not the slightest doubt, constantly protecting the Union against the faint of heart who might compromise on that issue in order to save free trade. His staunch Unionist friend Arthur Elliot illustrated this problem when he wrote in early 1906: "As to politics, we both agree that the two causes—The Union and Free Trade have to be maintained. This we ought to be able to effect in spite of rival ambitions, and rival caucuses."[38] Dicey could not accept that equation of the two issues. Free traders advocated their cause too fervently and lost sight of the primacy of the Union, so Dicey frequently reminded his correspondents that Unionism without maintenance of the Union was an empty formula: "It must in my judgment be placed above all other political considerations."[39] This advice fell on deaf ears, for few of his political friends matched Dicey in the absolute priority he accorded the Union. A stranger to the world of politics, he counseled repeatedly that Unionists must forego every other project in the name of a higher loyalty to the Union. The potential disaster if they did not close ranks caused him

37. Albert Venn Dicey, "The Paralysis of the Constitution," p. 311.
38. Elliot to Dicey, 12 February 1906, Elliot Papers.
39. Dicey to Elliot, 12 June 1907, ibid.

no end of despair: "I own I have little hope of the Union being maintained unless Unionists of every class are willing to make concessions even on matters upon which they feel strongly."[40] He preached the theme of compromise to any Unionist who would listen as the only successful resistance possible to the fatal policy of Home Rule: "It is not possible to revert to the simple Unionism of 1886, and on the subject of Free Trade or Protection let each man and each constituency follow his own ideas."[41] For the next years he cared little about the economic issues of the tariff reform debate, as his only interest lay in preserving whenever possible unity within the Unionist party.

By 1909, after the Lloyd George budget had raised political temperatures, Dicey thought more than ever that Unionist solidarity alone could prevent the destruction of Britain. The weakness of free traders in the Unionist party caused him to urge upon his free trade friends the necessity of concessions: "For a chance of success Unionists must act together as one united party. This in effect as things stand now means that Free Trade Unionists must at the next general election give in to Tariff Reformers. I am prepared to do this in order to avert Home Rule & to resist the encroachments of the H.C. But are the mass of Free Trade Unionists?"[42] Strachey replied that tariff reformers had become so confident of their ultimate success that they would seek unity of the party by the surrender of the free traders.[43] Undaunted by this forecast, Dicey pressed ahead with his campaign for party unity:

> The one essential thing is to reunite the Unionist party. There is nothing except Unionism itself, & the giving up of Woman Suffrage on wh. I am not prepared to make very considerable concessions. I preach as far as I can the same doctrine alike to Tariff Reformers & to Freetrade Unionists. Neither can dispense with the aid of the other & the truest sign of patriotism is willingness to surrender other ideas in order to promote union against a common danger. As a matter of wisdom Free-traders must I think recognise more than they seem to me to do

40. Ibid., 5 July 1907, ibid.
41. Ibid., 11 July 1907, ibid.
42. Dicey to Strachey, 22 July 1909, Strachey Papers.
43. Strachey to Dicey, 27 July 1909, ibid.

one or two patent facts. Whatever be the reason there is throughout the world a tendency in favour of state intervention & Socialism far stronger than anyone could have anticipated ten years ago, tho' a turn of the tide in this direction was even then discernible. . . . To come nearer home, we must admit that the distrust of state intervention wh. lies at the bottom of free trade, is not shared by the majority of the M.P.'s of whatever party or by their constituents. No working man objects to protection in his favour, tho', self interest makes him feel the objections to a tax on corn. My inference from this is that F.T. Unionists ought in transactions with Tariff Reformers to remember & even admit that F.T.U.'s have not the support, as Free Traders, of general opinion.[44]

This melancholy conclusion led him to accept the inevitable demise of free trade influence: "Reconciliation & combined action among all opponents of socialism & of Home Rule is to my mind the need of the moment & I expect that the Free Trade Unionists will have to make painful concessions for the attainment of this end."[45] He willingly accepted this sacrifice if it aided in the maintenance of the Union.

Dicey honored the pledge to put the same message to both factions of the Unionist party. To avid tariff reformer Leo Maxse he urged the virtues of compromise as bickering between the two groups "ought to be sedulously avoided."[46] Later he added to this message of conciliation:

I shall certainly not vote, as indeed I have never voted, for any man who is not a clear & convinced Unionist. . . .

The one thing on which I think you and I possibly differ, besides the question of Tariff Reform (taken in itself) is the absolute conviction I feel of the necessity, no less than the justice of making such concessions on all sides as may enable Unionists to act together in an attack on the Government. I have said to Strachey, & I say to you, that each division of Unionists must be prepared to surrender a good deal. The more each surrenders to Unionism the more patriotic it will be.

44. Dicey to Strachey, 16 September 1909, ibid.
45. Ibid., 22 September 1909, ibid.
46. Dicey to Maxse, 15 September 1909, Maxse Papers.

I quite agree in regretting the loss of Chamberlain's energy & vigour, but you must remember that leaders who have suffered a great defeat cannot claim the confidence due to successful generalship. On Lord Salisbury's retirement Unionists commanded a strong Parliamentary majority, after the last general election it was transformed into a comparatively insignificant minority. During this session the minority has fought admirably, but I don't feel the least confidence myself that a dissolution will restore the Unionists to power. I may well be mistaken—I trust I am.[47]

Dicey never truly forgave tariff reformers for having split the Unionist party, thus exposing the Union to danger. They had given to socialists and Home Rulers a strength not enjoyed previously. Moderate Liberals who might have become Unionists refused to join the party for fear of tariff reform.[48] Advantages of tariff reform in 1910 had to be balanced against the havoc caused by its own victories. In both elections of 1910 Dicey reiterated his plea that both Unionist wings must stand together lest both perish if the Liberals triumphed.[49] The arid debates about economic policy Dicey engaged in eventually had some effect. By 1912, with a Home Rule bill before the House of Commons, he had compromised his allegiance to free trade to this extent: he still insisted on free trade within the Empire, but could now accept a measure of protection against other countries. Without admitting it he had become a Chamberlainite. He modified free trade, though against his better judgment, in order to serve Unionist purposes.[50] Only the Irish Question could have brought that transformation.

Of all the legislation passed by the Liberal government prior to World War I, no act, save Home Rule, caused Dicey such distress as the Trade Disputes Act of 1906. In his view the grant of freedom from liability in tort to trade unions offended the rule of law as he had popularized it. In addition, he had just published in *Law and Opinion* a discussion of the right of association that disapproved trade unions as an artificial destroyer of natural economic laws and

47. Ibid., 14 October 1909, ibid.
48. Ibid., 15 January 1910, ibid.
49. Dicey to Strachey, 21 November 1910, Strachey Papers.
50. Dicey to Bryce, 31 July 1912, Bryce Papers.

The Vinerian Professor, 1907
(Courtesy of Victor Bonham-Carter)

a menace to true individualism. Furthermore, trade unions promoted class loyalties at the expense of national allegiance. His position as principal of the Working Men's College did not inhibit his opposition, for he devoted a series of letters in the *Times* to an examination of the bill. The crux of his protest involved the exemption from liability in tort: "This privilege is in reality the power to commit wrongs without incurring the risk of having to pay compensation to the victim of wrongdoing. Is it, I ask, the deliberate will of the nation that a privilege so opposed to every principle of justice should be conferred upon every trade union throughout the land?"[51] Dicey wanted the House of Lords to battle to the end on this issue but, as he learned later, Balfour had signaled to the Lords that no opposition be made.[52] The Trade Disputes Act represented a lost opportunity to Dicey, for he felt deeply that "it was opposed to the most elementary principles of equal law" and might have been beaten on those grounds.[53]

His fears about the act materialized in 1911 and after, when labor unrest caused numerous strikes and loss of production in various industries. These deplorable circumstances he thought ample justification for his fierce opposition. In a strike by miners in 1912 Dicey displayed a bellicose attitude, urging the enforcement of the law even if it resulted in bloodshed. A strong government must preserve order at all costs lest the next strike lead to a greater coercion of the nation. The root of the problem was the Trade Disputes Act: "Conceal the fact as you may, this Act is intended to give & does give unjust privilege to trade unions, & it has produced, or at any rate tended to produce, all the evil, & more than all the evil, that was predicted by every assailant of the Act. Privilege, whether it be given to a King or a trade union, is simply a decent name for despotism. I am in my own mind firmly convinced that nothing will go right until we get back to the rule of equal law."[54] Even though the strike ended without the bloody confrontation he contemplated, he was not satisfied: "No sane person can to my mind doubt that, if the miners return to work it will have ended in a sheer triumph of the use of force by the Miners against the nation. Personally I think it

51. *Times*, 29 October 1906, p. 8.
52. Strachey to Dicey, 21 March 1912, Strachey Papers.
53. Dicey to Strachey, 22 July 1909, ibid.
54. Ibid., 20 March 1912, ibid.

would have been wiser & better to have fought out the battle by insisting upon the right of every miner who chose to work in the mines."[55] At a later date, but hardly in a more judicious mood, he maintained that the law of the land must apply to trade unions, and "if trade unionists use their privileges to obtain power by force the time has come when they must be fought by the force of the State."[56] This anticipation of class war in the name of the nation showed how extreme his views had grown. Labor troubles formed another indication of the changes Dicey feared in contemplation of England's future.

The political agitation surrounding the introduction of the Lloyd George budget in 1909, the two general elections of 1910, and the passage of the Parliament Act of 1911 have been studied in detail by numerous authors; the purpose here is to examine these events from Dicey's perspective of deepening pessimism about the fate of Great Britain. Before the introduction of the budget, Dicey had suspected that the Asquith government planned new and dangerous programs: "There are dark days before us."[57] His first reaction to the Lloyd George proposals was predictable: "This Budget fills me with alarm. It seems to me to open a new method of working taxation so as to favour the classes who support the party in power."[58] By the end of June the battle for the budget had claimed practically his entire attention. At this point he thought the budget must be rejected if only to protest the exclusive rights over financial measures exercised by the Commons. The House of Lords should reassert its legitimate authority as guardian of the nation against rash legislation. Whether all or only a portion of the budget should be repudiated Dicey did not know, for he did not possess a "practical & experimental knowledge of public life."[59] This inexperience did not deter attentiveness to what Dicey now called "the crimes of the Government."[60] The bystander role soon gave way to an opportunity for positive action.

As the budget confrontation grew more serious, Strachey

55. Dicey to Bryce, 31 March 1912, Bryce Papers.
56. Dicey to Elliot, 28 March 1912, Elliot Papers.
57. Dicey to Eliot, 2 April 1909, Eliot Papers.
58. Dicey to Smith, 26 May 1909, Smith Papers.
59. Dicey to Maxse, 26 June 1909, Maxse Papers.
60. Ibid., 27 June 1909, ibid.

approached Dicey to lend his name to an article providing constitutional justification for destroying the Lloyd George budget.[61] Strachey hoped this support might stiffen the backbone of the Lords, although he admitted that Lord Cromer had already informed him that the Lords would reject the budget for political reasons, but wished to cloak this action with the reputation of an acknowledged constitutional authority. To his credit Dicey, though he sympathized with the Unionist opposition, refused such a discreditable transaction.[62] He acknowledged that precedent favored the Commons, but believed that the government stretched the rule in order to destroy the Lords. Parliament must conform to the will of the nation, he argued, therefore any step by king or Lords that safeguarded the rights of the nation was legitimate. No privilege of the House of Commons commanded respect if it limited the rights of the nation. Over the next weeks Dicey sent Strachey several suggestions to resolve the parliamentary deadlock. A referendum might ease the tension, he thought, though he preferred to reserve this device for protecting fundamental statutes.[63] Dicey evaded the invocation of his authority by focusing Strachey's attention on the technical point that the Lords had never formally accepted their loss of control over a money measure.[64] The Lords and Commons must eventually define fully their respective powers: "That this budget is the best ground on which to fight it is to me less clear."[65] To these dicta from Dicey Strachey was oblivious, wishing to concentrate on the land clauses to defeat the budget, because they introduced new principles into the fiscal system.[66] By this time it became clear that Dicey raised constitutional issues; Strachey fretted about narrow political issues. Dicey justified his position by appeal to the interest of the nation even against the force of constitutional conventions.[67]

61. Strachey to Dicey, 2 July 1909, Strachey Papers.
62. Dicey to Strachey, 2 July 1909, ibid.
63. Ibid., 4 July 1909, ibid.
64. Ibid., 12 July 1909, ibid.
65. Ibid., 20 July 1909, ibid.
66. Strachey to Dicey, 21 July 1909, ibid.
67. Neal Blewett, *The Peers, the Parties and the People*, p. 95, refers to Dicey's "remarkable flexibility" about rejection of the budget. In his own mind Dicey simply adhered to the maxim that the national interest was paramount; it is true, however, that Dicey identified the national interest with the Unionist party. In any event, as Blewett shows at p. 96, the Union-

He never realized, however valid his constitutional points were, that party tactics dictated different political moves.

After his customary summer vacation Dicey returned to the fray with an increased sense of urgency. He now believed "this socialist revolution" would have to be fought by the Lords in the first instance.[68] This seemed the best form of resistance, for the Liberals had gained great advantage from confusing the budget question with the different issue of the constitutional powers of the House of Lords. Unionists should cultivate old Liberals like Rosebery who had already renounced Home Rule in order to mobilize national opinion. Piecemeal opposition could not succeed, so every Unionist strength must be employed. As always Dicey made plain: "I ought perhaps to add that I am not prepared to make the remotest compromise about Unionism either to gain the Irish vote or for any other object." Either amending or rejecting the budget was justifiable as a "lawful means of resisting revolution & in that sense 'constitutional.'" Dicey now escalated his attacks on the government, not for any specific policy but for its general immorality.

Few Unionists, for example, protested against the bribes, such as old age pensions, offered the electors by the government. "It is quite certain," he wrote to Strachey, "that we are apparently in danger of a revolution which is none the less 'revolutionary' in the strict sense of the term, because it is in Great Britain at least likely to be carried thro' without the use of physical violence."[69] Dicey feared that a premature election, resulting from rejection of the budget, might increase Unionist seats only to the point where Liberals depended upon Irish votes. This circumstance would bring a new Home Rule bill sooner than anticipated. Apart from the specific fiscal provisions, the true objection to the budget was "that a singularly unscrupulous Minister [Asquith] has taken advantage of a singular condition of public opinion, to make a desperate bid for office wh. is by no means unlikely to obtain its immediate end."[70] There was no limit to the chicanery he suspected: "I don't doubt

---

ist leadership defeated the budget for electoral reasons, not constitutional considerations.

68. The quotations in this paragraph are from Dicey to Maxse, 15 September 1909, Maxse Papers.

69. Dicey to Strachey, 16 September 1909, Strachey Papers.

70. Ibid., 22 September 1909, ibid.

that Asquith or rather Ll. George & Churchill will offer some further bribe, (e.g. Old Age pensions at 60,) accompanied with a promise of H.R. as in Canada privately made to the Nationalists."[71] Unionists must fight the next election at a disadvantage because the Liberals had resorted to illegitimate political stratagems, so Unionists had every right to denounce the moral bankruptcy of the government. The Liberals had bribed the poorer element of the electorate in "violation of all constitutional morality."[72] Unionists battled dishonest adversaries, Dicey believed; the Liberals confounded every move, no matter how principled, by cheap political tricks. The duty of Unionists was unity above all else, the leadership must cease the internecine bickering over economic policy, and the entire party must participate in the fight.

Fear of Unionist losses at a new election led Dicey to counsel a policy of caution to his Unionist friends. He had little faith in those leaders who forecast major Unionist gains. All omens pointed to a bad result: "All I can say for certain is that as a contest is probable where the fate of many national institutions will be at stake, it is in my judgment the duty of Unionists of every class to cultivate union and conciliation among themselves, & above all not to add to the questions which divide the Party, & not to estrange help which may be got from men like Rosebery, who I suspect has practically given up Home Rule or at any rate won't stir a finger in its favour."[73] If Unionists did not fight to the last, a deluge of radical legislation might swamp the country. Faced with unpleasant alternatives on all sides, Dicey at the last urged that the Lords reject the budget even if this occasioned a general election.[74] He favored battling to the last instead of committing political suicide by approbation of the budget. As the climactic vote on the budget neared, he became more adamant in his opposition. By November he was now prepared, "if the Bill be rejected, to defend and support the action of the House of Lords."[75] He could not agree with Arthur Elliot that rejection was legally, politically, or morally impossible, though he again admitted either acceptance or destruction was fraught with danger.

71. Ibid.
72. Ibid., 25 September 1909, ibid.
73. Dicey to Maxse, 25 September 1909, Maxse Papers.
74. Dicey to Strachey, 29 September 1909, Strachey Papers.
75. Dicey to Elliot, 2 November 1909, Elliot Papers.

Four days before the Lords killed the budget, Elliot replied that "the Lords' claim is to my mind absolutely inadmissible, and with our constitutional system it cannot be made to work."[76] Such were the differences of opinion between forthright Unionists! The Lords refused the budget on 30 November, Asquith soon after carrying a motion in the Commons protesting this usurpation. The electorate had its chance to judge the events of 1909.

On the first day of polling, 15 January 1910, Dicey wrote he was certain of nothing except the uncertainty of the election. His suspicion that the electors cared for nothing but narrow class interests he thought confirmed. The 1909 budget had quickened this process by focusing the attention of the voters on class loyalties: country laborers would vote for the budget because they feared taxes on food; artisans because the budget embodied socialist ideas.[77] The Unionist objective must be "to deprive the Government if possible of office, & if we fail in this, of power. I am in short in every respect the impentitent & unconverted Unionist of 1886."[78] After the first results Dicey found little to celebrate because the electorate had not cared whether the Lords killed the budget or not.[79] Unionist gains at the first election of 1910 failed to lift his spirits, though in general other Unionists rejoiced. As Dicey had foreseen, the Asquith government owed its majority to Irish votes. That the Liberals had retained office was sufficient evil, for as long as they did so, every sort of danger was possible: "I could almost shed tears, tho' it is probably wiser to laugh at the way in wh. politicians have corrupted the people. I know of no act of Disraeli's so base as the policy of this new coalition."[80] The second election of 1910 left the Liberal government intact, surviving bloodied but unbowed, and still dependent upon the Irish.

In 1911 Irish affairs intruded increasingly into his correspondence. That the Union with Ireland formed the quintessence of his politics was demonstrated anew by the immediate denunciation of the Parliament bill after its introduction in February 1911. He opposed it immediately because it restricted the veto power of the House of

76. Elliot to Dicey, 26 November 1909, ibid.
77. Dicey to Maxse, n.d., but late December 1909, Maxse Papers.
78. Ibid., 15 January 1910, ibid.
79. Dicey to Bryce, 16 January 1910, Bryce Papers.
80. Dicey to Strachey, 19 January 1910, Strachey Papers.

Lords, removing the absolute veto the Lords possessed over Home Rule. At the outset he was a "die-hard," because "the passing of the Parliament Bill unaltered is the destruction of the Union between England and Ireland.."[81] If Unionists accepted the Parliament bill, then Home Rule would follow inevitably. Dicey based his opposition on four considerations: (1) Unionists could never pass Home Rule, for this would mean the destruction of the party itself, (2) the international position of England would be placed in the gravest danger, (3) betrayal of Irish Unionists would be the worst sort of treachery, (4) Unionists still believed the voters opposed Home Rule as in 1886 and 1893 and therefore had no fear of a creation of new peers. Strachey, to the contrary, had advised that the Parliament bill pass unimpeded while Unionists prepared to fight on other issues. Because of this attitude Dicey accused him, most unfairly, of softness on Home Rule. Strachey indignantly rejected any such suggestion.[82]

Dicey accepted the rebuke but still pressed Strachey for an answer to his objections. Dicey argued that passage of the Parliament bill meant Home Rule; Strachey believed the Union could endure even if the bill passed. What were the grounds for this belief Dicey inquired; "we are opposed by crafty & unscrupulous foes," so Dicey wished to clarify any potential misunderstanding.[83] To this Strachey replied that new peers created to pass the bill would be pledged to Home Rule, thus making it truly inevitable. By accepting the Parliament bill, Strachey argued, two additional years of fighting would be gained without an assured Home Rule majority in the Lords.[84] In turn Dicey objected that Irish Unionists must see this as an abject surrender to Home Rule. With what new weapons did Strachey intend to fight Home Rule in the years following? Political expediency might easily cause the abandonment of Ulster. "I fear more than I can say," Dicey wrote, "the habit of Englishmen to neglect the feeling of Irishmen even when they are men loyal to England."[85] His customary pessimism permitted little hope for the Union if the Parliament bill passed.

81. Ibid., 18 May 1911, ibid.
82. Strachey to Dicey, 19 May 1911, ibid.
83. Dicey to Strachey, 21 May 1911, ibid.
84. Strachey to Dicey, 23 May 1911, ibid.
85. Dicey to Strachey, 5 June 1911, ibid.

As the critical vote neared in the House of Lords, Dicey had a change of heart, now believing: "To speak plainly to you my judgment . . . is in favour of surrender whilst political feeling & instinct is in favour of the policy of resistance. I should, if forced, act upon my judgment. But instinct is of more importance in this case than in most because the feeling of one insignificant person is likely to be the feeling of thousands of insignificant electors. Still my judgment is in favour of yielding."[86] An opportunity to confirm his conversion to Strachey's counsel of reason over instinct occurred on 24 July when a concerted Unionist demonstration had denied Asquith a hearing in the Commons. This disgraceful Unionist conduct Dicey promptly deplored. In this case he felt such a performance gained sympathy for the Liberals and lost respect for the Unionists. Dicey sought approval from Strachey for his protest, because he thought the incident had done grave damage to the image of Unionism as the party of order: "I don't wonder at the folly because the Unionists are very angry, & not without cause, but it was the greatest folly that men could commit."[87] His Unionist partisanship could not obliterate completely his respect for the traditions of parliamentary politics.

Despite the passage of the Parliament Act in August 1911, Dicey did not abandon the battle so easily. He continued the fight with a last polemic before moving on to other issues.[88] By the revolutionary device of the Parliament Act, he wrote, the Asquith government had destroyed the last constitutional check on the power of the House of Commons. Any coalition could legislate in the name of the nation on matters they would not dare put before the electorate. The act would produce special-interest factionalism at the expense of the nation. And of course the act allowed the opportunity for Home Rule to succeed without an appeal to the country. Amid the turmoil of 1912–14 these arguments never attracted the public attention he hoped.

In a life marked by tenacious belief in the doctrines first adopted in youth, on one issue only did Dicey reverse his stand: women's suffrage. In his younger days as an advanced liberal he had supported

86. Ibid., 25 July 1911, ibid.
87. Ibid., 26 July 1911, ibid.
88. Albert Venn Dicey, "The Parliament Act, 1911, and the Destruction of All Constitutional Safeguards," in *Rights of Citizenship*, pp. 81–107.

movements for the enfranchisement of women. By the time the women's movement had acquired political notoriety in 1903, he opposed votes for women as passionately as he had previously backed the movement. Dicey explained this volte-face in the one book he published on the subject:

> The considerations which, independently of specific arguments, have in respect of woman suffrage told upon my own judgment may be summed up under a few heads: First, the movement for the maintenance of the union between England and Ireland brought me for the first time into something like active political life. For nearly a quarter of a century I have joined in resistance to every demand for Home Rule. This changed the way I looked upon the movement in favour of woman suffrage. My Unionism impressed upon me, as did my keen sympathy with the North in opposition to secession, the thought that Conservatism may in some instances be an effort to enforce the supremacy of common justice, and to maintain the unity of a great nation. It made me feel that the mere desire of a class, however large, for political power or for national independence affords no conclusive reason why the wish should be granted. It raised in my mind the doubt whether the Liberalism of the day, which I had fully accepted, had not exaggerated the wisdom and the justice of yielding, where possible, to every wish entertained by a large number of our fellow-citizens. Since 1885 I have never doubted that a majority of the inhabitants of Ireland are opposed to the Union with Great Britain. I have also never seen the least reason to doubt that the people of the U.K. ought to insist upon the maintenance of the Union.[89]

Here again it must be noted that concern for the Union triggered his change of attitude toward votes for women. No doubt he feared that women might side with Home Rule if entrusted with the franchise. When the demand for votes grew more insistent after 1903, Dicey had long since turned against the movement.

When disputing the claims of Suffragettes, Dicey placed great

89. Albert Venn Dicey, *Letters to a Friend on Votes for Women*, pp. 3–4.

weight on the distinction between civil and political rights for women. He endorsed the grant of equal civil rights to women, frequently citing with approval the advances made by women in control of property during the nineteenth century. He favored private emancipation of women through statute and judicial legislation, but not public emancipation through enfranchisement. As in other political stands before 1914, he thought votes for women probable as a result of party maneuvering.[90] If it must come, he hoped it would do so as a result of party consensus, not a tactic for party advantage. From an extension of the franchise to women he personally saw no benefit, worrying that it "may be a very grave peril & loss to England."[91] When the suffrage movement gained strength he found it necessary to make his opposition public.

Dicey first did so in a 1909 *Quarterly Review* article where he rehearsed the arguments in his book of the same year.[92] Since he had long deplored the effects of an extended male franchise, enfranchisement of women would intensify defects already troublesome to the political system. He added that many women resisted assuming this political burden, therefore the right to vote should be denied despite the outbursts of an outrageous minority. Furthermore, the basis of government was force and in the last resort physical strength, with law and sovereignty depending ultimately upon this fact. In classic Austinian logic, men constituted the effective political class, as they exercised a monopoly on physical force. The admission to the electorate of women, helpless to wield power, could only disrupt the orderly functioning of government. In his book Dicey made one other argument obviously intended as a *reductio ad absurdum*. Votes for women, he asserted, would not end domestic agitation; it would lead to increased turmoil as a result of demands for women in Parliament, Cabinet seats for women, and other unnatural political developments.[93] Each argument Dicey established by *obiter dicta* about the political ineptitude, emotionalism, and incompetence of women. An experiment so potentially dangerous to England, he concluded, was not feasible in the perilous times of 1909.

90. Dicey to Bryce, 23 December 1907, Bryce Papers.
91. Dicey to Eliot, 24 December 1908, Eliot Papers.
92. Albert Venn Dicey, "Women Suffrage," pp. 276–304.
93. Dicey, *Letters on Votes For Women*, p. 62.

The failure of a Women's Enfranchisement bill in 1908 resulted in a lull for most of 1909, a fact Dicey considered "a good thing for the country, but unlucky for my book."[94] In 1910 the campaign resumed with the introduction of a conciliation bill designed to enfranchise a small percentage of women. Dicey thought the new bill dangerous, because many Unionists believed the women eligible to vote would go Tory, a sentiment he did not share. He insisted to Strachey that a referendum be included in any suffrage bill: "It has been no pleasure for me to oppose a movement in which I at one time believed, but it is intolerable to think a question of supreme importance to the nation should be decided at last not by an appeal to the nation but by a parliamentary dodge."[95] Asquith might well place his party behind the conciliation bill, despite his consistent opposition to votes for women, if he thought he could derive political benefit from it. This would settle the question, rescuing Asquith from the attacks of Suffragettes.[96] Dicey thereupon joined the Men's Anti-Suffrage Society, one of numerous political associations to which he belonged in testimony of his beliefs.[97] Dicey was not satisfied when the Asquith government allowed the bill to die. He chided Strachey for not seeing the peril of Asquith suddenly shifting his position in order to recoup political credit.[98] After a relatively quiet year in 1911, Suffragettes heralded a new conciliation bill with a mass destruction of windows on 1 March 1912.

This demonstration alienated sympathetic public opinion. By the end of the month the bill had failed its second reading in the Commons. Dicey prophesied that the defeat meant the death of the suffrage issue for the next five years at least, a prospect immensely pleasing to him. To Bryce he defended himself against the charge that hostility to votes for women sprang from misogynist attitudes: "Now there are many faults, some patent to all my friends & some best known to myself, of which I ought to plead guilty, but contempt for women is not one of them."[99] Shortly thereafter, in writing to congratulate Lord Cromer on the success of his chairmanship

94. Dicey to Maxse, 19 June 1909, Maxse Papers.
95. Dicey to Strachey, 30 May 1910, Strachey Papers.
96. Ibid., 2 June 1910, ibid.
97. Ibid., 7 June 1910, ibid.
98. Ibid., 21 June 1910, ibid.
99. Dicey to Bryce, 31 March 1912, Bryce Papers.

of the Anti-Suffrage League, Dicey summarized his feelings on the subject:

> Even if at some future time it should turn out that England is prepared to adopt Woman Suffrage, which she certainly is not at present, I believe you will still be thought to have done a good work in withstanding the success of the present agitation. Never was there a time when a novel experiment in constitution making could be tried at greater risk to the country, and further it was absolutely necessary that both Englishwomen & Englishmen should be taught that a change in the constitution cannot be obtained by methods of illegal violence. The strange thing about many women who deserve the highest respect both morally and intellectually, was their incapacity to perceive that the existence of peace and progress really depends upon the permanent determination of a country to enforce respect for the law. I hope you will long be able to take your part as a legislator in guarding all that is valuable in the English Constitution.[100]

This remained his last word because, in spite of continued Suffragette violence, he had more important issues to ponder in the last two years before the war.

Throughout the tenure of the Liberal government Dicey faulted almost every legislative proposal. One aspect of this general disillusion with national politics was his vitriolic hatred for Asquith. Dicey never forgave Asquith for his role as defense counsel for Parnell in 1890, condemning him on the principle of guilt by association.[101] After 1890 Dicey had kept the future prime minister under surveillance, so that in 1908, when Asquith replaced the ailing Campbell-Bannerman, Dicey subjected the new Liberal leader to close scrutiny. In a unique fashion Asquith embodied Dicey's fears about the deleterious effects of the modern party system. This perception of Asquith was not entirely erroneous, for, as has been written of Asquith, he "was an obvious party man who firmly had believed in the party system of government."[102] For his part Dicey

100. Dicey to Cromer, 12 April 1912, Lord Cromer Papers. I am grateful to Mr. T. L. Ingram for making a verbatim transcript of this letter.
101. Dicey to Strachey, 26 April 1910, Strachey Papers.
102. H. C. G. Matthew, *The Liberal Imperialists*, p. 143.

always indicted party government for its compromises and lack of moral commitment.

Before the first year in office ended Asquith drew the wrath of Dicey: "In any matter of private life I should never think of doubting the word of either Asquith or Balfour. When either of them comes to deal with politics, I feel I may expect ambiguity, equivocation, and as much shiftiness as falls short of telling a distinct lie."[103] Asquith possessed no scruples about retaining office, therefore he had unlimited capacity for political mischief. In the midst of the budget controversy Dicey asserted: "The government is in moral character & conduct far below any government wh. has existed during my lifetime in England & above all that Asquith, whether he knows it or not, is practically ready to pay any price for keeping office & this Ll.G. & W. Ch. have perceived."[104] If Asquith lost the prime ministership, Dicey believed, he would soon be reduced to a political cipher; Asquith also recognized this fact, clinging to office at all costs. To this appetite for power Dicey customarily attributed Liberal sponsorship of social legislation, Asquith offending most by the ill-disguised bribes he offered the electorate.

Dicey thought the Asquith ministry undermined the traditional moral standards that had made the conduct of British public life so respected throughout the world. He complained of "the demoralising and degrading kind of government under men like Asquith who seem to be developing all that is worst in party government."[105] On another occasion Dicey wrote: "I think one can't exaggerate the extent to wh. this Ministry is lowering the tone of public life."[106] Strachey concurred with this denunciation of the prime minister, especially what he considered the lamentable decline in public morality.[107] Dicey had arrived at these conclusions before the specter of Home Rule had become disturbingly real; when that occurred his attitude toward Asquith grew even more violent.

After the passage of the 1911 Parliament Act, Dicey attacked Asquith more vehemently. In late 1911 Dicey wrote: "I am for the moment more out of heart than I can say about the tendency of

103. Dicey to Lowell, 23 December 1908, Lowell Papers.
104. Dicey to Strachey, 25 September 1909, Strachey Papers.
105. Dicey to Smith, 5 April 1910, Smith Papers.
106. Dicey to Strachey, 23 February 1910, Strachey Papers.
107. Strachey to Dicey, 24 February 1910, ibid.

national politics. The present government is in my judgment the worst government, . . . which has held office since the beginning of the nineteenth century."[108] As the Home Rule bill made its way through Parliament over the next years, Dicey sprinkled his correspondence with references such as "this government of dodges and dodgers."[109] By June 1914, with Home Rule in the immediate future, Asquith received the full force of Dicey's wrath. Strachey had termed Asquith an opportunist; this Dicey rejected as far too kindly: "Asquith is that worst & most contemptible kind of politician to whom politics is all a game & who plays the game unscrupulously. . . . I fully believe that at all costs he will pass the Home Rule Act. He will try to make such an offer of an Amending Act such as Ulster will reject & then say that the Unionists are to blame for all further trouble."[110] Dicey often contrasted Asquith with the political heroes of memory, especially Hartington, with Asquith of course being the antithesis of his idols. The political delinquency of Asquith represented still another facet of the deplorable trend of contemporary English politics; Asquith symbolized the political decay of England Dicey bemoaned before the advent of the war.

The next theme Dicey pursued relentlessly, closely related to several of his pet animosities, was the growth of socialism before 1914. Since 1885 he had harbored misgivings about the course of modern legislation. In 1897, in a eulogy of Lord Pembroke that might have applied equally well to himself, Dicey praised the deceased for devotion to absolute standards of individualism.[111] Lord Pembroke had criticized every innovation diminishing the discredit that ought to attach to pauperism; he would have nothing to do with schemes for protection. Most important of all, Pembroke believed firmly in the principles of laissez-faire and he would not sacrifice them to the claims of unscientific humanitarianism or the exigencies of party warfare. Preparation of the *Law and Opinion* lectures sharpened Dicey's perception of social questions. He concluded that the battle between individualism and socialism would last a long time and have momentous consequences: "Moreover it looks to me as if Socialism were likely to become the cause of wars in the 20th century

108. Dicey to Strachey, 26 October 1911, ibid.
109. Ibid., 27 January 1912, ibid.
110. Ibid., 8 June 1914, ibid.
111. Albert Venn Dicey, "Lord Pembroke," pp. 616–29.

as religion was in the 16th or 17th."[112] Sponsorship of alleged socialistic legislation by Conservatives amounted to a betrayal of Unionism for electoral advantage. The campaign against dissolution of the Union Dicey equated with that against socialism, so that the fight for the political status quo implied preservation of the economic system as well.

With the publication of *Law and Opinion* Dicey believed more than ever that public opinion favored some form of collectivism even as it had embraced individualism fifty years before. The harmful effects of the party system, by increasing the competition for place and power, encouraged the rashest socialist experiments.[113] The Asquith government typified this misuse of politics:

> The Ministry have played an iniquitous trick. They came into power as zealots for free trade. They are retaining office as socialists. Asquith & Grey give a respectable look to Government but its policy is fixed by Ll. George & Churchill. They are both adventurers & Churchill has shamelessly ratted. They have broken all constitutional understandings by using the control of the budget as a means of introducing changes of policy and legislation wh. they could not have carried thro' the H.L. in an ordinary Act of Parliament. They have further offered a bribe to the poorer electors & the bribe I suspect will be gladly accepted.
>
> But the true difficulty of the situation lies much deeper. A sort of semi-socialism is, I am convinced, widespread among all classes. It is curious but I am sure true that the disbelief in religious dogmas of Xianity is at this moment combined with the feeling that the economic doctrines, rightly or not, attributed to Jesus ought to be put into practice. To put the matter quite plainly political adventurers are taking advantage of a very peculiar & to my mind dangerous state of sentiment. But the sentiment right or wrong is genuine. No one can observe the ideas & the conduct of really good young laymen without seeing the strong belief in the duty of aiding the poor.[114]

In this concern of youth for the sufferings of the poor Dicey hoped he found a nonlegislative method for alleviation of the poverty he

112. Dicey to Bryce, 12 May 1898, Bryce Papers.
113. Dicey to Strachey, 20 May 1908, Strachey Papers.
114. Dicey to Smith, 24 September 1908, Smith Papers.

thought the main cause of socialist feeling. He praised "the energetic good will of our younger Englishmen towards the poorer classes,"[115] and prayed that such efforts might secure benefits to the poor without the evils of socialism. To the end he preferred voluntarism to state coercion.

Party rivalries encouraged the bidding for political power through appeals to the poor. This dangerous precedent might be defeated if good sense and moderation prevailed. Relations between classes could improve only "if politicians and demagogues did not deliberately try to set the poor against the rich."[116] The rush of events before World War I gave him little solace. He confessed to amazement at the "extraordinary rapid progress of unscientific socialism."[117] Dicey thought there was no inherent socialist disposition in England, only that the party system gave it artificial stimulus. Even if socialism did not triumph, it would cause grave problems: "I have no belief that England will in the long run be converted into a socialistic state. The rich and the educated will somehow get the upper hand, but I fear dreadfully long contests and dangerous experiments which may undermine the power of the United Kingdom and possibly ruin the British Empire, that is to say, the greatest and freest State which has ever existed."[118] Because he felt the issues at stake so crucial for the future of Britain, Dicey protested against every manifestation of the socialist spirit.

The clearest indication of how Dicey wished to combine social reform with the principles of individualism may be seen in his attitude toward the Old Age Pensions Act of 1908. Though certain that some system of relief for the aged must eventually come, Dicey wanted the Lords to reject the proposal or at least amend it to make the scheme contributory. The bill was ill timed, because its passage did not wait for the Report of the Poor Law Commission appointed in 1905. A delay would have impressed upon the middle classes the crushing financial burden they were about to shoulder.[119] Its hasty

115. Dicey to Jacob, 5 February 1911, Working Men's College MSS.

116. Dicey to Arthur Lupton, 26 July 1912, ibid. Lupton succeeded Jacob as Vice-Principal of the WMC in 1911.

117. Dicey to Macmillan, 24 February 1914, Macmillan Company Papers, B.M. Add. Mss. 55085.

118. Ibid.

119. Dicey to Strachey, 8 July 1908, Strachey Papers.

passage "shocked me more than anything which has happened in my time"[120] and precluded the careful evaluation the measure required. Only if the pensioners contributed to the system would Dicey accept the act; otherwise it constituted a massive bribe demeaning to both pensioner and government. The Lords had refused to act, because even the Unionist leaders dared not risk unpopularity by deferring what the electorate thought a boon.[121] Dicey trembled when statesmen of either party told the poor that poverty might be eliminated by state interference in the economy. Asquith and the Liberals might reform the Poor Law by establishing outdoor relief in a form freeing the recipient "from the taint of pauperism."[122] Afterwards Dicey approved grudgingly the National Insurance Act precisely because it incorporated the voluntary principle into its funding.[123] This example notwithstanding, he regarded modern legislation as invariably collectivist in essence, detrimental to the individualist code by which he had lived.

What conclusion should be drawn from this extensive list of political disappointments? Was Dicey merely a garrulous old man, a political fossil who spent his days in reactionary attacks upon men and programs he did not understand? This indictment is true to the extent that Dicey possessed little flexibility in his political outlook, never making any attempt to inquire sympathetically into modern developments. He preferred the prejudices of youth to a search for insight into contemporary society. By the turn of the twentieth century the sacrosanct faith of his mid-Victorian youth allowed no questioning of the values he had espoused for so long. It was therefore inevitable that the Edwardian age should appear so alien, so novel, and indeed so much a decline from the days he could remember.

In Dicey's case a geriatric interpretation of his political crusades helps explain his increasing isolation. He lived on into an era when the causes sacred in his youth ceased exciting later generations. Dicey himself recognized this basic fact: "There is something quaint, tho' sad, in realising that one belongs to a generation which is already part of the past & criticized with more severity than

120. Dicey to Smith, 22 March 1909, Smith Papers.
121. Dicey to Strachey, 4 July 1909, Strachey Papers.
122. Ibid., 25 September 1909, ibid.
123. Ibid., 25 November 1911, ibid.

justice as mid-Victorian or perhaps even as early Victorian."[124] This conclusion applies beyond his politics, for Dicey eventually admitted that the intellectual temper of Edwardian England eluded him as well: "Now in 1914 everybody seems to me to turn their minds towards psychical research & to incline to believe the sort of things to which the ablest men of the Mid-Victorian age refused to look upon as matters deserving enquiry."[125] The essential values of modernity also surpassed his comprehension, as he testified on another occasion: "I prefer personally the old fashions of my contemporary mid-Victorians who have passed away. I trust I may follow them till death."[126] To this resolve he remained true. Although remarkably free from obsession with the past, in the sense of constant yearning for a return to a simpler age, Dicey allowed his youthful politics to distort his perception of modern England. He insisted that changing conditions need not mean different values; he thought his mid-Victorian values valid for all time, no matter what material progress occurred. Only in his legal work did he display ability to merge past and present, remaining abreast of current developments: his work on successive editions of *Conflicts* proved his flexibility in this area. As a lawyer Dicey never accepted the state of the common law in 1860 as absolute, unchangeable for the ages; he saw the law as a growing body, adapting to meet the needs of society. He brought a diametrically opposed attitude to his politics, where the values of 1860 must not alter an iota in spite of great social and economic changes over half a century. In this difference lies the key to his enduring reputation as a lawyer and the deserved obscurity of his politics.

Did Dicey's fulminations have political influence? His primary political correspondents, the journalists Maxse and Strachey, though both Unionists, opposed each other on tariff reform, and neither had the stature of Unionist editor J. L. Garvin. Dicey was too impractical, too dogmatic, too opposed to compromise for the world of political routine. To the electorate his penchant for abstract constitutional issues exercised little influence when it came to voting. Thus John Sandars, private secretary to Balfour, wrote during the 1909 budget debate that the Conservative party

124. Dicey to Bryce, 4 August 1911, Bryce Papers.
125. Ibid., 11 January 1914, ibid.
126. Dicey to Elliot, 5 March 1913, Elliot Papers.

must stick to a simple policy of amendment: "I daresay this sounds rather like claptrap, but really it is election business proper. It may read like the plea of the wirepuller rather than the reasoning of a Dicey or an Anson. But it is practical politics."[127] Into this world of political reality Dicey never entered. Unionist leaders trotted out his constitutional arguments when it suited their purpose, but otherwise paid scant attention to their professorial supporter. Dicey's commentaries before 1914 had little political impact, but they do illustrate one segment of Unionist thought perhaps more important than historians have admitted. This consisted of a violent, uncompromising attitude in politics hidden behind the traditional picture of English consensus. If this hostility surfaced in full view only against Home Rule, it remained an enduring legacy of bitterness within English politics. In the years 1899–1914 Dicey complained of many developments, but Ireland grieved him beyond any other issue. To the Irish Question Dicey returned again and again as a moth to the flame.

127. Sandars to Lord Lansdowne, 6 November 1909, Balfour Papers, B.M. Add. Mss. 49730, cited in Blewett, *The Peers, the Parties and the People*, p. 432, note 63.

CHAPTER TEN

THE STRUGGLE FOR

THE UNION RESUMED

FOR MOST ENGLISHMEN in 1899 the Irish Question lay dormant, presumably rejected conclusively at the election of 1895. The Irish delegation was still divided sharply over the Parnellite heritage and, since the fall of Parnell, had engaged in bitter internecine warfare. Not until 1900 did some semblance of unity reappear in the Irish Parliamentary party under the leadership of Parnellite John Redmond. After that date it duplicated the Parnellite party: "a party predominantly Catholic but not subservient to the Church, and a party genuinely nationalist without being either sectional or sectarian."[1] Dicey never allowed himself the luxury of believing Home Rule dead, even though the majority of his countrymen had long dismissed the issue. He retained defense of the Union as the great political passion of his life, demanding the duty of eternal vigilance. For this reason he refused involvement in other public disputes lest he forfeit whatever standing he had acquired as a Unionist partisan: "I have always been anxious as long as the Unionist controversy lasts, not to mix myself up in other contentions. Nothing injures the weight of a writer for the public more than a reputation for taking up all sorts of questions or, in other words, for advocating all sorts of crochets."[2] To this principle he adhered, though he had produced polemics on other issues threatening in the long run, as he maintained, the permanence of the Union.

With Ireland subservient to a Unionist government, Dicey had few complaints about the state of the Irish Question. One aspect of this issue eventually gained his attention, rallying him to a new cause. In the aftermath of Unionist election victories in 1895 and 1900, Dicey thought a reapportionment of seats in the House of

1. F. S. L. Lyons, *Ireland since the Famine,* p. 203.
2. Dicey to Strachey, 18 August 1899, Strachey Papers.

Commons appropriate, in particular more seats for England at the expense of Ireland. "There is no subject on which I feel more strongly," he wrote in 1901, "and as to which I must add, I am more convinced I am right. . . . The arguments in any case against a necessary reform are arguments, not of prudence, but of pusillanimity."[3] The reasons for his strong insistence were the resurrection of boycotting in Ireland and the apparent failure of the Unionist government to uphold the supremacy of the law. A Unionist government should never accommodate itself to the demands of Irish Nationalists: "There must be fighting & incessant fighting, though the fight must be carried on fairly."[4] He pressed for a definite statement by the government that a redistribution of seats would be forthcoming: "I know we Unionists expected a reform & I at any rate was gravely disappointed that nothing was said of it after the victory in 1895."[5] Dicey prized consistency of principle above the demands of political contrivance, thus he could not accept the rationale that politics necessitated leaving Ireland unruffled when, as he felt, common justice required the increase of English seats. This loftiness of tone, compounded by failure to perceive the working of everyday politics with its many petty compromises, precluded the political influence Dicey so ardently desired.

His sense of civic duty caused him to place his thoughts before the general public.[6] The primary duty of a Unionist government, Dicey argued, remained in 1901 as in 1886: to maintain and strengthen the Union. Fidelity to Unionist principles implied the willingness of the ministry to provide England with her legitimate share of parliamentary authority. The disproportionate representation of Ireland increased the power of the minority Nationalists who had demonstrated anew disloyalty to the United Kingdom during the Boer War. Political leaders must put aside party considerations and carry through a reform essential to national unity. Not even the disavowal of Home Rule by Lord Rosebery, leader of the Liberal Imperialists, satisfied Dicey. He thought this a justification of Unionist policy since 1886, but, as he pointed out to Maxse, the

3. Ibid., 26 June 1901, ibid.
4. Ibid., 1 July 1901, ibid.
5. Ibid., 2 October 1901, ibid.
6. Albert Venn Dicey, "The Due Representation of England," pp. 359–82.

recantation was insufficient.[7] Rosebery had still talked of a dependent parliament for Ireland, but Dicey insisted this plan destroyed the Union no matter how proponents disguised that fact. The erstwhile Liberal leader had earned undying distrust by his support of the 1893 Home Rule bill, an act Dicey could never forgive. Until the intervention of Chamberlain's tariff reform campaign in 1903, the increased representation of England remained a primary goal. He believed the Union might be protected for all time by this device, calling it "an absolutely necessary reform."[8] But the split between Unionist free traders and tariff reformers made the timing inopportune, so Dicey failed again with a project he had cherished.

The division in Unionist ranks because of tariff reform and the declining strength of the Balfour government dominated the next years. Though a Liberal government became more probable, the specter of Home Rule did not necessarily follow. Bryce, Dicey's only contact with Liberal politics, wrote about Home Rule that "no one thinks it is possible to bring into the next Parliament a bill like that of 1893."[9] No doubt Dicey was aware of this sentiment, but it made no difference. He had not weakened in his dedication to the Union, for at the end of 1905 he wrote: "As a matter of personal experience I think my vehemence as a Unionist speaker has come nearer the truth than the more moderate tone of my conversation about Unionism."[10] This self-appraisal was soon confirmed by the rapidity with which Dicey pointed to the implications for Ireland of the landslide Liberal victory of January 1906. Just one month later he carefully assessed the dangers to Unionism in the aftermath of the Liberal triumph.[11] The impending threat to the Union should silence all controversy about economic policy within the Unionist party. The duty of Unionists demanded unity above all else until the Union was again secure. Unionism had suffered such a terrible electoral defeat because of the ill-starred fiscal question. Home Rule and Unionism opposed each other at every point, so under no cir-

7. Dicey to Maxse, 15 March 1902, Maxse Papers.

8. Ibid., 11 August 1903, ibid.

9. Bryce to Smith, 26 January 1905, Bryce Papers.

10. Dicey to Miss Agnes Fry, 29 November 1905, in Rait, *Memorials*, p. 192.

11. Albert Venn Dicey, "Can Unionists Support a Home Rule Government?," pp. 247–66.

cumstances should a Unionist support a Home Rule government as Dicey termed the new Campbell-Bannerman ministry. Unionism had arisen from the national condemnation of any compromise by an English party with conspirators and rebels. The long battle of Dicey with the Liberal government over Irish policy commenced at the outset of its tenure.

In the beginning Dicey need not have worried. Bryce became the Cabinet member responsible for Ireland, with Home Rule remaining in the background while the government pushed ahead with other measures. As Bryce put it: "We do not contemplate anything at all revolutionary in Ireland. At present my aim chiefly is to better the condition of the people materially & socially and to wean them from disorder."[12] For his part Dicey wanted nothing short of the most unbending preservation of the status quo. He made this plain to Bryce in stating that his opinion had not altered since 1886: complete separation of England and Ireland posed a lesser danger than Home Rule.[13] The only argument favorable to Home Rule he accepted was the "intense difficulty of ruling Ireland either with vigour or with consistency, which is almost the same thing as with justice."[14] Until 1886, Dicey recalled, the Union had provided great benefits to both countries because opinion in England agreed on the governance of Ireland. The recklessness of Gladstone had shaken the foundations of Irish government. Strict enforcement of the law became a political badge of Unionism; Liberals conciliated Nationalist opinion by relaxing the law. Though he remained as adamant as twenty years before, "I am afraid from signs I see that the Home Rule battle will have to be fought over again."[15] Dicey never appreciated the problem Home Rule meant for English Liberals. Some still marched to the Gladstonian clarion call, whereas others thought the issue dangerous. Many recognized that raising Home Rule could only lead to dissension and another era of political impotence. So, while Dicey fretted from the start, Home Rule did not become an ominous reality until 1909.

The absorption of Dicey in the Irish Question between 1909 and the start of World War I falls into two periods divided by the Parlia-

12. Bryce to Smith, 16 June 1906, Bryce Papers.
13. Dicey to Bryce, 2 September 1906, ibid.
14. Dicey to Norton, 30 December 1906, Norton Papers.
15. Ibid.

ment Act of 1911. Until that act passed into law Dicey remained as in 1886, a fiery partisan of the Unionist cause. During that period Home Rule still formed a potential threat, because the Lords retained a veto over any bill; so Dicey repeated his usual constitutional arguments in favor of the Union. After the passage of the Parliament Act, he abandoned positive arguments for an emotional negativism that led him into advocacy of dangerous political activities. Zeal for the Union turned him into a living negation of constitutional doctrines he had popularized. The total commitment to the Union prevented compromise, closed his mind to other alternatives, and in the end brought him, the greatest living constitutional authority, perilously close to the promotion of civil war.

At the beginning of 1909 Dicey realized reluctantly that opposition to Home Rule no longer commanded the public interest as in 1886 or 1893. About this distressing situation he wrote to Goldwin Smith: "The whole state of politics disheartens me. It is quite clear for the moment the English public has grown very indifferent about Home Rule. My own belief is that a Bill proposing an avowed scheme of Home Rule such for example, as that contained in the Bill of 1893, could not be passed, but meanwhile the mismanagement of Ireland by a party who sympathise with Home Rule and the failure of the Government of the U^d Kingdom to support the rule of law in Ireland will I believe turn Loyalists into Separatists."[16] Above all Dicey feared that the Liberals, by their toleration of Irish lawlessness and concession of influence to the Nationalists, would turn Ireland into such a shambles that Home Rule might well appear the only alternative to English public opinion. The Liberals had done more to weaken the Union by their misgovernment than Gladstone had done by his open affirmation of Home Rule. Unionists must therefore "pledge themselves to restore the rule of law in Ireland."[17] Dicey thought the Irish Council Bill proposed by the Liberals in 1907 had deliberately breached the understanding that Home Rule should not be raised during the 1906 Parliament; Unionists must respond to this challenge by reforming their ranks: "I think more of Unionism than anything else, & to my mind both divisions of the Unionist Party have been far too careless about the

16. Dicey to Smith, 22 March 1909, Smith Papers.
17. Dicey to Strachey, 26 July 1909, Strachey Papers.

one belief which really binds them together, namely their Unionism."[18] Because of the other pressing problems in 1909, Dicey experienced trouble making his correspondents aware of the urgency of the Home Rule question.

He importuned his friends repeatedly that there must be no concession on Home Rule, for a moderate policy would be more ruinous to England than an extreme form of Home Rule or even independence for Ireland. The prospect of a new controversy over Irish policy stirred his combative instincts: "The duty of Unionists is to my mind clear: Fight hard, &, above all, fight staunchly."[19] Dicey badgered Strachey to have the *Spectator* give prominence to the imminent danger of Home Rule. As Dicey read the political situation, the Nationalists had never relinquished their demand for independence, and the government was composed of men who had admitted the justice of that claim. The Liberals governed Ireland on Nationalist principles, particularly in refusing to enforce the Crimes Act. If the Nationalists ever held the balance of power in the Commons, this could lead to untold complications: "All I absolutely insist upon is the Unionist party shall put unionism before every other consideration."[20] This was a task easier encouraged than accomplished, though Dicey never faltered in the attempt.'

Unionist gains in the first election of 1910 wiped out the absolute majority enjoyed by the Liberals since 1906, making them dependent upon Irish votes for continuing in office. That the Liberals should depend upon the Irish delegation, logical as it was under the circumstances, Dicey believed completely cynical. It demonstrated anew that Asquith possessed "no moral feeling."[21] Unionist failure to oust the Liberals cast Dicey into a more pessimistic mood than usual. As the Irish policy of the Asquith government unfolded, this pall of gloom deepened: "About politics I am much out of heart. The Unionism for which I care seems to be in a very bad way."[22] If only tariff reform had not split Unionists, Dicey lamented to fellow free trader Strachey, none of this turmoil would have occurred. The only ray of hope was his faith that if the Union were put to a fair

18. Ibid., 29 September 1909, ibid.
19. Ibid., 1 October 1909, ibid.
20. Ibid., ? October 1909, ibid.
21. Ibid., 19 January 1910, ibid.
22. Ibid., 1 February 1910, ibid.

vote, it would gain a resounding majority. But elections covered many issues, so the problem became isolation of the Union question where it might be decided directly. The referendum thus appeared to Dicey the only political instrument by which this forthright vote could be obtained. Yet even he acknowledged that the feeling of 1910 did not equal the anti–Home Rule sentiment of 1886 and 1895. The battle would have to be fought over again, and "at 75 one knows that the future belongs to younger men."[23] Dicey might have taken consolation that on the government side Bryce complained of the "difficult political situation," worse than that of 1886 and 1892.[24] Because Dicey contemplated Unionist problems exclusively, he had little insight into the realities of the overall situation.

The political situation did not improve, even though the Liberals had lost seats in the first election of 1910. The dependence of the government on Irish votes illustrated the bankruptcy of Liberal policy:

> The present Government seems to me essentially lawless. I am far more indignant with the more or less moderate Liberals who ally themselves with the Irish faction & wish to create an absolutely uncontrolled House of Commons which may give instantaneous effect to the will of any party which has got a Parliamentary majority than with Irish conspirators who to give them their due have never pretended to feel any loyalty towards England. They have behind them such justification (if so one can call it) as is to be found in the misgovernment of Ireland during the centuries that preceded the Catholic Relief Act. I had never till this year supposed that any English Ministry would be guilty of the baseness exhibited by Asquith, Winston Churchill, & Lloyd George. I am so full of this matter that I have let myself overflow into it without due excuse.[25]

The unity of action by Unionists Dicey anticipated never appeared. He looked to Balfour for leadership, but his erstwhile hero equivocated on economic principles, ensuring divisions within the Unionist party. Dicey feared that the government might adopt the

23. Ibid.
24. Bryce to Professor Macy, 3 February 1910, Bryce Papers.
25. Dicey to Smith, 19 April 1910, Smith Papers.

referendum, misusing it to their own advantage as the plebiscites of France had aided tyranny.[26] Nowhere in England did there seem to be the true spirit of patriotism necessary for a troubled country; the Liberals had long since abandoned any pretense of national feeling, and even the tariff reformers would not "rise to the requisite height of public spirit."[27] This pessimism led to the publication of an article attacking in no uncertain language the evils of party government as practiced by Asquith and the rest of the Cabinet.[28] The abyss Dicey foresaw was the possibility that loyalty to party might supersede respect for the nation in the eyes of the government. Asquith had shown his firm commitment to the party system by his determination to impose an American-style "machine" on Great Britain. This process lowered the tone of English public life, because party considerations dictated government policy and could result only in the degradation of popular government. The power of the House of Commons must be reduced if the authority of the nation should survive.

The close of 1910 brought from another direction yet another crisis within the Unionist party. In October sections of the party, led by J. L. Garvin and F. S. Oliver, launched a campaign in the press for a federal solution to the Irish Question in hopes of obtaining a greater measure of Imperial unity.[29] This form of solution to the Home Rule problem Dicey had long dismissed, so its revival from within the Unionist camp he thought especially distressing. Such an ending to the Home Rule struggle, he wrote, meant that "the triumph of Redmond & his Dynamiters would be more disgraceful and perhaps not in reality more dangerous, than defeat by Germany."[30] The true Unionist alternative was bringing down the Asquith government. Dicey implored the *Spectator* to attack the federalist heresy, a point Strachey emphasized he had already done because the *Times* had flirted with approval of this federalist scheme.[31] The Unionist romance with federalism ended in Novem-

26. Dicey to Strachey, 20 April 1910, Strachey Papers.
27. Ibid., 25 April 1910, ibid.
28. Albert Venn Dicey, "On the Brink of an Abyss," pp. 779–85.
29. See Alfred M. Gollin, *The* Observer *and J. L. Garvin 1908–1914,* pp. 208–26.
30. Dicey to Strachey, 21 November 1910, Strachey Papers.
31. Strachey to Dicey, 22 November 1910, ibid.

ber, when the second election of 1910 focused the attention of all
politicians on practical matters. Dicey concluded: "I detest what is
called absurdly enough Federalist Unionism. It seems to me the
silliest, & because of vagueness, one of the most dangerous forms of
the Home Rule mania."[32] For the time being at least, political
circumstances had prevented dilution of the pure gospel of Unionism.

Federalism emerged in another guise in 1911 when some Tory
elements put forward proposals for a separate Imperial Parliament.
Dicey would not countenance these suggestions, urging Strachey to
see that Unionists gave no backing to such a scheme. Among many
objections Dicey feared Liberals would exploit this feeling to explain that Home Rule for Ireland formed part of an overall plan to
unify the British Empire.[33] Unionist stalwart Walter Long, for instance, solicited from Dicey, after carefully rejecting any idea of
federal Home Rule, approval of a design modeled with few exceptions after the South African Act.[34] This overture was doubly inopportune, for not only did Dicey reject federalism on principle, but
he had just published the second edition of *A Leap in the Dark*,
which retained his absolute condemnation of Home Rule as federalism. Shortly thereafter, Dicey wrote to Strachey that several persons in politics (no doubt he included Long) had contacted him "as
if I could possibly sympathise with this folly."[35] As at the outset
of his Unionist career, Dicey repudiated compromise even when
tendered by Unionist leaders. Federalism had never impressed
him, and he saw nothing in its latest manifestation to change his
mind.

In the aftermath of the passage of the 1911 Parliament Act, the
Home Rule situation became more critical for Dicey. From the
accession of the Liberals in 1905 to that point in 1911, he had witnessed "the gradual defeat of all that as a Unionist I care for."[36] He
admitted being shaken when Sir Horace Plunkett asserted that the
millions spent for land purchase had not diminished demands for
Home Rule. This revelation challenged directly the assumption

32. Dicey to Strachey, 23 November 1910, ibid.
33. Ibid., 14 June 1911, ibid.
34. Walter Long to Dicey, 1 July 1911, General Manuscripts 508(39),
Glasgow University Library.
35. Dicey to Strachey, 12 July 1911, Strachey Papers.
36. Ibid., 26 October 1911, ibid.

Dicey had cherished for a quarter century that unrest in Ireland sprang from economic motives and that consequently Irish nationalism was ephemeral and need not be taken seriously. Plunkett's statement made a fleeting impression on Dicey, but he soon returned to his stock arguments against Home Rule. His beliefs about Ireland had petrified to the point where no new evidence could dislodge the conclusions of a lifetime. His advice was, as always, that "we must resist Home Rule tooth & nail."[37]

Focus now shifted across the Irish Sea where the role of Ulster gained increasing prominence. Dicey had high hopes for Ulster's smashing Home Rule by virtue of strict adherence to lawful resistance, which might be contrasted to the lawlessness of the government.[38] No sooner had the position of Ulster become magnified than a new crisis struck the Unionist party with the resignation under fire of Arthur Balfour as leader. In spite of critical remarks he had aimed at Balfour as opposition leader, Dicey called Balfour's departure a "calamity for Unionism."[39] His first choice for successor to Balfour was Walter Long who, despite some temporary aberrations, had served the Unionist cause well. If that selection proved impossible, Dicey had nobody else in mind. He was concerned that the entire party support the new leader, whoever was chosen.[40] The eventual choice of Andrew Bonar Law as Tory chief proved eminently satisfactory, although the new leader's economic views did not coincide with Dicey's. He respected Bonar Law's devotion to the Union, the most important qualification for any Unionist leader.

Dicey then turned to the task of renewed lobbying in favor of the referendum, envisioned as a tactic to delay Home Rule until a new general election could be forced. He hoped a referendum would preclude passage of a Home Rule bill, allowing the electorate a final decision on the Irish problem.[41] In his worst moments Dicey considered the dispiriting likelihood that Home Rule might win in a referendum. About the chance of this result he wrote to Strachey: "I am sorry to say that I sometimes fear the electors are even stupider than you suppose."[42] Strachey ended these speculations when

37. Ibid.
38. Ibid., 30 October 1911, ibid.
39. Ibid., 8 November 1911, ibid.
40. Ibid., 10 November 1911, ibid.
41. Ibid., 2 December 1911, ibid.
42. Ibid., 4 December 1911, ibid.

he informed Dicey that the House of Lords would on principle never approve a referendum.[43]

Because the strategy to avert Home Rule depended upon the forcing of a dissolution before it could pass, Dicey reacted to the collapse of his referendum dream by raising for the first time the possibility that the king might and should play a role in the growing political drama. Dicey recommended that Unionist leaders announce their willingness to take office when a Home Rule bill was introduced, then have the king order a dissolution to bring the issue to the judgment of the nation.[44] The dictum of Burke that the royal prerogative might be used in any great crisis proved to Dicey's satisfaction that such an intervention was justifiable. He repeated it many times, acknowledging that it involved grave risks to the Crown and the political system.[45] Dicey, who in *Law of the Constitution* had provided the classic definition circumscribing the prerogative, now found himself forced to qualify the doctrine he had preached for over two decades. As Home Rule grew more probable, the remedies he endorsed became more radical, leading him to political positions at variance with his own constitutional teachings.

At the start of 1912 Strachey attempted to cheer Dicey by an optimistic assessment of Unionist prospects.[46] Strachey emphasized the unity behind Bonar Law while signs of Liberal factionalism multiplied. In dealing with the rosy picture painted by his friend, Dicey, who rarely did so, indulged in a retrospect of the Home Rule controversy since 1886. Why in 1912 was defense of the Union so lacking in popular appeal compared to the great outcry of 1886 and 1893? He proposed six different answers to this question which, taken in entirety, explained the modern failure of Unionism.[47] In the first place, Home Rule bored the electorate, who cared little for constitutional principles; social questions occupied the interest formerly held by weightier matters. Next, Dicey felt the increasing power of the party system had contributed to the effectiveness of the Home Rule campaign. In Ireland strict discipline had maintained the primacy of this goal; in England one party had sustained the movement through its support. The third reason presented was most surprising,

43. Strachey to Dicey, 5 December 1911, ibid.
44. Dicey to Strachey, 12 December 1911, ibid.
45. Ibid., 26 December 1911, ibid.
46. Strachey to Dicey, 1 January 1912, ibid.
47. Dicey to Strachey, 7 January 1912, ibid.

for Dicey rarely considered Irish affairs in discussing Home Rule. He admitted that the Irish agitation against the Union had continued unabated for nearly thirty years, surviving even the ruin and death of Parnell. Such consistency of purpose had made its mark on the English public. This concession was the more remarkable in the light of Dicey's low opinion of Irish Nationalists. In the next instance, he believed that the generation of 1912 did not understand that Home Rule was not merely a scheme for Irish government, but attacked all British constitutional arrangements. Furthermore, the conversion of Gladstone in 1885 and the hostility between free traders and tariff reformers during the election of 1906 had destroyed the belief that all England opposed Home Rule. And finally, the alternation of parties in England, with different views about the government of Ireland, made it intolerable that Irish affairs should depend on the vagaries of English party politics. Because of this situation opposition to Home Rule seemed the sole province of the Unionist party and not, as Dicey had always believed, of the entire British nation. He concluded this survey with the warning he had uttered from the beginning: "I suspect that in 1912, as in 1886, I shall have to come back to the alternative: Separation is better for England than Home Rule."[48] Dicey could not accept Strachey's promising assessment, for the cause to which he had devoted his life now faced the most serious challenge ever.

Given that circumstance, Dicey next inaugurated a correspondence with new Unionist leader Andrew Bonar Law. He trusted that Bonar Law would recognize his name from the work he had performed as Unionist writer and speaker. While the Unionist party rallied its forces for the decisive battle to preserve the Union, Dicey assured Bonar Law that he intended to follow his leadership as faithfully as he had done with the Duke of Devonshire and Balfour. After a review of Unionist prospects and the usual prescription of unity for Unionist woes, Dicey introduced one new element of concern.[49] Winston Churchill was scheduled to speak in Belfast on 8 February, but Unionist partisans denied him public facilities for the appearance.[50] Dicey termed this tactic the worst mistake possible for Unionists. Denial of free speech to Catholic Home Rulers in Belfast

48. Ibid.
49. Dicey to Andrew Bonar Law, 21 January 1912, Andrew Bonar Law Papers, Beaverbrook Library, London.
50. See Peter Rowland, *The Last Liberal Governments*, p. 145.

played into the hands of Churchill, who deliberately fomented strife to gain sympathy for the Home Rule cause. Unionists should not be so stupid as to fall into Churchill's trap. Dicey felt so strongly about this subject that he fired off a protest to the *Times*. To Strachey he defended this public rebuke to Unionism on the grounds that if Belfast Unionists denied free speech to Nationalists, then resistance to Home Rule might easily be portrayed as revival of the Protestant ascendancy.[51] Hatred of religious fanaticism, Catholic or Protestant, stirred a desire to cleanse Unionism of this ugly taint before it vitiated Unionist policy. Respect for law had been a cardinal principle of Unionism, therefore: "It seems to me madness for Unionists to break the law for the sake of stopping freedom of debate. Just because I can imagine circumstances in wh. Ulster ought to fight, I feel sure that Ulster should, when she has not been deprived of any legal right, not join in a row."[52] A scrupulous regard for law could help convince the public of the righteousness of the Unionist crusade; anything less invalidated the moral aspirations of Unionism.

In February Dicey approached Macmillan's about the publication of a selection of his letters to the *Times*, to be entitled *Thoughts on the Parliament Act*. The purpose of the proposed book was to prove "that the House of Lords, tho' from one point of view almost destroyed, retains a suspensive veto, wh. may turn out of considerable power, & lastly insist upon the fact that the whole policy of the Unionist party must be governed by the existence of the Parliament Act."[53] Though Macmillan declined the offer politely, the reason for refusal caused Dicey great dismay. *Unionist Delusions* had sold well in 1887, because the public had cared about the Home Rule question; in 1912, as Dicey sadly acknowledged, neither it nor any political topic excited much interest.[54] Public indifference or even resignation to Home Rule astounded Dicey, for whom the Union had been a way of life: "I hear expressions used by men I should have thought sound Unionists which make one stand aghast. There seems to be spreading an idea that Home Rule must come. I cannot tell you the pain that this sort of delusion causes me. I do not think

51. Dicey to Strachey, 27 January 1912, Strachey Papers.

52. Ibid., 30 January 1912, ibid.

53. Dicey to Macmillan, 4 February 1912, Macmillan Company Papers, B.M. Add. Mss. 55085.

54. Ibid., 6 February 1912, ibid.

any man can exaggerate the moral calamity which will befall English statesmanship if Unionists do not fight to the last in defense of the Union."[55] The public mood of apathy surpassed Dicey's understanding, though every passing month confirmed its increasing strength.

On the eve of the introduction of the 1912 Home Rule bill, Dicey predicted that, whatever the outcome, it would inaugurate the last Home Rule campaign, because Asquith and the Irish Nationalists would remain allied through every vicissitude in order to pass the bill before new elections. Only a dishonest politician like Asquith would try to carry Home Rule without an appeal to the electorate, so Asquith "ought not be allowed to retain office for a day."[56] Once the new bill became public Dicey examined its provisions with meticulous care. He admired the cleverness of the bill while feeling nothing but horror at its contents. Asquith proposed the bill to keep his unholy coalition together, for this maintained him in office and no other consideration meant as much to him. Unionists had to place their arguments before the public through discussion and debate as never before. Would the electors see the madness of Home Rule? Dicey doubted it, because the generation of 1912 needed the political education common in 1886.

If all else failed, the king must prevent Home Rule by insisting on a general election before the bill was submitted to the Lords for a third time. Dicey appreciated the perils to the Crown inherent in this maneuver, but believed that, if approved by Unionist leaders in advance, the plan might work. The only drawback was his doubt that the king possessed sufficient will to see the plan through to the end. Everything must be subordinated to maintenance of the Union, so Unionist leaders must form a consistent policy around which the Unionist public could rally.[57] As he wrote to Bryce, now aloof from Liberal plans: "I shall fight on on my old line—to recall Grant's dictum—for the whole summer or more. It is to me the natural & the right line. I am the old Unionist of 1886 & remain unchanged & unrepentant."[58] Dicey soon learned how isolated this attitude left him, for Strachey, now his lone political confidant, had advised

55. Dicey to Elliot, 20 March 1911, Elliot Papers.
56. Ibid., 9 April 1912, ibid.
57. Dicey to Strachey, 13 May 1912, Strachey Papers.
58. Dicey to Bryce, 17 May 1912, Bryce Papers.

Dicey how little regarded Strachey was by Unionist leaders. Tariff reformers dominated the party and thought him a loathsome free trader.[59] In spite of the disheartening information, Dicey knew his duty required continuation of the good fight.

A complex problem arose for Dicey when Ulster Unionists made plain that under no circumstances would they accept Home Rule. He believed Ulster would fight, and civil war would be the result of the government pushing the Home Rule bill. How far could Dicey support Ulster resistance? Specific conditions would dictate his answer, for he would not conjure up constitutional cases merely for the sake of argument.[60] When the necessity arose for such a painful choice, he would decide on the basis of the facts as he then understood them. Ulster did not possess an absolute veto on the will of the British nation. If Home Rule passed without an appeal to the people, then the Ulster case would be strengthened. If the protest of Ulster degenerated into attacks on Catholics, then he must abandon Ulster. To this argument Strachey replied by justifying the legitimacy of resistance to laws altering the status of a citizen. "I must obey the captain of the boat while I am in the boat," Strachey wrote, "I think I have a moral right to resist being thrust out of the boat."[61] Ulster must follow the path of passive resistance, Dicey countered, until the nation had been consulted.[62] If the British electorate by a clear majority sanctioned Home Rule, Ulster could not expect a full veto.

Strachey, ever the realist, told Dicey that Ulster would defy a Dublin parliament, she would organize a provisional government. Then what would be the duty of an English Unionist?[63] Strachey argued that Unionists must avert this situation by forcing a dissolution through raising the inevitability of civil war. In rejoinder Dicey still would not commit himself, for the grievance was potential and would remain so until at least May 1914. Lawful Unionist resistance might prevent passage of Home Rule by use of the Parliament Act; to this end English Unionists should pour out money like water. In the meantime Ulster must act with intense self-discipline.

59. Strachey to Dicey, 14 May 1912, Strachey Papers.
60. Dicey to Strachey, 30 June 1912, ibid.
61. Strachey to Dicey, 2 July 1912, ibid.
62. Dicey to Strachey, 7 July 1912, ibid.
63. Strachey to Dicey, 9 July 1912, ibid.

Dicey held out little hope for Ulster in this regard: "Recent events have justified my fear that Ulster has not the self-control necessary for carrying out the very difficult policy of passive resistance within the limits of the law, tho' I believe it would be successful."[64] The arming of Ulster had already begun, and Dicey doubtless referred as well to the 12 July Belfast speech of F. E. Smith assuring Ulster of permanent Unionist support.[65] Dicey feared that these developments confused two questions he thought best kept separate. How far had Ulster the right to carry resistance by constitutional means was not the same problem as to what length could a Parliamentary minority go in resisting by physical force.[66] Answering these difficult moral and constitutional questions could not be postponed forever, as Dicey eventually learned.

By October 1912 the private debate between Dicey and Strachey took on greater urgency as the political atmosphere grew more heated. Dicey contended that if after a dissolution a majority of electors favored Home Rule, Englishmen must bow to the dictates of the nation.[67] He insisted on the important difference between this approval of Home Rule and a bill passed only by virtue of the Parliament Act.[68] Strachey reserved his opinion about that situation, having a more belligerent attitude against the coercion of Ulster. He could not accept the relevance of Dicey's distinction. For Strachey political realities counted more than constitutional niceties; he hated Home Rule, and the manner of its passage paled when compared to the injustice it fastened upon Ulster.[69] Both men eventually agreed that Unionists should not bind their future action by rigid allegiance to a single course of action. The duties of Ulstermen and Englishmen would differ significantly with the advent of Home Rule, so no benefit could arise from anticipation of the future. The sole commitment Unionists might make was the pledge that they would repeal Home Rule if successful at the next election, assuring the moral consistency of their position.[70] Events in Ulster and Lon-

64. Dicey to Strachey, 14 July 1912, ibid.
65. Rowland, *Last Liberal Governments*, p. 175.
66. Dicey to Elliot, 21 November 1912, Elliot Papers.
67. Dicey to Strachey, 13 October 1912, Strachey Papers.
68. Ibid., 19 October 1912, ibid.
69. Strachey to Dicey, 21 October 1912, ibid.
70. Dicey to Strachey, 22 October 1912, ibid.

don repeatedly mocked the unreality of such calm reflections about the volatile Irish situation.

On 13 November, for example, a famous scene of disorder in the House of Commons ended with Churchill's being struck by a copy of the standing orders, hurled by an enraged Ulsterman. Dicey was scandalized by such behavior, so much so that he immediately fired off a letter to the *Times* protesting this lamentable Unionist indiscretion. Unionists should meet Liberal provocations with "dignity, sometimes by silence, & constantly by contempt."[71] Unionist misconduct placed the government in a strong moral position and gained public sympathy. His protest probably would lose him his last political friends, so he begged Strachey's support for his stance as well as for the general advice that Unionists refrain from further riot. Dicey received no solace from Strachey, who maintained that the Asquith government deserved a hard knock, and this outburst had raised the morale of the Unionist party.[72] On the same day Strachey sent this assessment to Bonar Law: "I do not think you need feel any concern about dear old Dicey's outbreak. He is a splendid Unionist, but a man apt to be carried away by phantom fears."[73] Unaware of this condescending reference so indicative of his political impotence, Dicey insisted to Strachey that such parliamentary actions, even if useful in the short run, damaged the Unionist cause in the final analysis.[74] Dicey never resolved the quandary of what to advocate when the Unionist party, the vehicle necessary for preservation of the Union, did not live up to the elevated moral standards he thought mandatory for the ultimate success of Unionism.

Dicey then sought Arthur Elliot's approval of the protest, because several Unionists had written to him denouncing the letter. This criticism had been painful to accept, for he had never consciously done anything to harm Unionism. Dicey now wondered whether he had acted too quickly, confessing that he was "really perplexed in my own mind."[75] Unionists had endured many Liberal irritations since 1905, and on this occasion the rowdiness had rallied the spirits of the party. But Unionists had defied the authority of the Speaker

71. Ibid., 14 November 1912, ibid.
72. Strachey to Dicey, 15 November 1912, ibid.
73. Strachey to Bonar Law, 15 November 1912, ibid.
74. Dicey to Strachey, 17 November 1912, ibid.
75. Dicey to Elliot, 18 November 1912, Elliot Papers.

to score this triumph, earning little credit for a party dedicated to law and order. The use of violence to terminate debate, Dicey argued, was the worse possible precedent Unionists could help establish. If they repeated these untoward activities, surely the moral position of Unionism must suffer. What reply was possible if the future Irish Nationalists or Laborites imitated Unionist actions? As he wrote to Elliot: "I do not believe that any man living has more at heart that this Home Rule Bill should be rejected, & this Home Rule Government be expelled from office. I am an old man—I have lived into a generation of which I probably fail to understand the sentiment, but I cannot bring myself to believe that any party will, or ought in the long run to gain anything by substituting Parliamentary shouts for Parliamentary debate. The next step will be to substitute fisticuffs for arguments." [76] Elliot proved more receptive than Strachey to Dicey's transparent honesty, praising him for long service to Unionism. When every emotional element in the Home Rule controversy had disappeared, his work would endure: "At the bar of reason you have, in my opinion at all events, annihilated the Home Rule cause." [77] This approbation from an old friend, while rewarding, assuaged his despairing mood about the future very little.

In January 1913 Dicey published the last of his jeremiads on Home Rule. [78] The new book repeated in slightly amended form the arguments Dicey had first advanced in 1886. As he admitted: "I doubt whether human ingenuity could now produce on Irish Home Rule either a new argument or a new fallacy." [79] *A Fool's Paradise* would lose money because English opinion was thoroughly sick of Home Rule; if Unionists succeeded in this last campaign, however, he was convinced that Home Rule would not trouble Britain for a generation. [80] Dicey thought the book "really nothing more nor less than the voice of 1886 addressing the new generation of 1913. One cannot in these circumstances expect to achieve much. The young on the whole must decide the course of present and future events." [81] The true interest of this latest work rested in the constitutional

76. Ibid.
77. Elliot to Dicey, 20 November 1912, ibid.
78. Albert Venn Dicey, *A Fool's Paradise.*
79. Dicey to Bonar Law, 12 February 1913, Bonar Law Papers.
80. Dicey to Strachey, 18 January 1913, Strachey Papers.
81. Dicey to Eliot, 22 April 1913, Eliot Papers.

doctrines upon which Dicey based his political conclusions. If the political arguments against Home Rule had not altered, the constitutional justification for resistance had changed dramatically from the 1885 *Law of the Constitution.*

In the 1913 discussion of the duty of Unionists, for example, Dicey asserted that if the Asquith government passed the Home Rule bill without a dissolution, then Unionists should regard the Home Rule Act as lacking constitutional authority and moral validity. The problem of English resistance would be considerably simplified, for resistance to an unconstitutional law presented no moral dilemmas. These arguments merit closer study. On the question of constitutional authority, Dicey was by 1913 renowned as the constitutional expert who had publicized fully the doctrine of the absolute supremacy of Parliament. By his own definition the laws Parliament passed were constitutional; Dicey himself had done most to banish the idea of unconstitutionality from English law. For him to argue that the mode of passage of a law could in any way affect its validity breached a fundamental principle of the constitution as he had described it. The politics of Home Rule now led him to the conclusion that the bill would be unconstitutional if a special set of circumstances did not precede its passage. This selective application of rule theory was indeed strange constitutional dogma from a scholar of Dicey's eminence.

That a Home Rule Act might lack moral validity was also a remarkable doctrine from a lawyer who, when it suited his purposes, had adhered rigidly to the Austinian separation of law and morality. Dicey had taught that legal obligation under English law never depended on moral content or lack thereof. Though Dicey had frequently insisted upon the close relationship of law and morals, this belief had seldom animated his constitutional writings. How far Dicey strayed from his own principles of constitutional law may be seen by comparison with his views a few years later on the position of conscientious objectors under English law. In 1918 Dicey stated unequivocally that it was a primary duty of every citizen of a state to obey the laws.[82] This statement was authentic Dicey, quite in spirit with his constitutional creed. In the service of Unionism, however, he jettisoned his usual jurisprudential creed and in the

82. Albert Venn Dicey, "The Conscientious Objector," p. 359.

process violated the spirit as well as the letter of his own legal doctrines. In the case of both constitutional authority and moral validity Dicey acknowledged that the constitutional practices he advocated were unusual, justifying them on the grounds that the Liberal government had indulged in immoral and unconstitutional acts first. Not only was this assertion dubious in itself, but even if true, that fact hardly called for the remedies Dicey now endorsed. These novel doctrines contradicted a career of rare distinction in constitutional scholarship; as such they were not worthy of Dicey. Deeply committed to the Home Rule question, he allowed his emotions to interpret the constitution instead of his intellect.

In *A Fool's Paradise* Dicey returned to his basic premise about Irish affairs: "I am an old, an unconverted, and an impenitent Benthamite. I hold to the belief that where, in one State, the welfare of 40,000,000 has to be weighed against the welfare of 4,000,000, the welfare of the greater number ought to prevail, and in this case my utilitarianism is confirmed by the reflection that of the 4,000,000 residents in Ireland, 1,000,000 do not demand, but on the contrary abominate, Home Rule."[83] From start to finish Dicey never wavered in the presumption that Ireland formed no separate nation. To admit the nationhood of Ireland would have switched the Benthamite calculus dramatically. If it were solely a question of four million Irish citizens, then surely Home Rule must win, as a clear majority favored it. By insisting on the place of Ireland within the United Kingdom, based on the denial of separate nationhood, Dicey avoided awkward challenges to his Benthamite values. The Irish Question meant economic or political issues, never was it a problem of conflicting nationalisms.

A Fool's Paradise gained the customary praise in Unionist circles. Austen Chamberlain termed it "at once an encouragement and an armoury for the struggle" while professing depression about the public apathy over Home Rule.[84] Sir Edward Carson desired that "anyone who cares about the country would read this book & the previous ones."[85] Given the tensions of 1913, this book had even

83. *A Fool's Paradise*, p. ix.
84. Austen Chamberlain to Dicey, 13 February 1913, General Manuscripts 508(41), Glasgow University Library.
85. Sir Edward Carson to Dicey, 19 July 1913, General Manuscripts 508(35), ibid.

less influence than his earlier ones. Dicey admitted that "controversial work is essentially dreary."[86] He was prepared for the slight ripple the book caused; still, he could have accepted fiery Liberal denunciations better than indifference. Refusal to take the Home Rule problem seriously added another piece of evidence that the new generation did not value resistance to Home Rule as highly as Dicey.

Throughout 1913 Dicey maintained his unflagging epistolary efforts at preserving the spirit of Unionism. His correspondence with Bonar Law and Strachey grew even more voluminous as he followed the politics of the day closer than ever before. He stressed continually the necessity for Unionists to press for a dissolution before the Home Rule bill passed. Dicey surpassed himself in the number of detailed letters devoted to this single requirement, particularly those addressed to the Unionist leader. The only excuse for them, he wrote, was "my zeal for Unionism."[87] During the year Dicey, distressed by public disinterest, became more introspective about his singular devotion to the Union. He explained that "there is something in me which makes Home Rule and its evils possess my mind. My contemporaries seem, I know not why, to have become quite indifferent about a matter which haunts me as much as it did in 1887."[88] On account of this attitude Strachey bestowed upon him the recognition as "the staunchest of Unionists."[89] Dicey's private contemplation brought forth no new conclusions, for he retained his customary pieties about the danger to England and the Empire. He admitted his fanaticism on the subject, but excused this on the grounds that time drew short for opponents of Home Rule. The Asquith government had no intention of allowing the people to choose before the bill passed into law.[90] Thus he felt it imperative that a dissolution be forced upon the government as soon as possible.

How this difficult assignment might be accomplished Dicey carefully explained to Bonar Law: by the collection and presentation of petitions, by the constant holding of Unionist meetings to demand

86. Dicey to Holmes, 15 July 1913, Holmes Papers.
87. Dicey to Bonar Law, 3 January 1913, Bonar Law Papers.
88. Dicey to Mrs. Litchfield, 4 April 1913, in Rait, *Memorials*, p. 218.
89. Strachey to Dicey, 18 February 1913, Strachey Papers.
90. Dicey to Strachey, 11 May 1913, ibid.

it, by clamoring for it at each by-election, by making every effort to win by-elections, by subordinating every other political object to this demand, *"The announcement in some more or less public fashion of the readiness on the part of the Unionist leaders to take office for the sake of holding a dissolution, even if this involves taking in the face of a hostile majority in the House of Commons."*[91] The advantages of such a campaign Dicey thought obvious. Unionists should pose as defenders of the rights of the electorate, attracting many non-Unionists to the cause. It would strengthen the hand of Unionists to assail Home Rule if passed without a dissolution. The agitation would open the eyes of the king to his constitutional powers, a point on which Dicey placed great emphasis. This campaign provided a policy all Unionists might back without reservation.[92] Bonar Law politely noted the counsel of Dicey, then proceeded along the path the realities of politics demanded. This result produced in Dicey an intensification of despair as his hopes of defeating Home Rule declined.

The failure of party leaders, with the exception of Bonar Law, to fight to the death on Home Rule earned them severe censure. According to Strachey they placed greater importance on tariff reform than preservation of the Union.[93] With this analysis Dicey sadly concurred. The Unionists could not lead "because they cannot trust either themselves or their followers. They are neither men of light nor men of leading."[94] Unionist leaders preferred threats of civil war to force a dissolution instead of the less dangerous path Dicey had suggested. Bonar Law agreed with the insistence upon a dissolution but thought the best hope of avoiding civil war lay in convincing the government that Unionists were deadly serious about its prospects.[95] The Unionist chief added that this policy had already taken effect, that the Liberals could not persevere in the forcing of Home Rule, and a dissolution would soon be forthcoming. The prominence granted to the need for a dissolution pleased Dicey, but he qualified his acquiescence to Bonar Law's logic with the obser-

91. Dicey to Bonar Law, 28 March 1913, Bonar Law Papers. Italics in the original.
92. Dicey to Strachey, 27 April 1913, Strachey Papers.
93. Strachey to Dicey, 29 April 1913, ibid.
94. Dicey to Strachey, 11 May 1913, ibid.
95. Bonar Law to Dicey, 12 June 1913, Bonar Law Papers.

vation that any sort of desperate political conflict over a dissolution was preferable to civil war.[96] For this reason he emphasized an alternative solution to the problem facing Unionism.

Many times before he had alluded to the possibility of a royal intervention to break the impasse between a government pushing ahead with Home Rule and an opposition talking of armed resistance. Dicey now stressed the constitutional duty of the king to call to office a Unionist government "wholly and solely for the purpose of referring the Home Rule Bill to the electors for their sanction or rejection."[97] At the same time Dicey deplored Unionist rhetoric about resuscitation of the royal veto, because such talk would destroy Unionism at the polls. He urged that Home Rule must be fought before the bill passed, and Unionists must not rely on the veto after it had become law.[98] "Strong or fanatical Unionist as I am," he wrote, "I would not venture to advise at this crisis the use of the Veto."[99] On one occasion, while lauding the "noble work" of Carson in battling Home Rule, he pressed Bonar Law to clarify the folly of Carson's endorsement of the royal veto. Dicey never denied the existence of this power, but argued that a sufficient crisis had not yet arisen for its application. When the occasion demanded, "I am fully prepared as a constitutionalist, to defend the employment of the Veto."[100] In the meantime Unionists should harp upon the moral necessity of a dissolution, keeping a discreet silence about the royal veto. If political conditions required a choice, however, "Personally I should prefer the use of the Veto to the outbreak of civil war and the use of cannons and rifles."[101] This flirtation with royal power once again illuminated the constitutional morass into which Dicey sank. He maintained that the one constitutional principle binding on the king was "that he shall not oppose the undoubted will of the nation."[102] This claim ignored the tenor of constitutional development in the nineteenth century, when the Crown was removed from politics; the monarch was excused from

96. Dicey to Bonar Law, 13 June 1913, ibid.
97. Dicey to Strachey, 19 February 1913, Strachey Papers.
98. Dicey to Bonar Law, 28 March 1913, Bonar Law Papers.
99. Ibid., 25 March 1913, ibid.
100. Ibid., 13 June 1913, ibid.
101. Dicey to Strachey, 21 May 1913, Strachey Papers.
102. Ibid., 18 August 1913, ibid.

the task of ascertaining the popular will. So positive was Dicey that the country opposed Home Rule that he never thought that the nation might approve Home Rule. Royal intervention might then be construed as partisan action on behalf of the Unionist party, destroying the constitutional position of the monarchy. To this possibility Dicey was blind; if necessary the king must be enlisted in the fight against Home Rule no matter what the consequences.

The avowed purpose of some Unionists to resist Home Rule after it had become law caused grave concern to Dicey. Fighting the government tooth and nail before it became law seemed the only sensible course to him. He agonized over the moral problems of Ulster defiance when a decision appeared imminent. Charles Eliot had already cautioned him that *A Fool's Paradise* had gone too far in encouraging obstruction to law; Dicey told Holmes frankly that he retracted no statement in his book.[103] His perplexity found little resolution in the cries of Unionists who would launch civil war "when this accursed Bill is the law of the land & when there is from a legal point of view no Union to defend."[104] Once again searching his conscience, Dicey presented this uneasiness to Strachey in the form of hypothetical questions. If the Home Rule bill passed without a prior dissolution, could English Unionists abet the resistance of Ulster?[105] Dicey believed this treason. What if Asquith dissolved Parliament before the Act took effect, then after the election still had a majority dependent upon Irish votes? What if, in the same situation, Asquith acquired a small majority of his own? Strachey, ever the political realist, had little trouble in answering two of Dicey's queries.[106] In reply to the first, whether treasonable or not, he would aid the resistance of Ulster by as large and as open a subscription as he could afford. The second question Strachey considered too problematical and offered no opinion. If the last eventuality occurred, then he had no right to encourage Ulster but must instead discourage opposition to the law as best he could. These answers by his friend allayed Dicey's anxiety little, for thoughts of treason did not come lightly to him.[107] For the rest of the year this

103. Dicey to Holmes, 15 July 1913, Holmes Papers.
104. Dicey to Strachey, 18 May 1913, Strachey Papers.
105. Ibid., 21 May 1913, ibid.
106. Strachey to Dicey, 22 May 1913, ibid.
107. Dicey to Strachey, 23 May 1913, ibid.

difficult moral problem continued to plague him: "My own mind is full of doubt and I do not wish to come without the greatest deliberation to any decision. This is in the strictest sense private."[108] This circumspect attitude Dicey adhered to scrupulously when, for example, he donated £50 to the Irish Unionist Alliance: he specified that the money be devoted to speakers only, in order that he should not support in any way the prospect of civil war.[109] The predicament remained, to be faced again in the future.

Dicey maintained that under no circumstances should Unionists assent to Home Rule, even with Ulster excluded, because by this act they made the repeal of Home Rule impossible. They could not agree to its passage one year and then repeal it whenever they returned to office.[110] By such a charade Unionists themselves would sanction "the surrender of all that Unionists have fought for since 1886."[111] Unionists could not, even for the sake of averting civil war, cooperate in the passing of any form of Home Rule. He retained his hard line on Ireland as firmly as ever, compromise on the issue impossible. The Union outweighed every consideration, for, once lost, it could never be restored. He appealed to Strachey to abandon the exemption-of-Ulster plan, which "seems to me nothing else than holding out the White Flag of surrender."[112] Strachey, who favored the Ulster formula as a moderate solution to an immoderate problem, held his ground, unapologetic for his stance; only the future could decide who was correct.[113]

Nineteen fourteen continued the dreary saga of political conflict. Dicey condemned the Unionist argument that Asquith would not pursue Home Rule to the bitter end; failure to do so, Dicey thought, spelled ruin for Asquith's political future: "Personally I am convinced that Asquith will never now advise a dissolution."[114] He reiterated his demand that every legal tactic available to the opposition should be used in forcing an appeal to the electors before Home Rule became law. He laid his views before the public with all

108. Ibid., 6 October 1913, ibid.
109. Dicey to Elliot, 23 October 1913, Elliot Papers.
110. Dicey to Strachey, 10 October 1913, Strachey Papers.
111. Ibid., 14 October 1913, ibid.
112. Ibid., 16 October 1913, ibid.
113. Strachey to Dicey, 16 October 1913, ibid.
114. Dicey to Bonar Law, 18 February 1914, Bonar Law Papers.

the vigor customary in these efforts.[115] Despite his frenetic activity there seemed to be no stopping Home Rule.

In this context Dicey was among the original signers of the British Covenant when it first appeared on 3 March 1914. A. M. Gollin has written of Dicey as "in the grip of an agitation of a kind that occasionally seizes upon the academic mind and produces curious, extraordinary and even violent results."[116] The story of Dicey's long involvement with Irish affairs should have sufficiently demonstrated that his emotional state in March 1914 was no occasional event, but the logical result of a three-decade preoccupation with the Home Rule controversy. Dicey embraced the covenant as a new test of loyalty to Unionist principles. Every Unionist and every patriotic Englishman ought to sign, though he feared the hesitation and stupidity of ordinary citizens might prevent such a response: "I am sure it is now or never for the Union."[117] Association with Lord Milner and the British Covenant marked the climactic point of his involvement with potentially treasonable activities. Dicey had wrestled with the theoretical problem of Ulster defiance of the law for several years without arriving at an answer to the moral and constitutional dilemmas it posed. Milner, a man of action whose plans for the defense of Ulster rapidly took shape, forced a final decision. In the long history of Dicey's connection with Home Rule, many parts unflattering to the jurist, he salvaged a modicum of respect by shrinking from treason, the final betrayal of his own constitutional precepts:

> I am afraid that I cannot do much in the direction towards which you quite naturally point. . . . I have not the least doubt that if the Home Rule Act is passed, defiance of it will be crime and probably treason. I can go a good way in defending this action on the part of the Ulstermen. About the part to be taken by Englishmen after the passing of the Home Rule Act, I have my doubts. I trust and hope that I may be able to act together with the whole Unionist Party, but much will depend upon

115. Albert Venn Dicey, "Facts and Thoughts for Unionists," pp. 717–23; "The Appeal to the Nation," pp. 945–57.

116. Alfred M. Gollin, *Proconsul in Politics*, p. 197.

117. Dicey to Lord Milner, 3 March 1914, Lord Milner Papers, Bodleian Library, Oxford.

circumstances. On one point, which if I wrote on the matter at all I should be forced to mention, I suspect I dissent from many Unionists. I am pretty certain that all members of the Army, officers or soldiers, will obey orders. My opinion is that it is their duty to do so. I am certain that the English public will never tolerate the dictation of the Army. I think the public are in this right.[118]

The talk of civil war by British covenanters, Dicey soon realized, harmed the Unionist cause. Other Unionists found the movement ill timed and ill organized; as Elliot informed Dicey: "All these lists of Duchesses and Primrose League Dames, with a *small* sprinkling of rational, non-party and patriotic men, will not impress the public."[119] It is to Dicey's credit, however small the merit a negative act earns, that he dissociated himself from the pugnacious factions of the Unionist party.

About the role of the Army in the Ulster controversy, for instance, Dicey had been forthright. He was convinced that Army meddling in government would fail, as the example of Oliver Cromwell showed, because the English people would not tolerate such activity.[120] Dicey disapproved Unionist threats to tamper with the Army, "for I have always entertained the strongest conviction that in a civilised country obedience to lawful orders was the absolute duty of soldiers and that the British Army would, in circumstances however painful, fulfill this duty."[121] Though he suspected every manner of Liberal treachery in the confusion known as the Curragh Mutiny in March 1914, this did not excuse Unionist activities. Spreading sedition in the army did little to forestall Home Rule; only a dissolution could accomplish that.[122] The Asquith government had gained sympathy by portraying itself as the guardian of civilian control over the military. Dicey recognized that constitutional fastidiousness mattered little in Ireland, where both Protestants and Catholics busily armed for war. In spite of this he again

118. Ibid., 6 March 1914, ibid.
119. Elliot to Dicey, 12 March 1914, Elliot Papers. Italics in the original.
120. Dicey to Strachey, 14 July 1913, Strachey Papers.
121. Dicey to Sir Edward Carson, 9 December 1913, in Ian Colvin, *Carson the Statesman*, p. 238.
122. Dicey to Bonar Law, 28 March 1914, Bonar Law Papers.

impressed upon Milner that a dissolution was preferable to civil war: "At the present moment [7 May 1914] my doctrine is probably of little importance. I am glad to have put my convictions on record, they may either soon or on some future occasion become of importance."[123] The flirtation with Milner demonstrated that he would not take the final step by which legal resistance turned into treason. At the final moment common sense and constitutional propriety prevailed over his Unionist sympathies.

This hesitation at criminal action did not otherwise moderate his tone about political affairs or ease his apprehension about the impending Home Rule clash. In a long plea to Balfour in April Dicey urged his former hero to keep Ulster in a defensive position lest the importation of arms alienate English opinion. An appeal to the moral sense of British electors alone could save Ulster, and false steps might easily forfeit this sentiment. Balfour must perform this task and "thereby save the Union between Great Britain & Ireland."[124] Balfour could do little, so events moved inexorably forward into the summer of 1914. To the last Dicey recommended that the king should intervene to force a dissolution upon the government and secure the authority of the nation, a suggestion completely impossible in the political context.[125] "I confess," he wrote, "that I am utterly out of heart when I perceive that the Amending Act if passed, will in effect be the repeal of the Act of Union between Great Britain & Ireland and sacrifice that Union when it had really begun to produce good effects in Ireland."[126] This latter conclusion must be attributed more to Unionist faith than to an objective appraisal of the situation; his old friend Bryce provided a better analysis to A. Lawrence Lowell:

> Our situation in England is not only interesting but extraordinary and, I must add, deplorable. Five years ago no one would have dreamed that such things were possible as the open advocacy of civil war and the toleration by Government of two armed and drilled bodies of men threatening one another, under

123. Dicey to Milner, 7 May 1914, Milner Papers.
124. Dicey to Balfour, 28 April 1914, Balfour Papers, B.M. Add. Mss. 49792.
125. Dicey to Strachey, 14 June 1914, Strachey Papers.
126. Ibid., 24 June 1914, ibid.

circumstances which might precipitate them into a conflict such as has not been seen since 1798 or perhaps even 1689. It would take too long to explain how this state of things has been brought about, and perhaps you have watched our politics long enough to understand the causes. Most of us here think that the Government has been strangely negligent, or over sanguine, in allowing the Ulster volunteers to arm and drill and threaten action, palpably illegal. However, as things stand now, Ministers seem to have concluded that Home Rule could not be imposed by force without the risk of serious bloodshed, which would not only discredit us in the eyes of the world, and damage the Ministry heavily, but would make the working of Home Rule more difficult, reopening old wounds which we had supposed to be long closed. There has, of course, been a great deal of bluff, but the Ulster volunteers have now bluffed themselves into a position when their blood is up and their feeling is real. They are prepared to fight and they count upon the reluctance of a considerable section of the Army to take action against them. The situation is darker at this moment than it has yet been, because the leaders of both sides are not in command of the position. Carson is believed to be uneasy at the point to which he has led his men, and willing to enter into an arrangement but he dare not do it except upon terms which the Nationalists cannot be expected to accept. Redmond himself would, I believe, be willing to go a long way to meet Carson, and he would be right in doing so, because, from his point of view, the vital thing is to get his Home Rule Parliament established in Ireland, even if it only includes three fourths of Ireland. The exclusion of Ulster could hardly be permanent. If the Home Rule Parliament works well, the situation will somehow change, and the Imperial Parliament will again intervene. The sentiment of the Ulster volunteers is quite genuine, although their apprehensions of the increase in the power of the Roman Catholic Church, or of any kind of religious persecution, are absolutely groundless, and the Tory leaders in England, most of whom must know how groundless these religious terrors are, seem to me to be merely using Ulster as a pawn in their party game. Although the best of them feel that it is a very dangerous game, their feeling is so bitter that it looks as if they would continue to play it. The worst part of the whole business is, that it is liable to sap still further the respect for law and order, which used to be a distinguishing feature of our people. There is, I am afraid, something in your tribute to our management of our political affairs, written six years ago, which would not be true today, so rapidly have events moved.[127]

This state of opinion made rational discussion of the issues all but impossible.

The last act of the Home Rule drama came on 21 July 1914, when the Conference of Eight met in a frantic effort to resolve Irish difficulties.[128] On its eve Dicey warned again that Asquith sought only party advantage from the conference. This provided the final opportunity for Unionist leaders to demand a dissolution before the bill became the act, since "Unionism must naturally come to an end when there is no longer a union to defend."[129] On the same day Dicey sent Bonar Law a long memorandum detailing the dangers the Unionist chief would face on the morrow.[130] Asquith looked for further delay; he wished to involve Unionist leaders in passing the Home Rule bill; he wanted to prevent the king from forcing a dissolution. As always Dicey enumerated the steps necessary to escape these Asquithian snares. Unionists must insist upon the right to a dissolution; if Carson desired, the total exclusion of Ulster must be obtained; Unionists should not pledge no repeal of Home Rule if the act passed before a dissolution. The conference soon broke down amid an atmosphere of mutual distrust. Dicey thereupon repeated in the *Times* his insistence that a dissolution must precede passage of Home Rule.[131] Even the darkening international scene could not focus his attention elsewhere; on 31 July he sent a final caveat to Bonar Law that opponents of Home Rule must remain vigilant because "ever since he became Prime Minister Asquith has never sacrificed any party advantage to considerations of patriotism."[132] To the end of peacetime Dicey fought for the defense of the Union.

127. Bryce to Lowell, 17 June 1914, Bryce Papers.
128. The eight were: Asquith and Lloyd George for the Liberals, Bonar Law and Lansdowne for the Conservatives, Redmond and John Dillon for the Nationalists, and Carson and James Craig for Ulster.
129. Dicey to Strachey, 20 July 1914, Strachey Papers.
130. Dicey to Bonar Law, 20 July 1914, Bonar Law Papers.
131. *Times*, 27 July 1914, p. 10.
132. Dicey to Bonar Law, 31 July 1914, Bonar Law Papers.

What answer may now be given to Dicey's own question about the extraordinary hold the Home Rule question had upon his time and work? His antipathy to Irish nationalism may best be interpreted in the twin context of his youthful idealism about the heroic nature of nationalism and the equation of nationalism with territorial integrity. In the first sense, the long years of maturity had shown him how nationalism played a role in the modern world far different from that envisioned by the undergraduate Dicey. Dicey described this process in old age when he wrote that any ideal has defects unperceived by the proponents of that ideal.[133] Throughout his life intense dedication to the lofty aspirations of nationalism could not permit inaction while the enthusiasms of youth were destroyed. Dicey's political creed deserves study because he was that *rara avis* of English life, a devoted nationalist from mid-century who paid scant attention to later imperialist rhetoric. His hopes for the future remained pinned to the redeeming value of nationalism as expressed in the political configuration of Great Britain. But nationalism did change, Dicey himself analyzing the long process of disenchantment:

> Everybody I think who has thought over the matter at all must admit that while the so-called principle [of nationalism] contains an amount of truth which explains the influence it exerted over some of the best men who preached it to the world sixty or seventy years ago, it clearly needs very careful definition. It is further I think pretty clear to anyone who marks the influence of Nationalism during the last fifty years, that a sentiment which seemed to Mazzini and to Cavour almost wholly good, contains in it a good deal of possible evil, and that at best nationalism which was preached as the basis of moral unity may also well be the means of disuniting a people who have come to live happily and prosperously as the members of one State.[134]

Nationalism as moral and political unity defined the Union for Dicey, with the result that Irish nationalism, because it attacked the unity, had to be fought at all times and with every weapon. The

133. Dicey to Rait, 11 February 1920, in Rait, *Memorials*, p. 278.
134. Dicey to Bryce, 19 December 1918, Bryce Papers.

integrative tendency in nationalism, as Dicey assumed nationalism must always be, could not abide the centrifugal force of Irish national feeling. In fighting Home Rule Dicey defended the Union as a symbol of British nationalism, a major tenet of his mid-Victorian faith.

How typical was Dicey's intransigent opposition to Home Rule? Because his attempts to influence politics invariably proved futile, was he therefore a solitary figure set against the currents of an age he could not comprehend? In his analysis of Unionist addresses for the second election of 1910, Neal Blewett concluded that Unionists "verged on the hysterical." [135] If that description applied to 1910, what phrase properly conveys their state of mind in the spring of 1914? How serious was the threat of civil war over Ulster? The study of Dicey's attitudes for this period allows some provisional judgments on a small portion of this problem. In the Unionist circles he frequented, opposition to Home Rule approached an Armageddon mentality by the summer of 1914. The British Covenant had gained two million signatures by July 1914; and Dicey complained that many university Unionists of his acquaintance refused to sign on the grounds it would commit their college, a reservation unknown in 1886. [136] On Home Rule Dicey stood alone in the sense that he continued to argue the issue in constitutional terms; but many others followed the Unionist banner as fiercely for mundane political reasons. The influence of Dicey came in legitimatizing Unionist resistance, sheltering other motives under his umbrella of constitutional arguments.

The question of aiding Ulster defiance caused anguish among English Unionists, and many, like Milner, prepared to see the contest through. As has been described, Dicey could not accept that. The assertion that "most of the Ulster Volunteers would probably have melted away as rapidly as they had materialised" [137] Dicey and his Unionist cohorts would have considered patently ridiculous. Dicey feared Ulstermen were too ferocious, not that they lacked courage. Too much reliance on Dicey alone would be wrong, but this account of his activities in the die-hard wing of the Unionist party suggests that this faction of Unionists were in earnest prior to

135. Neal Blewett, *The Peers, the Parties and the People*, pp. 326–29.
136. Dicey to Milner, 6 March 1914, Milner Papers.
137. Rowland, *The Last Liberal Governments*, p. 350.

August 1914. The political significance of Dicey lay in reflecting a Unionist mood of no compromise on Home Rule. What effect this feeling had in Ulster remains problematical, but it should not have weakened the will of Ulster to fight Home Rule by every means possible. Only such a cataclysmic event as the Great War could have diverted Dicey from Irish affairs, and at that the war took some time before this happened. So at first the Irish Question still occupied his attention.

CHAPTER ELEVEN

THE IMPACT OF WAR,

1914–1918

T HE NECESSITY OF strong support for the war did not initially take precedence over the battle against Home Rule. Before the end of August 1914 Dicey urged Bonar Law to obtain an authentic truce on Irish affairs or else the absolute exclusion of Ulster from the Home Rule bill still pending. Distrust of Asquith made Dicey "dread that the Government should make national patriotism the means of securing a party triumph."[1] While he praised the "magnificent outburst of national and patriotic feeling" the war occasioned, this display should not obscure the Unionist duty to ensure that a fundamental issue like Home Rule should not be settled by private arrangements among government officials.[2] Any proposed resolution of the Home Rule controversy required the assent of the electorate to have validity. Dicey faced an uncomfortable dilemma, because obstruction on Home Rule might dilute the mood of national unanimity; yet how else could one remain true to Unionist principles? Bonar Law might accept the bill without betrayal of Unionism if he could obtain a concession of Home Rule's coming into operation only by specific address of the House of Commons.[3] In any case, Unionists must make their policy clear to the country lest the idea of a corrupt bargain harm the reputation of the party.[4] Either a true truce must prevail or Unionists must continue their opposition as before.

Caught between the demands of Redmond for Home Rule and the solid defiance of Protestant Ulster, Asquith, who was never so desirous of Home Rule as Dicey alleged, placated both sides by putting the bill on the statute book but suspending its operation. Dicey opposed this strategem, because it established Home Rule as

1. Dicey to Bonar Law, 24 August 1914, Bonar Law Papers.
2. Dicey to Strachey, 28 August 1914, Strachey Papers.
3. Dicey to Bonar Law, 1 September 1914, Bonar Law Papers.
4. Ibid., 7 September 1914, ibid.

the law of the land; its nonoperation afforded him little consolation. In light of this disheartening development, Dicey urged that Bonar Law assert the just claim of Ulster to exclusion, and the injustice of irritating Ulstermen who had rallied to the defense of the country. Yet Bonar Law must avoid any appearance of lack of patriotism.[5] Precisely how Bonar Law should accomplish these goals Dicey did not specify. Dicey proclaimed the essential unfairness of Asquith's cloaking Home Rule in the guise of patriotism, a view with which Bonar Law agreed, but Unionists had no alternative to supporting the government.[6] Dicey would have preferred that the Home Rule bill remain in legislative limbo until after the war had ended. The bill passed into law with the proviso that amending legislation would be required before it took effect.

This final step by the government brought a predictable reaction from Dicey, who wrote of his "bitter regret" that the bill had become law even with the various stipulations about its practice.[7] Asquith was guilty of the worst perfidy for violating the political truce supposed to last for the duration of the war. That Asquith's action justified the vituperation Dicey had aimed at the prime minister over the years mollified him little; to Dicey it was yet another proof the Liberal leader would turn any situation to his political advantage. He wrote to Bonar Law that Unionists must perform the patriotic though painful duty of aiding the government.[8] A few days later he reported to Bonar Law that the *Times* had not published his letter in agreement with Bonar Law's protest against the passage of Home Rule. The paper had done so, he thought, to prevent partisan strife from harming the war spirit; Dicey certainly had not that intention, wishing only "that all my friends should know that I stood firmly by the Unionist Party and its leaders till the last."[9] Few could have believed otherwise.

Eventually this long letter, or really a personal statement of the kind Dicey often made, appeared in the Belfast *Northern Whig.*[10]

5. Ibid., 10 September 1914, ibid.
6. Ibid., 15 September 1914, ibid.
7. Dicey to Macmillan, 16 September 1914, Macmillan Company Papers, B.M. Add. Mss. 55085.
8. Dicey to Bonar Law, 16 September 1914, Bonar Law Papers.
9. Ibid., 21 September 1914, ibid.
10. *Northern Whig,* 5 October 1914, clipping in the Milner Papers.

He wrote as a Unionist of 1886 in order to brace the morale of Ulster, demonstrating that the battle for the Union, though not yet won, had not been entirely lost either. As proof he cited ministerial statements that the Home Rule Act as it stood would never be enforced. Asquith had conceded in the House of Commons that the coercion of Ulster was absolutely unthinkable. Finally, the men of Ulster had given to the United Kingdom a splendid model of patriotism, so no government, in view of Ulster self-sacrifice, could violate the no-coercion pledge. This address to the Unionists of northern Ireland put a more optimistic interpretation on events than Dicey felt privately. In lamenting the existence of the inoperative Home Rule Act, Dicey found to his dismay that Arthur Elliot had turned into a "win the War" man with no time for phantom issues like Home Rule.[11] This discovery caused great pain, for he counted Elliot among the most steadfast of his Unionist friends. Dicey revealed to Strachey his true feelings about the enactment of Home Rule:

> I know you will sympathise with my intense disappointment & to you, I may add indignation, at the passing of the H.R. Act. It should in common fairness have remained the H.R. Bill till after end of the War, in my judgment, till the meeting of the next Parliament. In this case, as in every other, Asquith has preferred the interest of his party, or rather, his own interest as a party leader to the welfare of the Nation. Silence is now right: his own interest and the interest of the nation coincide. *But I implore you never trust him or use language wh. implies he can be trusted.* . . .
>
> I don't believe that the H.R. Act with Ulster either excluded or included, is the final settlement of the relation between England and Ireland. But the Union as we have known it, is I fear gone forever.[12]

The belief that he must abstain from political controversy destructive of the war effort diminished severely his writings about Home Rule: "I hate writing anything about the Home Rule Act; it simply reminds me of wasted labour and energy for more than 25

11. Dicey to Elliot, ? October 1914, Elliot Papers.
12. Dicey to Strachey, 25 October 1914, Strachey Papers. Italics in the original.

years of my life."[13] On one issue he could not restrain himself: the possibility that certain clauses in the Suspensory Act might be interpreted by the government in such a way that Home Rule could come into operation without further reference to the House of Commons. Strachey assured him that not even Asquith would outrage public opinion by such a blatantly partisan maneuver before the end of hostilities.[14] Dicey dissented from this assessment of Asquith, still distrusting the prime minister's "supreme skill and extreme unscrupulosity as a party leader."[15] The fear of Asquithian duplicity led him to send a memorandum about this possibility to Bonar Law. Dicey warned the Unionist leader that no greater delusion existed than the belief that the Asquith government would wait until the end of the war before again acting on Home Rule.[16] Bonar Law must watch the government at all times lest the truce end abruptly with a surprise move. The best precaution against this possibility lay in amending the Suspensory Act to preclude another of Asquith's sharp maneuvers.[17] Dicey's anxiety proved groundless in September 1915, when the 14 September Order in Council reaffirmed the provisions of the Suspensory Act. Still Dicey could not shake his uneasiness that Asquith might yet stoop to additional political chicanery.[18] The long years of opposition had left Dicey suspicious of every aspect of the Home Rule controversy.

Other than this outburst Dicey adhered consistently to his vow of silence about Irish matters. He managed this difficult feat primarily by constant reminders to his correspondents that he had undertaken this uncharacteristic quiet from a sense of patriotic duty.[19] The frequent mention of his self-denying ordinance showed Dicey had not lost interest in Home Rule. Nevertheless, when compared to the flood of letters on Ireland prior to August 1914, the self-imposed restraint was indeed remarkable.

Perhaps the best proof of fidelity to this pledge lay in the silence

13. Ibid., 4 January 1915, ibid.
14. Strachey to Dicey, 7 January 1915, ibid.
15. Dicey to Strachey, 9 January 1915, ibid.
16. Dicey to Bonar Law, 5 February 1915, Bonar Law Papers.
17. Ibid., 10 February and 19 May 1915, ibid.
18. Ibid., 20 September 1915, ibid.
19. Ibid., Dicey to Strachey, 14 November and 10 December 1915, Strachey Papers.

about the 1916 Easter Rebellion. On past evidence it is easy to conjecture the feelings of outrage with which Dicey greeted the news, his demands for immediate suppression of this treasonable action at all costs, and the stern approval in the interests of justice of the subsequent execution of the rebel leaders. Nowhere is there direct proof of these emotions. Not until June 1916 did he end his silence about Ireland. The occasion was Lloyd George's attempt to engineer a Home Rule compromise between Carson and Redmond in the aftermath of the Rising. Dicey sent Bonar Law a letter plus a long memorandum, almost completely underscored for emphasis.[20] In the letter he showed that the Easter Rebellion had not altered his views at all. Resolving Home Rule solely by agreement between Irish Unionists and Irish Nationalists violated the understanding held by English Unionists since 1886, Dicey maintained, that the settlement of Irish affairs concerned the entire United Kingdom. Dicey denounced the work of Lloyd George, as it could only weaken the chance for success against Germany. Further, he reminded Bonar Law that he had abstained purposely from writing on Home Rule, but he had watched the conflict with great care for thirty years and would not be silent if the Irish Question terminated in this solution. In an atmosphere necessary for delicate negotiations to flourish, Bonar Law could not totally disregard the implied threat to publish something inflammatory.

In the accompanying memorandum Dicey indicated that two facts now dominated the Home Rule question: the Easter Rebellion in Dublin and the Home Rule Act already on the statute book at Westminster. He therefore put five arguments to Bonar Law in an effort to dissuade him from approval of the Carson-Redmond talks: the sudden popular emotion for conciliation between Irish parties and reconciliation between Great Britain and Ireland provided no sound foundation for an enduring settlement; concessions to Ireland as a result of rebellion and murder would only strengthen Sinn Fein by fostering the impression that violence and treason alone could bring about desired changes; the Home Rule Act of 1914, with its abolition of the lord lieutenancy, would destroy the supremacy of the Imperial Parliament, and in addition, the exclusion of Ulster would be a legislative and practical problem; Home Rule introduced

20. Dicey to Bonar Law, 10 June 1916, Bonar Law Papers.

in wartime would betray those Ulstermen who had volunteered for service abroad on the understanding the question would remain in abeyance until peacetime; a hurried settlement in wartime might contain provisions ultimately fatal to the authority of the Imperial Parliament. Each of these considerations Dicey felt sufficient for rejection of the Lloyd George proposals. Collectively these arguments demanded resistance to any form of Home Rule.

Dicey repeated this line of reasoning to Strachey two days later. If Britain's bitterest foe schemed to ruin the country, he could not improve on the plan Lloyd George suggested. Lloyd George suffered "from that delusion which is common to dreamers of a certain type, that when you find a definite question which it is hard to settle, it is wise to make it part of a far more wide and more difficult question which you fancy may be easy to deal with because you have not as yet realised its immense practical difficulties."[21] To the various objections raised by Dicey, Strachey replied that English Unionists could not appear more Ulsterite than Ulstermen themselves. If Ulster could accept the Lloyd George proposals, how could Englishmen presume to veto the agreement?[22] Strachey conceded the policy of dividing Ireland involved risks but saw no other policy possible.

This argument of inevitability Dicey rejected at once. He insisted that the electorate had never agreed to Home Rule, so why must Unionists now stampede toward acceptance?[23] Home Rule negotiations must increase rather than lessen the problem of prosecuting the war. Once again Dicey depended less on the actual merits of the case than the alleged future difficulties a certain action must surely bring. Strachey retorted that the Home Rule experiment must be tried, for failure to do so would ruin the Unionist party.[24] Every Unionist leader backed a compromise on Home Rule. Unionists must preserve unity of action because the party was the hope of the country; the Liberals, Strachey wrote, were smashed to pieces. Since the Liberal and Irish Home Rule leaders desired a settlement, the country would doubtless ratify a decision reached by all parties. Dicey still would not capitulate. He would never accept the necessity of Home Rule:

21. Dicey to Strachey, 12 June 1916, Strachey Papers.
22. Strachey to Dicey, 14 June 1916, ibid.
23. Dicey to Strachey, 3 July 1916, ibid.
24. Strachey to Dicey, 5 July 1916, ibid.

The Unionist party will with the passing of this settlement into an Act of Parliament, come inevitably to an end. Whether the Liberal Party is smashed I know not. It will probably turn into a more or less Socialistic and what is worse, an anti-English party. I bitterly regret that the turn events have taken have filled me with distrust for all our parliamentary leaders. I believe that the best Unionists have been mainly influenced by their fear of destroying the Coalition Gov't. and thus injuring the country. This fear I believe to be misplaced. Not a German soldier less would perish if a Government were formed with two policies only. The maintenance of the war with the utmost efficiency and the maintenance of order in Ireland. It is their want of courage to see to these two things only which has ruined, and I fear will disgrace, the Unionists. I am absolutely certain that in such a policy they would have had the support of the country.[25]

The Carson-Redmond negotiations faltered and soon collapsed altogether. Ireland receded into the background, as Bryce noted: "Now everything is adjourned till the end of the war."[26]

For the remainder of the war Dicey more or less honored his vow of silence about Ireland. At the end of 1916 he warned Strachey that the introduction of conscription into Ireland might lead to another rebellion, thereby stirring up trouble needlessly.[27] In 1917 Dicey published two articles on Ireland, after that nothing. In the first, he repeated his opposition to Home Rule before peace and before the meeting of a new Parliament elected after the conclusion of a final peace treaty.[28] In the wake of the Easter Rebellion, Dicey urged, differences between Sinn Feiners, Parliamentary Nationalists, and Ulstermen precluded a lasting constitutional arrangement. The Home Rule Act of 1914 was already dead before it had ever taken effect. The Parliament elected in 1910 possessed no mandate to legislate on Home Rule, therefore not tampering with the troubled Irish situation remained the best policy. In the other article, Dicey asserted that a grant of dominion status to Ireland could not suc-

25. Dicey to Strachey, 6 July 1916, ibid.
26. Bryce to Eliot, 7 September 1916, Bryce Papers.
27. Dicey to Strachey, 24 December 1916, Strachey Papers.
28. Albert Venn Dicey, "Is It Wise to Establish Home Rule before the End of the War?," pp. 1–25.

ceed.[29] To support this position he again used the hoary arguments of 1886, particularly the contention that since the Irish did not wish this constitutional status, the whole idea was an exercise in futility and doomed to failure. These writings aside, Dicey made no mention of Ireland for the next year. This may be attributed to two factors: the increasing fascination of Dicey with the epic struggle on the Continent, and the military rule clamped on Ireland that prevented additional disturbances. The process by which World War I superseded even Ireland as his primary interest testified to the tremendous impact the war had upon him.

In August 1914 Dicey believed the war an inconvenient intrusion into the Irish Question. Shortly thereafter the heroic dimensions of the struggle began to make a profound impression, beginning the change of his priorities. This process may best be seen in a letter to Strachey in October 1914 when, after the usual bemoaning of the Irish situation, he added: "Nevertheless I am glad to have lived [to] witness this splendid outburst of national spirit."[30] From that point forward, the war occupied an increasing proportion of his attention, liberating him from the pall Ireland cast over his life. Against the melancholy record of politics, Dicey sensed the return of the heroic element to English life. As he wrote to W. P. Ker: "Do you feel as I do that the present war, terrible as it is, and fearful as are its results to many of one's friends, is the most instructive experience which I have ever gone through? I had no idea how much a just war, to those who felt it just, was a cause of new national unity."[31] Gradually it dawned on Dicey that a new dedication had gripped the country.

For an individual who had prized patriotism and national spirit above other civic virtues, the war offered many compensations: "I have never seen before and neither of us is likely to see again, such unanimity about any serious political topic as we see today about the War."[32] By the end of 1914 the redemptive aspects of the fighting offset the carnage suffered on the field of battle. The spirit of national unity had created sympathy among all classes of English-

29. Albert Venn Dicey, "Ireland as a 'Dominion'," pp. 700–26.
30. Dicey to Strachey, 25 October 1914, Strachey Papers.
31. Dicey to W. P. Ker, 16 November 1914, in Rait, *Memorials*, pp. 230–31.
32. Dicey to Bryce, 12 November 1914, Bryce Papers.

men, an unlikely occurrence in peacetime.[33] In early 1915 the gratitude occasioned by this outpouring of national strength found fullest expression in the conclusion to the new introduction in the eighth edition of *Law of the Constitution*. He had worked on this for months prior to the outbreak of the war, but the ending focused on the regeneration wrought by the war where the tremendous spirit "may console old men whom political disillusion and disappointment which they deem undeserved may have tempted towards despair, and enable them to rejoice with calmness and gravity that they have lived long enough to see the day when the solemn call to the performance of a grave national duty has united every man and every class of our common country in the determination to defy the strength, the delusions, and the arrogance of a militarised nation, and at all costs to secure for the civilised world the triumph of freedom, of humanity, and of justice."[34] The themes touched upon here anticipated Dicey's future attitude toward prosecution of the war: total victory or national death were the only alternatives, and the barbarism of the Germans required every exertion against this threat to European civilization. As was his wont, he divided the issue of the war into neat categories, throwing himself into unquestioning support for the conflict. Therefore .he resolved to rouse public support to the best of his ability.

Dicey did not share the optimism of contemporaries who believed the war would be short and decisive. He decided early that the struggle against Germany might last longer than the Napoleonic wars.[35] The protracted battle Dicey forecast convinced him of one fact: he would not live to see the triumph of Great Britain. As the fighting developed into a stalemate, the more positive he became that the war would last far longer than the ordinary Englishman suspected. The only advantage to this presumed length was that this would spare Dicey the problems sure to come at its end: "I am somewhat glad to believe I may not be mixed up with many of the

33. Dicey to Bryce and Mrs. Bryce, 31 December 1914, in Rait, *Memorials*, p. 231.

34. *Law of the Constitution*, 8th ed., .p. cv.

35. Dicey to Holmes, 11 January 1915, Holmes Papers; Dicey to Ker, 18 February 1915, in Rait, *Memorials*, p. 235; Dicey to Eliot, 26 April 1915, Eliot Papers.

hopeless controversies which will occupy the first years of peace."[36] As the need for sustaining enthusiasm grew, Dicey volunteered with the only weapon at his disposal, the pen.

This decision to participate in promoting patriotism was the more remarkable because Dicey, though enjoying good health, suffered inevitably from the infirmities of advancing age. He had grown quite deaf, to the point where ordinary conversation proved difficult. Nevertheless, Bryce described him in 1916 as "vivacious and active minded as ever."[37] Even at the end of the war when he was eighty-three, his wife wrote that he still enjoyed wonderful health.[38] The real problem was the drain on his energy his work caused: "I think that somehow though I am very well for my years, I have not yet properly learned to adjust my arrangements to the fact that everything seems twice as difficult to get done as it did to me even ten years ago."[39] As the war progressed, Dicey admitted reluctantly that the experience of old age counted for less "than the comparative vigour of youth or middle age."[40] He realized that his work must go slower if it were not to exhaust him, making all effort impossible.

In addition to the predictable problems of old age, Dicey found wartime Oxford, largely denuded of faculty and students, lonely and isolated. He had outlived most of his closest friends, many of those surviving now enfeebled: "I am most thankful that I still have power to write intelligibly. It is really an undeserved blessing when I think of the many men among our friends who have broken down."[41] This personal situation combined with his alienation from politics to reinforce the feeling of distance from his own times: "Pretty nearly every one older than myself with whom I was intimate has passed away. It is also impossible not to perceive that I myself belong in reality to the mid-Victorian age much more than to 1914."[42] Once he decided to serve his country by his writings, however, his strong devotion to duty spurred his efforts.

The first fruit of his resolve was an address at the Working Men's

36. Dicey to Bryce, 27 September 1916, Bryce Papers.
37. Bryce to Holmes, 14 September 1916, ibid.
38. Mrs. Dicey to Mrs. Bryce, 11 July 1918, ibid.
39. Dicey to Bryce, 12 November 1914, ibid.
40. Dicey to Strachey, 27 November 1916, Strachey Papers.
41. Dicey to Bryce, 27 July 1917, Bryce Papers.
42. Dicey to Bryce and Mrs. Bryce, 31 December 1914, in Rait, *Memorials*, p. 232.

College on 21 November 1914.[43] His purpose, as he informed Bryce, was to "try, if I can, to make it consist in the enforcement of the necessity of justice and of the duty of hope."[44] The duty of justice he defined as the imposition of judicial severity upon Germany. The Allies must obtain retribution, not retaliation, on behalf of the victims of German oppression. Great Britain must also secure that German aggression should not be repeated. The duty of hope meant that Britain must do everything possible to end German militarism and never despair of ultimate victory even in the face of German success. Dicey described this exhortation to Oxford acquaintance H. A. L. Fisher:

> I send you enclosed a copy of my pamphlet on the War. I dare say you have seen it, but it is a satisfaction to let one's friends know as far as one can how one stands as regards this terrible though, to my mind, absolutely necessary War, as far as England is concerned. There is certainly nothing new in the pamphlet. All it contains is an attempt on my part to express, as simply and clearly as I can the truth as I see it. But who will venture to assert that he sees the truth on any matter worth thinking about as it actually is? Certainly no man will venture upon this assertion who possesses common sense and has attained my age.[45]

In his search for analogies to lend weight to patriotic appeals, Dicey fastened upon the Napoleonic era about which he could remember his parents having talked. Great Britain must exhibit the same tenacity as a century earlier. Interest in the Napoleonic wars led him to discover that the political writings of Wordsworth during the Napoleonic era were relevant to the struggle begun in 1914.

His two major wartime publications examined the lessons Wordsworth might teach to the present generation. In 1915 the first, an introduction to the text of the tract on the Convention of Cintra, gave a preliminary account of Wordsworth's politics.[46] Dicey often

43. Albert Venn Dicey, *How We Ought to Feel about the War.*

44. Dicey to Bryce, 20 November 1914, Bryce Papers.

45. Dicey to H. A. L. Fisher, 12 February 1915, H. A. L. Fisher Papers, Bodleian Library, Oxford.

46. Albert Venn Dicey, "Introduction," in *Wordsworth's Tract on the Convention of Cintra,* pp. vii-xl.

admitted his shortcomings at literary criticism, so he avoided any attempt in this direction: "Thro' life I have sedulously fought shy of verses & poets."[47] Focusing on the political content of Wordsworth's work, Dicey praised him as a prophet of the nationalism dominant from 1815 to 1870 that had been so admirable. Mazzini was still a special hero for Dicey, and he expressed surprise that the Italian had not recognized Wordsworth as an early herald of nationalism.[48] This first work merely scratched the surface of the subject, for not until 1917 did Dicey publish his complete reflections.

The Statesmanship of Wordsworth aimed at two points: to establish the wisdom of the poet's writings and to show that his policies contained valuable lessons for Great Britain.[49] Dicey hoped the book might raise flagging spirits as the war lengthened and casualties mounted. On the eve of publication, as was customary with his books other than the political polemics, he held out small hope for its success: "It is not a satisfactory production. I found rather to my surprise, that having published two or three things which in substance make up the essay, did not so much help as perplex me when I tried to blend them into one whole. I was also a good deal tired whilst getting the book prepared. It is not a good, though certainly it is a very odd, piece of work to be done by me. The only thing in which I think I have succeeded is the avoiding of any attempt to criticise Wordsworth's poetry."[50] Dicey knew well that the topic lacked popular appeal, although he felt the effort expended well spent if it placed emphasis on the underlying issues of the war. Nevertheless he concluded: "It will do me little credit tho' or perhaps because I laboured a good deal at it."[51]

The message of the book came in the final chapter, where Dicey argued that Great Britain should imitate the policies Wordsworth had proclaimed a century earlier. In particular the country must manifest self-discipline, respect the spirit of nationalism, and reject any peace not providing complete victory. In addition, she must preserve the national independence of smaller countries against the aggression of Germany. This activity had formed the cornerstone of

47. Dicey to Strachey, 11 April 1915, Strachey Papers.
48. Dicey to Cromer, 12 December 1915, ibid.
49. Albert Venn Dicey, *The Statesmanship of Wordsworth*, p. 5.
50. Dicey to Bryce, 27 March 1917, Bryce Papers.
51. Ibid., 8 April 1917, ibid.

British foreign policy since the Napoleonic era, Dicey asserted, so Britain should not alter this traditional policy at such a crucial moment. Despite his best efforts, the book made little impact indeed. The price of the book was so high that, in order to stimulate sales, Dicey offered to forego his royalties if the cost could be halved.[52] Too late he perceived that the hortatory chapter might have succeeded if published separately as an inexpensive pamphlet. This realization apparently guided his wager that the book would sell closer to 500 than 5000 copies. Unfortunately, Dicey won the bet without difficulty.[53]

Despite the disappointing sales of the book, Dicey did take satisfaction from the critical acclaim it received. His preliminary pessimism gave way to genuine delight upon the appearance of the book. Dicey reaped the reward of praise from his friends: "It is a very strange thing, the S. of W. which will I expect never repay the Clarendon Press, which I most sincerely regret, nor get into a 2nd edition, has from the appreciation of friends, & the interest of the subject itself, given more of joy, than any book I have ever written."[54] Bryce, for example, called the book "striking," recommending it to A. Lawrence Lowell for its application of Wordsworth's teachings to the present war.[55] Another testimonial which gratified Dicey immensely came in a note from President Woodrow Wilson, a friend from the 1898 trip to America, who wrote that "I receive the book very gratefully as the work of a valued friend."[56] At Dicey's advanced age these sentiments amply compensated for his labors. Though he had correctly surmised that the book would earn no increase in reputation, still he concluded: "When one has reached the age of 82 one naturally feels that any book one gets published may be one's last. I should be well content as a writer & a man if the S. of W. occupied this position."[57] The writing of these wartime books indulged his sense of duty, making him feel part of

52. Dicey to A. L. Smith, 21 May 1917, Miscellaneous MSS, Balliol College. A. L. Smith was Master of Balliol from 1916 to 1924.
53. Sir Charles Oman, *Betting Book of All Souls,* p. 176. The sale was under 1000 copies.
54. Dicey to Bryce, 25 July 1917, Bryce Papers.
55. Bryce to Lowell, 20 July 1917, ibid.
56. Woodrow Wilson to Dicey, 5 September 1917, General Manuscripts 508(46), Glasgow University Library.
57. Dicey to Strachey, 17 June 1917, Strachey Papers.

the effort to save "all that is worth having in life."[58] Participation in the war, however remote, caused him to follow its progress carefully by the start of 1915.

In his daily monitoring of the war Dicey soon developed predictable opinions. From the start, for instance, he subjected Asquith to a withering stream of abuse for his alleged defects of character and mistakes in guiding the national effort. So ingrained was the distrust of Asquith that Dicey often warned he might sacrifice the interests of the nation for personal political gain. The advent of the 1915 coalition eased Dicey's suspicions little. Asquith's political past militated against the firmness of his leadership, Dicey thought, so he could never make the coalition a success.[59] By the end of 1915 the fortunes of the war convinced Dicey that Great Britain was in the gravest peril, only the brief period in 1857 during the Indian Mutiny compared to the extent of national danger. He inclined less than ever to extend to Asquith a charitable interpretation of events: "You will think perhaps that my distrust of Asquith is an obsession. It has however very little to do directly with his belief in Home Rule. . . . It does mean that I believe him absolutely devoted to the wretched arts of party management. His skill as a manager is no doubt the foundation of his success, and not one man in a thousand ever believes that confidence in the talent in which he is supreme may be and often has been the ruin of much greater men than Asquith, and may be an extraordinary peril to the nation whom he leads."[60]

If Ireland remained the most vital of his concerns in Great Britain, then the most disturbing aspect of the home scene was the union militancy in vital industries, which endangered the spirit of class and national unity. This development justified the vehement attacks he had made upon the Trade Disputes Act of 1906. The best solution to strikes in wartime, Dicey argued in his usual uncompromising fashion, was the arrest of strikers on charges of treason, for this action alone could adequately safeguard the interests of the nation.[61] Loyalty of trade unionists had shifted from its rightful object, the nation, to the trade unions. The Trade Disputes Act had promoted this detestable process, according to him, with unions

58. Ibid., 13 December 1915, ibid.
59. Ibid., 1 August 1915, ibid.
60. Ibid., 17 December 1915, ibid.
61. Ibid., 1 August 1915, ibid.

exercising the tyrannical privileges of an aristocratic class. Since the government possessed the authority to combat the power of the unions, the first use of that authority should protect blackleg workers who wished to stay on the job.[62] The state must act as strikebreaker, as in France, if the nation were to escape intolerable coercion from the unions.[63] This autocratic attitude toward trade unions stemmed from Dicey's belief in the paramount necessity of subordinating every consideration to winning the war. That some other institution might have supplanted the state as object of primary loyalty he found unbearable. National allegiance must prevail over class allegiance if England should triumph.

In 1916, after Lloyd George had settled a strike by Welsh miners, Dicey denounced the agreement, for the miners had again put loyalty to their unions above that due the nation. Thereupon he wrote to Strachey:

ENCLOSED MEMO ABOUT DELETERIOUS
EFFECTS OF SETTLEMENT

(1) it adds immense strength to Unions
(2) advantage has been won by fear of Welsh miners breaking the law in a way fatal to the conduct of the war
(3) combined with Trade Disputes Act 1906, it adds strength to bodies accustomed to defy the law of the land
(4) loyalty to union was substituted for loyalty to nation
(5) it makes a direct advance towards direct Socialism. It will soon be plausibly (and perhaps soundly) arguable that all kinds of work on which the safety of the nation may depend, must be placed in the hands of the nation, i.e. of State officials
(6) it will soon make the protection of the right to work in its true sense, i.e. the right of e.g. a woman, to take work on terms fairly agreed upon by herself and her employer, a moral, if not a legal impossibility.[64]

This statement was vintage Dicey: fearful of socialism, solicitous of the right of contract, seeking national unity above all else, and zealous for the rule of law as he conceived it. He attributed the propen-

62. Ibid., 9 January 1916, ibid.
63. Ibid., 16 January 1916, ibid.
64. Ibid., 18 March 1916, ibid.

sity of working men to place loyalty to their union above loyalty to the nation to the fact that they had never suffered a German-style invasion. Trade unionists indulged their selfishness whenever union goals conflicted with national aims: "This is the saddest and most dangerous feature of our times."[65] Throughout the war the trade union problem troubled Dicey. A strike in Coventry confirmed "the fear I have long entertained that the loyalty of the artisans has been diverted from the country to their trade unions. I am at least sure that difficulties in the U.K. are essentially of much greater peril to England than even failures on the Continent."[66] The pervasiveness of this deplorable sentiment strengthened his resolve to protest trade union tyranny whenever the opportunity arose.

As the necessity to sacrifice everything for the sake of victory increased, he joined several campaigns of social discipline aimed at fostering a sense of participation on the home front. One cause was the attempted suspension of racing for the duration of the war; the failure of racing authorities to cooperate caused him to attack bitterly their lack of public spirit.[67] The issue that most disturbed him was the campaign encouraging total prohibition of drink. Dicey sympathized with the object of this movement, for early in 1915 he had taken a pledge of abstinence. However, he disapproved of any effort to enforce this policy by statute. Prohibition must be entirely voluntary or else it would cause more harm than good.[68] The "glasses down" movement might create grave divisions in society, for the working classes would view government coercion as class legislation. Dicey so feared class antagonisms that he thought this possibility could not be risked when national unity must prevail over other goals. From this position Dicey never wavered. He criticized the campaign to make grain available for bread only and not beer, lest a controversy detract from patriotism.[69] As always, he preferred voluntarism to government compulsion on social issues.

By 1916 Dicey no longer believed patriotism impelled silence about government direction of the war. Criticism of Asquith shifted

65. Ibid., 24 December 1916, ibid.
66. Dicey to Bryce, 2 December 1917, Bryce Papers.
67. Dicey to Strachey, 21 March 1915, Strachey Papers.
68. Ibid., 4 April 1915, ibid.
69. Ibid., 4 February 1917, ibid.

from his personal defects as party leader to dissatisfaction with his war leadership. This led eventually to the remarkable (for Dicey) statement that despite all misgivings about Lloyd George, he would prefer the Welshman as head of a cabinet composed of a small number of trustworthy Liberals and Unionists.[70] "Wait and See" promised defeat, so he rebuked Strachey for writing in the *Spectator* that Asquith was indispensable to victory.[71] The resignation of Asquith could only benefit Great Britain, for his phlegmatic style prevented an aggressive prosecution of the war. On the eve of Asquith's displacement in late 1916, Dicey still maintained a steady barrage of criticism, convinced that the prime minister would lead the country to ruin.[72] The accession to power of the Lloyd George coalition in December 1916 altered Dicey's outlook dramatically about the prospects of eventual victory.

By the beginning of 1917 Dicey thought the triumph of England closer than he had anticipated. This turned his attention to the shape of society after the end of hostilities: "I am glad to have witnessed the nobility and self-sacrifice of our troops, and my one great hope for the State is that if a good peace is obtained, the civilians who have been soldiers during the war, whether officers or men, may have great influence after the peace."[73] The war, as terrible as it was, had made clear one fact: "The fine spirit of our armies is proof that the corruption of peace may go far less deep than one sometimes has feared & that there are many more heroes living around one than one supposed."[74] The entry of the United States into the war clinched this euphoric mood. Aid from America would enable the Atlantic powers to defeat the strongest Continental power. He could barely restrain his enthusiasm at the news in the belief that Great Britain must now triumph.[75] All doubt that the Allies would eventually win the war vanished.

So pervasive had Dicey's interest in the war become that he published just one article pertaining to changes in the constitution caused by the war. This examined the formation of the war cabinet

70. Ibid., 17 March 1916, ibid.
71. Ibid., 17 April 1916, ibid.
72. Ibid., 27 November 1916, ibid.
73. Ibid., 30 January 1917, ibid.
74. Dicey to Jacob, 18 February 1917, Working Men's College MSS.
75. Dicey to Lowell, 18 April 1917, Lowell Papers.

soon after Lloyd George replaced Asquith as prime minister.[76] From the start of hostilities Dicey had lobbied, because of his hatred for Asquith's indolence, for such a new constitutional body: "For War purposes a small Cabinet several of whom were experts combined with a large Ministry is the ideal I should aim at."[77] The sole function of this smaller group would be the efficient prosecution of the war. Dicey repeated this suggestion several times, usually in conjunction with attacks on Asquith. At the beginning of 1916 he wrote: "I am afraid that what we really need is something in the nature of a Dictatorship, that is to say, a small Cabinet constructed solely for the purpose of carrying on the war with success, and even small enough to make a sense of responsibility a reality."[78] When the war cabinet materialized, Dicey congratulated Bonar Law on his membership, writing that his presence and that of Milner ensured that the new coalition government would act in a national spirit.[79] In view of his anticipation of the war cabinet, it was not surprising Dicey praised the cabinet experiment for the vigor it would breathe into the government. His only reservation concerned the effect this innovation might have on existing constitutional conventions surrounding the cabinet. Secrecy and lack of accountability were not principles Dicey approved, but as with so many other wartime developments, expediency proved the strongest argument of all. In the end he hoped the common sense of British statesmen would make the necessary adjustments in governmental relationships to preserve the essential spirit of the cabinet system.

Nothing could detract from the final victory of Great Britain. This conclusion, on which he had pinned all his hopes, evoked a joyfulness seldom expressed by Dicey. The triumphant end to the conflict, an event he doubted he would live long enough to enjoy, justified the great sacrifices of the previous four years: "One hardly knows what to say about these stunning events. I think the only words which can occur to any serious man are 'Bless God for a victory of righteousness, and for England having fought on the right side and on the whole having fought with calmness, courage, and

76. Albert Venn Dicey, "The New English War Cabinet as a Constitutional Experiment," pp. 781–91.
77. Dicey to Strachey, 14 August 1915, Strachey Papers.
78. Dicey to Bryce, 31 January 1916, Bryce Papers.
79. Dicey to Bonar Law, 14 December 1916, Bonar Law Papers.

honour.' Something of this kind must I think come into every man's mind. History has from a moral point of view for once been dramatic in the assertion of justice."[80] For the moment the satisfaction of victory more than compensated for the personal and national travails endured; the various disappointments of World War I could not dampen the exhilaration of triumph. Dicey experienced few such moments in his life.

80. Dicey to Bryce, 12 November 1918, Bryce Papers. For similar sentiments see also Dicey to Eliot, 14 November 1918, Eliot Papers, and Dicey to Mrs. G. C. Crump, 5 December 1918, in Rait, *Memorials*, p. 263.

CHAPTER TWELVE

THE LAST YEARS,

1918–1922

D ICEY'S FINAL YEARS saw no diminution in his intellectual strength, although his physical capabilities continued to deteriorate. His deafness became more of a handicap so that conversation, the great joy of his life, was all but impossible. In 1919 he complained to Bryce that he recognized few faces anymore and could hear nothing unless words were spoken directly to him.[1] The privations of old age made visits to All Souls infrequent. On these rare occasions when he found the strength, he missed almost all the conversation. In college debates he could not intervene effectively on behalf of opinions he thought deserved support. The result was utter frustration.[2] Adding to the pain of these last years was the personal isolation as more friends passed away. Especially distressing was the death of Bryce in early 1922, about which an acquaintance wrote Dicey that it "leaves, for both of us, a gap which cannot be filled."[3] In compensation for his enforced physical inactivity, Dicey maintained the keen interest in public affairs he had demonstrated throughout his life. His infirmities reduced the torrential flow of letters of the pre-1914 era, but did not entirely prevent Dicey from expressing his opinions when the occasion demanded. As always, where politics were involved, this meant constant attention to developments in Ireland.

For most of 1919 the escalating violence in Ireland troubled him little. Throughout that year events in England predominated, with the peace conference, the continuation of the Lloyd George coalition, and the economic adjustment to peacetime more than enough to occupy his time. Only twice did he stir, on both occasions pro-

1. Dicey to Bryce, 17 June 1919, Bryce Papers.
2. Dicey to Lady Farrer, 5 November 1920, in Rait, *Memorials*, p. 269.
3. C. P. Ilbert to Dicey, 25 January 1922, General Manuscripts 508(4), Glasgow University Library.

testing discussion of dominion status for Ireland.[4] This particular solution to the Irish Question he found as preposterous as ever, citing the reasons he had repeated since 1886. These letters were the last addressed to the *Times*, ending nearly forty years of correspondence during which he had often graced the pages of the paper with his forthright stands on political issues.

When in 1920 the level of hostilities in Ireland rose dramatically, Dicey again feared for the permanence of the Union. Most disturbing was the cooperation of many erstwhile Unionists in the government plans for a compromise on Irish policy. Such a modification of traditional Unionist resistance to Irish demands and a departure from the tested principles of 1886 could result only in disaster.[5] The government intention to pass the 1920 Government of Ireland Bill was thoroughly misguided, for it was a concession England must forcibly impose upon Ireland, as few in that country desired it at all.[6] Dicey added that the era had long since passed when such a policy might satisfy Irish aspirations. He based his opposition to government proposals not on the necessity for a more realistic solution, however, but on the stubborn conviction that the Unionism of 1886 still had validity and that Ireland might yet become a contented partner in the United Kingdom: "The firm and continuous determination of the British Parliament both to remedy actually existing grievances, such as the state of the Irish land law, and to refuse decisively any modification by way of Home Rule in the Act of Union would have preserved, and probably strengthened, the unity of the United Kingdom."[7] Dicey added that Unionists had failed before 1914, because they had neither reduced the number of Irish representatives at Westminster nor made Unionism the basic premise of their policy.

Since 1886 Dicey had learned nothing and forgotten nothing. In a letter to the *Spectator* he adhered to the line he had propagated from the start of the Home Rule controversy.[8] He never acknowledged that Unionist emphasis on economic prosperity for Ireland had been

4. *Times*, 3 May and 15 July 1919.
5. Elliot to Dicey, 6 February 1920, Elliot Papers.
6. John Venn to Dicey, 29 March 1920, General Manuscripts 508(29), Glasgow University Library.
7. Dicey to Rait, 7 April 1920, in Rait, *Memorials*, p. 268.
8. *Spectator*, 27 March 1920.

mistaken from the outset; still less did Dicey understand in 1920 that the political situation in Ireland meant the British government no longer held the initiative for a settlement.

Persistence in maintaining the simplicities of 1886 reinforced his lack of confidence in Lloyd George's Irish policy. Dicey despaired of any constitutional formula to unite all Ireland. The majority of Irishmen were Sinn Feiners, he now asserted, or at any rate governed by those who believed assassination a lawful form of rebellion. The imposition of a settlement unacceptable to Irishmen would repeat with far less excuse the original error of Pitt when carrying the Act of Union. Therefore Dicey advocated the repeal of the 1914 Home Rule Act, withdrawal of the government-sponsored 1920 Home Rule bill, and the governing of Ireland "in a firm but orderly manner by the power of the United Kingdom."[9] He saw no other alternative save one. If British coercion failed, then Dicey pondered one other innovation:

> I sometimes think—but the dream is too wild a one—that if a tremendous constitutional experiment is to be tried, the independence of Ireland guaranteed by Great Britain, and by Great Britain alone, might be the least perilous of wild plans.
> I thought this and expressed the thought in 1887, and in one respect I was right. Great Britain with gun-boats and with a Parliament to which Ireland sent no members, and with the avowed policy of treating any foreign power who interfered in the government of Ireland as exposing itself to the hostility of Great Britain, might conceivably protect itself against the dangers of Irish hostility.[10]

This thought remained what it had always been for Dicey: wild. He had devoted too much of life to Irish matters for him to abandon precepts formed more than three decades earlier.

Dicey insisted, as he had always done, that equal application of the law must prevail if peace and prosperity were to bless Ireland. The rule of law must be enforced against Irish rebels; therefore he opposed strenuously the release of Terence MacSwiney, the hunger-striking mayor of Cork who eventually died in prison, and

9. Dicey to Strachey, 14 September 1920, Strachey Papers.
10. Ibid.

denounced Asquith for suggesting that MacSwiney be released. At the same time he insisted that the rule of law must apply to the army and Royal Irish Constabulary as well. Retaliatory atrocities were understandable in view of rebel provocations, but culprits must suffer severe punishment. He deplored especially "lawless retaliation when committed by the men whose special duty it is to maintain the rule of law."[11] Balfour alone had administered the law equally in Ireland, and only Balfour had enhanced his reputation while in charge of Irish affairs. Dicey denounced negotiations with Sinn Fein on the grounds that this would tacitly admit that murder for a political object was no more crime than open rebellion.[12] Was English law to allow political motivation in justification of murder as a principle of the criminal law? The atmosphere of violence in Ireland made no change in his presuppositions.

When at last the warfare ended in 1921, the truce between de Valera and the government filled Dicey with horror: "Does it not mean the practical condonation of so-called rebellion supported by outrage and murder?"[13] In England the effect would be catastrophic, for how could acts acceptable in Ireland be punished as murder at home? He believed the 1920 Ireland Act could not succeed any more than the 1914 act had done. Between the Nationalists who demanded independence and coalition leaders who should not concede it, there could be no satisfactory compromise. Dicey saw military enforcement of the Union as the only alternative. As Arthur Elliot wrote to Dicey: "We must make up our minds to occupying militarily Dublin, Cork, Limerick and one or two other centres: and disperse any *large* collection of hostile force which may take the field."[14] In approving this recommendation, Dicey believed this action could not worsen the already bad state of feeling between the two countries. He regretted only that lifelong Unionists in the coalition, like Balfour, who should never have trusted Lloyd George, had played a role in the deterioration of the Irish situation.[15] With renewed fervor Dicey now berated Lloyd George, since his claim as the leader who won the war had long since lost its magic for Dicey.

11. Ibid., 24 September 1920, ibid.
12. Ibid., 7 December 1920, ibid.
13. Ibid., 11 July 1921, ibid.
14. Elliot to Dicey, 2 December 1921, Elliot Papers. Italics in the original.
15. Dicey to Strachey, 10 March 1922, Strachey Papers.

He never comprehended how the prime minister could mesmerize staunch Unionists into following his Irish policy.

The last detailed exposition of views on the Irish Question came from Dicey in December 1921, less than four months before his death:

> The turn of events in England fills me as you will easily believe, with despair. I hope I overrate the probable ruin to be caused to England, or rather Great Britain, by a surrender without dignity, or in reality of generosity, and to Ireland by a victory gained not by civil war, but by organised murder. . . . A perfectly fair account of the events which have led to the miscalled treaty which is really the final surrender of conflict against Home Rule by men who have made their fame as Unionists, it would be right to dwell, as mitigating circumstances in the acceptance of defeat, upon the effect of the war, and a change in public opinion in England no less than the world over, which no Government could anticipate. . . . You will understand at least the terrible moral and political depression which the present circumstances bring upon me. If you want to measure the depth of this feeling, compare the defeat and surrender of England, when concluding a real treaty with the representatives of the United States and the surrender of England to the Sinn Feiners after a victory abroad and a defeat at home by a policy not of civil war but of organised murder. To sum the matter up from my point of view, in the latter case, England has been degraded and Ireland corrupted.[16]

In this apocalyptic frame of mind Dicey played out the last act of his preoccupation with Ireland.

In the last months Dicey concerned himself with the Irish Free State Bill, approving only the provision that Ulster could not be brought under the sovereignty of a common Parliament unless the assemblies in both northern and southern Ireland passed an identical act. Dicey could never be complacent about any Irish issue, so he counseled Strachey: "I constantly fear lest the present Government should use defects or errors in the Bill to deprive the Parlia-

16. Dicey to Holmes, 19 December 1921, Holmes Papers.

ment of Northern Ireland from placing Ulster outside the Bill."[17] Dicey's reputation as the last of the great Unionist polemicists caused Carson to approach him for an article on Ireland. The elder statesman of Unionism replied via Strachey: "Would you let him know that though from my age and from my state of health, I feel I cannot write anything worth publishing with regard to Irish affairs, I am still neither more nor less than an absolutely unconverted Unionist of 1886–7."[18] On this occasion he repeated his warnings about safeguards for Ulster in preserving independence from Dublin. This potential problem bothered him greatly, for, in his last letter about the Irish situation, written just eleven days before his death, he again advised Strachey: "I am haunted by a suspicion which is almost too bad a one to entertain, that Lloyd George or the Government mean in some unexpected fashion to mix together the question whether the whole of Ireland or the majority thereof, will not accept as a Free State every part of that island without an opportunity of leaving open to Ulster any opportunity of voting herself out of such Free State, of which she has always refused to form part."[19] To the end Ireland remained the foremost of his interests.

The "absolutely unconverted Unionist of 1886–7"—seldom has a self-portrait rung so true. From start to finish of the Home Rule controversy, Dicey opposed steadfastly every permutation that threatened the treasured unity of Great Britain. That he should not survive the conclusion of that enduring problem was altogether fitting, particularly a solution making permanent the destruction of all that he had prized. Mrs. Dicey, recounting the last years of her husband's life, wrote: "I can feel thankful that he did not live on with weakened powers & to be probably more and more oppressed by the state of the world & Ireland above all. For the last few years he had refrained from writing anything for publication about Ireland, feeling that he was not able for it & the law book & another before that helped him to keep his thoughts from dwelling too much on the war & its results."[20] "Ireland above all"—the motif dominated Dicey's life from 1886 onward. Death freed him from the fascination that had governed the latter half of his life.

17. Dicey to Strachey, 17 March 1922, Strachey Papers.
18. Ibid., 22 March 1922, ibid.
19. Ibid., 27 March 1922, ibid.
20. Mrs. Dicey to Holmes, 14 September 1922, Holmes Papers.

If the preceding account has not sufficiently convinced that Ireland dominated Dicey's life, one additional episode should clinch this argument. On two occasions in 1920 Dicey refused the grant of honors. His reasons were calculated carefully, as he explained in responding to Bryce's inquiry whether he had been tendered a Privy Councillorship:

> I have never by any Government, or on any occasion, been offered a seat on the Privy Council. Hence I have never in fact declined the offer. But had it been offered I should have certainly declined it as I have now twice declined the offer of a Knighthood. The two reasons which would now apply to every title are these: —At the age of nearly 86 I am quite indifferent to any title whatever, even to one which I most gladly would have accepted when we were in the midst, (say 25 or 30 years ago) of the Home Rule conflict. The second reason is that at the moment when the policy for which I fought to the best of my ability, and with my whole heart, has finally failed, does not seem to me an appropriate time for receiving any title.[21]

From this account Dicey, it seems clear, never believed that his constitutional scholarship merited such recognition as a knighthood. He measured the achievements of his life primarily in political terms, and the sole criterion was defense of the Union. No other aspect of his life mattered as much to him. Thus when the Union at last shattered under the impact of forces Dicey could not comprehend, only a pervasive sense of failure remained, symbolized by his refusal of honors.

His two close friends, Elliot the Unionist and Bryce the Home Ruler, commended him for the sincerity of his action. Elliot praised his attitude: "The moment of passing such a measure as this H.R. Act, against whose principle you have fought so splendidly and so consistently since 1886 to the present time, is hardly the one for you to receive from the Ministers who have passed it, what they call a political honour."[22] Elliot rejoiced in Dicey's decision, lauding especially the arguments and language he had used in the process. Bryce consoled Dicey with the argument that Unionist politicians

21. Dicey to Bryce, 6 January 1921, Bryce Papers.
22. Elliot to Dicey, 29 December 1920, Elliot Papers.

had never offered a Privy Council seat, because they had never realized what a strong case Dicey had made against Home Rule.[23] Unionists had never appreciated the sophistication of his constitutional reasoning. Neither of his friends pointed out that Dicey had rarely adduced pragmatic, politically useful weapons against Home Rule. He had phrased his polemics in the language of the detached constitutional lawyer without understanding the emotional content of the Irish issue. Dicey had attempted to unite constitutional expertise with political ambition, but the combination had not worked. Politicians had seldom responded to his weighty logic. For that reason, despite great exertions, he had not gained the influence he sought in political circles. He wanted a reputation in both the world of constitutional scholarship and the arena of practical politics, but earned it only in the former.

Although Ireland remained the primary external problem of the postwar years, labor unrest at home continued to cause Dicey distress. The root of labor discontent, Dicey contended, lay in two or three passionate beliefs that were a strange mixture of half-truths with noxious delusions: "The partial truth is that men start in life with very unequal chances, not as much as wealth as, what is much worse, of welfare. On this partial truth is grounded the feeling, which is not in itself unreasonable, that more ought to be done than English Liberals have hitherto attempted for lessening this inequality."[24] Precisely this sort of uninformed opinion backed the dangerous rise in socialist and Bolshevist sentiment throughout the country. He denounced vehemently the strike movement that disrupted production throughout 1919. About the strike of coal miners, for instance, he maintained that action so harmful to the nation was in effect treason and should be punished as a crime: "It is the claim of a particular class to have & use a power to compel the State to obey its wishes, and a power beyond that conceded to any other class."[25] Dicey was not indifferent to conditions causing the unrest, but held with Burke, whom he often cited, that as at the 1797 mutiny at the Nore, miners must end their strike before any inquiry into their grievances could be undertaken. When labor difficulties persisted, Dicey expressed indignation at the cowardice of politi-

23. Bryce to Dicey, 21 January 1921, Bryce Papers.
24. Dicey to Bryce, 13 November 1918, ibid.
25. Dicey to Strachey, 10 March 1919, Strachey Papers.

cians who failed to discipline the working class and put it under proper restraint.

When Lloyd George settled the miners' strike in 1920, Dicey argued that the prime minister had inaugurated the rule of revolution by caving in to the demands of the unions.[26] This grave warning of imminent national disaster must be set against the failure of revolutionary ideologies within the Labor party and the dominance of a leadership dedicated to parliamentary tactics and electoral persuasion.[27] To these developments Dicey was oblivious. More isolated than ever and analyzing labor troubles in terms of an earlier age, he used his remaining strength to attack the phantoms of socialism he thought lurking throughout England.

In 1921 a new and insidious threat to the England he revered emerged in reading the work of J. L. and Barbara Hammond, with Dicey both fascinated and outraged by the tone of their books.[28] He found remarkable their "quiet assumption that everything that was wrong was the result of human injustice. Bentham, Adam Smith, and all their pupils or descendants, are tacitly treated as wrongdoers."[29] Such criticism of the heroes of his youth could not pass unanswered. He defended the enclosure movement, for example, by pointing out that it provided improved cultivation, and that proponents of enclosure, who promoted the good of the nation, never perceived the burdens imposed upon commoners. That the total wealth of the country could increase dramatically without benefitting the ordinary citizen Dicey would not admit: "I cannot but think that free trade, whatever its defects, did in England between 1850 and 1870 go a good way towards lightening the burdens, to say the very least, which fell upon the large class of wage earners."[30] As with so many other of his beliefs, no questioning of his assumptions was permissible, lest the intellectual security he required be demolished in the process. Because they contradicted memories of youth and condemned the generation he admired, Dicey could not ignore

26. Dicey to Lady Farrer, 5 November 1920, in Rait, *Memorials*, p. 277.
27. Maurice Cowling, *The Impact of Labour 1920–1924*, p. 40.
28. Dicey never specified what work or works had drawn his wrath, but possibilities included: *The Village Labourer* (1911), *The Town Labourer* (1917), *The Skilled Labourer* (1919).
29. Dicey to Bryce, 21 May 1921, Bryce Papers.
30. Ibid.

the Hammonds. On one occasion he used them as an example of the extent to which Bolshevist ideas had permeated Great Britain. The Hammonds meant to write with objectivity, but socialistic misconceptions vitiated the attempt.[31] Their interpretation of English history betrayed "belief in the delusions of Bolshevists."[32] The attitude of the Hammonds symbolized all that he feared for the future of the nation.

Like the Irish Question, the labor issue eventually became too painful for discussion. Dicey lamented the political power workers had obtained, because Bolshevist doctrines had gained a stronger hold on the electorate than he had hitherto suspected. The most pernicious Bolshevist idea maintained that votes plus violence were morally justifiable in attaining working-class goals. Modern socialism in England had undermined reverence for the will of the nation, respect for law, and the realization of equal political rights, which should have become the strong feature of democracy. Dicey had lived long enough to witness the destruction of the values he held most dear; only the commitment to his writing sustained him during the difficult postwar years.

The appearance of Dicey's last book, *Thoughts on the Union*, in collaboration with Robert S. Rait, when Dicey was eighty-five testified to his enduring intellectual vitality.[33] Dicey's interest in the 1707 union had previously focused on its role as a model for the union with Ireland. The Scottish Union had worked so well in uniting the two countries that Dicey frequently cited it in support of his contention that similar benefits might yet emerge from the Irish Union. Not until 1906, after reading *The Scottish Parliament before the Union of the Crowns* by Rait, did Dicey become interested in the Scottish Union for its own sake. At that time he promised himself that he would eventually publish something on the subject, because he already had his conclusion about 1707 firmly in mind: "The statesmanship of the Whigs was both far more vigorous & far more skilful than any piece of parliamentary policy I can recall."[34] By the next year he had formulated plans with Rait, then

31. Dicey to Strachey, 11 July 1921, Strachey Papers.
32. Ibid., 14 July 1921, ibid.
33. Albert Venn Dicey and Robert S. Rait, *Thoughts on the Union between England and Scotland.*
34. Dicey to Bryce, 18 March 1906, Bryce Papers.

at New College, Oxford, for a book on the union with Scotland.[35] These plans fell into abeyance for the next years when the political controversies of Edwardian England claimed virtually all his attention.

The start of World War I presented Dicey with the leisure time necessary for a return to the Scotland project. In wartime Oxford he lectured on the subject, and the more information he gathered, "the more I admire the wisdom of British statesmanship in both parts of the island."[36] He described this process to a friend: "I am trying to expound to a class mainly of ladies the nature of the Scottish Parliament & its connection with that Act of Union wh. was the first and noblest feat of British Statesmanship."[37] As usual with Dicey's historical writings, these judgments predated the research upon which they were ostensibly based. The use of the *Thoughts* motif—a general statement then explained and elaborated—paralleled closely the technique employed in legal writings of reducing a complex topic to a few general principles. This reductionist approach, so useful in legal studies, proved less successful in this historical essay.

The *Thoughts* device suited Dicey well, for "my object has always been to draw together pretty well admitted facts, or at any rate facts of which I feel no reasonable doubt."[38] Whenever he required expert advice on specific problems in Scottish history, he called upon Rait or Bryce for the information. He often tested his hypotheses on Bryce, for example, when he suggested to his old friend that after 1690 the General Assembly and Parliament in Scotland practiced the doctrine of separation of church and state with each institution supreme in its own sphere. The union of 1707 had passed so easily because both institutions had agreed on its necessity, ensuring a near unanimity of opinion on the issue.[39] Dicey published his preliminary impressions in 1917 in the only article of his ever to appear in a professional historical journal.[40] This reluctance was not sur-

---

35. Ibid., 30 July 1907, ibid.
36. Dicey to Rait, 16 April 1915, in Rait, *Memorials*, p. 237.
37. Dicey to Jacob, 26 December 1915, Working Men's College MSS.
38. Dicey to Bryce, 14 June 1916, Bryce Papers.
39. Ibid., 27 September 1916, ibid.
40. Albert Venn Dicey, "Thoughts on the General Assembly of the Church of Scotland under the Constitution of 1690 (1690–1707)," pp. 197–215.

prising in the light of his comment: "That dullest of Scottish periodicals the Sc. Hist. Review contained I think the dullest article I ever wrote. But yet I look upon it as rather a good piece of study."[41] For the most part this article rehearsed arguments which would form the second chapter of the subsequent book.

Thoughts on the Union has not stood the test of time well. Dicey's determination to prove the Union a triumph of statesmanship while passing over the seamier sides of the negotiations has not impressed later historians. The chief glory of the Union Dicey found in the creation of a new unitary state without the destruction of either English or Scottish identity. This buttressed his lifelong belief that nationalism expressed itself best in the creation of larger political units, while the spirit of nationality created discord and led to the dismemberment of larger states. The union of England and Scotland was the prototype of everything he valued in nationalism. The 1707 union represented the aspirations for national unity and common patriotism Dicey embraced all his life. Historical accuracy was again sacrificed to the need of reinforcing his own beliefs.

In an essay on Dicey, H. G. Hanbury remarked that the share of the book between Dicey and Rait could not be ascertained.[42] Dicey gave ample testimony to the division of labor in his private correspondence: "It is I think certain that I and Rait each contribute a good deal to the book which neither of us could without a good deal of additional trouble, have provided if we had been working alone."[43] Dicey supplied the principles while Rait contributed the facts of Scottish history to support those *Thoughts*. As Dicey phrased it: "I naturally took mainly to the constitutional side thereof as it was part of our law in which from having been brought up in a very good Whig circle, I had been from my youth perpetually though unconsciously, educated."[44] Dicey admitted the dearth of research and that little in the book was original, but thought the partnership had made "certain undoubted facts obvious to a somewhat uninterested public."[45] Cooperation between the two men had resulted in a book "never more truly shared between two friendly

41. Dicey to Bryce, 8 April 1917, Bryce Papers.
42. H. G. Hanbury, *The Vinerian Chair and Legal Education*, p. 162.
43. Dicey to Bryce, 25 March 1920, Bryce Papers.
44. Dicey to Holmes, 19 December 1921, Holmes Papers.
45. Dicey to Bryce, 11 November 1920, Bryce Papers.

partners."[46] The organization, bulk of the writing, and main conclusions of the book may be attributed to Dicey, even if Rait supplied the historical evidence in support of those assertions.

Preparation of the third edition of *Conflict of Laws* proved the last great intellectual effort of his life. In this endeavor he received the assistance of A. B. Keith. The exertion this revision required taxed his strength fatally, for it meant constant correspondence with Keith in Edinburgh, with the attendant aggravation this circumstance caused. Dicey persisted in this inconvenient arrangement so that a trained scholar would be available to complete the task if he did not survive. Mrs. Dicey wrote of the last days of her husband: "I knew well & so did our good Doctor that it would have been worse than useless to tell him to stop working altogether & everyone who could judge said that his work did not show any signs of weakened power. He had the satisfaction of seeing the book published & in his hands just three days before he failed & in a week he passed away without any great suffering. In spite of my having been sadly incapable for the last few years I was able to be at times with him during that last week."[47] Only when he had completed this last work, and not before, did Dicey die peacefully at age eighty-seven. Dedication to the work at hand lasted to the very end, for he left no unfinished scholarly business. He had obeyed his personal work ethic to the last.

46. Ibid.
47. Mrs. Dicey to Holmes, 14 September 1922, Holmes Papers.

CHAPTER THIRTEEN

CONCLUSION

IN THE FINAL ANALYSIS, on what achievements should the reputation of Dicey rest? In his contributions as an academic lawyer he carved out a formidable niche for himself in the history of English law. Harold Laski wrote that Dicey was the "most considerable figure in English jurisprudence since Maitland" and as an Oxford professor exercised more influence in the outside world than any teacher since T. H. Green.[1] James Bryce thought that most characteristic of Dicey's legal writings was "the power of bringing out certain main points with perfect clearness & convincing force. . . . Your manner is simple & therefore better." Bryce likened his friend to the great Blackstone in his facility "for wedding Law to the Muses. There are not two or three other law books that can be read with the same pleasure as yours."[2] An additional testimonial came when Arthur Elliot reported to Dicey a conversation with Lord Haldane, who had said: " 'Dicey's is much the biggest legal mind we have.' That from an ex-Chancellor is worth recording."[3] Such praise for his legal career could be easily multiplied, for he had dominated the study of constitutional law in his own lifetime. But his exploits in academic law never satisfied his ambition; the law was not his entire life. So when Dicey reviewed his own career, impressive as it must have appeared to others, he concluded that he had not lived up to the high standards set for himself. In turn this led to a persistent self-disparagement surprising in a life so outwardly successful.

Dicey measured success in life by the extent to which an individual attained the goals formulated as a young man.[4] Because he had at one time aspired to either a judicial or a political career, and in

1. Harold Laski, "Obituary of A. V. Dicey," p. 77.
2. Bryce to Dicey, 24 February 1917, Bryce Papers.
3. Elliot to Dicey, 5 August 1917, Elliot Papers.
4. Dicey to Bryce, 8 April 1918, Bryce Papers.

his own mind had only settled for a professorial life, Dicey never overcame his deep disappointment despite ample examples of success. One major reason for this frustration lay in Dicey's belief that such reputation as he had gained came too late for him to enjoy. In 1896 he wrote: "In the main my life has been a very lucky one. Yet I have always felt that the one piece of ill-luck, which I may add clearly depends as much on character or to speak plainly natural defects, as upon chance, is that everything has chanced to come to me a little too late. . . . And in ways you can easily trace out I have always been & no doubt now shall be to the end rather behind time. In my own case the matter is not of any great personal consequence even as a personal question."[5] The obvious case was Dicey's participation in the Home Rule controversy after 1886; his great political opportunity came when he was over fifty and already committed to the Vinerian Chair. He referred to this sense of failure when he wrote in an autobiographical vein:

> But I do believe that among men not the victims of some tragic mischance, happiness is more diminished by indulging in the sense of disappointment than by almost any other cause. The insidiousness of the thing lies in the fact that hardly any man who does not rise greatly above, or sink greatly below, the ordinary level of human nature, can fail to feel his life to be in truth disappointing. The happiness thereof, and I must add the real goodness thereof, almost always falls below his legitimate hopes or expectations, and hence the disappointment is always in a sense justifiable. But on the other hand I believe there are few sources of unhappiness which to so great extent can be cured by what used to be called a little philosophy, by which I think was really meant the application of good sense and of thought to the measurement of things which concern your own personal feeling. A very little of such reflection will show you that in most lives the number of foes who have injured you, or have thwarted one's efforts to gain some desired object are few. The plain truth is that most persons are from the nature of things indifferent but not hostile to one's welfare. Friendships are surely as common—myself I think far more common—

5. Ibid., 9 March 1896, ibid.

than settled hostility. . . . In many things I have failed as every one else has failed in accomplishing the ends I most desired. But I cannot I am glad to think ascribe this to anyone's hostility.[6]

Friendships could partially soothe professional disappointments, but a void remained where Dicey allowed himself no excuses. Near the end of his life he wrote: "All I can ask of my friends is to think of me at my best, and to believe that I knew even better than they *how much I fell short even of what I might have been.*"[7] If Dicey fell victim to the high standards he applied to himself, other more concrete factors also played a role.

The greatest frustration resulted from the long battle against Home Rule into which Dicey put disproportionate time and effort. No Unionist meeting was too small for him to address; no aspect of Irish affairs too insignificant for him to analyze as part of the overall Irish problem. Yet by 1900 he recognized: "I fear that I myself have given more of my powers to controversy of a direct-kind than controversial labours are ever worth."[8] Too emotionally involved to heed his own diagnosis, Dicey could not divorce himself from the political engrossment he found so exciting. Later he admitted that "the books against Home Rule have clearly failed of their object," proving his original caveat of 1900 all too true.[9] The Irish Question emphasized the failure of political ideas he had admired since youth. The redemptive spirit of nationalism, for example, which he had hoped would lead to a peaceful European community, had in Ireland destroyed his dreams. The passage of years had perverted nationalism into an ideology of war, revolution, and national rancor. At the end this feeling of disillusionment pervaded his outlook: "There is hardly a single movement which excited the enthusiasm of the best men of the 19th century, including even the abolition of negro slavery, which has not to say the very least, disappointed their hopes."[10] The commitment to his political beliefs went unrequited; pessimism about the politics to which he had given allegiance,

6. Ibid., 31 January 1917, ibid.
7. Dicey to Mrs. Litchfield, ? 1920, in Rait, *Memorials,* p. 274.
8. Dicey to Godkin, 26 June 1900, Godkin Papers.
9. Dicey to Strachey, 22 February 1915, Strachey Papers.
10. Dicey to Bryce, 16 October 1921, Bryce Papers.

especially Home Rule, blighted his last years and affected profoundly his view of the success he had attained.

In addition, Dicey commented frequently on his uneasiness about the future of Great Britain. The certitude of his mid-Victorian values suffered under the increasing attacks of the twentieth century. In 1914 Dicey wrote that "I seem to have lived on into another age with new criteria of belief tho' what they are I know not."[11] Alienation from the world of the new century made him draw more than ever upon the ideals of his youth to cushion him against the disappointments the advancing years brought. Upon the death of Lord Cromer, for example, Dicey wrote: "The plain truth is that I have lived into a different generation and into a different world from that under which I was born and educated."[12] In the year before his death he returned to this theme: "Remember that my words, right or wrong, are those of an old Victorian who belongs to the past not to the present age."[13] Dicey, steadfast in his loyalty to the values of youth, became increasingly at variance with the world as it changed and he did not. Inevitably he felt isolated in an age he could not comprehend.

One aspect of this loneliness was the realization that society in general paid less homage to the theoretical study of constitutions, the field to which he had dedicated his scholarly life. What had appeared to young Dicey a career important for its own sake declined sharply in prestige throughout his lifetime. By 1900 he could write to Holmes: "I sometimes doubt a good deal whether in the present state of the world legal study & law itself retain quite the interest or the importance it has possessed in other ages."[14] Dicey found himself in the unenviable position of becoming a greater figure in an area less appreciated by the general public. He regretted not the initial decision so much as the lack of personal satisfaction resulting from changed circumstances. On another occasion he wrote: "Still I think there are always solid reasons at given periods for preferring some particular field of mental or moral activity. The logical sciences in which I include law, legislation, jurisprudence, and the like, seem to have lost their hold on the

11. Ibid., 11 January 1914, ibid.
12. Dicey to Strachey, 30 January 1917, Strachey Papers.
13. Ibid., 14 July 1921, ibid.
14. Dicey to Holmes, 3 April 1900, Holmes Papers.

world."[15] These reflections deepened the mood of failure, which his obvious constitutional reputation could not assuage.

A further blow resulted from the difficult personal labors required for the writing of his scholarly books, followed by the declining interest in his legal and constitutional works. Throughout his life Dicey maintained a reputation for brilliant conversation, leading his friends to assume that the lucid expression of his books flowed just as easily. This was certainly not the case. As he himself wrote: "In fact writing of all kinds is difficult and labourious to me, & I should have done rather better in a world where people use their tongues rather than their pens."[16] The primary obstacle he encountered in composition was the lack of "a sort of compression and also precision which is not needed in a speech, or at any rate the want whereof can in speaking be a good deal concealed, and these qualities are not bestowed upon my by nature."[17] In his scholarly endeavors Dicey repeated his material several times in lecture form before he thought it worth publishing. The result was a long period between conception and fulfillment of a project. As he put it: "The truth is I am a slow worker & have to think or rather dream over any work for years before I can get it done. People don't perceive this because the only thing I do quickly is to talk & everyone knows myself included that I talk too quick in every sense of the expression."[18] The feeling that he expended increasing labor on topics of decreasing importance played its part in Dicey's diffidence about his professorial work.

About his polemical books Dicey had no such doubts. The contrasts between his political and constitutional works were instructive: the scholarly books took years to germinate, but his polemical work appeared in months. He never doubted his political conclusions, yet worried constantly about his constitutional theories even after his reputation was assured; and he thought the political writings more influential than the legal treatises. His own estimate of his influence contradicted that of posterity. His constitutional volumes were the permanent source of his fame, but this fact Dicey never realized. The humility many observers remarked about Dicey

15. Dicey to Bryce, 19 March 1910, Bryce Papers.
16. Dicey to Eliot, 6 November 1899, Eliot Papers.
17. Dicey to Jacob, 22 December 1917, Working Men's College MSS.
18. Dicey to Bryce, 19 November 1921, Bryce Papers.

applied to his scholarly work, not his political philosophy. Confidence about his work was not unwarranted, but simply misplaced.

The final recognition in Dicey's low opinion of his own success was that his cherished method of abstracting basic principles from complex legal material led, in the last analysis, to a superficiality he had not anticipated. "I do not believe that I have ever got hold of a strictly original thought in my life," he once wrote, "even in the form of a new error."[19] His special vocation he considered "the not very exalted one of repeating to dull men the truisms they refuse to notice."[20] Dicey called himself the "prophet of the obvious," though admirers usually termed this a genius for clarifying constitutional issues others had allowed to remain in doubt.[21] This lack of profundity Holmes alluded to when he wrote of Dicey: "The only qualification that I should put in to his greatness is that he could not think like a devil and therefore could not touch the deepest complexities of the exquisite."[22] In a real sense his intellectual strengths were his weaknesses. The legal works remain among the most readable in the literature of the law, yet elegance of style cannot conceal that Dicey's foremost contribution lay precisely in making obvious areas of the law previously obscure. Thus his work, while extraordinarily influential, was derivative and not strictly original. He utilized the Austinian method of analysis, but added little to the Austinian tradition of English jurisprudence.

At the outset it was stated that Dicey's reputation and enduring influence must be assessed from his major works. From this perspective *Conflict of Laws* constituted the greatest of his books, for it exercised a decisive formative influence upon this important branch of modern law. Dicey succeeded so admirably because this field suited best the methodology of legal positivism he invariably employed. His ability to abstract fundamental principles from a mass of undigested judicial decisions worked well, because private international law had developed in haphazard fashion. In the area of constitutional law, *Law of the Constitution* must rank slightly behind, because it, though wearing well since 1885, was narrowly

19. Ibid., 17 May 1912, ibid.
20. Dicey to Strachey, 4 April 1915, Strachey Papers.
21. "College Notes," *Working Men's College Journal,* 17 (June 1922): 288.
22. Holmes to Laski, 20 February 1925, in *Holmes-Laski Letters,* 1: 712.

conceived and never synthesized its field as *Conflicts* had done for its topic. *Law of the Constitution* was and is a classic treatise, but the principles enunciated therein, meant by Dicey to be unchanging, have been reinterpreted by each succeeding generation. His ideas, glossed by many commentators, have endured but at the price of redefinition by modern authorities.

For the reasons detailed in chapter 8, *Law and Opinion* must be rated much lower, for it has misled historians of Victorian England ever since its publication. The materials for the history of Victorian opinion were diverse and complex, so his reductionist technique distorted more than enlightened when applied to historical causation. Modern investigation into the data Dicey so cavalierly researched has terminated its influence. The political works failed most abjectly, retaining too much of the legal scholar to have wide appeal. They lacked the passion Dicey felt for the Home Rule issue but could not express, for he despised the demagoguery of politicians and their indifference to constitutional principles. Dicey never comprehended that public opinion cared little for the discussion of emotional issues like Ireland in constitutional terms. His fame rests squarely on the legal and constitutional books that best utilized his approach to the law.

For a man whose private life was remarkably free of personal disaster, there existed one tragic element in Dicey's career. There were two Diceys, the famous lawyer and the frustrated politician; the tragedy lay in the predominance of the latter over the former. C. H. S. Fifoot has written that Sir Frederick Pollock was for sixty years at the heart of the law in England: "Rooted in the virtues that have come, with whatever truth, to be called Victorian, the fruits of his scholarship were harvested by men who were themselves the products of a new legal education."[23] But for the lure of politics, especially the Irish Question, Dicey might well have claimed that position. Where Pollock corresponded with Holmes for decades on every conceivable legal subject, Dicey filled his letters to Holmes with discussions of contemporary politics. That difference of emphasis was significant. As Dicey eventually realized, he had wasted much time on fruitless crusades dictated by his dogmatic politics. As Pollock himself noted of Dicey: "In the 1860's he and

23. C. H. S. Fifoot, *Judge and Jurist in the Reign of Victoria*, pp. 136–37.

Bryce were university Liberals together, but his ideas remained fixed on all material points while Bryce's mind was open to the last."[24] This facet of Dicey's character led to a rigid political creed, whereas in the law, where his achievement was greatest, he was unduly humble about his influence: "His outstanding characteristic was extreme modesty, and a complete lack of dogmatism in a subject [conflict of laws] in which any English-speaking court in the world would have accepted his views unhesitatingly, in the absence of any controlling authority."[25] If those years spent criticizing Home Rule had been devoted instead to the law, Dicey's professional career would certainly have been even more fruitful. If he merited the praise due a great lawyer, how much greater might he have become? The mid-Victorian code to which he adhered explained Dicey's priorities. Arthur Elliot wrote of him that "he never forgot the great end for which he was working—his country's good."[26] If, in retrospect, one might wish that he had allotted his labors differently, nevertheless Dicey lived in obedience to the values embraced in his youth. To this mid-Victorian faith he remained loyal all of his life.

24. Pollock to Holmes, 10 April 1922, in *Holmes-Pollock Letters*, 2: 93.

25. F. F. Russell, cited in F. H. Lawson, *The Oxford Law School*, p. 71, note 1.

26. Statement by Elliot, n.d., affixed to Dicey-Elliot correspondence, Elliot Papers.

BIBLIOGRAPHY

Manuscript Sources

The collections used may be divided into those essential for the life of Dicey and those of marginal interest. Of primary importance were:

Arthur Balfour Papers, British Museum, London
Bodleian Manuscripts, Bodleian Library, Oxford
Andrew Bonar Law Papers, Beaverbrook Library, London
James Bryce Papers, Bodleian Library, Oxford
Charles William Eliot Papers, Harvard University Archives, Cambridge, Mass.
Arthur Elliot Papers, National Library of Scotland, Edinburgh
General Manuscripts, Glasgow University Library, Glasgow
E. L. Godkin Papers, Houghton Library, Harvard University, Cambridge, Mass.
Oliver Wendell Holmes, Jr., Papers, Harvard Law School Library, Cambridge, Mass.
A. Lawrence Lowell Papers, Harvard University Archives, Cambridge, Mass.
Macmillan Company Papers, British Museum, London
Leo Maxse Papers, West Sussex County Record Office, Chichester
Charles Eliot Norton Papers, Houghton Library, Harvard University, Cambridge, Mass.
Goldwin Smith Papers, John M. Olin Library, Cornell University, Ithaca, New York
J. St. Loe Strachey Papers, Beaverbrook Library, London
Working Men's College Manuscripts, Working Men's College, Crowndale Road, London

Of secondary importance were:

Oscar Browning Papers, Hastings Public Library, Hastings
Joseph Chamberlain Papers, Birmingham University Library, Birmingham
8th Duke of Devonshire Papers, Chatsworth, Derbyshire
H. A. L. Fisher Papers, Bodleian Library, Oxford
William E. Gladstone Papers, British Museum, London
Thomas Hill Green Papers, Balliol College, Oxford

Thomas W. Higginson Papers, Houghton Library, Harvard University, Cambridge, Mass.
William James Papers, Houghton Library, Harvard University, Cambridge, Mass.
Viscount Milner Papers, Bodleian Library, Oxford
Miscellaneous Manuscripts, Balliol College, Oxford
3rd Marquess of Salisbury Papers, Hatfield House, Hatfield, Herts.
Earl of Selborne Papers, Lambeth Palace Library, London
Somerville College Manuscripts, Somerville College, Oxford

Books by Albert Venn Dicey

Can English Law Be Taught at the Universities? London: Macmillan, 1883.
A Digest of the Law of England with Reference to the Conflict of Laws. London: Stevens & Sons, 1896.
England's Case against Home Rule. London: John Murray, 1886.
A Fool's Paradise: Being a Constitutionalist's Criticism on the Home Rule Bill of 1912. London: John Murray, 1913.
How We Ought to Feel about the War. London: John Murray, 1915.
Introduction to the Study of the Law of the Constitution. London: Macmillan, 1885.
The Law of Domicil as a Branch of the Law of England, Stated in the Form of Rules. London: Stevens & Sons, 1879.
A Leap in the Dark: A Criticism of the Principles of Home Rule as Illustrated by the Bill of 1893. London: John Murray, 1893.
Lectures on the Relation between Law and Public Opinion in England during the Nineteenth Century. London: Macmillan, 1905.
Letters on Unionist Delusions. London: Macmillan, 1887.
Letters to a Friend on Votes for Women. London: John Murray, 1909.
The Privy Council: The Arnold Prize Essay 1860. London: Whittaker, 1860.
The Statesmanship of Wordsworth: An Essay. Oxford: Clarendon Press, 1917.
With Robert S. Rait, *Thoughts on the Union between England and Scotland.* London: Macmillan, 1920.
A Treatise on the Rules for the Selection of the Parties to an Action. London: Maxwell & Son, 1870.
The Verdict: A Tract on the Political Significance of the Report of the Parnell Commission. London: Cassell & Co., 1890.
Why England Maintains the Union: A Popular Rendering of "England's Case against Home Rule." London: John Murray, 1887.
Wordsworth's Tract on the Convention of Cintra. London: Humphrey Milford, 1915.

Articles by Albert Venn Dicey

Dicey wrote on a wide variety of topics, so numerous that it would be impossible to list everything. The most important writings have been separated into articles on legal and constitutional topics, those on contemporary politics, and those of a more general nature. Not included are the 285 reviews and articles contributed by Dicey to the *Nation;* these may be found in the *Haskell Index* published by the New York Public Library. Also not listed are the approximately 130 contributions to the *Times,* which may be found in the *Times* index.

Legal and Constitutional Articles

"Blackstone's Commentaries." *National Review* 54 (December 1909): 653–75.
"Chetti v. Chetti." *Law Quarterly Review* 25 (April 1909): 202–5.
"The Combination Laws as Illustrating the Relation between Law and Opinion in England during the Nineteenth Century." *Harvard Law Review* 17 (June 1904): 511–32.
"Comparison between Cabinet Government and Presidential Government." *The Nineteenth Century and After* 85 (January 1919): 25–42.
"Conflict of Laws and Bills of Exchange." *American Law Review* 16 (July 1882): 497–512.
"Constitutional Revision." *Law Quarterly Review* 11 (October 1895): 387–92.
"The Criteria of Jurisdiction." *Law Quarterly Review* 8 (January 1892): 21–39.
"The Development of Administrative Law in England." *Law Quarterly Review* 31 (April 1915): 148–53.
"Development of the Common Law." *Macmillans* 24 (August 1871): 287–96.
"*Droit Administratif* in Modern French Law." *Law Quarterly Review* 17 (July 1901): 302–18.
"The Extension of Law Teaching at Oxford." *Harvard Law Review* 24 (November 1910): 1–5.
"Federal Government." *Law Quarterly Review* 1 (January 1885): 80–99.
"His Book and His Character." In *Memories of John Westlake,* pp. 17–42. London: Smith, Eldon & Co., 1914.
"Hyams v. Stuart King." *Law Quarterly Review* 25 (January 1909): 76–80.
"Introduction." In Emile Boutmy, *Studies in Constitutional Law: France—England—United States,* translated by Elinor Mary Dicey, pp. v-viii. London: Macmillan, 1891.

"Introduction to English Law." *Working Men's College Journal* 7 (December 1901): 189–91.

"Judicial Policy of England." *Macmillans* 29 (April 1874): 473–87.

"Law-Teaching, Oral and Written." In *A Memoir of the Right Honourable Sir William Anson,* edited by H. H. Henson, pp. 84–101. Oxford: Clarendon Press, 1920.

"The Legal Aspects of Disestablishment." *Fortnightly Review* 39 (1 June 1883): 822–40.

"The Legal Boundaries of Liberty." *Fortnightly Review* 9 (1 January 1868): 1–13.

"Legal Education." *Macmillans* 25 (December 1871): 115–27.

"Legal Etiquette." *Fortnightly Review* 8 (1 August 1867): 169–79.

"Locus Regite Actum." *Law Quarterly Review* 26 (July 1910): 277–79.

"The New English War Cabinet as a Constitutional Experiment." *Harvard Law Review* 30 (June 1917): 781–91.

"Note." *Law Quarterly Review* 3 (January 1887): 102–4.

"On Private International Law as a Branch of the Law of England." *Law Quarterly Review* 6 (January 1890): 1–21; and 7 (April 1891): 113–27.

"The Paradox of the Land Law." *Law Quarterly Review* 25 (January 1909): 221–32.

"Professor Dicey's Opinion." *Canada Law Journal* 45 (July 1909): 459–62.

"Sovereignty." *Working Men's College Journal* 8 (January 1902): 224–28.

"The Study of Jurisprudence." *Law Magazine and Review,* Fourth Series 5 (August 1880): 382–401.

"The Teaching of English Law at Harvard." *Contemporary Review* 76 (November 1899): 742–58.

"Will the Form of Parliamentary Government Be Permanent?" *Harvard Law Review* 13 (June 1899): 67–79.

Political Articles

"The Appeal to the Nation." *The Nineteenth Century and After* 75 (May 1914): 945–57.

"The Balance of Classes." In *Essays on Reform,* pp. 67–84. London: Macmillan, 1867.

"Burke on Bolshevism." *The Nineteenth Century and After* 84 (August 1918): 274–87.

"Can Unionists Support a Home Rule Government?" *Contemporary Review* 89 (February 1906): 247–66.

"The Conscientious Objector." *The Nineteenth Century and After* 83 (February 1918): 357–73.

"The Defence of the Union." *Contemporary Review* 61 (March 1892): 314–31.

"The Due Representation of England." *National Review* 38 (November 1901): 359–82.

"The Duties of Unionists." In *The Case for the Union: A Collection of Speeches, Pamphlets, and Leaflets on Home Rule for Ireland,* Third Series. London: Cassell, 1887.

"English Party Government." *Quarterly Review* 210 (April 1910): 604–27.

"Facts and Thoughts for Unionists." *The Nineteenth Century and After* 75 (April 1914): 717–23.

"Home Rule from an English Point of View." *Contemporary Review* 42 (July 1882): 66–86.

"How Is the Law to Be Enforced in Ireland?" *Fortnightly Review* 36 (1 November 1881): 537–52.

"Ireland and Victoria." *Contemporary Review* 49 (February 1886): 169–77.

"Ireland as a 'Dominion'." *The Nineteenth Century and After* 82 (October 1917): 700–26.

"Is It Wise to Establish Home Rule before the End of the War?" *The Nineteenth Century and After* 82 (July 1917): 1–25.

"New Jacobinism and Old Morality." *Contemporary Review* 53 (April 1888): 475–502.

"On the Brink of an Abyss." *The Nineteenth Century and After* 67 (May 1910): 779–85.

"Ought the Referendum to Be Introduced into England?" *Contemporary Review* 57 (April 1890): 489–511.

"The Paralysis of the Constitution." *Contemporary Review* 88 (September 1905): 305–16.

"The Parliament Act, 1911, and the Destruction of All Constitutional Safeguards." In *Rights of Citizenship: A Survey of Safeguards for the People,* pp. 81–107. London: Frederick Warne & Co., 1912.

"The Protest of Irish Protestantism." *Contemporary Review* 62 (July 1892): 1–15.

"The Referendum." *National Review* 23 (March 1894): 65–72.

"The Referendum and Its Critics." *Quarterly Review* 212 (April 1910): 538–62.

"To Unionists and Imperialists." *Contemporary Review* 84 (September 1903): 305–16.

"Two Acts of Union: A Contrast." *Fortnightly Review* 36 (1 August 1881): 168–78.

"The Unionist Outlook." *Publications of the Irish Unionist Alliance* 3 (1894): 463–84.

"Unionists and the House of Lords." *National Review* 24 (January 1895): 690–704.

"Woman Suffrage." *Quarterly Review* 210 (January 1909): 276–304.

Miscellaneous Articles

"Alexis de Tocqueville." *National Review* 21 (August 1893): 771–84.

"Bryce's American Commonwealth." *Edinburgh Review* 169 (April 1889): 481–518.

"The College as It Is Now." In *The Working Men's College 1854–1904: Records of Its History and Its Work for Fifty Years*, by *Members of the College*, edited by J. Llewelyn Davies, pp. 236–54. London: Macmillan, 1904.

"A Common Citizenship for the English Race." *Contemporary Review* 71 (April 1897): 457–76.

"Democracy in Switzerland." *Edinburgh Review* 171 (January 1890): 113–45.

"E. L. Godkin." *Living Age* 255 (9 November 1907): 335–42.

"England and America." *Atlantic Monthly* 82 (October 1898): 441–45.

"England in 1848." *Quarterly Review* 234 (October 1920): 221–42.

"History." *Working Men's College Journal* 6 (March 1900): 193–98.

"Introduction." In *The Legal Sufferings of the Jews in Russia*, edited by Lucien Wolf, pp. i-x. London: T. Fisher Unwin, 1912.

"Lord Pembroke." *National Review* 28 (January 1897): 616–29.

"Louis Napoleon: 1851 and 1873." *Fortnightly Review* 19 (1 February 1873): 197–204.

"Mill 'On Liberty'." *Working Men's College Journal* 7 (February, March, April, May 1901): 17–21, 35–38, 58–62, 81–86.

"Professor Edward A. Freeman." *Archaeological Journal* 49 (1892): 86–88.

"The Reform Act of 1832 and Its Critics." *Fortnightly Review* 39 (1 January 1883): 116–31.

"The Republic and Christianity." *Undergraduate Papers* 1 (December 1857): 16–19.

"The Right Hon. Arthur Cohen, K.C. (1830–1914)." *Law Quarterly Review* 31 (January 1915): 96–105.

"Strength and the Weakness of the Third French Republic." *The Nineteenth Century and After* 68 (August 1910): 205–19.

"Suggestions on Academical Organisation." *Fraser's Magazine* 80 (October 1869): 407–30.

"Thomas Edward Dicey." In *The Bi-Centenary Record of the Northampton Mercury 1720–1920*, edited by W. W. Hadley, pp. 49–54. Northampton: privately printed, 1920.

"Thoughts on the General Assembly of the Church of Scotland under the Constitution of 1690 (1690–1707)." *Scottish Historical Review* 14 (April 1917): 197–215.

"Thoughts on the Parliament of Scotland." *Quarterly Review* 225 (April 1916): 438–55.

"Was Pitt a Prophet?" *Contemporary Review* 70 (September 1896): 305–14.

"Wordsworth and War." *The Nineteenth Century and After* 77 (May 1915): 1041–60.

"Wordsworth on the Revolution." *The Nineteenth Century and After* 78 (October 1915): 870–91.

Secondary Works

The following list is by no means exhaustive, but it indicates the works that have proved most useful for this biography.

Books

Abel-Smith, Brian, and Stevens, Robert. *Lawyers and the Courts: A Sociological Study of the English Legal System, 1750–1965.* Cambridge, Mass.: Harvard University Press, 1967.

Amery, Leo. *Thoughts on the Constitution.* London: Oxford University Press, 1953.

Annan, Lord. *Leslie Stephen: His Thought and Character in Relation to His Time.* London: MacGibbon & Kee, 1951.

Anon. *The Northampton Mercury 1720–1901: A Popular and Illustrated History of "The Northampton Mercury" from the Early Part of the Eighteenth Century to the Commencement of the Twentieth Century.* Northampton: Privately printed, 1901.

Ashton, John. *Chap-Books of the Eighteenth Century.* London: Chatto & Windus, 1882.

Beloff, Max. *The Intellectual in Politics and Other Essays.* London: Weidenfield & Nicolson, 1970.

Birks, Michael. *Gentlemen of the Law.* London: Stevens & Sons, 1960.

Blewett, Neal. *The Peers, the Parties and the People: The General Elections of 1910.* London: Macmillan, 1972.

Bonham-Carter, Victor. *In a Liberal Tradition: A Social Biography 1700–1950.* London: Constable, 1960.

Bruce, Maurice. *The Coming of the Welfare State.* 3d ed. London: Batsford, 1966.

Burgin, E. Leslie, and Fletcher, Eric G. M. *The Students Conflict of Laws: Being an Introduction to the Study of Private International Law, Based on Dicey.* 3d ed. London: Stevens & Sons, 1937.

Carr, Sir Cecil T. *Concerning English Administrative Law.* New York: Columbia University Press, 1941.

Castel, J.-G. *Conflict of Laws: Cases, Notes and Materials.* 2nd ed. Toronto: Butterworth's, 1968.

Childers, Erskine. *The Framework of Home Rule.* London: Edward Arnold, 1911.

Clarke, P. F. *Lancashire and the New Liberalism.* Cambridge: Cambridge University Press, 1971.

Cohen, Lucy. *Arthur Cohen: A Memoir by His Daughter for His Descendants.* London: Biekers & Sons, 1919.

Cooke, A. B., and Vincent, John. *The Governing Passion: Cabinet Government and Party Politics in Britain 1885–1886.* Brighton: Harvester Press, 1974.

Cowling, Maurice. *The Impact of Labour 1920–1924: The Beginning of Modern British Politics.* Cambridge: Cambridge University Press, 1971.

Crump, Lucy, ed. *Letters of George Birkbeck Hill.* London: Edward Arnold, 1906.

Curtis, Jr., L. P. *Anglo-Saxons and Celts: A Study of Anti-Irish Prejudice in Victorian England.* Bridgeport, Conn.: Conference on British Studies, 1968.

———. *Coercion and Conciliation in Ireland 1880–1892: A Study in Conservative Unionism.* Princeton: Princeton University Press, 1963.

De Smith, S. A. *Judicial Review of Administrative Action.* 2nd ed. London: Stevens & Sons, 1968.

Drescher, Seymour. *Tocqueville and England.* Cambridge, Mass.: Harvard University Press, 1964.

Emden, Cecil S. *The People and the Constitution: Being a History of the Development of the People's Influence in British Government.* 2nd ed. Oxford: Oxford University Press, 1956.

Faber, Geoffrey. *Jowett: A Portrait with Background.* Cambridge, Mass.: Harvard University Press, 1957.

Fifoot, Cecil H. S. *English Law and Its Background.* London: G. Bell & Sons, 1932.

———. *Frederic William Maitland: A Life.* Cambridge, Mass.: Harvard University Press, 1971.

———. *Judge and Jurist in the Reign of Victoria.* London: Stevens & Sons, 1959.

———. *Law and History in the Nineteenth Century.* London: Bernard Quaritch, 1956.

Fisher, H. A. L. *James Bryce (Viscount Bryce of Dechmont, O.M.).* 2 vols. New York: Macmillan, 1927.

Foulkes, David. *Introduction to Administrative Law.* 2nd ed. London: Butterworth's, 1968.

Fraser, Peter. *Joseph Chamberlain: Radicalism and Empire, 1868–1914.* London: Cassell, 1966.

Fry, G. K. *Statesmen in Disguise: The Changing Role of the Administrative Class of the British Home Civil Service 1853–1966.* London: Macmillan, 1969.

Garner, J. F. *Administrative Law.* 3d ed. London: Butterworth's, 1970.

Geldart, W. M. *Legal Personality.* London: Stevens & Sons, 1911.

Ginsberg, Morris, ed. *Law and Opinion in England in the 20th Century.*
  London: Stevens & Sons, 1959.
Gollin, Alfred M. *The* Observer *and J. L. Garvin 1908–1914: A Study in a
  Great Editorship.* London: Oxford University Press, 1960.
———. *Proconsul in Politics: A Study of Lord Milner in Opposition and in
  Power.* New York: Macmillan, 1964.
Goodhart, A. L. *English Contributions to the Philosophy of Law.* Oxford:
  Oxford University Press, 1949.
Graveson, R. H. *The Conflict of Laws.* 5th ed. London: Sweet & Maxwell,
  1965.
Griffith, J. A. G., and Street, H. *Principles of Administrative Law.* 4th ed.
  London: Pitman Publishing, 1967.
Guest, A. G., ed. *Oxford Essays in Jurisprudence: A Collaborative Work.*
  London: Oxford University Press, 1961.
Hamer, D. A. *Liberal Politics in the Age of Gladstone and Rosebery:
  A Study in Leadership and Policy.* Oxford: Clarendon Press, 1972.
Hamson, C. J. *Executive Discretion and Judicial Control: An Aspect of the
  French Conseil d'Etat.* London: Stevens & Sons, 1954.
Hanbury, Harold G. *The Vinerian Chair and Legal Education.* Oxford:
  Basil Blackwell, 1958.
Harrison, Brian. *Separate Spheres: The Opposition to Women's Suffrage in
  Britain.* London: Croom Helm, 1978.
Harrison, John F. C. *A History of the Working Men's College 1854–1954.*
  London: Routledge & Kegan Paul, 1954.
Hart, H. L. A. *The Concept of Law.* Oxford: Clarendon Press, 1961.
Harvey, J., and Bather, L. *The British Constitution.* 3d ed. London: Mac-
  millan, 1972.
Harvie, Christopher. *The Lights of Liberalism: University Liberals
  and the Challenge of Democracy 1860–1886.* London: Allen Lane,
  1976.
Heuston, R. F. V. *Essays in Constitutional Law.* 2nd ed. Oxford: Oxford
  University Press, 1964.
Heyck, Thomas W. *The Dimensions of British Radicalism: The Case of
  Ireland 1874–1895.* Urbana: University of Illinois Press, 1974.
Holdsworth, Sir William S. *Charles Viner and the Abridgments of English
  Law.* London: Stevens & Sons, 1923.
———. *The Historians of Anglo-American Law.* New York: Columbia
  University Press, 1928.
———. *Some Makers of English Law.* Cambridge: Cambridge University
  Press, 1938.
Hood Phillips, O. *Constitutional and Administrative Law.* 3rd ed. Lon-
  don: Sweet & Maxwell, 1962.
Howe, Mark DeWolfe, ed. *Holmes-Laski Letters: The Correspondence of
  Mr. Justice Holmes and Harold J. Laski 1916–1935.* 2 vols. Cam-
  bridge, Mass.: Harvard University Press, 1953.
———. *Holmes-Pollock Letters: The Correspondence of Mr. Justice*

Holmes and Sir Frederick Pollock 1874–1932. 2 vols. Cambridge, Mass.: Harvard University Press, 1942.

Hurst, Michael. *Joseph Chamberlain and Liberal Reunion: The Round Table Conference of 1887.* London: Routledge & Kegan Paul, 1967.

Hynes, Samuel. *The Edwardian Turn of Mind.* Princeton: Princeton University Press, 1968.

Ions, Edmund. *James Bryce and American Democracy 1870–1922.* London: Macmillan, 1968.

Jackson, R. M. *The Machinery of Justice in England.* 6th ed. Cambridge: Cambridge University Press, 1972.

Jennings, Sir W. Ivor. *The Law and the Constitution.* 5th ed. London: University of London Press, 1959.

Jones, Gareth Stedman. *Outcast London: A Study in the Relationship between Classes in Victorian Society.* Oxford: Clarendon Press, 1971.

Keeton, G. W., and Schwarzenberger, G., eds. *Jeremy Bentham and the Law.* London: Stevens & Sons, 1948.

Keir, D. L., and Lawson, F. H. *Cases in Constitutional Law.* 5th ed. Oxford: Clarendon Press, 1967.

Kendle, John E. *The Round Table Movement and Imperial Union.* Toronto and Buffalo: University of Toronto Press, 1975.

Knight, William. *Memoir of John Nichol.* Glasgow: James MacLehose & Sons, 1896.

Laski, Harold J. *Reflections of the Constitution: The House of Commons, the Cabinet, the Civil Service.* Manchester: Manchester University Press, 1951.

Latham, Richard T. E. *The Law and the Commonwealth.* London: Oxford University Press, 1949.

Lawson, F. H. *The Oxford Law School, 1850–1965.* Oxford: Clarendon Press, 1968.

Lawson, F. H., and Bentley, D. J. *Constitutional and Administrative Law.* London: Butterworth's, 1961.

Litchfield, Henrietta. *Richard Buckley Litchfield: A Memoir Written for His Friends by His Wife.* Cambridge: Cambridge University Press, 1910.

Long, Walter. *Memories.* London: Hutchinson & Co., 1923.

Lubenow, William C. *The Politics of Government Growth, 1833–1848.* Hamden, Conn.: Archon Press, 1971.

Lyons, F. S. L. *Charles Stewart Parnell.* London: Collins, 1977.

———. *Ireland since the Famine.* 2nd ed. London: Collins, 1973.

MacDonagh, Oliver. *A Pattern of Government Growth, 1800–1860: The Passenger Acts and Their Enforcement.* London: MacGibbon & Kee, 1961.

Marshall, Geoffrey. *Constitutional Theory.* Oxford: Clarendon Press, 1971.

———. *Parliamentary Sovereignty and the Commonwealth.* Oxford: Clarendon Press, 1957.

Marshall, Geoffrey, and Moodie, Graeme C. *Some Problems of the Constitution.* London: Hutchinson & Co., 1959.

Matthew, H. C. G. *The Liberal Imperialists: The Ideas and Politics of a Post-Gladstonian Elite.* Oxford: Oxford University Press, 1973.

McCarthy, Justin. *The Case for Home Rule.* London: Chatto & Windus, 1887.

Mitchell, J. D. B. *Constitutional Law.* 2nd ed. Edinburgh: W. Green & Son, 1968.

Morris, J. H. C., general editor. *Dicey and Morris on the Conflict of Laws.* 8th ed. London: Stevens & Sons, 1967.

Norton, Sara, and Howe, Mark DeWolfe. *Letters of Charles Eliot Norton: With Biographical Comment.* 2 vols. Boston: Houghton Mifflin, 1913.

O'Brien, Conor Cruise. *Parnell and His Party 1880–1890.* Oxford: Clarendon Press, 1957.

O'Day, Alan. *The English Face of Irish Nationalism: Parnellite Involvement in British Politics 1880–86.* Dublin: Gill and Macmillan, 1977.

Ogden, Rollo. *Life and Letters of Edwin Lawrence Godkin.* 2 vols. New York: Macmillan, 1907.

Oman, Sir Charles, ed. *The Text of the Second Betting Book of All Souls College 1873–1919.* Oxford: Privately printed, 1938.

———. *Things I Have Seen.* London: Metheun, 1933.

Palmer, Sir Roundell. *Speech at the Annual Meeting of the Legal Education Association.* London: Butterworth's, 1871.

Parris, Henry. *Constitutional Bureaucracy: The Development of British Central Administration since the Eighteenth Century.* London: George Allen & Unwin, 1969.

———. *Government and the Railways in Nineteenth Century Britain.* London: Routledge & Kegan Paul, 1965.

Rait, Robert Sangster, ed. *Memorials of Albert Venn Dicey: Being Chiefly Letters and Diaries.* London: Macmillan, 1925.

Rempel, Richard A. *Unionists Divided: Arthur Balfour, Joseph Chamberlain and the Unionist Free Traders.* Hamden, Conn.: Archon Press, 1972.

Richter, Melvin. *The Politics of Conscience: T. H. Green and His Age.* London: Weidenfield & Nicolson, 1964.

Robson, W. A. *Justice and Administrative Law: A Study of the British Constitution.* 3d ed. London: Stevens & Sons, 1951.

Rowland, Peter. *The Last Liberal Governments: Unfinished Business 1911–1914.* London: Barrie & Jenkins, 1971.

Schreiner, O. D. *The Contribution of English Law to South Africa Law, and the Rule of Law in South Africa.* London: Stevens & Sons, 1967.

Sieghart, M. A. *Government by Decree: A Comparative Study of the Ordinance in English and French Law.* London: Stevens & Sons, 1950.

Southgate, Donald. *The Passing of the Whigs 1832–1886.* London: Macmillan, 1962.

Stevens, Robert. *Law and Politics: The House of Lords as a Judicial Body, 1800–1976.* Chapel Hill: University of North Carolina Press, 1978.

Street, Harry. *Justice in the Welfare State.* London: Stevens & Sons, 1968.

Sutherland, Gillian, ed. *Studies in the Growth of Nineteenth-Century Government.* London: Routledge & Kegan Paul, 1972.
Wade, E. C. S., and Bradley, A. W. *Constitutional Law.* 8th ed. London: Longmans, 1970.
Wade, H. W. R. *Administrative Law.* 3d ed. Oxford: Clarendon Press, 1971.
———. *Towards Administrative Justice.* Ann Arbor: University of Michigan Press, 1963.
Wallace, Elisabeth. *Goldwin Smith Victorian Liberal.* Toronto: University of Toronto Press, 1957.
Yardley, D. C. M. *Introduction to British Constitutional Law.* 2nd ed. London: Butterworth's, 1964.
Young, Kenneth. *Arthur James Balfour.* London: G. Bell, 1963.

Articles

Annan, Lord. "The Intellectual Aristocracy." In *Studies in Social History: A Tribute to G. M. Trevelyan,* edited by J. H. Plumb, pp. 243–87. London: Longmans, 1955.
Anon. "College Notes." *Working Men's College Journal* 17 (June 1922): 288.
———. "The Liberal Unionist Conscience." *Spectator* 66 (7 February 1891): 193.
———. "Professor Dicey: Portrait and Sketch." *Journal of the Society of Comparative Legislation* 17 (1917): 1–4.
———. "A Word of Warning from Professor Dicey." *Spectator* 62 (1 September 1888): 1187–88.
Arndt, H. W. "The Origin of Dicey's Concept of the Rule of Law." *Australian Law Journal* 31 (1957): 117–23.
Boyce, D. G. "Dicey, Kilbrandon and Devolution." *Political Quarterly* 46 (July-August 1975): 280–92.
———. "Public Opinion and Historians." *History* 63 (June 1978): 214–28.
Brebner, J. B. "Laissez-Faire and State Intervention in Nineteenth-Century Britain." *Journal of Economic History* 8, Supplement (1948): 59–73.
Bristow, Edward. "The Liberty and Property Defence League and Individualism." *Historical Journal* 18 (1975): 761–89.
Buckland, P. J. "The Southern Irish Unionists, the Irish Question, and British Politics 1906–1914." *Irish Historical Studies* 15 (March 1967): 228–55.
Cosgrove, Richard A. "A. V. Dicey at the Harvard Law School, 1898: A Study in the Anglo-American Legal Community." *Harvard Library Bulletin* 26 (July 1978): 325–35.
———. "The Relevance of Irish History: The Gladstone-Dicey Debate about Home Rule, 1886–1887." *Eire-Ireland* 13 (Winter 1978): 6–21.
Crouch, R. L. "Laissez-Faire in Nineteenth Century Britain: Myth or Real-

ity?" *Manchester School of Economics and Social Studies* 35 (September 1967): 199–215.

Davis, Peter. "The Liberal Unionist Party and the Irish Policy of Lord Salisbury's Government, 1886–1892." *Historical Journal* 18 (1975): 85–104.

Dicey, Edward. "The Plea of a Malcontent Liberal." *Fortnightly Review* 44 (1 October 1885): 463–77.

Dike, Chijioke. "The Case against Parliamentary Sovereignty." *Public Law* (Autumn 1976): 283–97.

Fanning, Ronan. "The Unionist Party and Ireland, 1906–1910." *Irish Historical Studies* 15 (September 1966): 147–71.

Ford, Trowbridge. "Dicey's Conversion to Unionism." *Irish Historical Studies* 18 (September 1973): 552–82.

———. "Dicey as a Political Journalist." *Political Studies* 18 (1970): 220–35.

Goodhart, Arthur L. "The Rule of Law and Absolute Sovereignty." *University of Pennsylvania Law Review* 106 (May 1958): 943–63.

Graveson, R. H. "Philosophical Aspects of the English Conflict of Laws." *Law Quarterly Review* 78 (July 1962): 337–70.

Gray, H. R. "The Sovereignty of Parliament Today." *University of Toronto Law Journal* 10 (1953): 54–72.

Hart, H. L. A. "Legal Positivism and the Separation of Law and Morals." *Harvard Law Review* 71 (February 1958): 598–625.

Hart, Jenifer. "Nineteenth Century Social Reform: A Tory Interpretation of History." *Past and Present* 31 (July 1965): 39–61.

Harvie, Christopher. "Ideology and Home Rule: James Bryce, A. V. Dicey and Ireland, 1880–1887." *English Historical Review* 91 (April 1976): 298–314.

Holdsworth, Sir William S. "The Conventions of the Eighteenth Century Constitution." *Iowa Law Review* 17 (January 1932): 161–80.

Hood Phillips, O. "Constitutional Conventions: Dicey's Precedessors." *Modern Law Review* 29 (March 1966): 137–48.

Jennings, Sir W. Ivor. "In Praise of Dicey." *Public Administration* 13 (April 1935): 123–34.

Laski, Harold. "Obituary of A. V. Dicey." *Nation and Athenaeum* 31 (15 April 1922): 77.

Lawson, F. H. "Dicey Revisited." *Political Studies* 7 (June and October 1959): 109–26, 207–21.

Lefcowitz, Allen B., and Lefcowitz, Barbara F. "James Bryce's First Visit to America." *New England Quarterly* 50 (June 1977): 314–31.

Lucas, Sir Charles P. "Albert Venn Dicey." *Working Men's College Journal* 17 (April 1922): 223–25.

MacDonagh, Oliver. "The Nineteenth-Century Revolution in Government: A Reappraisal." *Historical Journal* 1 (1958): 52–67.

MacLoed, Roy M. "Statesmen Undisguised." *American Historical Review* 78 (December 1973): 1386–1405.

Monsman, Gerald C. "Old Mortality at Oxford." *Studies in Philology* 67 (July 1970): 359–89.

Montrose, J. L. "Return to Austin's College." *Current Legal Problems* 13 (1960): 1–21.

Newman, Gerald. "Anti-French Propaganda and British Liberal Nationalism in the Early Nineteenth Century: Suggestions toward a General Interpretation." *Victorian Studies* 18 (June 1975): 385–418.

Nicholls, David. "Positive Liberty, 1880–1914." *American Political Science Review* 56 (March 1962): 114–28.

Orth, John V. "The British Trade Union Acts of 1824 and 1825: Dicey and the Relation Between Law and Opinion." *Anglo-American Law Review* 5 (1976): 131–52.

Parris, Henry. "The Nineteenth-Century Revolution in Government: A Reappraisal Reappraised." *Historical Journal* 3 (1960): 17–37.

Perkin, Harold. "Individualism versus Collectivism in Nineteenth-Century Britain: A False Antithesis." *Journal of British Studies* 17 (Fall 1977): 105–18.

Pillet, Antoine. "Professor A. V. Dicey." *Working Men's College Journal* 18 (February-March 1923): 38–40.

Pollock, Sir Frederick. "Our Jubilee." *Law Quarterly Review* 51 (January 1935): 5–10.

Simpson, A. W. B. "The Common Law and Legal Theory." In *Oxford Essays in Jurisprudence (Second Series)*, edited by A. W. B. Simpson, pp. 77–99. Oxford: Clarendon Press, 1973.

Soldon, Norbert C. "Individualist Periodicals: The Crisis of Late Victorian Liberalism." *Victorian Periodicals Newsletter* 6 (December 1973): 17–26.

Tulloch, Hugh A. "Changing British Attitudes towards the United States in the 1880s." *Historical Journal* 20 (1977): 825–40.

Wade, H. W. R. "The Basis of Legal Sovereignty." *Cambridge Law Journal* 13 (November 1955): 172–97.

———. "Quasi-Judicial and Its Background." *Cambridge Law Journal* 10 (1949): 216–40.

Winterton, George. "The British Grundnorm: Parliamentary Supremacy Re-Examined." *Law Quarterly Review* 92 (October 1976): 591–617.

Yntema, Hessel E. "Dicey: An American Commentary." *International Law Quarterly* 4 (1951): 1–10.

INDEX